THE WAY

OF

A SHIP

Books by Alan Villiers

The Way of a Ship
Sons of Sinbad
Captain James Cook
Give Me a Ship to Sail
Posted Missing
Sailing Eagle
The Quest of the Schooner Argus
The Set of the Sails
Cruise of the Conrad
By Way of Cape Horn
Falmouth for Orders
The Bounty Ships of France
The War with Cape Horn
Grain Race

Books for Younger Readers

And Not to Yield
Joey Goes to Sea
Stormalong

The Way of A Ship

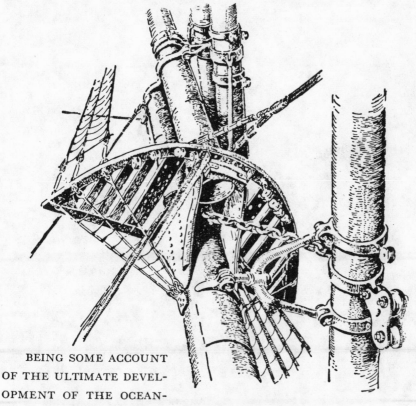

BEING SOME ACCOUNT
OF THE ULTIMATE DEVEL-
OPMENT OF THE OCEAN-
GOING SQUARE-RIGGED SAILING VESSEL, AND THE
MANNER OF HER HANDLING, HER VOYAGE-MAKING, HER PERSON-
NEL, HER ECONOMICS, HER PERFORMANCE, AND HER END

By ALAN VILLIERS

*Illustrated with the Author's Photographs
and Diagrams and Drawings by* HAROLD A. UNDERHILL

New York CHARLES SCRIBNER'S SONS

Contents

LIST OF ILLUSTRATIONS

Introduction to the New Edition

I GREW up in the Sailing-ship Era and my life has coincided with its passing. I have tried to do something more than watch it pass. As a young boy in Melbourne, the deepsea square-rigged ships from America and Northern Europe were part of the daily scene—English, United States and Canadian, Chilean, French, German, Russian (most of these actually Finnish, for Finland was then a Russian province) and our own Australian. Most of ours were ships grown too small to carry paying cargoes in the Cape Horn trade, and now Tasman Sea and Pacific traders. To me they were all adventurous and wonderful, and the sound of strong wind in their high rigging was imperious and challenging. I studied them and, even as a small boy, went aboard, talked with the seamen, and tried climbing aloft. I read all I could find about them, fiction and non-fiction, from Marryat and Melville onwards.

It dawned early on me that ships like these had been very important in the story of Man. All his major discoveries had been by sea, made in sailing-ships, from Dias and da Gama, Columbus and Magellan to Cook, Flinders, Vancouver, and the ice pioneers Franklin and Ross. Down there in Australia before the flying age, one was aware of the sailing world's immensity, and could appreciate what a great achievement the voyages of a man like Captain Cook had been. He had to have a seaworthy ship able to keep the seas for years and survive hurricanes, ice-hazards, and occasional bumping on coral reefs. The ship was no use without competent crews of seamen trained, disciplined, and fit to serve her for years if need be, far from any hope of leave or base. He must also be supremely competent himself and maintain that competence in all matters and in all men's view, for the sailing-ship was a very public place to her own people. He had also to control his mariners' frequently deplorable eating habits lest they die of scurvy, or he could lose the lot and his voyage just for that.

I put the ship first. No one man no matter how gifted could create that essential instrument. It was the product of slow, courageous growth nurtured by many men down the centuries. I wondered later, when I noted the skills of such able seamen as the Arabs, Indians, Malays, Chinese and the Japanese (who though much farther to the north, were still within an island-hopping sailing-ship passage of us) —why had not any of these discovered and developed Eastern Australia. Or California, Central America, Peru? They all had ships of a sort, some of them of long proven worth for Indian Ocean monsoonal voyages of thousands of miles. Indeed, at least the Chinese and the Semitic seamen had developed ships far better than the European of the Early Christian Era: obviously, they were not good enough. There were vague rumours that one or two wandering or blown-away Asians had reached our country and California: but they had certainly lacked the ships and seamen to follow up. (Maybe they'd lacked a sufficiency of continuous political stability at home, too. Successful voyaging must mean successful trading, which was not to be fostered in war-torn nations nor by inward-looking, despotic rule.)

I spoke English 14,000 miles from England because James Cook had good ships and seamen, and skill in all the science and know-how that go with sailing them. But, I reflected, the development of these *could* have been elsewhere. Those shadowy ancient mariners the Phoenicians, after all, had been groping right round Africa in Europe's Dark Ages, though they had taken several years to do it and, apparently, made such a voyage only once. Then they had flung their know-how away.

Other attractions in the big sailing-ships I knew were more obvious. Their masts and yards towered over the waterfront from miles away. I observed that, unlike steamships—squat, fat smoking beasts, low with their stumpy masts and funnels—the Cape Horner was *all ship*. Your eye took in the whole of her with one sweeping look at her stirring stance, even beside a dock. She was both strong and beautiful: power, grace and loveliness flowed in her lines from the curve of her seakindly cutwater to the harmony of her elegant stern. She was the way she was because men had slowly learned to fit her to the natural ways of the wind and the sea. To use efficiently the forces of nature she had to have nature's beauty too. She was an art-form, as well as a fascinating creation of skilful engineering. She was these things because she had to be, to keep the seas and make long voyages with endurance, strength, and supreme seaworthiness in the service

xii

of Man—and to go on doing this so long as he had the skill to serve her and the sense to keep her. But how much longer, in the middle of the second decade of the twentieth century, was this likely to be?

Soon after the first World War, I became aware that they were doomed. So I hurried to begin my service in them, and I stayed with them then wherever I could find them, under many flags. I learned all I could, made friends with old-timers whose experience went back to the clipper days and the Chilean nitrate-men—real experience, not briefly sought for the sake of a book or a passage somewhere. By the 1920's I was doing well to find one of these in each ship, none at all in the Finnish vessels which were manned by boys. I sailed wherever I could, regardless of flag or trade—from the Gulf of Finland to the Red Sea, from the Grand Banks of Newfoundland and the Greenland fishing grounds to the Tasman Sea, from the Horn to Hatteras and Good Hope, Land's End to Zanzibar—round and round, without benefit of canals or engines. My ships became more difficult to find: but in fact they lasted a surprisingly long time. The last to survive as working-ships earning their keep were the Finnish four-masted barques *Viking* and *Passat*, and the (then) New Zealand *Pamir*: it was 1950 when the last of them sailed past the Horn. There had been successful powered ships then for well over 125 years.

The *Passat* and *Viking* still survive at permanent berths in 1969, but the *Pamir* was lost with heavy casualties in a North Atlantic hurricane in September, 1957. She was an auxiliary vessel then, not at all the independent stout Cape Horner ready to take the odd hurricane in her stride. She was trying to carry a big cargo most of which was loose grain. Knocked over on her beam ends with that, she could not get up again. Fitting engines into Cape Horn ships and dragging propellors behind them was no way to 'save' them. . .

I was seven years old when the *Preussen* was lost, that mighty culmination of the Sailing-ship Era: I had barely managed to get to sea when the *Potosi* was burned out. I never saw either of these great ships but I knew of them early, knew some of their Masters later, and studied them when I could—first, by listening to the talk of seamen. As for that, I was not learning much about other ships during my first several voyages. It was as much as I could do to absorb what I should aboard the ship I served, then: when one is doing the donkey-work alow and aloft one doesn't bother much about the reason why. How the officer of the watch could see when the wind was about to change or show such uncanny awareness of the fact that I had allowed the old barque to wander a little from her course, I had no idea. I began to learn the serious business of the sailor's calling only when I managed to get abaft the mast, in the officers' part of the ship, and could understudy a consummate seaman like Ruben de Cloux. By then it was 1930. All the big American and British sailing-ships were gone from the sea and, except for a few old bo's'ns, sailmakers, and a carpenter or two, old seadogs had gone forever from the forecastle. By 1934, I had the ship *Joseph Conrad*. Then I learned, fast.

Realising that the ships I knew were the last of their kind on earth and the men even more surely doomed (for the odd ship may be restored and preserved), I cultivated old masters—men like the Britishers Jervis, Learmont, Fearon, David Williams; the Americans MacDonald, Reynard, Klebingat; the Germans Piening, Miethe, Krage, Clauss, Hauth; the Finns, Portuguese, and Swedes. I got to know an owner or two and I had some experience of that myself. Foremast hands were more difficult to find for indeed they had faded away. Fortunately there was still old Charlie Müller, that concentrated essence of all good Cape Horn bos'ns and wandering AB's who at 92 still flourishes: through him I met a few more before they picked up their last moorings, and others in Wales, Tasmania, Hamburg, Alaska, Port Adelaide, New Zealand.

In the *Parma* in 1931, I found some of the remarkable German books and records with which those thorough seamen had documented what they learned—the books of the Deutsche Seewarte such as their meticulous Sailing Directions for the Atlantic and the Pacific Oceans, and other works. These were gold-mines. I became aware that, although we'd had splendid sea writers in English (the best a Polish ship-master) there were certain gaps in our recorded knowledge. This was all very well while there was a living tradition of Cape Horn voyaging and ship-handling: but very soon there would be nothing of the kind. So I tried to do something on this side, too, to prepare for the gap.

There were and there still are the sailing school-ships, of course, and there are a few real Cape Horners in various states of preservation here and there about the world. There may well be several added to this fleet which now has representatives in Finland, Sweden,

Hawaii, California, Portugal, Germany, England, New York and New England. All the school-ships are engined, many of them as minor motor-ships as well as sailers: ordinarily none goes near Cape Horn. They must fit into the curricula of naval or mercantile academies: few now venture near the Roaring Forties, though the German barque *Gorch Fock,* the Danish ship *Danmark,* and some of the Russians make winter voyages, and the Argentine ship *Libertad* skipped across the North Atlantic coast-to-coast in 1966 in six days 21 hours with no use of her engines. She has a complement of nearly 400 men; not because she needs them but it is her business to train them.

As memory of the real ships fades, here and there one notes a growing fleet of odd and useless monstrosities, catch-penny 'galleons' congregated in the ports of Florida and curious craft trying to pass themselves off as square-rigged ships in the dude-sailing business. One quick look at most of these would make an albatross sea-sick, but they do not venture where an albatross may see them. They had better not, for the souls of old salts—the seadogs said—fly with the albatross.

I saw the ships all go. I did what I could to save at least some knowledge of their ways, and I saved one or two of them, when I could. For I felt that with the passing of these great and sometimes glorious ships went a noble skill nobly developed, though practised by plain men of whom the world did not often hear—and, when it did, too often only when they were in trouble.

ALAN VILLIERS

Oxford
September, 1969

Preface

THIS book is intended to make the big square-rigged sailing-ship comprehensible, now that all such vessels have disappeared from the commercial world and only school-ships remain. I have not attempted to prepare a treatise on seamanship, for there are many of these, and I have not gone into too great detail in my technicalities. I have tried to present a clear exposition of the manner of working the sails and handling the ships, and to set down, in plain language, the stories of some outstanding shipmasters, ships, and owners. I have tried to select those who had a real contribution to make to the story of the big sailing-ship.

I owe thanks to many, particularly in recent years to Mr. Erich F. Laeisz and his Marine Superintendent, Captain Herman Piening; to Captain Ernst Römer, of the Deutsches Hydrographisches Institut, and to Captain Erwin Kornitzer, the well-known sailing-ship historian, of Hamburg; to Sir Thomas Devitt, of Messrs. Devitt and Moore; to Captain James S. Learmont; to Boatswain Charles Müller; and to many excellent masters and good seamen, now dead. Their names appear in these pages, and that is my tribute to them.

I wish also to thank the Portuguese Minister for Marine, His Excellency Admiral Americo Tomás, for his kindness in arranging my passage in the barque *Sagres;* and also the Danish Committee for the ship *Georg Stage,* especially Captain J. B. Junker.

I am very grateful to Mr. Harold A. Underhill, of Glasgow, for his clear diagrams and sketches.

A list of books I have found useful appears at the end.

ALAN VILLIERS

April, 1953

Part I

———◆———

THE

ULTIMATE DEVELOPMENT

Chapter one

THE GREATEST SHIP OF ALL

AT FIRST the pinpoint breaking the horizon astern might have been the first emergence of the upper-works of a steamer, so fast did it come up and grow. The southeast trade wind was blowing fresh and the blue sea ran with whitecaps. The sturdy little barque was carrying every stitch she could, staggering along with the water gushing from her scuppers as she rolled. Her two thousand tons of nitrates from the west coast of South America was being hurried homewards at her maximum speed of nine and a half knots. The pinpoint astern grew into a pyramid and, catching the sun, turned to purest white. It was at once obvious that this white could belong to the upper-works of no steamship. This was a sailing-ship, a square-rigged ship. Yet what ship could be coming up at such a terrific speed? The year was 1910. There were no clippers left. This was a huge ship, a giant among sailing-ships.

Sail after sail lifted above the horizon to disclose at last the swift black hull of a nitrate ship. Within the hour, the overhauling ship was beside the little barque, to windward of her, rushing by in a smother of foam. Those aboard the barque felt that their ship was standing still. They saw that the ship to windward was a five-masted full-rigged ship. She was lying over a little, with her lee scuppers awash, and the sea was gushing from her wash-ports. She was a great lofty vessel with masts 200 feet high towering upon the sea, dwarfing the 1500-ton barque whose astonished apprentices counted forty-three sails, all set magnificently and pulling like horses. The flag at the short gaff on the aftermost mast was German. The name on the high flared bows was

1

Preussen. As she passed and drew steadily ahead, they could read her name again on the shapely counter, and her port of registry. *Preussen,* Hamburg, they read.

Before the watch was out the great five-master was a pinpoint breaking the horizon again, this time ahead. No one aboard the little Limejuice barque would ever forget the grace and glory of that great ship, racing past them, while they lived. There was one *Preussen* only—a supership, a swift giantess among all sailing-ships, the ultimate expression of deepwater Sail.

The five-masted full-rigged ship *Preussen* was the only ship of her type ever built. She was a steel ship four hundred and thirty-three feet long with a beam of nearly fifty-four feet, displacing over eleven thousand tons and carrying eight thousand tons of cargo. She was propelled entirely by her 60,000 square-feet of canvas, and the only power aboard her was for working her cargoes and raising her heavy anchor when she was getting under way. She set thirty square sails, six on each mast, and from fifteen to eighteen fore-and-afters. Her mainyard was over a hundred feet long. Her best speed was a shade over seventeen knots—no more. Tank experiments made with a model of her, years after the ship herself was lost, showed that, to shift her 8000 tons of cargo through the sea at a speed of seventeen knots, her sails had to develop more than six thousand horse-power. The whole great fabric of her tremendous driving power was controlled by a total crew of forty-seven officers and men. Excepting perhaps the steward, cabin-boy, and two cooks, every one of these was a sailor in the true sense of that word. Her master was a veteran of the Laeisz Flying 'P' Line, a man trained in the *Potosi* under the genius Hilgendorf.

The *Preussen* was without a doubt the greatest sailing-ship the world has seen. Her career was brief, for a blundering steamer, unable to judge speeds or to comply with the International Rule of the Road, knocked her down at the Channel mouth when she was outward-bound on the voyage after passing that little barque. She was built in 1902. She sailed only a short eight years. But in that time she moved large cargoes faster through the water, over long distances, than they had ever been shifted under sail before.

She was economic in her need of man-power. She consistently defied Cape Horn, and beat round to the west'ard voyage after voyage in an average of little over a week. She *consistently* made splendid passages, not with odd bursts of speeds and prodigious days' runs, the chance reward of occasional highly favouring circumstance, but with unblemished averages throughout the whole of the run from the Channel through both Atlantics right down to the Horn, and round and to the West Coast ports, and home again by the same long way. She was a hard-working ship, a cargo-carrier. She showed no kites of studding-sails and she knew no tricks. Her great voyages impressed no passengers, for there was no passenger business under sail to the ports where she traded. Her voyages were reported only in the specialised shipping press. The speed with which she was able to deliver eight thousand tons of nitrate from Iquique to Hamburg did not matter much, except to her owner and her officers and crew—to her owner, for quick turn-round in port and smart passages at sea meant that she could make two round voyages a year, instead of three in two years as other ships did, and so earn more freights. And to her officers and crew, because they took a fierce pride in their ship and exulted in her great performance. Excellence bred excellence: the better voyages the big ship made, the faster they tried to sail her.

And yet, in the twentieth century, surely she was an anomaly upon the sea? What hope had she of surviving against the might of powered competition? What hope had *any* sailing-vessel? How did it come about, indeed, that the *Preussen* was ever built as late as 1902, to sail at all? Steamships of a kind had existed in Scotland and in America since 1788, and had been proved practical seagoing vessels since 1810. The first British steam navigation company was formed in the 1820's, and the development of the screw—to replace the vulnerable paddle-wheel—in 1836, and the use of iron and, later, steel in ship construction, had enabled steamships to leap ahead.

But the wind was free, and its use well understood by men and by nations which had traditionally sent their ships under sail across the seven seas. The science of square-rigged ship-handling

The Preussen

HAROLD A UNDERHILL.

and of voyage-making under sail, built up over many centuries, was not so lightly thrown away. Since man had first sat astride a floating log and noted that a branch of foliage held aloft gave way to his craft in a breeze, the sailing-ship had developed, slowly —sometimes halting for several centuries—but surely, and, in a wild spurt, to the gracious clippers and then, at last, the great clipper-carriers, the mighty ships which still could 'clip' along though they stowed four thousand, five thousand, six thousand, even eight thousand tons of cargo down below. It was of these that the *Preussen* was the undisputed queen, the last, most perfect, and most useful development. There had been great four-masted barques before her—American, British, French, and German. There had been a few five-masters, too. These were five-masted barques, of which the greatest was her company-ship *Potosi*—Hilgendorf's command.

The *Preussen,* in a sense, was a gesture of defiance flung at the mechanical age, an affirmation of her owner's belief that the great sailing-ship still had a place if she could compete with powered vessels on their own terms, if she could safely deliver large cargoes regularly, at a reasonable and predictable speed. She served a trade which was difficult for steamships. The ports of the West Coast of South America then were arid places, little better than open roadsteads, where water for boilers was scarce and costly, where cargo-handling dawdled on with painful and expensive slowness. The cargoes these ports offered had to be loaded almost bag by bag.

Nor was there any Panama Canal for steamships to slip through. The route from and to Europe lay around Cape Horn, with the Straits of Magellan the only possible alternative. It was a question which was worse. The Cape Horn route was notoriously stormy. The mountainous spine of South America dips far to the south, down into the abode of the great west winds which rush upon the continent's tip in a ferment of gale after gale, almost as if they wished to bar entry to the Pacific by that route. Passage-making there was difficult for steamships and sailing-ships alike, and the Straits of Magellan abounded in navigational dangers.

Moreover, once she had passed the bunker-port of St. Vincent in the Cape Verde Islands, coal was an expensive item for a steamship on that long haul, and she might burn prodigious quantities of it. A general cargo out to Chile or Peru would scarcely pay when a month or two might well be lost discharging it. Steamships were expensive vessels with much more capital invested in them than in the average sailing-ship. They had larger crews, a considerable proportion of whom contributed little or nothing to the ship's earnings in ports. On the West Coast, sailing-ship crews worked cargo. The men were all earning members of their ship's company. Sailing-ships bought no coal beyond the galley's meagre requirements, and they used very little fresh water. It was not so important to them as to steamships that they should get rid of their outward cargoes with the utmost possible dispatch. Cargo-handling by lighterage at open roadsteads did not bother them. If the weather got too bad they could slip out to sea, without the time-wasting preliminary of raising steam.

And, if the worst came to the worst, and no cargoes offered for loading at any West Coast port, a square-rigged ship could up-anchor and sail off before the Pacific trade winds over to Australia, to try her luck there for a cargo of Newcastle coal or South Australian grain, or she could sail up to Puget Sound for North American lumber. She could do these things without buying bunkers or anything else, beyond her few necessary sea stores. At the turn of the century and for at least a decade before, there was a fair prospect that the sailing-ship, having arrived at a Chilean port, would get a cargo homewards without difficulty. At first the demand for copper ore and later the demand for nitrates seemed insatiable, in northern Europe. Intensive industrialisation, with its resultant growth of cities and heavy demands on farming soil, led to an expanding market for nitrates of which there seemed no end.

And so there were the cargoes, there were the ships, and there were a few owners with enterprise to exploit them and men with the skill to sail and to handle them. It was against this background that the *Preussen* was developed. She was no freak. Her building was the logical outcome of a belief on her owner's part that there was still useful work for the sailing-ship to do, at any rate in the carriage of bulk cargoes over long distances on routes where advantage could be taken both of the regular trade winds and of the almost equally regular westerly gales of the great Southern Ocean.

Even in the opening decade of the twentieth century, this belief was reasonable. There *was* work for well-designed and well-sailed square-rigged ships to do, despite the inroads of the powered vessels. The average speed of too many tramp steamers then was about seven knots. Indeed, eight knots was their usual top speed, and they made long voyages at an average nearer six. Under really adverse conditions, such as when bound to the westward on a winter North Atlantic passage, it was not at all unusual for a tramp to take six weeks or more to battle the few thousand miles between the Channel and, say, Halifax, or even to run out of bunkers altogether and stagger into Bermuda burning her last dunnage boards, or be towed in by a tug. Such ships as the *Preussen* and *Potosi* could average better speeds than six knots in the Europe-to-Chile voyage, out and home, and the best of the 'P' four-masted barques did almost as well. A captain like Robert Hilgendorf, in ten years in command of the four-masted barques *Placilla* (2780 tons), *Pitlochry* (2971 tons), and the five-masted barque *Potosi* (3854 tons) kept up a steady average of 7.6 knots outwards and 7.4 knots homewards, on twenty Chilean voyages during which his vessels were loaded to capacity on each run. The *Potosi* and the *Preussen* averaged eight knots in the trade winds; both ships made Chilean voyages at this speed.

This was at a time when the clippers had long been run off the seas, and both American and British owners—with very few exceptions—had discarded sail as outmoded. The British shipping genius had turned early to the development of the powered vessel, especially the passenger-carrier and the cargo-liner. Clipper-ships as such had gone inevitably, for they were racehorses of the days of sail, not competitors with steam. They were the fast ships which took the cream of the cargoes at premium rates, and carried passengers to their distant destinations more swiftly than other sailing-ships or the early auxiliary steamers could. They were costly to maintain and run, and they had to have large earnings. There was a limit to their development. They were essentially big ocean-going square-rigged yachts, with a grace of line that prohibited the stuffing of enormous cargoes into them, and tremendous sail areas which, to work them properly, called for double crews. Without an assurance of premium cargoes the clippers could not pay and, of course, it was the premium cargoes which the powered vessels first took from them. The opening of the Suez Canal, the crossing of the American continent by railroad, and the improvement in ships' boilers and engines put an end to them. Most of the clippers were wooden ships, first American, then British. Only a few British clippers were built of iron, though a modified clipper-form lasted in some of the earlier steel ships.

There has been a lot of confused thinking about this whole subject of the clipper-ship, even among seafarers. Argument has raged interminably on just what a clipper was, who built the first clipper, and so forth. It is probable that there always were some types of fast sailing-vessel. Some Arab dhows, with their beautiful hulls and great lateen sails, could outsail, for instance, any swift frigate which tried to inquire too closely into their cargoes or their passengers, and early explorers in the Pacific speak of swift canoes and catamarans which could sail at twenty knots. There is no doubt that some Micronesian canoes, especially in the Ladrones and the Gilberts, were capable of sailing at fantastic speeds. But they were skimmers and not ships. They flew across the surface of the water, under ideal conditions, and they could carry nothing which could not sit upon them and act, as the occasion required, as live and swiftly adjustable ballast. The Arab dhows were ships and so were Indian dhows, and Chinese sea-going junks. But these dhows had one great asset which was denied European sailing vessels. They had the wonderful monsoon winds. In the north-east monsoon, over the whole of the tropics in the western Indian Ocean, they had an assurance of good weather with a nice breeze and ideal sailing conditions. Their seafarers developed a hull form which was swift and grace-

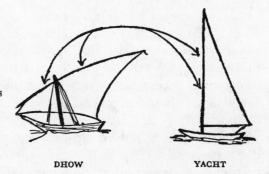

Same sail, rigged differently, with long leading-edge and excellent aero-dynamic qualities

DHOW   YACHT

ful in the sea, but it was weak, for it was not ordinarily called upon to do battle with really bad weather. They developed a sail-form, too, which was magnificent under good conditions, for the Arab lateen sail is essentially the modern high-aspect-ratio Bermuda rig with the leading-edge—the luff—of the sail bent to the lateen yard carried on a leaning mast, instead of travelling on the mast itself, as it does in yachts. The lateen, under the severe conditions of North Europe, had to become a square sail, and its yard had to be shortened for strength, and properly supported.

European seafarers, having to contend in the North Sea and the Bay of Biscay with truly dreadful conditions of wind and weather, were compelled to develop ships along different lines. The only certainty about their sailing conditions was their appalling uncertainty, and a hull-form had to be devised which was above all strong and seaworthy. This did not develop fast sailing qualities, nor could it be expected to do so. Such vessels as the North Sea colliers and—long before them—the Portuguese caravels were good weatherly sailing-ships. They could beat to windward well enough. They were strong, small, and manoeuvrable. But they were not fast. It was sufficient for their purposes if they made successful voyages at all, and remained afloat to deliver their cargoes no matter what the sea and the iron-bound coasts tried to do to them. As vessels ventured out upon deepsea voyages

—and after all, it took the Europeans, led by the Portuguese, a mighty long time to do that—they still had to be, above all else, strong, seaworthy, and able.

The ancients had their favourable monsoons in the Indian Ocean and throughout the eastern seas. They could haul their ships ashore when the stormy monsoon blew. Indeed, in the mid-1950's, they still do so. The alternating monsoons were well understood by eastern mariners long before the time of Christ. But nobody then understood the system of the trade winds. No European and no Asiatic knew how to make real global voyages. The Portuguese had to grope through many weary decades down towards the tip of Africa in their quest for a sailing route to the East, before they understood the use of the south-east trade wind, though they did understand the science of ocean voyaging—at any rate as far as the Atlantic was concerned— before Da Gama sailed for the Cape, and before Cabral publicized the finding of Brazil. Compared with other European mariners, they had at least the advantage that the summer northerlies down the Portuguese coast would blow a ship quickly to the trade wind zone, when she could head either west for the Americas or south for the Line, and thence down the South Atlantic and where she willed.

The Portuguese, too, had to develop strong ships, to stand up to the gales and general treacherous weather of the Cape of Good Hope. But they had at first a monopoly of deepsea sailing, except to the West Indies and Central America, and so speed scarcely entered the picture at all. It was sufficient that a ship could run, beat, and go about, and survive the occasional gale. She had to be roomy to stow her cargo and her sea stores, and to accommodate all the people then necessary to sail and to fight a long-voyage ship. The tendency in Europe, then, was to develop deepsea merchant ships along the lines of long, deep, and beamy boxes, with barrel-bows to shove the sea away before them and comfortable fat after-bodies to carry their great stern-windowed balconies high out of the reach of breaking water. Since there were no towboats, they had also to be reasonably manoeuvrable in confined waters, and the best way to assure this was to keep ships small. There were great Chinese junks capable of carrying hundreds of passengers—Marco Polo speaks of these—and enormous Arab and Indian dhows, long before there were sizable European sailing-ships.

The development of the European sailing-ship was further handicapped by the growth of monopolies. The opening of new lands and the expansion of trade were for long regarded as royal monopolies. Enterprising spirits could not just build themselves a ship and set off to trade somewhere. Discoveries were expensive and zealously guarded. First, Portugal and Spain divided the world's trade, as they knew it, and disregarding all that part of it which still remained in Eastern hands. (This was considerable.) Then, in turn, the British, the Hollanders, and the French fought for a share. What each really wanted was a monopoly and, when none could control all, they soon developed their own 'spheres of influence' where they proceeded to set up favoured companies which could continue as before, sending out barrel-bowed sailing warehouses which took a year to make one Indian round voyage, which were quite content to carry on with an appalling wastage of human life, and satisfied if they made a voyage at all. As time went on, many of these ships did develop good under-water bodies, as far as their capacious hull-forms would permit. But they were still short, and they were too beamy and deep to sail really well. Their standing rigging, too, was cordage, and their lighter spars were broomsticks.

As for ships of war, the notorious conservative outlook of navies is no recent development. At first any merchant-ship could serve a turn as ship-of-war when called upon but, later, with the development of greater and heavier fire-power, a war-ship had to be above all a stable gun-platform. Having developed such ships, most navies were very loth to look ahead or even to contemplate the idea that what they had evolved could possibly be improved. Small privateers and other pirates had need of faster ships, but they did not have to be very fast to overhaul the merchantmen of any period up to the early nineteenth century. Hurrying is a modern idea, in all its forms. Ships and voyages alike were leisurely, and they stayed that way for centuries.

Why not? It was a good way, eminently satisfactory. There was a great tradition behind it. Moreover, as far as competition with the swifter ships of the East was concerned, this hardly existed, for the Asiatic ships soon concerned themselves with their own trade, and the Europeans with the commerce of Europe. The European ships had the great advantage of superior fire-power and a better understanding of naval warfare. European conservatism was further bolstered by monopolistic legislation and restrictive practices of all kinds.

It was the virile Yankees, really, who changed all this. The challenge of their great continent was a tonic to the early pioneers. Unhindered—after the Revolution—by European monopolies and practices, with unlimited supplies of the best of all ship-building materials in the forests of Maine and New England, with an abundance of good harbours to provide slip-ways in close proximity to the magnificent forests, it was little wonder that the New Englanders took early to shipbuilding, and soon excelled at it. There was no valid reason why the hull-forms of seagoing sailing-ships should be built to resemble a large herring barrel. The New Englanders, too, were early converts to the philosophy of speed. Perhaps the shortness of their summers and the fresh, clean air had something to do with that. There was moreover a good financial reward in fast ships. They were used as privateers, first, in the War of Independence. Afterwards they became traders, ranging the length and breadth of the great Pacific and making venturesome voyages to China and the East, whose success founded many a New England fortune. Then they cut in on the China trade to England, after the repeal of the British Navigation Laws, and soon 'clipped' weeks and months from the average China voyages.

The discovery of gold in California in 1848 and in Australia three years later gave a great impetus to the faster, larger sailing-ship, and the New Englanders met the demand. In the China trade, it was essential to get the tea each season to the main centres as quickly as possible, both to catch the early auctions and to minimise the supposedly ill effects of too long a stowage under hatches. The discoveries of gold led to gold-rushes in earnest, and thousands of enterprising spirits literally 'rushed' out round the Horn to San Francisco, for they were unable to cross the continent quickly or indeed at all, without making an expedition out of it. Later, thousands more hurried out from Europe and America round Good Hope to Melbourne. Yankee clippers carried the great majority of them. British shipowners found themselves compelled to order New England clipper-ships, 2000-tonners like the *James Baines* and the beautiful *Champion of the Seas*, and it was some years before British builders caught up with the strong American competition. When they did, it was to produce masterpieces.

A series of circumstances combined to make the American success with clippers short-lived—the American Civil War with its accompanying financial stringencies in New England and its serious difficulties for American shipowners generally, the opening up of the rich American hinterland with its unlimited opportunities for landbound trading, the political failure to appreciate the importance of shipping and seafaring generally which was so curiously marked a feature of the Washington scene for the best part of a century, and the rapid growth of European iron and steel ship-building—these spelled the death-knell of the American clipper, indeed of the American sailing-ship in general. After importing the plates for a steel four-master or two (and turning out some good but very expensive ships), the Maine shipbuilders had to turn their hands to big schooners which, though useful in the coastal trades, were never really suitable for making continuous global voyages. There was a limit to the size of practical wooden sailing-ships, though at least one giant six-masted schooner was built which was three hundred and fifty feet long. This was the *Wyoming*, built in 1910. The *Great Republic*, an early four-masted barque built by the famous Donald Mackay at Boston, was 335 feet long with a beam of 53 feet, but both she and the *Wyoming* were strengthened with straps of iron.

One other great improvement the New Englanders made, and that was in the cut and the set of sails, both square and fore-and-aft. Through the slovenly centuries, European ships had been content with sails which set like large white bags, big-bellied, flapping tent-like things which were altogether crude and inefficient. The Yankee clippers set sails of purest cotton-canvas, milled from cotton grown in the southern states. This was strong material and durable, but it was always much more difficult to 'hand' than the flax and the hempen sails of Europe. Cotton sails had to be cut well to do their work at all, and it was soon obvious to racing shipmasters interested in speed that the set of their sails was a matter of first importance. Such ships as the *James Baines*, the *Lightning*, and the *Red Jacket*—and their predecessors—kept their canvas set in perfect symmetry. Square sails and fore-and-afters alike were as flat as possible, and, as far as the designers' rather elementary ideas of aero-dynamics would allow, they were kept set always in such a way as to exert their maximum power.

This, of course, was old knowledge in a Chinese junk or an Arab dhow, which always had understood the business of sailing. It is only to the eye of the modern steamship seafarer that the junk looks lubberly. Her battened, heavy sails always set and pulled well, and so did the lateen sail of a dhow. If a lateen was the fore-runner (and by thousands of years) of the modern Bermuda rig, the classic Chinese sail combined the advantages of the fore-and-after with the square sail, for the battens can give the same effect as the European yards, with one-tenth the trouble.

According to what generally are accepted as the records, ships like the *James Baines* and *Lightning* were the fastest ocean-going sailing-ships which were ever built. According to no less an authority than Lloyd's Calendar,* which in its 1953 edition still had a section dealing with sailing-ship records, the fastest day's run ever recorded under sail was made by the American-built clipper *Champion of the Seas*, which, when sailing for the

* See Appendices.

ABOVE The five-masted, full-rigged ship *Preussen* was the greatest sailing-ship ever built.

BELOW The *Preussen* under all plain sail. She was a 'three-island' ship, like most of the Laeisz vessels, with a big midships superstructure.

Two views of the loss of the *Preussen*.
She drove ashore in the Straits of Dover,
helpless after a steamer had run into her.

↑ A nitrate port on the west coast of South America, in the old days.

Black Ball Line, once claimed to have made good 465 nautical miles in a day. The evidence in support of this run is an extract in the ship's own newspaper, the "*Champion of the Seas Gazette.*" (Most of those crack clippers produced their own newspapers.) The master of the *Champion*, a Captain Alexander Newlands— said to have been a modest and reserved seaman of great integrity—was in the habit of presenting his passengers with a weekly statement of progress, in this newspaper. From the noon of December 11 to the noon—ship's time—of December 12, 1854, while running her easting down, he reported the ship to have made 465 miles.

If she did make this run, then the *Champion of the Seas* was indeed champion of the seas, for she had been hurtling along at a shade better than twenty knots for a full 24 hours. I hate to do it, but I gravely doubt this 'record,' and for these reasons. The positions of the ship are given for noon on December 11, when she was reported as being in 47 01 South latitude and 88 31 East longitude, and for noon on December 12, by which time she had reached—the passengers are told—49 58 South and 99 15 East. True enough, the distance between these two positions is 465 miles made good on a course of S 67½E. But were they *observed* positions? If they were, how well were the observations made? The captain speaks of a heavy NW gale blowing at the time. In the Southern Ocean these came with rain, usually, and very murky weather, which did not clear up until the wind jumped to the SW and blew very hard. Such winds brought up enormous seas, and though the *Champion* was a big ship for those days and was not heavily laden, it is most improbable that she would be able to run at maximum speed for a full twenty-four hours through a gale-whipped sea which would of necessity be an ever-increasing menace to her. She must have been steered, too, with an uncanny perfection. Running heavy under conditions such as those, the usual square-rigged ship was inclined to yaw badly and, to make good 465 miles, she would have to sail at least 480 through the water. To cover that distance was, I think, impossible. It is far more probable that the alleged run was between an assumed position upon the 11th to an observed position on the 12th, and the computed position on the 11th was considerably to the westwards of where the ship actually was.

This would be reasonable. At the best, observations snatched hurriedly from the storm-tossed deck of a fleeing clipper in a down-south gale could not have been entirely reliable. I do not doubt for a moment that the ship made a tremendous run those twenty-four hours. But I do doubt that it was all of 465 miles, or anything like that. The following day the master reports 'no observations,' perhaps to signify that the previous positions were by observation; but he doesn't say so. Moreover, for the two days, December 13 and 14, he claims to have made good only 341 miles, and 1829 for the week. The *Champion* was in all 67 days under canvas on the voyage Liverpool to Melbourne, which gives her an average of 199 miles a day—a shade over eight knots. This was extremely good and she was without doubt a wonderful flyer. But it was not a record. The little Scots clipper *Thermopylae*, half her size, raced from London to Melbourne in 1868 in 60 days, and repeated the performance in 1870. A dozen ships, at least one of them a modern four-masted barque, made Australian passages better than the *Champion's*. Indeed, she does not appear in the lists of record-making passages at all, which seems odd for a vessel which could make a better day's run than ever was made by any other. If he drove her at anything like that speed, it is certain that Captain Newlands was a sail-carrier who would have done his best to break the record.

It is perhaps significant that the 465-mile run was reported only in the ship's own newspaper and, copied from that, in the Melbourne *Argus* on the ship's arrival. Passengers liked to read such things. I do not say they were concocted for them, but the temptation to put the best foot forward was always there. The Black Ball Line had many rivals. Captain Newlands may genuinely have believed that his ship had covered the distance, but I would like to see his private journal and the workbooks in which the sights—if any—were worked up. In those days, it was usual to use a slate.

Claims for other great runs are made by several Black

Ball liners, the *Lightning*, the *Donald Mackay*, and the *James Baines*. The *Lightning* claims day's runs of 436 and 430 miles, noon-to-noon, on different occasions, once in the North Atlantic and once in the Roaring Forties. The *James Baines* put in a claim for 420 miles, also made running the Easting down, in her case as part of a 63-day run from Liverpool to Melbourne. The *Lightning*, under Captain Enright, once ran 920 statute miles in 46 hours 48 minutes. In a report to the passengers aboard at the time Captain Enright wrote, under date March 21, 1857:—

> I cannot help informing you of the extraordinary run we have made during the last 48 hours—or rather, allowing for change of time, 46 hours 48 minutes. During this time we have run, by thoroughly good and trustworthy observation, not less than 790 knots or 920 statute miles, being an average of nearly 17 knots or more than 19½ statute miles an hour. Yesterday our noble ship made not less than 430 knots, amounting to an average during the 24 (23½) hours of more than 18 knots. Our change of longitude has amounted to 18 degrees, each degree being equal to 44 miles. I firmly believe this to be the greatest performance a sailing-ship has ever accomplished. I hope this information will in some degree compensate you for the inconvenience which the heavy weather has occasioned you.

In 1856 the *Lightning* covered 2188 miles in the seven-day period from June 28 to July 4. This has a genuine ring, though I doubt all those over-400-mile days. There is another point about these which makes them doubtful. Without exception, the terrific runs are claimed for ships bound eastwards, either in high latitudes of the North Atlantic or down in that part of the watery world which sailors used to know as the Roaring Forties. The ordinary method of obtaining longitude then was by means of a so-called time sight which provided data for the solution of a problem in spherical trigonometry, the answer to which gave—or was supposed to give—the ship's longitude, east or west of the Prime Meridian, in time, and this was converted into arc. At the best, such a method was dependent on two serious uncertainties. The first was an assumption of a probable latitude as part of the data for working the problem, and the second was the accuracy of the ship's chronometer. Masters provided their own chronometers then, and for many years afterwards. They may or may not have been accurate, and there was no means of checking them. It was the general practice to leave the final working of the time sight until noon, when it was hoped the ship's latitude might be established by catching a quick altitude of the sun just as it came to its zenith. But at the very best, the method was liable to a fair amount of honest error. It is a significant thing that no ship except the *Lightning* ever claimed to have run 400 miles or more for more than one day.

There was a claim, too, that the *James Baines* once touched 21 knots in the course of a day's run of 420 miles. She may have done so, though evidence is lacking as to how her speed was measured. It is possible that there was a considerable element of guess-work in it.

I do not for a moment wish to indicate a belief that the case for most sailing records may rest upon inadequate grounds, or that I doubt the integrity of those who claimed them. Yet it is significant that when the passengers went, so did the more extravagant claims. Speeds in the *Preussen* and *Potosi* were accurately measured and thoroughly checked and verified. They were also recorded, with typical German thoroughness. The greatest speed that either ship ever logged was 17½ knots, and that was under ideal conditions. These big 'P' ships were very much more powerful than any clipper. The *Preussen* once kept up a speed of 17 to 17½ knots for a four-hour watch, but at the end of that time the increasing sea cut her speed down, despite her enormous length, her great power, and the fact that she was still being driven under every stitch of sail. And despite, too, the fact that she was a ship especially designed to make use of strong gales, strengthened in every way, with steel masts and yards and wire and chain rigging, and with a steel hull which was strengthened to accept any stress the great masts might put upon it, or the sea. The *Preussen* had a built-up deck amidships which was ninety-three feet long, and this effectively kept any dangerous weight of water from her main decks. The older type of sailing-vessel, running in a gale of wind, would fill her decks from rail to rail if she were pressed too hard, and her high bulwarks, unable to shed the sea fast enough as it came aboard, would soon be a source of danger. The long midships super-structure saved the *Preussen* and the *Potosi* from this risk.

Accurate measurement over a period of years showed that the mean speed of the *Preussen* with a beam wind of Beaufort Force 8—that is, a moderate gale—and deep-loaded, was 13.7 knots, while the *Potosi* under the same conditions had a mean speed of 13.1 knots. These huge ships were more deeply laden than any clipper ever was. They could also stand a great deal more punishment from the sea. The usual clipper at the height of the clipper era was called upon to move a round thousand tons of cargo through the water, with a sail area of some 40,000 square feet and a crew which averaged at least a man for each thousand square feet of canvas. The *Preussen*, with the same crew as a small clipper and 60,000 square feet of canvas, moved 8,000 tons of cargo.

This is in no way to belittle the clipper ships, for they were beauties and they did magnificently. But all too often theirs is regarded as the culminating era of deepsea sail. They are commonly thought to be the ultimate in the development of the ocean-going sailing-ship. My point is that in fact they were not. Just when sailing-ships could have been further developed and the science of the use of the ocean winds brought really near perfection, the concentration of too many competent ship-owners on the development of engined vessels—an easier way to progress—handicapped the sailing-ship off the face of the sea. The clippers were ephemeral and their day was soon gone. For a while afterwards—perhaps for another twenty years after the opening of the Canal at Suez—cargo-carrying steam-ships were still handicapped in their efforts to compete with long-voyage sail.

But in the interval too many owners who were still interested in sailing-ships turned in the wrong direction, towards the devel-opment of under-canvased hogs of ships which broke good men's hearts and drove bad men to drink. Sailing-ships became larger and larger, clumsy great wall-sided warehouses, all too often—drifters, as their predecessors had been, centuries earlier, with their designers and their owners blinded by the imagined need for cargo capacity before all else. True, a four-masted barque with stump t'gall'nt rig * and a bit of a donkey-engine to raise steam in ports could lurch about the world with a crew of 24 men, and carry 4500 tons of cargo when she could get it. Far too often she couldn't *sail*; even more often, she was not properly sailed. In America the pioneering stock which had produced the great clipper captains and crews turned their eyes inland, towards the development of their own country. In Britain, the best seafarers soon turned to steamships. Many an older captain, of course, and a considerable number of the older able seamen, stuck to sailing-ships. But, more and more, the oncoming officers looked upon sailing-ships merely as a training-ground, an initiation which they would profit from, in steam.

There were plenty of magnificent British steel and iron square-rigged ships at the turn of the century, and three hundred of them still sailed that day in 1910 when the *Preussen* walked by the little *Inver* barque. But they were a doomed three hundred. Not a single shipowner either in Britain or America believed in them, as practical ships. The building of such ships had ceased entirely in British yards and had long been finished in America. In Britain, a few lines carried on each with a handful of ships which were still of use in specialised trades, such as the carriage of case oil from the eastern seaboard of the United States to the Far East, or they sent old ships tramping, seeking bulk cargoes of coal or wheat or lumber or guano wherever they could be found. Steadily more and more such ships were sold to Scandinavian flags where, under-capitalised and sailed by steady-going, competent masters who generally had some financial interest in them, they continued for a decade or two to make a meagre living. But they accepted the increasing inroads of the powered ship. They were not fighting back. They had taken the second place and were well on the way to no place at all. All hope of the fast parcel trade, of passenger-carrying, of any sort of liner trade, had been abandoned. Despite the efforts of a

* A somewhat squat vessel with shorter masts than usual, and no royals.

few far-sighted men, square-rigged sailing-ships had been allowed to decline, after the clipper era, except in size.

It need not have been so. The French and a few Germans still saw the opportunity for real sailing-ships, but the French, having built a fleet of magnificent steel four-masters, spoiled them with politics, bolstered them with bounties which, being essentially unsound in a business so fiercely international as deep-sea shipping, led to their ruin. When the bounties stopped the French sailing-ships stopped too.

It was left to the Germans to carry on—above all, it was left to the Flying 'P' Line of the Hamburg House of Laeisz. The House of Laeisz fought back with a fleet of splendid ships in a trade its owners and its masters thoroughly understood. The day the *Preussen* was launched might have ushered in a new era of sail, though, a few years later, the crew of the little *Inver* barque had gazed at her with astonishment amounting almost to awe, as if she were an apparition from another age. It was their barque, indeed, which belonged to another era. She was a nice little barque and her master was a fine old man. At least two of her apprentices were to rise to positions of distinction, though not at sea. But she was of use as an earning entity in the shipping world only while her fabric lasted, only as long as the metal she was made of survived the perils of rust and the sea. Beyond that, she had no future—neither she nor any of her kind. She was a sailing acceptance of the supremacy of steam and as such she was doomed.

But the *Preussen* could—and should—have founded a new sailing dynasty.

Chapter two

THE LAEISZ STORY

THERE were many beautiful ships built towards the end of the sailing era, especially in Scotland. Square-rigged ships did not easily yield to the encroaching steamers. After all, it took the powered vessels over a century and a quarter finally to drive the engine-less cargo-carrier from the face of the sea. Many beautiful and able ships were built in Great Britain during the 1880's and some, too, in the 1890's. But many even among the best of them suffered grave disadvantages. In order to be fast, they had to be too fine-lined to carry big cargoes. If they were not fast, they often were poor sailing-ships. Far too many of them could not sail and, of those which could, far too many were not sailed properly either because of shortage of crew, poorness of gear, or, as time went on, the sad deterioration in the quality of officers, especially of masters. Soon almost every owner was either changing over to steamers, or at least he kept the idea in mind. All the sailing liners went—the splendid fleets of the *Lochs*, the *Glens*, the *Clans*, and the rest of them. A very few Scots and a few more Liverpool owners kept sailing-ships for a while but, except for the Scots, they did not keep regular lines. They competed with the Scandinavians, buying up old ships and running them to death.

By the first decade of the twentieth century, only Devitt and Moore's still maintained anything like a real line of sailing-ships from anywhere in Britain, and they had few ships left by that time. Those they had were used for training, and splendid ships they were. For a while, the great steamship companies

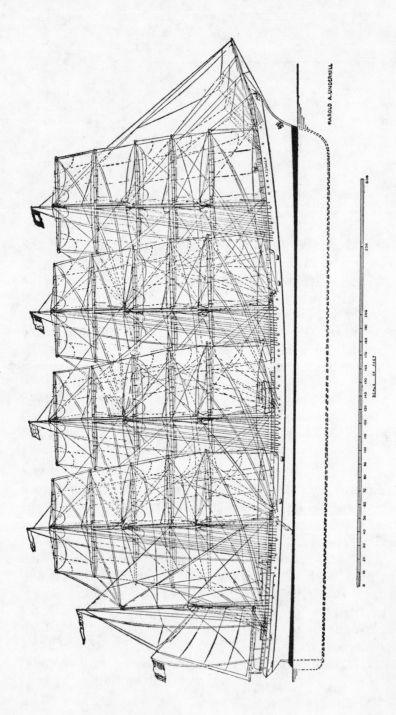

SCALE OF FEET

HAROLD A. UNDERHILL

The France

who had themselves been among the first to discard sailing-ships insisted that their officers should be trained under sail. Almost all important pilotage services kept the same requirement, for pilots never knew when they might have a big sailing-ship to handle. But, as far as the liner companies went, the '14–'18 war put an end to their interest even in sail-training. A decade or so later, most pilotage services had followed suit. By the 1950's, few serving masters who had ever been in a sailing-ship, and almost no sail-trained mates, remained in British ships, though the masters of the great Cunarders, even in 1953, were men who had begun as apprentices in square-rigged ships. So were a few senior masters in other lines, and a sprinkling of marine superintendents ashore and Elder and some of the Younger Brethren of Trinity House. But by 1950—if not long before—it had become impossible to man a Cape Horner (if there had been one to man) with experienced British officers and crew less than fifty years of age.

As for the splendid French fleet of big steel sailing-ships, they found themselves handicapped out of existence by the very advantages of the system under which they had been nurtured. Building subsidies and a bounty on mileage sailed were all very well while they lasted. But first the building subsidy stopped and so did the building. Then the bounties were stopped, and so did the sailing. At the end of the '14–'18 war, many French ports were literally jammed with magnificent big ships and barques lying two and three abreast, which no one could run any longer because owners, masters, and crews alike had been too long accustomed to artificial aids, and then could not do without them. The high freights ruling during the war had disguised the truth for a while, but when the freight market collapsed the whole science of deepwater sailing in France came almost at once to an end.

It was a pity. The French had built good ships and they knew how to sail them. They were the first, indeed, to develop the five-masted square-rigger. The five-masted French barque *France* was built in Scotland in 1890, and she was a vessel of 3784 gross register tons (compared with the *Preussen's* 5081 and the *Potosi's* 4026), 361 feet in length with a beam of 48.8 feet and a depth of 25.9. The *France* was a strong, magnificently built vessel which could sail, and she was well-handled by good masters and officers, with a very able crew. She could load little short of 6000 tons, and on her maiden voyage she ran from Barry Dock to Rio in a day more than a month. Later, she sailed from the Channel to Valparaiso in 63 days, which was very good. But she barely managed to survive into the twentieth century. On a passage outwards towards Chile with a full cargo of Tyneside coal in 1901, she went missing. There was a report later that a little barque named the *Josepha* had sighted the great five-master, on her beam ends with the sea washing along her whole main deck, and no one aboard, just two months after she had sailed from the Tyne. That was the end of the *France*.

After that, the French built one more five-masted barque, the 5633-ton *France II*, which was 419 feet long with a beam of 55.8 feet and a depth of 24.9. She was an auxiliary but she did not last more than ten years, either. I remember seeing her towing up the River Yarra at Melbourne and thinking that she looked a rather big and clumsy ship. She had a tremendous sheer most of which was in her very long forecastle-head, which reared up like a ski-run. She had a rather squat rig for so large a ship. She was supposed to be able to do 17 knots, but in fact her logs showed that she seldom passed 14 and, despite the help of her twin screws, she did not break any sailing records. She was a powerful vessel which could stand a lot of driving. The auxiliary engines were taken out of her after the '14–'18 war, but not long afterwards she got on a reef off the coast of New Caledonia, and stayed there. The year was 1922.

Auxiliary five-masted barques, indeed, did not do very well. There were only four ever built—the *France II*, the German *Maria Rickmers* and *R. C. Rickmers* (which were auxiliary steamers), and the Danish East Asiatic Company's *Kjøbenhavn*. The *R. C. Rickmers* was built in 1906 and was a handsome model of a ship, spoiled by a squat funnel. Rickmers were enterprising sailing-ship owners, and so were the Vinnens of Bremen. Rickmers, Vinnens, and Laeisz all developed the big sailing-ship with enterprise, determination, and ability. The *R. C. Rickmers* registered 5548 tons and was 410.5 feet long between perpendiculars—a truly enormous sailing-ship (even with her bit of a steam engine). The Rickmers Line was interested in the Far Eastern trade, which it had developed very well. All these German lines (like all other lines which could do so) worked with companies of their own nationals established ashore, and there was a considerable German interest in the East. So the *R. C. Rickmers* spent most of her time under the German flag trading to the East, either with case oil from American ports or bulk cargoes such as cement and coal from northern Europe. Then, if she could find such a cargo, she loaded rice in Burma for the homeward passage. Sometimes she had to go tramping, taking whatever cargoes she might find. She sailed steadily from 1907 until the outbreak of the first World War, but though her steam engines and boilers took up good space in the hold which could better have been filled with cargo and she had to carry additional crew to steam, her passages, on the whole, were simply good sailing-ship passages. Her best passage, for example from Taltal in Chile to Hamburg, was 57 days. Both the engineless *Potosi* and *Preussen* did as well as that, without paying any engine-room crews. The *R. C. Rickmers* was taken in a British port at the outbreak of war in 1914 and, not long afterwards, a German submarine sent her to the bottom.

The *Kjøbenhavn* was built in 1921 and went missing in 1928-29 when on a passage from Montevideo towards Australia to load grain. She was a magnificent big five-masted barque, built in Scotland, registering 3901 gross tons, 369 feet long with a beam of 49.3 feet and a depth of 26.9. She was equipped with wireless and every possible aid to navigation which could have been of use to her. She was well manned and ably sailed. She was kept up magnificently, as all the Danish East Asiatic ships always have been. She had a splendid crew which included forty cadets. Yet she sailed off on what should have been a commonplace passage, a ballast run through the Roaring Forties with everything in her favour, and, from that day onwards, she disappeared from the face of the sea. Perhaps she was too big? All these five-masters had to face that charge. Yet size had nothing to do with the drifting ashore of the *France II*, and certainly nothing whatever to do with the loss of the *R. C. Rickmers* (except perhaps to make her a better target). The *Kjøbenhavn* had shown herself to be a good sailer and a fine, able vessel. She could have been caught by-the-lee, of course, in a sudden shift of wind (as happens in the Roaring Forties), and blown over. That is indeed her most likely fate, in the opinion of Cape Horn seamen. But size would have nothing whatever to do with that. It could happen to any ship.

An earlier auxiliary five-master, the Rickmers five-masted barque *Maria Rickmers,* also went missing. The *Maria Rickmers* was built in 1890, perhaps to rival the first *France*. She was built by Russell's at Port Glasgow and was a little larger than the *France*, and was very heavily rigged. She carried three skysails which added to the weight aloft far more than they were worth. Her first voyage was to be with coal from South Wales to Singapore, and then with rice from Saigon homewards. She took 82 days to reach Singapore which was no better than sailing-ship time. Her owners sent a reprimand so severely worded to the poor master that as soon as he had read it, he fell dead on the spot. The mate—a most experienced man—took the big ship up to Saigon and loaded the rice. The *Maria Rickmers* sailed from the Cochin-China port on July 14, 1892, and passed Anjer ten days later. She has not been heard of since.

Auxiliary fóur-masted barques have not done any better than their outsize sisters, as far as sailing goes. There have not been many of them, built as such. The big *Magdalene Vinnen* was perhaps the best of them. She was in the Australian trade when I was in that run in the four-masted barques *Herzogin Cecilie* and *Parma* and the ship *Grace Harwar*, but though she was a good ship and had a useful diesel engine for which she had been designed, she never made better than good sailing-ship voyages. In 1933 we beat her easily, with the *Parma's* 83-day run from Spencer Gulf to Falmouth.

Indeed no auxiliary square-rigged ships did much good in the deepwater trades. The advantages which the auxiliary was thought to possess were largely imaginary on long deepsea voyages, and the engines wasted space and added to both capital and running costs. A real square-rigged ship had too great a windage in her masts and yards and tremendous array of wire and cordage to be pushed easily against a head wind; indeed the power necessary to give her a useful speed in such conditions would make her a full-powered motor-ship. Then what sense would there be in sailing? The temptation to a master to use the power with which he was provided would be altogether too great. Engines powerful enough merely to kick the ship ahead in a calm were of no real use; indeed, they could be a menace, for two reasons. In the first place, any propeller must cause drag and upset the ship's sailing qualities to greater or less degree, and even if the propeller's blades were feathering, the run of the ship would still be spoiled to some extent. In the second place, a master, knowing that he had the help of the engine, might very well come to rely upon it to help him off a lee shore, or help to push the ship's head round when beating under adverse conditions, and a fault in the engine or a greater strength in the set than the engine could push against could lead to the loss of the ship. At least one of the Vinnen five-masters was lost in this way, in the English Channel. Undeterred by the losses both of the *Maria* and *R. C. Rickmers,* the Vinnen Line built five five-masted auxiliary sailing-ships of an unorthodox rig, during the 1920's. They were really big schooners with square tops'ls on the foremast and the middle-mast. Sailors spoke of them as five-masted bastards. The theory was that they would be ideal for such trades as that between Northern Europe and the River Plate, with its good trade winds and its zone of calms. But they were not. They did not sail very well and they did not handle well and, after one was lost, at least one of the others was converted into a full-powered motorship.

No, there was no answer to powered competition in putting power in the sailing-ships themselves. That way lay total failure. It was a complete delusion. Internal combustion engines were small when they were first put into sailing-ships—too weak to be of real use. And so the tendency was to reduce the windage—

to cut down the sailing-ship's rig. This happened widely on the British coast, and before very long most of the few surviving schooners were regarded as motorships with auxiliary sails, not sailing-ships with auxiliary motors. From that, it was an easy step to becoming full motor-ships in fact and, though some of the Scandinavian countries continued to develop a form of alleged auxiliary schooner even after the second World War, in fact the over-riding consideration was to maintain a pretence of being auxiliaries in order to defeat certain manning provisions in the engine-rooms, and so keep down running costs. The vessels were not real sailing-ships at all. Any serious defect in their motors kept them in port.

The House of Laeisz, unlike the French House of Bordes and the Vinnens and Rickmers—the last great German sailing-ship lines—was never deluded by the auxiliary motor fallacy. The way to develop better sailing-ships was by doing just that—by developing better *pure* sailing-ships. In this there was one other factor, too, of incalculable importance—indeed it was the very keystone of the whole structure of shipping everywhere. That was the men. Power spoiled good men just as it spoiled the ships which tried to use it. Power spoiled masters, and it spoiled crews. Once power was introduced there could never be enough—more and bigger engines became the cry, and sailing qualities and abilities went on the discard. It was fatally easy to start up the internal combustion engine. Once started, there was no end to it.

The father of Ferdinand Laeisz was a merchant in Hamburg before 1800. Hamburgers were always enterprising business-men who kept an eye on the sea. The Germans were late-comers in the general expansion of overseas trade, though there were German sailors in Da Gama's ships and in others of the early Portuguese pioneering ships in the Indian Ocean. On the whole, the disunited states of the country which later became Germany were interested in land development, and seafaring was left to the river ports of Hamburg and Bremen, and the ancient Baltic ports. But when the Germans did turn their attention to the development of overseas trade, it was with typical Teuton

↑ The firm of F. Laeisz was sailing Cape Horners for a century. This is the *Peking,* one of the last. Note the raised midships superstructure, which prevented the main deck from being heavily swept by the sea.

This is what happened aboard the usual Cape Horner—main deck awash and dangerous to work; but all the gear led here, and it must be used.　　　　　　　　→

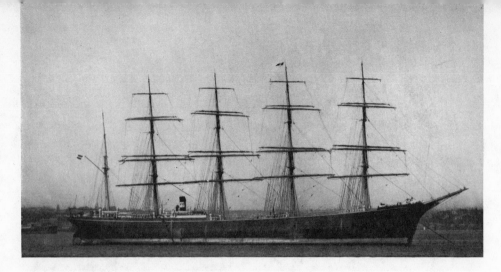

thoroughness. Business houses spread to South America, to China and Japan, to the east and west coasts of Africa, to the South Seas. All this activity led to an increased employment for German ships, which then flew a variety of flags.

The older Laeisz—Ferdinand, founder of the great sailing-ship line—built his first ship, the 220-ton wooden brig *Carl*, in 1839, and the firm was still sailing two four-masted barques in 1939 when the outbreak of the second World War put an end to all such activities. The Laeisz Line was sailing its own ships for a century, though Ferdinand Laeisz probably had an interest in other vessels before he built the *Carl*. He was a man of enterprise and terrific energy. In the 1840's he was interested in South Seas whalers. He was a pioneer in the Japanese trade. He made ventures in all sorts of things, including silk top-hats, and the success of those ventures helped to bring in the money for a ship or two.

The *Carl* was built by Jacob Meyer in Lübeck and her first voyage was from that port to Pernambuco—later called Recife—on the coast of Brazil, with a cargo of general which included a consignment of hemp rope and a parcel of silk hats. Later she made a very successful voyage to Guayaquil with much the same sort of cargo, and Laeisz bought other ships to carry his ventures over the East. In those days, small sailing-ships did not so much carry goods to earn freights. They carried their owners' own merchandise in which they traded. Small Laeisz brigs and minute barques began to drop into odd ports from Singapore to Vladivostok and from Sydney to Yokohama, with a comprador aboard, usually, to do the actual trading. Those were the days when a little ship could sail to fortune, as the New Englanders well knew. She might begin, say, by taking a general cargo which could be sold readily to German firms established at Pernambuco, and move up from there to lift rum in the West Indies bought for sale to the military clique in Sydney (rum was the early currency of New South Wales) and, in Sydney, change

ABOVE   The auxiliary five-masted barque *R. C. Rickmers*. Sailors held that the funnel spoiled her.

CENTER   The *Kjøbenhavn* went missing in 1928/29. She was the last of the five-masted barques.

BELOW   The big *France* was lost on a reef off New Caledonia.

←

part of her cargo for trade goods which in turn she would use to buy sandalwood in the Fiji Islands, filling her hold with *bêche-de-mer* and such aphrodisiac stuff, all of which was readily saleable in China. Everything was grist to the little ship's mill. She was a travelling warehouse which profited—usually considerably—on her own goods. She might handle a parcel of opium (though this was a specialty for fast ships), or get herself a cargo of jerked beef from some hot Madagascar roadstead by the simple process of building a corral ashore and rounding up the cattle. The world was hers and the trade thereof, and an enterprising man who could see his opportunities and had the energy and the integrity to follow them could make a fortune. It was usual to establish some sort of 'factory' ashore in the ports where trade was good and likely to be permanent. The Germans were sometimes handicapped by the prior claims of others but, in the great Pacific, throughout the East, and upon the vast rich continent of South America, there were opportunities for all.

But conditions were constantly changing, politically, industrially, in every way. Powerful combinations of merchants, of one nationality or another, were always trying to monopolise certain trades. Often, they succeeded. A firm of enterprise had always to be on the lookout for changed opportunities. In the middle nineteenth century, there were three trades of importance on the west coast of South America in which there were obvious fields for great expansion. These were in copper-ore, guano, and nitrates. Much of the copper-ore was already going to South Wales (in a fleet of magnificent little wooden ships of which we have not heard anything like enough). The guano was wretched stuff, the droppings of millions of sea birds, and to get a cargo meant scraping the stuff from rocks and taking it aboard at exposed roadsteads off desolate islands, literally sack by sack, boatful by boatful. It was a trade that would obviously come to an end when the deposits were dug through. It was not the birds' current efforts which produced the stuff in commercial quantities, but the discovery of enormous rookeries where the birds had been undisturbed for ages. The guano business scarcely

seemed a trade worth organising, in a big way. But nitrates
were different. So in 1867 Ferdinand and Carl Laeisz bought
six wooden barques which had been built for a German firm
in Valparaiso, and that was their beginning in the nitrate trade.
The six barques were each between 450 and 600 tons, and their
names were the *Rosa y Isabel, Henrique Teodoro, Mercedes,
Ricardo, Carolina,* and *Don Julio.* They were built by the Hamburg firm of Stülcken, and they were good ships. They were
already in the nitrate trade round the Horn. Germany needed
nitrates for fertilisers, and Hamburg was the depot, too, for the
distribution of such things deep into Europe and even to much
of Scandinavia. As for outward cargoes, there was usually plenty
of general cargo for German firms in Chile and Peru or, at the
worst, bulk cargoes of coke. The day had gone then when ships
traded in their own right, though, to some extent, many ships
still carried cargoes in which their owners had an interest. It
is probable—I do not know—that the House of Laeisz acquired
an interest in some nitrate mines, or in the nitrate business some
way or other. I know that the firm bought whole cargoes of
nitrate even until the end of the 1920's. Such interests naturally
helped to assure a continuance of cargoes.

There were also plenty of German interests in Mexico and
Ecuador, and in Central America. Ships took out goods for these
firms, and then moved down to the Chilean nitrate ports to load
for home. Or they took, perhaps, a bulk cargo of coke or other
fuel for Valparaiso, or to Corral, and then carried coastal
cargo—at a good rate—up to Iquique, with calls at half a dozen
places on the way. An interest in a firm or firms ashore helped to
obtain these coastal cargoes, which were worth having.

It was by no means left exclusively to Laeisz ships to exploit
the trading opportunities for sailing-ships all along the west
coast of South America. But—apart from such worthy special-
ists as the Swansea copper-ore men—the West Coast charters
were generally looked upon as a last resort. The earning of a
freight from such parts was too often accepted as a forlorn,
wearisome business of spending months at an open roadstead,
exposed to the hazards of earthquakes and the odd northerly

gale, and suffering throughout the extreme and expensive dila-
toriness of the local inhabitants. The result of this attitude was
that ships of other nationalities (apart later from the subsidised
French) avoided the place, if they could, and served it poorly
if they had to serve it at all. Hundreds of British ships flocked
there from time to time, but on the whole they took things as
they found them. They had other trades which paid better
and were more pleasant. What Laeisz had the business sense
to foresee was that the nitrate trade would continue to be of
value to sailing-ships for many years. It was worth building for.
It was worth organising. He did not look upon it merely as a
means of providing the odd and difficult cargo for an outmoded
type of ship. Far from it!

And so, beginning with those six small barques, the Laeisz
Line built up the nitrate trade from the west coast of South
America until they were employing not only the greatest
fleet of big sailing-ships in the world, but the greatest ships.
It was profitable. The Laeisz family was able, among other
things, to build a great concert-hall in Hamburg and present it
to the city. Even after all the bombs of the second World War,
the Laeisz concert-hall still stood in Hamburg, though it was no
longer known by its proper name and half of it was then used as
studios for the British Forces radio network in occupied Germany.
The scroll-work round the shield with the name F. Laeisz was
still there.

At first, as he expanded, Laeisz bought good sailing-ships
wherever he could find them, and built others. At least one of his
early wooden ships was a small brig which was built in North
America, the *Los Hermanos* ex *North Point,* which was built at
Williamsburg, New York in 1855. He bought Dutch ships and
he bought Swedish ships, but above all, he bought Britishers.
One quartette of lovely barques he bought from British owners
included the little *Puck,* of just under 500 tons, built in Sunder-
land in 1863 as the *Peep-o'-Day,* as well as three others which
he renamed the *Pluto, Poncho,* and *Paquita.* Why the Laeisz
family chose the initial P for their ships nobody can say. Perhaps
it began from the choice of the nickname, *Pudel,* for a beautiful

and especially favoured little barque, in 1856. The tradition is that the *Pudel* was given that name because it was the pet-name of the goodlooking Mrs. Carl Laeisz, who was famed for her magnificent curly hair. On this account, Mrs. Laeisz was known to her family and friends as Pudel, and *Pudel* became the name of the barque. The *Pudel* enjoyed a long and highly prosperous career, mostly in the Eastern trade, and it was not long after this that all the Laeisz ships were given names beginning with the letter P.

By the 1880's, the line was building its own steel sailing-ships of over a thousand tons. Among these were the long-lived barques *Plus* and *Prompt*. I knew the *Plus* very well, in after years. She was a vessel with very good sailing qualities. When I knew her she was owned in Finland, and Captain Ruben de Cloux had some shares in her. It was in her saloon in the London docks that small group of us finalised our plans for buying the Laeisz four-master *Parma,* in 1930. De Cloux had command of the *Plus* then and looked upon the experience as a holiday, for his usual command was one of the big undermanned four-masters in the Australian trade. He said the *Plus* was a lovely ship and a splendid sailer. She was the kind of ship, he said, that a master felt could almost understand what he said to her. She handled like a yacht and moved through the water like a clipper, and she had no vices at all. Many of the Laeisz ships were like that, both big ships and small.

As the size of metal ships steadily increased, the Laeisz Line built 1500-tonners, then 1700-tonners—all full-rigged ships. Several of these ships, built in the 1880's, survived until after the '14–'18 war, mostly then under the Norwegian or the Finnish flags. Of these I remember personally the *Parchim* and the *Pampa,* both Finns when I knew them. These ships had made great passages in the West Coast trade for the House of Laeisz. It was nothing unusual for them to make the voyage out to Chile from the English Channel in little over two months.

It was the advent of the four-masted barque which really gave the Laeisz Line the chance to leap ahead. As the size of

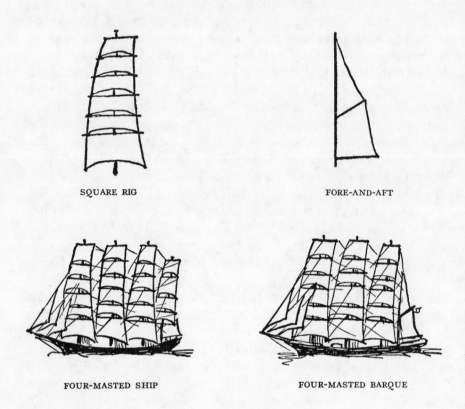

SQUARE RIG   FORE-AND-AFT

FOUR-MASTED SHIP   FOUR-MASTED BARQUE

ships increased it became necessary to give them four masts, instead of what had been for several centuries the traditional three. A ship with a water-line length of 300 feet or so required disproportionately high masts and long yards, if she were rigged with three masts, and the stresses were enormous. She was too easily dismasted. To rig her with three square-rigged masts and an after-mast fore-and-aft rigged gave her a good balance, and made her more manageable and much more manoeuvrable. At first, some owners (Rickmers was one) experimented with four-masted full-rigged ships which were square-rigged on all their masts. There were some beautiful big ships of this rig, of which a notable example was the skysail-yarder *Peter Rickmers*. But it

was soon obvious to the masters of these ships that the yards on
the fourth mast were not really much help. A ship was much
more manageable with the jigger-mast carrying only fore-and-
aft canvas, and she was just as fast—or very nearly so. In bad
weather it was customary to reduce sail on the aftermost mast
first, because canvas set there could cause the ship to fly up into
the wind, or at least to steer badly. So the four-masted ship rig
soon went out. It never was adopted by the Laeisz ships, for it
was not a good rig for Cape Horn. (Indeed, it is probable that
the great *Preussen* would have done equally as well rigged as a
five-masted barque.)

The first Laeisz four-masters were the powerful *Pisagua* and
Placilla, a pair of massive beauties. Each registered little short of
3000 tons. They were built by Tecklenborg—the German-built
Laeisz sailers were practically all built either by Tecklenborg at
Geestemunde or by Blohm and Voss at Hamburg—and they
began to make names for themselves on their maiden voyages.
On her first passage outwards, the *Pisagua* drove from the Channel to Valparaiso in 70 days. She continued to make splendid
passages for the following eighteen years. Then in 1910 she was
struck in the English Channel by an outward bound P. and O.
liner which was so badly damaged by the heavy-laden nitrate
ship that she sank. It was just after 4 o'clock on a windy March
morning. The *Pisagua* was beating up-channel under a press of
sail and the liner did not give her the right of way, as she should
have done, for sailing-ships had the undisputed right-of-way
over powered vessels at sea. The weather was clear, and the navigation lights of both ships were burning brightly. In such circumstances it was the duty of the ship which had the right of
way to keep her course and speed; otherwise the ship which had
the duty to give way might become confused. So both ships stood
on, and for once it was the steamer which went down. But the
Pisagua was very badly damaged and she did not sail for Laeisz
again.

As for the *Placilla,* it was her privilege to be taken from the
stocks by Robert Hilgendorf. This great seaman immediately
proceeded to drive her from the Channel to her port in Chile in

58 days. Only the *Preussen* could beat this record, and then by just one day. From the West Coast back again was a much longer route, for sailing-ships had first to stand out from the Chilean coast to get well out of the current sweeping northwards there, and then make a long board down to the westerlies which blew them to the Horn. The outward route in the South Atlantic, too, was shorter, for the outward-bounder hugged the land. (The chart on page 39 shows the difference clearly.) Nonetheless Hilgendorf raced the *Placilla* back from Iquique to the Channel in 75 days. Then he was out again in 62, and home in 70; Hilgendorf never made a bad passage.

The *Placilla* and the *Pisagua* showed the superiority of the big four-master in the nitrate trade, and Laeisz built up his fleet with similar ships. His little barques were dispersed and most of the full-riggers soon followed them. He bought strong four-masters from Great Britain and he had Blohm and Voss and Tecklenborg build more, usually each yard furnishing a new ship —or a pair of ships—alternatively. The *Pitlochry* and the *Persimmon* were two British-built Laeisz four-masters. The *Pitlochry* was built for Laeisz by Stephen and Sons at Dundee. She was of 3088 tons gross register, and she sailed under the Flying 'P' house-flag from 1894 until 1913. Hilgendorf had command of her for a while, and she could sail. The *Persimmon* had been the *Drumrock,* built by Ramage and Ferguson at Leith in 1899. She was an unusually fine ship, the last of the *Drums* and the best of them. She was a big fellow, 3100 tons, and a three-skysail-yarder. What was most unusual in ships of that time, she had excellently planned accommodation for the crew which even included a bathroom. This was hitherto unheard of, for the sailing-ship sailor was expected to take his ablutions in a bucket or, preferably, naked in a Doldrums rain-squall.

The *Persimmon* could sail, too, and her passages both outwards and home again were consistently less than two and a half months. Laeisz sold her to the Vinnens in 1913, when she was renamed the *Helvig Vinnen,* and, under this name, she was one of the many fine German sailers to become American prizes in the first World War, which found them on the west coast of

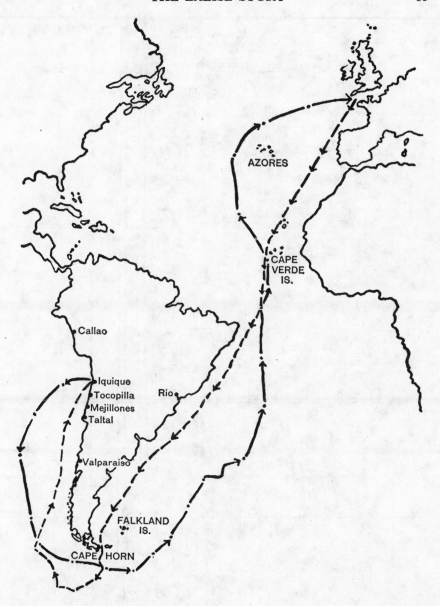

Outward and homeward routes between the Channel and Chile.
Actual voyages are plotted.

The Potosi

'HAROLD A.UNDERHILL'

North America. The Dollar Line of San Francisco ran her for a while—one voyage, I think—and then she went to Canadian lumber interests to be used as a lumber barge, in tow. Feeling, perhaps, that such lowly employment was beneath her, the old ship took a wild sheer one day and stranded herself on the rocks in Queen Charlotte's Sound. She thumped herself on the rocks good and hard, and there she remains.

But before the *Pitlochry* and the *Persimmon* joined the Flying 'P' Line, the great five-masted barque *Potosi* had been built by Tecklenborg's at Geestemunde, and under Hilgendorf was sailing magnificently. The *Potosi* was undoubtedly the best five-masted barque and one of the best square-rigged ships ever built. Her long midships house, the enormous strength of her hull and her rigging, and her splendid masters and good crews combined to make her outstanding. In a way, she was a better ship and a greater ship even than the *Preussen,* though the *Preussen* was the larger and was proved statistically to be half a knot faster, under some conditions. If the *Preussen* sailed, in 1903, from the Channel to Iquique in 57 days, the *Potosi* then had already made the run to Valparaiso in 59, and she did it twice. That very year she romped homewards round the Horn from Iquique to the Channel in 57 days, and the *Preussen's* best homeward passage was 61 days in 1904.

The *Potosi* was said by some critics to be a German answer to the five-masted barque *France,* but indeed she was a logical development in the story of the Laeisz Cape Horn ship. As barques and full-riggers had had to develop into four-masted barques when sailing-ships increased in size, so inevitably did the four-masters grow into five-masters. The *Potosi* was not the first German five-masted barque, for the *Maria Rickmers* had preceded her by five years. The *Potosi* was a beamier and deeper ship than the *Maria Rickmers,* though she was not quite so long. She carried a little over 6000 tons, and her hull was designed to stand any stresses which the combination of the Cape Horn seas, her enormous nitrate cargo, and the tremendous spread of her great sail area could impose upon it. All her running rigging, except the necessary tackles of best manila or Europe hemp, was of chain or wire. Even her royals—her uppermost sails, which are the first to be taken in—were of double-strength Cape Horn canvas. She had the long midships house, in which her people were accommodated. This house was more than a solid super-structure handy for providing reasonably dry quarters. It pro-vided a safe working platform for the sailors and an unassailable place of control for the officers. It was high up out of the sea and, under Cape Horn conditions, its openings to the maindeck could be secured, giving then entry only through scuttles in the deck. This kept the sea out—or most of it—and the galley dry, and gave the sailmaker and the carpenter good places to work.

Many a long steel sailing-ship lost a whole watch of her crew —half the crew—over the side in the Cape Horn seas. Men had to work on deck because the gear that controlled the sails and yards all led there and could lead nowhere else. When a deeply loaded ship was rolling badly, running before a great wind and sea, she would often fill her decks with green water from rail to rail. Under such conditions a slip could well mean death. In the *Potosi* and all the other big Laeisz ships this was not so, for the midships house kept the men out of the sea to some extent, and broke the force of the water sweeping aboard. Where the men had to work on the exposed main deck, heavy netting was lashed up six feet above the bulwarks, to keep them from being washed over the side. Strong steel netting was rigged permanently be-neath the jibboom, and this used to be one of the hall-marks of the German ships. Brace-winches—the largely neglected inven-tion of an able Scots shipmaster named Jarvis—were installed, and these had two great advantages. They simplified the heavy work of bracing (of manipulating those wires and ropes which controlled the angle of the yards) and they kept men from the dangerous proximity of the ship's side. Brace-winches were in-stalled immediately abaft the fife-rails of the masts and, if a big sea threatened to engulf the men while bracing, they could simply put on the brake and leap for the safety of the gear leading to the belaying-pins all round the fife-rail.

Such things saved lives. They boosted morale, which was always good in well-found and well conducted ships. They enabled a ship to be driven—*safely* driven—to the last. Any fool could hold on to sail in a rising wind and force his ship along, for a while. But the *Potosi* and her kind were designed for all-out driving and the roar of the gale in their massive riggings—how it roared!—was power and speed. They could be driven and they would not go under. They could be driven and they would not be dismasted. No such Laeisz four-master or five-master ever was dismasted, though the waters and the shoreline round the Horn are littered with the wrecks of ships which drove their masts out, or foundered when overwhelmed in gales. Many, many a square-rigged ship went missing off the Horn. The ice took some. Many had their hatches smashed in by the sea, and foundered. No Laeisz ship ever was overwhelmed in the seas off Cape Horn, or anywhere else. No 'P' ship is missing there. No 'P' ship foundered with her hatches stove, or staggered broken from the tumult of the Horn to run off eastwards before the westerly winds and so reach Chile the easier way, after sailing in high latitudes right around the world. (A good many square-riggers did that, too.)

The tradition the 'P' ships sought always to establish and maintain was reliability. Their shippers—the merchants who sent their cargoes by them—must know that any 'P' ship would arrive more or less when she was expected, with her cargo intact and in good order. The 'P' ships were still carrying general cargo when most other sailing-ships were tramping for such bulk cargoes as they could find. Laeisz made the Chilean a liner trade, with his sailers. In that, I think, was his great merit. Long after other owners gave up the deepsea sailing-ship as doomed, he showed that such vessels if properly conducted and well sailed, could still do their share of the world's work and do it splendidly. He had to build up not only his ships and the trade. He had to build up a lighterage system in the Chilean ports. He introduced the revolutionary idea that a sailing-ship could and should have quick despatch at a West Coast roadstead. Not for him ill-fed, discontented crews, laboriously grinding up one coal-basket at a time with an antiquated, back-breaking dolly-winch—he installed donkey-engines and steam winches, or oil winches if they were better, to handle the cargo in and out mechanically. Most sailing-ships in those last days—if the truth be told—took things easily, if they could. They were on the way to oblivion. Why should they bother to fight against the inevitable end? So they would arrive and anchor, and prepare themselves for a long stay, and be content at poor deliveries, slow cargo-handling. Not so the ships of the Flying 'P'!

"My ships can and *will* make rapid voyages!" * That was the maxim, and it applied in port as well as at sea. The 'P' four-masters would come storming in to the crowded anchorages off Valparaiso or Iquique, a cloud of ordered sail, and the sailors would be rigging the cargo gear as soon as they had spare time from securing the sails. The boys were opening hatches. The donkey-boiler was ready and the winches turning over. Agents ashore would have lighters already waiting at the appointed anchorage. The great four-master would come running in from sea, shortening sail, and, as her anchor ran out and she spun head-to-wind under a backed mainyard, the lighters would already be crowding alongside and cargo-handling would begin at once, as in the smartest steamer. They were days at anchorage where other sailing-ships were weeks, and even months. When they were ready for sea, they sailed. No idling, no waiting for a fair wind! It was a common sight to see a 'P' ship getting under sail and moving through the roadsteads still with the last lighter alongside and the last slings of cargo going in.

With these traditions—good crews, good ships, good owner-ship and management, a good and reliable trade well organised —it was not to be wondered at that the Laeisz Line dared to build great five-masters, despite the fate of the *Maria Rickmers* (which had shocked the shipping world), and despite all the jeremiahs who kept prophesying that deepsea sail was irrevocably doomed. Yet there was also one other factor to be considered, and that the most important of all. That was the men, the officers, and above all else, the masters. There was a pool of good sailing-ship sailors in Hamburg, and had been for centuries. There was an apparently inexhaustible supply from the Baltic ports, from the Friesian

---

* This was the opening sentence in the Laeisz "Instructions For My Captains." See Appendices.

Islands, and from Scandinavia, especially Denmark. There were plenty of first-class officers. But really outstanding masters, fit to get the best out of a super-ship such as the *Potosi* or the *Preussen,* making not only good voyages but the best possible voyages— *always*—these might be understandably scarce. There has always been more knowledge than men able to make use of it. No creation man ever achieved was more in the hands of its master than the ocean-going sailing-ship. He was more than her brains. He was her *character,* her resolution, her hope of integrity. If he failed, she failed. If he did not know his business, it was no use giving him the best ship in the world. If he had a defect of character, in the long run that would affect his ship and the men in her. The big square-rigged ship can be compared to a great orchestra, needing an inspired conductor really to bring it to full life. The wind was the score and the sails the instruments. Lesser conductors might do something, of course, but with a real master the performance could be magnificent.

In Erich Laeisz's office by the Trostbrücke in Hamburg, one photograph hangs upon the wall. It is not of Ferdinand or Carl Laeisz, nor any other ancestor, illustrious as they were. It is a photograph of a man with high cheekbones and a hawk nose, a grim-looking, determined man, with a firm hard mouth, wide-apart all-seeing eyes (which in life were the hardest of cold blue), a strong but not pugnacious jaw. It could, with a darkened skin and a head-dress of eagles' feathers, be some great Red Indian chief of long ago. It could be a great statesman, a great admiral. In fact it is the face of that great master of Cape Horn ships, Robert Hilgendorf. With Hilgendorf to entrust with her command, the House of Laeisz dared build the *Potosi* with an assurance that, under God, she would succeed.

Chapter three

ROBERT HILGENDORF

ROBERT HILGENDORF was without a doubt one of the really great sailing-ship masters, if not one of the greatest, of whom any record remains. He was born in the little town of Schievelhorst on the Gulf of Stettin, by the shores of the Baltic, on the last day of July, 1852. His father was a respected shipmaster, sailing in small brigs and barques out of Stettin. In the summers he sailed with his father, as a child and, at the age of fifteen, Robert Hilgendorf went to sea professionally. He learned his business in the Baltic trade and the hard North Sea. The ships sailing in those trades were usually old and leaky. They were sailed with woefully small crews, who knew no privileges. Captain's son or no captain's son, a boy in such ships learned the hard way—the hardest of hard ways—and, before he was passed as fit to perform the duties of an able seaman, he had to satisfy the prolonged and meticulous scrutiny of his more experienced fellow-seamen, jealous of the high standards of their calling. Yet Hilgendorf was an able seaman at seventeen. He mastered thoroughly every detail of his profession, for the little Baltic ships laid up when the seas iced over and their crews then became their riggers, shipwrights, sailmakers, and general maintenance men.

Like all his countrymen who followed the sea, Hilgendorf was conscripted for a term of service in the Imperial Navy, in which he rose to become a boatswain's mate. This advancement was unusual and was evidence of outstanding character. The old Imperial Navy did not look kindly upon conscripts drawn from the Merchant Service and set itself out, above all else, to impress them with their appalling inferiority. So long and so thoroughly did this attitude persist that, upon the outbreak of the first World War in 1914 when the reserves were called up, some masters of famous German liners were compelled to come back to the colours, at first, as ordinary seamen. Hilgendorf must have impressed somebody of influence, and impressed him profoundly.

With his mate's certificate from the Steuermannsschule at Altona—he graduated with honours—Hilgendorf went at first back to the Baltic trade. It was not that he preferred the dumpy brigs and the leaky old barques, but he knew that a young officer would at once attain a position of responsibility there, and it was his plan to profit by the experience. He could have signed away as junior officer in some deepsea ship, with no difficulty at all. But he wanted his master's license before going deepsea. His plans were made. The young Hilgendorf shipped as mate—only mate—of the Baltic barque *Nautik,* a tough little ship which earned her living hard. Her crew were her stevedores as well as her seamen. They handled the cargo in and out, and there were barely enough of them to do that. They sailed her in the Baltic in the spring, summer, and autumn and, in the winters, moved into the grim North Sea. There were just enough of them to handle the ship. The master was old—very old—and Hilgendorf gained invaluable experience. Most of the time it was he who sailed the ship.

After two years of that, he took his master's certificate. Then, as he had always intended to do, he left the Baltic barques for ever. He went to Hamburg and presented himself, with his certificates and his credentials, at the office of Herr Laeisz. There were other good sailing-ship owners in Hamburg then. Hilgendorf chose Laeisz, and he knew what he was doing. The Laeisz Line had the name of being hard but fair. Ferdinand Laeisz and his son Carl Heinrich encouraged good service by a system of bonuses. They were constantly adding to their fleet. Command came quickly to competent masters, in their ships in the Cape Horn trade. The Laeisz Line above all had a reputation for granting advancement by competence and by no other criterion. That was enough for Hilgendorf.

Carl Laeisz took an immediate liking to the tall, slim, hard-eyed young seafarer from the Baltic. Many good Laeisz officers and masters had come from there, and others from the Friesian Islands. Hilgendorf was appointed at once to be mate of the barque *Parnass* and, on the first voyage, he showed himself to be an outstanding officer. It was 1876 when he graduated from the Officers' School at Altona. Within five years he had command of this same *Parnass*. From that time onwards until his retirement from the sea in 1901, Hilgendorf commanded Laeisz square-riggers in the Cape Horn trade, and he rounded Cape Horn with them sixty-six times.

The records of all these voyages—the actual records, not some old-timer's hazy recollection set down years afterwards, or old newspaper clippings—are to be found today in the offices of the Deutsche Seewarte at Hamburg. The German Hydrographic Office began very early to collate comprehensive records of sailing-ship voyages and to encourage masters to send in reports of their ships' performances. The idea was the sensible one of carrying on a systematic study of ocean winds and currents, and all relevant data, for the general purpose of improving the standard of sailing-ship passages everywhere. With every ship providing data, then in due course all would stand to benefit from the increase in knowledge. Every master was required to report, for example, where he met the trade winds—on what latitude and longitude—and their strength, how far they took him (for the trade winds can vary quite a lot, and of course a sailing-ship wanted to get maximum value from them and to steer such a course as to ensure this). He reported, too, how he crossed the Doldrums and those other areas of exasperating calms which the older seamen used to call the Horse Latitudes (why I don't know, though it is said it was because the trying conditions of calm and stifling weather caused severe losses among horses in sailing troopships). He had to furnish detailed accounts of how he got his ship to the westward round Cape Horn, or through the South China Sea against the monsoon; how he found the sailing conditions in the Straits of Malacca or the Straits of Bali or along any other highway that he had to use or chanced to be blown through. All this information was assembled painstakingly and, on top of similar research which had been done before—though there was not a great deal available of this—it was used to prepare voyage-plans for any master who cared to ask for such a thing, on any voyage he was called upon to make. Well aware of the value of the work the Hydrographic Office was doing, masters sent in their reports comprehensively. Through his reports in this manner the whole sailing career of Robert Hilgendorf—and most other German sailing-ship commanders—can now be traced without much trouble.

Hilgendorf's record is magnificent. There is no other word for it. Ship followed ship—the lovely barque *Parsifal* followed the *Parnass,* and the *Professor* and *Pirat* came after that; then the *Pergamon, Palmyra,* the four-masters *Placilla* and *Pitlochry,* and then at last the mighty *Potosi*. Nine square-rigged ships, barques, ships, four-masted and five-masted barques, ranging from 650 to above 4000 tons, with one thing only in common, that they all flew the Laeisz house-flag. Hilgendorf drove them all. On eighteen round voyages, his average outward passage from the Channel to his port in Chile was 64 days, and his average homewards was 74. The average passage outwards meant sailing some 11,500 miles—the usual distance he actually logged was 11,440—and homewards, 12,000. In almost twenty years in command, Hilgendorf sailed those nine square-rigged ships, deep-loaded in both directions—at an *average* speed of seven and a half knots. He beat all nine, passage after passage, to the westward round the Horn in from seven to ten days. After Hilgendorf retired from active command in 1901—he retired as soon as he was fifty, for he knew that a Cape Horn shipmaster should not stay in that trade to grow old—it took tramp steamers another quarter of a century to improve upon his average, and that without any of the tremendous effort of beating round the Horn.

Hilgendorf's ships were not clippers. They were strictly the products of the post-clipper era. They had adequate crews, but no one would call them over-manned. Even the *Potosi* carried only twenty able seamen and a total crew of forty-four. Hilgendorf knew also adversity, for he lost the *Parsifal*. Her nitrate cargo shifted and she foundered, her people getting off in the boats just in time. He knew what it meant to be adrift. When the *Parsifal* sank, Hilgendorf saved his crew. No one was lost. Nor did he over-drive his ships. The *Parnass* was a wooden barque built in 1878 but she was not sunk until a submarine got her in 1916, and she was still a good ship then. If that wooden ship had been over-driven, she certainly would not have lasted half as long. Yet Hilgendorf got clipper passages out of her.

Before Hilgendorf, any passage to a Chilean port in less than 90 days was reckoned good, and it was usual to allow at least three weeks for getting round the Horn. (Sailors in the sailing-ship era, when they spoke of rounding the Horn, meant to sail westwards from the latitude of 50 South in the Atlantic, down past the Horn, and then to fight up to 50 South latitude in the Pacific: nothing else was counted as a Cape Horn rounding, for the eastwards passage before the westerly gales was reckoned no rounding at all. The distance a sailing-ship had to travel to get from 50 S to 50 S past the Horn was at least 1200 miles—every mile of it almost invariably a bitter fight.)

A glance at the face of Hilgendorf, with those cold steel-blue eyes and general impression of indefatigable determination, shows that he had the proper temperament to defeat Cape Horn. There had been fast passages around before his time, of course, and some of the American clippers in the California gold-rush days had hurled themselves to wind'ard past the Horn in splendid style. So had some of the little Welsh copper-ore carriers. It was Hilgendorf's astonishing consistence that was new. It was a fresh contribution to the whole science of conducting voyages under sail. In his way, Hilgendorf was a scientist—a sailing scientist. Some called him the Devil of Hamburg—devil in the sense that he controlled the winds, so often would the wind work right for whatever passage he was making. There was an old belief, which indeed persisted as long as sailing-ships, that certain individuals could control the wind. The quality was more often ascribed to Finns, and Captain de Cloux was alleged to be a 'devil' in that sense, too. These allegations came almost entirely from brother shipmasters who failed to make as good passages as he did. 'De

Cloux kan *troller*,' they said with a shrug, as if that disposed of the matter. 'De Cloux can *troll*'—in other words is a bit of a witch, in league with the satanic forces which (according to the old salts at any rate) controlled far too much of the ocean winds and the ways of the world. In the same way Hilgendorf was a *troll*, too, according to the less successful of his critics.

Some said he was called the Devil of Hamburg because he was a hard man on his crews. He *was* a hard man, and there is no doubt of that. But he was a fair man, and there is no doubt of that either. He was a successful man, and success breeds envy. He held the respect of his subordinates. Men did not desert from his ships. The crew lists of the *Potosi* (they were still in the Laeisz office in 1953) show the same men coming back voyage after voyage. I have not consulted the lists for the other ships. Charlie Müller—a man who rounded the Horn a dozen times (reckoning roundings as sailors counted them) and served in twenty deepsea sailing-ships from South Seas brigantines to the great *Potosi*— paid this tribute to Hilgendorf: "He certainly was a driver but he knew what he was doing. He was a hard man, but fair. He looked after his crew. In the *Potosi* I was never called out in my watch below." * Charlie Müller was in the *Potosi* as a young able seaman in 1901, on Hilgendorf's last voyage.

It was not everybody who wanted to sail with Hilgendorf. He had one standard, and that was perfection. He expected perfection from his officers and his men, and he saw that he got it. There were some who said he lacked humanity, but the only story

* Charlie Müller's own account of this experience is in the Appendices. Here is his opinion of the *Potosi* and of Captain Hilgendorf: "The *Potosi* was about the handiest vessel I've ever been in (for her size). We never got called out on our watch below; the watch on deck could handle her in the heaviest weather. The sails clewed up that snug, they were nearly fast just by hauling the bunt-lines close up. Capt. Hilgendorf (the Devil of Hamburg) was a very hard master to please, but he was a splendid captain and navigator and he knew just exactly where the right winds would blow. We went through the Strait of Le Maire, which was a dangerous thing with such a big ship. But he knew what she could stand and on the whole voyage we never lowered the upper topsail yards. Of course, she was a wet ship and when he drove her through heavy seas, she was fully up fore and aft. His quickest voyage was 54 days from Iquique to the entrance of the channel. The *Preussen* was not so handy, I was told. It's a pity those ships are all gone, they were a splendid school for future Captains and Officers."

I have heard which is handed down in Hamburg to support this is an account of how he left three members of the *Potosi's* crew, once, to languish in a Chilean jail, and hired three locals to do their work and then charged the cost of the hire against the others' wages, after they had been released on sailing-day and helped to sail the ship home. There was nothing unusual in a few liberty-men—or indeed, a great many liberty-men—landing in a Chilean jail, from other ships. But Hilgendorf would not have it. Other masters used to bail their men out on the Monday morning, take them back to their ships, log them a day or two's pay (in accordance with the Act) and then let them get on with their work. But not Hilgendorf, and I do not see that he was wrong. He did not expect anyone from his crews to behave so stupidly ashore that he had to be imprisoned, however briefly. The men had erred and they must take their punishment. No one from the *Potosi* ever erred in that way again while Hilgendorf was there. I should say he was a good disciplinarian. As for his humanity, no one could fight the big *Potosi* round the Horn with a smile. As for crews, it was the style then in German ships to work them hard and not to pay them much (though the wages were about the same as those ruling in British ships), but to feed them well. The foremast hand had few rights and was treated brutally as a matter of course in too many American ships, and stupidly in too many British. Laeisz ships had no mutinies. That is evidence enough.

In the working of a great sailing-ship the cooperation of every man aboard was a real necessity. Good sailors would work to their last gasp when they felt they were handled by a *man,* when they felt the ship was worth fighting for. Hilgendorf would never have made his splendid voyages if, among all the other things he was, he had not been also a magnificent leader of men. He extended his men to the utmost of their ability. He called upon them—never by word of mouth but always with the ship— to fight to the last ounce of their strength. The *Potosi* was a heavy ship. With ten able seamen, two ordinary seamen, and two boys in a watch, she was by no means over-manned. (Clipper ships a fourth her size had twice her crew.) Those men and those

boys gave their best always for the ship, and no amount of
bullying, no inhumanity, could have sustained an effort like that
or ever have brought it into being.

It was the same in port. Clippers rested in port, and this indeed became altogether too much of a sailing-ship tradition. They
waited for cargoes to come down, or to ripen or be harvested,
while their masters acted the part of the distinguished gentlemen
they were, with their tophats and their cabs, and—far too often—
their rooms ashore in the best hotel in town. Their crews were
sufficiently employed tending the ship, looking after her wooden
masts and spars, setting up her hempen rigging, looking after her
cordage. The *Potosi* and her kind had masts and yards of steel
tubes even to the royal yards, which were fifty-foot pieces of
tubular steel strong enough to withstand anything. Their standing rigging was massive iron wire set up to steel rigging-screws,
as fat as a man's thigh. Setting this sort of thing up was a dock-
yard job, normally requiring attention only when the ship was
reclassed or surveyed for some reason. Running rigging, too, was
wire and chain wherever these could be used. The boltropes of
the sails were heavy steel wire. The gear on the sails—the array
of lines by which the square sails could be muzzled from the deck
—was wire. These things were attended to at sea. In ports the 'P'
ships worked their cargoes with the utmost despatch, under all
conditions. The *Placilla,* the *Pergamon,* the *Potosi* and the rest
were working cargo-ships pure and simple. They were engaged
in a prosaic piece of the world's carrying business, shifting coke
and coal and cement and general cargoes from North Germany
out to Chile, and carrying nitrates back again. The shore lighterage system which Laeisz built up had a great deal to do with
the rapid turn-round of his ships, but in this, too, the spirit of the
crews was of importance. General cargoes such as those carried
by the *Potosi* included every sort of German manufacture—pianos,
machinery, cube sugar, liquors, toys. Landing this sort of thing
undamaged, unbroached, and with maximum speed called for
crew loyalty, and Hilgendorf commanded that in abundance.

One of the remarkable things in his astonishing record is his
average of five months and 19 days for the whole voyage, from

↑ Hilgendorf loved gales. Looking down on the main deck
of a 'P' ship driving before a gale near Cape Horn.

The *Potosi* off Cape Horn,
holding on to all her
lower topgallantsails
in a gale of wind
←

Robert Hilgendorf—
the picture from the Laeisz office

←

The five-masted barque *Potosi*
↓ was a magnificent ship.

The Flying 'P' Line bought good ships from others, as they became available. This is one of the case oil carriers, bought in 1910—the former *Arrow*.

The Laeisz ships were always sailed hard, and beautifully kept up. They were the most consistent good-passage-makers in Cape Horn history.

the Elbe and back to the Elbe again. This was the average round voyage that Hilgendorf made, handling two cargoes—sometimes three, for there was a good deal of coastal traffic the Laeisz ships built up along the coast of Chile. Five months and 19 days! Think for a moment just what such a voyage meant. Deeply laden— right down to her loadline—and with her freshly signed-on crew just aboard (it was the custom to take the majority of the crew aboard at the last possible moment) the ship would be towed down the Elbe. Though it was later Laeisz practice to tow the larger ships such as the *Potosi* and *Preussen* clear of the Straits of Dover unless the wind was fair, the usual thing was for the tug to let go the tow at the earliest possible moment. The outward-bound square-rigger would begin her passage at the mouth of the Elbe, with the North Sea and all the English Channel to fight through first. Far too often the westerly gales of the North Atlantic, funnelling through the narrow seas, would at once roar their defiance at her, trying to force her eastwards where she must go west, with 700 miles to make to wind'ard, with shoals and sands and a dangerous coastline all about her, and the complicated tidal system of the English Channel as a further enemy. She had nothing whatever in her favour but her own excellence, the character of her commander, and the good spirit and competence of her crew. Out she must fight until she had cleared Land's End before she could feel herself free of the hindering proximity of too much land—and then, fight westwards still, keeping out of the indraught into the Bay of Biscay and well clear of Finisterre. Then she might find northerly winds to blow her to the Trades, and she might have to fight her way down the Portuguese coast too.

The Trade winds once found would blow her to the doldrums calms, where the skill of her master and the excellence of his voyage-brief from the Hydrographic Office—and his luck— must bring her through, and she might spend days pulling the yards round to every catspaw, the steel ship near stagnant on the glassy and inhuman sea. Sooner or later—the sooner the better— she must find the south-east trades to drive the ship along again, but the allegedly south-east Trades often began in the south-south-east or even in the south, and a square-rigged ship, south-bound, must stand on with the wind on her port side and do her best, and not be jammed upon the coast of Brazil. A skilful man would see his ship across the Line where even a deal of westing would not bring her to leeward of Cape San Roque, and a courageous man would sail on boldly, knowing the Trade would work fair in due course.

Always there were problems, difficulties—the Horse Latitudes after the Trades, and perhaps 2000 miles of latitude to make before the ship could turn west to fight to wind'ard of the Horn. Latitude was always harder to gain than longitude. So long as she was south of 50 South the savage onslaught of the westerly gales, the roar of the great winds and the smashing of the seas, the shortness of the days and the threat of ice, made life hellish enough. Then she must make her northing along the Chilean coast, and take care she did not drift past her harbour, at the end, in the north-setting current which at times was stronger than the wind. Then in from sea, bowling in with the morning wind, and the ship to moor in a crowded tier—no tugs to help! If there were tugs they were weak: in any event, owners took a poor view of masters who needed towboats to help moor their ships at an open anchorage. It was not the owner's judgment which chose the right second—*precisely* the right second—to round up and stand in among the lines of moored ships, with the great four-master or five-master placed exactly where she must be, with just the right amount of way to take her to her berth without over-running, without collisions, without damage.

As soon as she was moored, the cargo must be worked out. (Here Laeisz ships had a great advantage, for at least lighters were waiting for them and a good shore organisation was ready to assist.) Then ballast, and coastal cargo in, and move up to the loading port—handle the coastal cargo out—get rid of the ballast —stow 4000, 5000, 6000 tons of nitrate down below (and stow it well, avoiding all fire risks, all fear of the heavy bags shifting). Then away again, getting well off the coast to avoid that current again, and stand down for the Horn, this time to run along what sailors called down-hill way, though the down-hill way gave trouble enough and sank many ships. There was ice, too—or there might be—and after that, there was the long road home through both Atlantics and, at last, the romp through the congested Channel where the risk of colliding steamships was greatest for a sailing-ship handled ably and sailing with speed. (Three Laeisz ships were knocked down there by stupid steamers which contemptuously misjudged their speed, and others were badly damaged.) And so to port at last, after sailing at least 24,000 miles (including the passage on the Coast) without ever the aid of tugs from the setting-out to the end, without the aid of anything but supreme ability and confidence, and a well-found ship and the ocean winds.

All this in five months and nineteen days! At an average speed of seven and a half knots! *Pirat,* Channel to Valparaiso, 68 days—*Pergamon,* Channel to Valparaiso, 65 days—*Palmyra,* Channel to Valparaiso, 63 days—*Placilla,* Channel to Valparaiso, 58 days —*Potosi,* off-Channel to Valparaiso, 55 days! This was the Hilgendorf record.

What Robert Hilgendorf did was to establish a tradition. For him no flags flew; no golden cocks were hoisted to the maintrucks of his great steel ships. There were no trapperies. Whether he was able to sail a four-masted barque or a five-masted barque or any other kind of ship from the Elbe to Valparaiso in 58 days or 88 days affected nobody and nothing, except the fortunes of the House of Laeisz and his own good name. No bonus was paid for general cargoes quickly delivered, nor for nitrate (except the bonus the owner paid for work well done).

Much has been written of the clipper ships, the great China tea races, the Australian wool derbies, the great days of the Yankees in the San Francisco trade. Hilgendorf knew about them and he respected them. But the clippers' day was done when he had his first command, and it had been very brief. A few real clippers and some semi-clippers continued to carry Australian wool home round the Horn for another twenty years. The clippers' contribution to the art of sailing had been made. What Hilgendorf did was to show—and to show conclusively—that it was not final, as it was generally accepted as being. The lovely clippers were by no means the ultimate development in sail. Their good passages, their occasional great days' runs, their comparatively rare bursts of great speed were well publicised and well known. What was often forgotten was that they made many poor passages, too, even the best of them. Where they excelled was in their yacht-like grace, their perfect ability to ghost along in light winds, their splendid handiness. The China tea trade was known to old sailors as a Flying-fish trade, and the term was applied with some good-humoured contempt by the Cape Horners. The tea clippers with their studding-sails set ghosted graciously upon the azure airs of the summer monsoons. The big Americans—the *James Baines, Lightning* and her kind—and Britishers like the *Thermopylae* and the *Cutty Sark,* could storm along in the wild west winds, too. The ships which Donald Mackay built for the Baines Black Ball line were indeed great ships, clippers among the clippers. Donald Mackay, working in steel and encouraged to go on producing great sailing-ships, could have achieved perfection. Indeed his ships in their prime *were* perfection of their kind, or as near to that as man is likely to get. But Donald Mackay had to go out of the clipper-building business.

If the tea clipper excelled in light winds, so did the steamer, and the sailing-ships were soon ousted from the China trade. Nor was it of any use for the wool clipper to storm towards the Horn and race home with her wool if the steamer could cross the Indian Ocean, slip through Suez Canal, and steal at least a month on the best sailing time. A clipper had a good chance of catching the wool sales if she allowed herself 90 days to get there. But the steamer was certain to make the sales in 60. As for the clippers, a good many failed to make the passage from Sydney or Melbourne to London in 90 days or less, though this was a down-hill run.

Not every clipper in that business was a *Cutty Sark* or a *Thermopylae.* The records show many a passage homewards among the racing wool fleet of 100 days and more, some of them over four months. Even famous ships made more than enough poor passages. In 1877 the *Romanoff, John Duthie, Ben Voirlich,*

Loch Garry, and *True Briton* were all over 100 days with their wool, and the year's best passage was the *Mermerus'* 80 days. The *Mermerus* herself took 109 days a year or two later, though she was a beautiful ship and a consistent sailer. The same year the *Thomas Stephens* and *The Tweed* were 100 days and more, though the *Cutty Sark* was only 72. This was with the wool clip from the 1885–86 season. Twelve out of twenty-seven of the fastest sailing-ships in the world were 100 days or more on the run home from Australia that season. Nor was this as unusual as one might be led to imagine by the sailing-cards and other advertising material of the period. The previous season, eleven in much the same field had been equally dilatory; the following season there were nine and, in 1890, again eleven, which included the *Samuel Plimsoll,* a couple of *Loch* ships, and the lovely *Hesperus* and *Harbinger.* After that season the sailing wool races steadily declined, and even the wonderful *Cutty Sark* was sold foreign by the mid-nineties.

The point is that at no time did the clipper-masters or owners make a systematic and concerted study of the best way to make use of the ocean winds, at all times of the year. They were confirmed individualists. The odd good passage with a perfect cargo —and not much of that—was not good enough. Neither was dependence upon the vagaries of the ocean wind without any organised attempt to correlate the painfully acquired knowledge of this source of all sailing-ships' power. There were good masters, of course, who made such individual study as they could, and the broad principles of the winds' behavior were well understood. But broad principles were not enough. Children in their geography lessons in elementary school were taught the alleged 'limits' of the trade winds, and the west wind zones, and the behavior of hurricanes, and so forth. Too many clipper-masters acted as if they knew little more than the children did. They had good general sailing directions available to them. Maury had laid them down. That great seaman, James Cook, after one westwards rounding of the Horn in a Whitby ship laid down the general principles as well as anyone did, and he beat round in 1769.

They had also the immense background of their individual experience, but there was no organised pool of such knowledge for them to use.

Hilgendorf's main contribution was, in its way, scientific. What he most wanted to avoid was continued calm. Calm was the curse of sailing-ships, the great handicap of voyage-making—above all, zones of calms such as the doldrums and the Horse Latitudes, and after them, almost as bad, any calm. By making a systematic study of the records at the Hydrographic Office which soon were covering the experience of hundreds of ships sailing at all seasons of the year, a master like Hilgendorf could choose those places on the Line and elsewhere where his ship was likely to encounter the minimum of calm. Experts in the office, too, were constantly grappling with this problem of improving the sailer's chances of making consistent good voyages, and Hilgendorf paid close attention to them. He was an avid student and a thorough observer. More than that, he was a natural meteorologist. He was a master of the complicated and highly necessary art of so placing his ship at all times that she was able to get maximum use out of every puff, every flutter of the wind. Currents helped, too, and, like the Trade Winds, they were by no means the confined streams in the sea which the text books laid down. Currents varied greatly, as did the Trade Winds, and a sailing-ship seaman must know them intimately. What his critics called 'trolling' and sailing by black magic was Hilgendorf's skilful application of his knowledge.

There were no weather forecasts then, apart from long-range plans furnished by the Hydrographic Office. A master had to estimate the probable daily changes of the weather for himself, from his experience, the scant data available to him, and what signs he could see and understand. There was nothing uncanny in reading the signs rightly. Off the Horn, too, Hilgendorf's genius was outstanding. Too many masters before his day—and afterwards—approached the grim area of Cape Horn with alarm and trepidation, and shortened down their ships at the first icy blast from the demon wind, and kept them shortened down until the wind hauled fair or fell light, or, despairing that this would

ever happen, they gave up the fight and ran the other way around
the world. There was one reason only for Hilgendorf's remarkable
defeat of Cape Horn. (Cook could have done—would have done
—the same thing, and indeed counsels it.) He *used* the wind—
all winds. He was a genius at so using the violent winds that he
made them benefit his ship and assist her passage, instead of
hindering her. If he emerged from the Straits of le Maire to find
a violent westerly gale off the pitch of the Horn, then he did not
shorten down (he was fortunate that he had command always
of strong and well-found ships) and hope for the best. He kept
a press of sail—not all sail, for that would be mere stupidity.
(There are myths about in Hamburg that Hilgendorf never took
a sail in: he let them blow away. He is alleged to have padlocked
the sheets, to have stood by the halliards with a six-shooter—and
so forth. All this is nonsense. It was not possible to padlock the
Potosi's sheets, even if some megalomaniac fool wanted to exhibit
his ignorance by so stupid a gesture, and the halliards came down
to steel hand-winches. Blow away the sails? He took them in,
when he had to. The Laeisz Line required its masters to keep
histories of all sails in their ships, in a special book prepared by
the marine superintendent and handed in at head office at the
end of each voyage. In Hilgendorf's books there is no record of
any unusual number of sails being blown out. "We did not take
in an upper tops'l while I was in her," says Charlie Müller of
his voyage in the *Potosi*. "And we rarely took in a lower topgallant." That is the truth, but it is not a picture of insensate sail-
carrying.)

By keeping such press of sail as his ship could well stand,
Hilgendorf prevented her from driving to leeward. He would
storm on across the gale, taking the wind and the weather on his
starboard beam (that big midships superstructure would be most
valuable then) and making such compass course as he could,
preferably with some west in it as the wind worked round. The
Potosi would go to windward in a gale, sailed like this, and hold
a good course six points from the wind. So Hilgendorf would
storm down to 59 or 60 degrees South, if he had to. Unless it
was necessary, he would not tack the ship—not beat in a series

of short and futile tacks, trying to get to windward. If it was the best thing to do, he would storm right down to 60 S. at once, and *then* go on the other tack. Sometimes such a course was advisable, sometimes not. He seemed to know. There were no rules, or if there were, they have not yet been discovered. Every rounding was a tremendous battle, and the victory was to the shipmaster who, with confidence in his ship and in himself, fought back with tireless skill and, preferably, a touch of weather-judging genius. "He knew just exactly where the right winds would blow," says Charlie Müller of his old master.

What Hilgendorf had to do was to have his ship on such tack as was always that which would benefit her most, as the wind changed. Wearing or tacking a big ship too often in the Cape Horn seas wasted time and lost hard-won ground. He wore ship and he tacked ship when he had to. If for example he found himself in 59 South down off the pitch of the Horn and the wind was, say, west-south-west, he would go about and stand on the port tack though his ship at first would of necessity make such a course which, if continued, would make all Tierra del Fuego a lee shore, and so a very grave danger. But his knowledge and the weather-signs showed him when he did a thing like this that the wind would—must—change to south-west or south-south-west. Therefore he had the nerve to stand on and to continue standing on, even though the loom of the iron-bound, mountainous land might be under his lee before an appreciable wind-change did come. This kind of sailing took nerve and knowledge. Even to think clearly in those screaming, roaring hurricanes took a great deal of courage. Hilgendorf had these qualities in abundant measure. Nor did he take any foolish risks.

It was the exercise of his meteorological skill that gained him his name of the Devil of Hamburg. It was by the exercise of that skill and in furthering it at all times in the general interest of his profession, that Hilgendorf made his contribution to the science of deepsea sailing—a contribution which was made possible, too, by the strength and good sailing qualities of the ships he commanded, the foresight and sound management principles of his owners, and the astonishing endurance, skill, and infinite ability of that so often misrepresented figure, the foremast hand, of any nationality. Hilgendorf was the Toscanini of Cape Horn— the Beethoven, if you like—and his officers and men were superb instrumentalists.

There were other masters who could handle a big sailing-ship as well as Hilgendorf could. One hundred thousand seamen— from America, Britain, France, Scandinavia, Portugal, Poland, Italy, Japan—could probably have done as well as the chosen band which formed the crew of the *Potosi* or *Placilla,* under his leadership. But Hilgendorf was in truth a genius. It was not just that he sailed heavy-laden sailing-ships at an average speed of seven and a half knots over a period of more than twenty years though indeed no clipper master could come near that record. It wasn't just that he brought down the average time for a round voyage to Chile under sail to less than six months. His true genius lay rather in the fact that he showed how others could do like-wise, with ships which were good cargo-carriers, were not par-ticularly fine-lined, and were never over-manned. He founded a tradition, and he advanced the science of deepsea sailing to heights it had not known before. It was not his fault, though it was ironic, that circumstances over which he could not possibly have the least control would defeat his every effort, and that before he died he would see European deepsea sailing-ships of all kinds driven from the seven seas, apparently for ever.

Hilgendorf left the sea after the *Potosi*'s tenth voyage, and retired ashore. He was just fifty years old. He did not seek to go to sea in steam, though he had no scorn for steamships as such. His belief was that the two forms could continue to exist together, the sailing vessel and the powered vessel. But he left it to others to assist the steamers. He could have had command of the *Preussen,* which was launched the year after his retirement. He felt she should be commanded by a younger man. Hilgendorf was 43 years old when he took command of the new *Potosi.* He had trained many good officers. There were plenty to carry on his tradition. The *Preussen* went to Captain Boye Petersen, then aged 33. Boye Petersen was a scientific driver in the Hilgendorf manner, and so was Nissen, who took over command of the *Potosi*. Nissen was then 39 years old. Boye Petersen and Hinrich Nissen were great sailing-ship masters and they proceeded to carry on the Hilgendorf tradition. Nissen, after being mate with Hilgendorf in the *Placilla*, commanded the Tecklenborg ship *Parchim*. Here he proceeded to show what he could do by sailing that big steel ship 4871 nautical miles in 19 days on his first voyage, which was an average—allowing for the difference of time as he was making easting—of almost 11 knots. Nissen had the *Pitlochry*, too, and did very well with her. But it was difficult for him to follow in the steps of the master in the great *Potosi*, and his average over seven outward passages to Chile was six days more than Hilgendorf's had been on his ten voyages. His average homewards was four days more. His voyage homewards in 1903—the year that I was born—was 56 days from Iquique to the Lizard. Indeed that was the best homewards passage which not only the *Potosi* but any sailing-ship ever made in that trade, for it stands as the record.

If Nissen made his name with the *Potosi*, Boye Petersen served the *Preussen* very well. When Nissen was driving the *Potosi* home at an average speed of over 8.6 knots, Boye Petersen was sailing the *Preussen* from the Channel to Iquique in 56 and a half days, at the same speed. In thirteen days he had her cargo discharged and full stowage of nitrates under hatches and, 68 days later, was in the Channel again. Boye Petersen was second mate with Hilgendorf in the *Placilla*, and mate with him in the *Pitlochry* in 1894. He was a brilliant pupil in a great tradition, and Hilgendorf recommended him for his first command, the barque *Pestalozzi*. This was in 1896, when Petersen was 27 years old. In later years he became Marine Superintendent for Laeisz at Hamburg, and it was he who handled the sale of the four-masted barque *Parma* to our syndicate in 1931. The second World War killed him. His home in Hamburg was bombed to the ground, his only son was a war casualty, and in December, 1943, Boye Petersen died. He was 74 years old. Nissen sailed Laeisz ships almost as long as there was a Laeisz square-rigger

to sail, and had command of the *Parma* and *Pamir* between the
wars. He took the *Peking* on her last German voyage. He was
a Laeisz officer from 1892 until 1926, nearly all that time in
command. He died in 1943.

As for Hilgendorf, when he retired he became a marine
surveyor and an appraiser of shipping and of cargo damage,
for several marine insurance companies. For over thirty years,
his dignified figure and strong seaman's countenance were familiar on the Hamburg waterfront and at the boarding points
along the River Elbe. He would come aboard quietly and go
about his business, which concerned such things as the proper
securing of hatches and the general seaworthiness of ships and
competence of ships' companies. Hilgendorf could step aboard
a ship and, at a glance, have a very good idea of how she was
run. His insurance appraising job called for complete integrity,
too. He did very well at it.

In February 1937, Robert Hilgendorf died. His ships had
long predeceased him. The floundering propellor and the clank-
ing piston-rod had defeated them, after all. Yet it was not really
theirs which was the last victory. The obliteration of the deepsea sailing-ship was in the last analysis due to the blindness and
stupidity of men. There was work for both types of ships to do.
It was foolish to throw away a great art, deliberately. Hilgendorf had been right to try to preserve and to extend sailing
skill. It was his reward that at least he delayed for a few years
the onrush of the demoralising power age at sea and, through
his efforts and his unrivalled genius, kept the square-rigged ship—
that loveliest of all man's working creations—going for at least
another decade, and kept the science of real sailing alive a little
longer than it otherwise might have been. Hilgendorf blazed
the way. He showed what could be done. He opened up vistas
of possible progress. It was not his fault that, within his own
lifetime, the lesson was neglected and the science he had
helped to build and to nourish so splendidly was thrown away.
The onrush of the mechanical world was too great to be with-

stood. Man thought himself ready to run a world without benefit of natural things like sailing-ships, and no Hilgendorf, no
Laeisz, no *Potosi* and no *Preussen* could stop him.

Yet Hilgendorf's was a grand life. He was given great instruments and he handled them magnificently. He showed what man
could do and could go on doing, had he the sense to retain his
own clear skills while he pursued the illusion of the mastery of
power.

What became of Hilgendorf's and Laeisz's great work? If the
Potosi and the *Preussen* were such super-ships, why were not
more of their kind launched, to sail successfully? These ques-
tions might well be asked, but the answer is plain enough. The
Potosi sailed for Laeisz until the outbreak of the first World War
and continued to do splendidly. Typical of her good sailing
qualities were her average of eleven knots for eleven consecutive days when homeward-bound in 1908, with Nissen command-
ing, and her passages of 62 days Channel to Taltal and the same
number of days homewards again, in 1909. She had to stay in
her Chilean port when the war began, and she was at Valparaiso
continuously from 1914 until 1923. This did her no service. She
had been awarded to France as reparations but the French, having
many sailing-ships laid up of their own, made no attempt to sail
her. The Chileans then sailed her for a year or two under the
name of *Flora*, but by 1925 they had lost her by fire. She was in
Hamburg early in 1925 and was then offered back to Laeisz,
but she was strained and damaged by that time—she had been
ashore somewhere, too—and though Mr. Laeisz was rebuilding
his fleet, a great ship which had been allowed to become weakened
was no use to him.

By that time, too, it was hopeless to replace her by rebuilding.
In 1895, the *Potosi* had cost 695,000 Reichsmarks; seven years
later, the *Preussen* cost over 900,000. Where before 1914 a splendid four-masted barque could be built by the best yards for
round £40,000, the price afterwards was more than £70,000.
The nitrate trade had slumped. The Chilean coastal trade was lost.
This used to cover local costs and, as such, was valuable. There

was no fortune to be made in running the nitrate ships. They had to survive on narrow margins. Other factors affected the ship's earning capacity. The Chileans were developing their own coke and subsidising their own cement industries. Outward cargoes shrunk and continued to shrink; the production of nitrates by chemical process in factories in Europe and America, very naturally, caused the freight in Chilean nitrates to slump badly, too. A five-masted barque costing, then, £100,000 or more had no longer much hope of paying. Laeisz did not give up the idea of replacing his *Potosi* and *Preussen*, but he had to shelve it.

These big ships were heavy on sails and gear and cost considerable sums to keep in the splendid condition they had to maintain. They could pay only if they kept a share of general cargo, which returned much higher freights than such bulk stuff as coke and coal. But they could hope to handle first-class general cargo only as long as they kept shippers' goodwill, and the shippers had in fact no surer means of transport open to them. When the *Preussen* was lost, she had her tween-decks full of best pianos. These were for the Chilean Christmas market. They were salved, of course. But the market was lost. After that, shippers began to prefer power, and the goodwill which the Laeisz Line had so painstakingly built up was largely lost. Though the loss of the *Preussen* was due to her collision with the steamer *Brighton*, which ran into her and caused her to become unmanageable, the *Brighton* did not sink her. The steamer merely caused structural damage so serious as to reduce the big ship's seaworthiness to such an extent that, in a gale soon afterwards, she was driven ashore, broke her back, and was lost. The litigation following her loss dragged on for months and the whole matter had not been cleared up when the World War came.

Then the Panama Canal was opened, and this gave steamships an immense advantage over sailing-ships in the Peruvian and Chilean trades. The Panama Canal was of no use to sailing-ships, for its approach on the Pacific side was through a notorious belt of calms which no amount of statistical research, no sailing skill, no lion-hearted courage could make of use to a big square-rigged ship. Even before her loss, the *Preussen* had had to seek cargoes elsewhere than in the Chilean trade. She was in New York in 1908 to load a cargo of oil for the Standard Oil Company, which she delivered to Japan. She was 33 days beating from Cuxhaven to New York, 73 days from New York to Lombok Straits, and only 112 days for the whole passage. She attracted a great deal of favourable attention in Yokohama (the Japanese were particularly interested in the value of square-rigged ships for officer-training). From Yokohama she crossed the Pacific to the Chilean nitrate ports and took up her old run. She had to cross in ballast, earning nothing, and she had to break the regularity of her Chilean voyages to earn the freight on the case oil. Bulk installations for storing and distributing oil put an end to the sailing trade in oil cased in tins. The *Preussen* was not a tanker.

After the first World War the Laeisz Line continued to develop the 3000-ton four-masted barque. The first war was a serious break in the sailing tradition but, to some degree, that was overcome. The second World War broke it down entirely. Laeisz ships between the wars had recruited crews to some extent because all Germans who wished to qualify as officers in sea-going ships were required first to serve a minimum of twenty months in a square-rigged sailing-ship, and the last four-masted barques had accommodations for thirty or forty such cadets. They were good crews and the system worked well. But it had to be given up during the second World War, and it was not revived afterwards. Again, after this second war the few surviving ships of the Laeisz Line were dispersed and the men who sailed them were penniless and unemployed.

This time it was final. The tradition had been broken once too often.

Part II

───────◆───────

TECHNICALITIES

Chapter four

GLOBAL SAILING CONDITIONS

THERE are plenty of books about sailing-ships and the life aboard them—histories of ships and of companies, personal reminiscences, general books about sailing-ships, and so on. I have read all I could get hold of during the past forty years. Many are of so general a nature that, while interesting, they are of little value to the student who seeks more detailed knowledge of how sailing-ships went about the efficient performance of their share of the world's work. The best of the books—and there are many good ones—are written on the assumption that a public already knowledgeable in the ways of sail will read them. They are addressed to mariners and others who are so familiar with sailing-ships that they take the whole sailing background for granted. Indeed, some of the writers—among them the best of the sailing-ship historians—make no secret of the fact that they address their works to fellow sailing-ship men, and their contempt for the rest of the world is thinly veiled. It is a healthy contempt, perhaps; but speaking broadly, the sailing-ship men have gone now. A new generation of seafarers has looked with astonishment on the few surviving sailing-ships, while these were still with us, as relics misplaced from some myth, wondering that men ever dared go to sea in them or, having gone, ever made successful voyages. Since 1950 the engineless deepsea commercial sailing-ship has disappeared from the face of the sea, like the morning mist—gone with the wind, indeed.

A moment's reflection is sufficient to recall that the world's commerce must *all* have been conducted in sailing vessels for

71

thousands of years. But how? The development of big sailing-
ships can be traced from the histories, and there are enough
of them. But it is of not much use to understand how the rigs
were changed and to be able to follow the broad principles of
ships' progress, if the whole art of handling them and the science
of voyage-making with them are not also comprehended. How
were their voyages made? Did they just emerge hopefully from
some port on a windy day, and contrive somehow to be blown
in the course of time to the neighbourhood of the port to which
they were bound, there to be plucked in from the sea by some
industrious tow-boat?

The answer is, of course, that they did not. The study of
ocean sailing conditions is as old as the story of discovery by
sea itself, for the two went hand in hand. A sailing-ship on an
ocean voyage was not at all concerned with making the shortest passage between two points, measured in miles. What she
sought was the best and shortest usable passage, measured in
terms of winds and weather. What Columbus did in 1492, in addition to stumbling upon some of the islands of the West Indies,
was to open the best sailing route to that area and, from there,
to all North America, for ships which reached the West Indies
were bound, sooner or later, to observe the useful movement
of the Gulf Stream northwards along the American coast.
Indeed, the great silent river of the warm Gulf Stream flowing
northwards and eastwards made possible the early return voyages towards Europe, for just as the north-east Trade winds
blew sailing-ships westwards, the Gulf Stream drifted them gently
north and east to the areas where they could profit from the
westerly winds, and variables. Speaking very broadly, the water
and the winds went round and round, and men learned to use
them.

The existence of the north-east winds—they were called
Trade winds because of their great value to the sailing trade of
the world—was previously known to the Portuguese, for in summer these winds usually begin with northerlies down the Portuguese coast, and sailors from that country had been going at
least to the nearer Atlantic islands for over half-a-century be-

fore Columbus sailed. What was imperfectly understood was the limits of the Trade wind, and its seasonal variations. Such knowledge could be acquired only painfully, over many voyages, and one of the great contributions of Prince Henry's school of navigation at Sagres was to assemble and correlate this knowledge, as it grew.

In their own spheres, the Arabs, the Indians, the Chinese, the Malays, the Persians, and the Polynesians were ahead of the Europeans. The alternating monsoons of the western Indian Ocean, the seasonal winds of the eastern seas, and the trade winds in the Pacific were of great help to migratory and trading voyages in those areas, as soon as they were understood. The only certainty about such voyages is that they are very ancient. So are sailing directions of some sort or other, from primitive charts made of shells sewn with palm-fibre on to reeds, to written directories, lists of courses and distances and drawings of landmarks and remarks on winds and currents, and so forth. With a schoolboy's knowledge of the wind systems of the world, it is easy to understand how the ancient Arabs and Indians were able to make their long trading voyages to the east coast of Africa, Madagascar, and the Persian Gulf. The same knowledge is enough to comprehend that people living along the coasts of Peru, if they had vessels of sufficient seaworthiness, could drift off westwards before the Trade winds of the South Pacific and land among the South Sea islands, whereas people coming the other way—from Malaya and through the chain of Indonesian islands—must have understood very thoroughly the art of working a vessel to windward, for the Trade wind was right in their faces. The swift canoes and the fore-and-aft rig which the Asiatic seafarers developed so well were in fact ideal for windward voyaging, and there is no doubt that the sailing peoples of Indonesia did venture into the South Seas, taking their good canoes with them.

In Europe, ocean sailing was a slow development. The vagaries of the sailing winds in the stormy Western Ocean are I think sufficient to account for that. The trade wind zone of the North Atlantic is remote from the hardy mariners of Northern

Europe. Though the Portuguese could blow down into it, there was no reason why they should, until Prince Henry opened up the trade with the west coast of Africa in the fifteenth century. Why blow off the coast when there was nowhere to go? When to be blown away meant to be lost? European voyages were coastal and short sea voyages—up to Iceland for dried cod, to the Baltic with wool, from Norway with more dried cod or salted herrings, to Cornwall for tin and lead, from the Mediterranean with Eastern products, brought there in part by land caravan and in part by Arab dhows. Sailing conditions in the Mediterranean could be severe and there was an absence there, too, of the kinder monsoons of eastern seas. Earlier sailing vessels in the eastern Mediterranean were narrow-gutted things unfitted for ocean voyaging. They were meant to be propelled by oars as auxiliary to their sails, and many of them could be hauled ashore at the approach of bad weather. Countries bordering the North Atlantic had to develop *ships*. From the Portuguese coasts northwards, conditions were often stormy and frequently perilous, and ships stout enough and weatherly enough to cross the Bay of Biscay and to go up to Iceland had to be good. With such vessels available, European mariners were ready to pierce the veil which, to the end of the Middle Ages, clouded ocean sailing.

The Vikings had learned very early how to make westing in the high latitudes of the North Atlantic with their square-sailed big boats, and their trade to Iceland was an ancient one. They knew how to cross the North Atlantic by the tenth century— probably well before—but those grim northerners, true to character, confined themselves to the cold north where even they soon had enough of transatlantic voyaging, and were content with the trade with Iceland. What they learned to use was the easterly part of the circular movements of wind which passed more or less regularly across the North Atlantic. The wind spirals across, between 37 North and 60 North latitude—speaking very broadly—, and the popular opinion that the wind is more or less constantly from the west (apart from a few odd easterly spells in spring and summer), like most popular ideas, is quite wrong. The wind, twisting itself across from west to east with a procession of clockwise spiralling motions (interspersed now and then by anti-cyclones), blows most often from south-west and west in the most used latitudes today—between 40 and 55 North—but, north of that, the east-blowing part of the cyclonic semicircle is most encountered.

The Vikings did not know why the wind often blew from the east to help them towards Iceland (and to Greenland too, if they wanted to go there) but they knew that it did, and that was knowledge enough. The recommended sailing route for square-rigged ships bound from east to west at certain times of the year is still * to make first from the North Sea up to 55 North or so, not far from Cape Farewell at the tip of Greenland, using the easterly half of the wind's cyclonic movements to get that far and then, profiting from the Arctic current, to sail on to destination. From off Cape Farewell, a north-westerly wind is favourable to make for Halifax or New York, and even a westerly gale would be on the starboard beam and usable.

As men learned that there were ocean voyages worth making, they learned also how to make them. It was a slow process. Through at least three-quarters of the fifteenth century, Portuguese navigators were trying to push down the west coast of Africa towards the Cape of Good Hope, in order to find the sailing route to India. Theirs was the immense task of discovering, first, that there was a southern extremity to Africa round which they could sail and, secondly, how to make successful voyages round it, if it were there. The extremity was there and there was clear water south of it, but to try to grope right down the whole west coast of Africa, following the trend of the land, was an almost impossible thing in a sailing-ship. Both the winds and currents, in the main, were adverse. By ghosting along with land and sea breezes, by somehow negotiating large areas of calm, by patiently exploiting every favourable slant in the variables along the coast, a ship *may* at last have come to the Cape of Good Hope, after a long and exceedingly trying voyage. A few hardy pioneers almost did this, but it was not

* In the British Admiralty publication *Ocean Passages for the World*.

until Bartolomeo Dias, either by accident or design, stood off the coast and then ran back in further to the south that the Cape of Good Hope was actually found.

Between the voyages of Dias and Da Gama's first passage to India, some Portuguese had made a more important discovery than the mere whereabouts of the Cape of Good Hope. He discovered the way to make use of the Atlantic's Trade winds. This was the key to all subsequent voyages. How and upon what data this great step ahead was made we do not know, for the records so far brought to light are silent about it. It might have been the logical sequence of the oceanographical work begun by Prince Henry at Sagres. It might have been tried out by some bold pioneer who, a better navigator than most and unafraid to leave the vicinity of the land, stood boldly out to make the best of the persistent head winds blowing in his face and, taking the wind on his port beam, let his ship bowl along until she came to the limit of the south-east wind. At least she could sail south that way, and hope to make easting later. After the passage through the Trade winds, the variables would let him go as he willed, though he might take a little time about it.

However the proper way to use the wind-system of the Atlantic may have been discovered, the fact remains that the sailing directions given to Vasco Da Gama in 1498 were such that he had only to follow them and he was making the best possible sailing passage between Europe and the Cape of Good Hope. From that, and from the exploitation of Columbus' down-hill run westwards before the north-east Trades of the North Atlantic, all European long voyages under sail evolved. The Trade wind system of the Atlantic, the monsoons of the eastern seas, the mixture of Trades and monsoons of the Indian and the Trades of the Pacific—slowly, painfully knowledge was built up of them all, and used. In this, as in so many important phases of European maritime history, the Portuguese were the true pioneers.

The English navigator Dampier, though perhaps best known as a buccaneer, made such study as he could of the behavior of the ocean winds, and wrote a book about them. He called it a "Discourse on Winds" and it was a useful piece of work, for Dampier managed to get about a good deal of the globe. Other famous navigators slowly added to the store of sailing knowledge, and so did many whose names are not recorded—Spaniards, sailing the North Pacific in the early days; English, in the ships of the East India Company; Dutch, sailing between Holland and Indonesia, and finding that instead of trying to shape a course more or less direct from the Cape of Good Hope towards Jakarta (or anywhere else in Java or India) it saved weeks to sail first in the west winds zone to the longitude of the port to which they were bound, and then the south-east Trade wind would carry them northwards.

James Cook, the Yorkshire seaman who became the greatest sailing explorer of history, added his quota of knowledge. Cook did not sail anywhere without noting everything that would be of sailing value to those who came after him. He is always describing those things that matter to the sailor—the appearance of the land, prominent landmarks, wind and weather. Before Cook, some of the discoverers had preferred the Straits of Magellan as the better route to reach the Pacific. Like the good seaman he was, Cook scorned this idea and properly so, for it was a laborious, dangerous, and foolish waste of time to try to sail a square-rigged ship that way, when there was good open sea to beat in south of Cape Horn.

Here is Cook on the subject in his own Journal,* spelling and all (he is worth reading, for this is the very essence of sailing directions) :

> I am no advocate for the Straits of Magellan, but it may be expected that I should say some thing of Strait le Maire through which we pass'd, and this is the more incumbant on me as it was by choise and contrary to the advice given by Mr. Walter the ingenious Author of Lord Ansons Voyage who adveiseth all Ships not to go through this Strait but to go to the Eastward of Staten land, and likewise to Stand to the Southward as far as 61° or 62° South before any endeavour is made to get to the westward; With respect to the passing of Strait Le Maire or going round Staten land I look upon of little consequence and either

---

* Cook's complete Journal is being published in full, for the first time, by the Hakluyt Society in London.

one or the Other to be pursue'd according to circumstances: for if you happen to fall in with the land to the westward of the Strait and the winds favourable for going through it certainly must be a piece of folly to loose time in going round Staten land, for by paying a little attention to the directions I have already given no ill concequences can attend; but, on the contrary if you should fall in with the land to the eastward of the Strait or the wind should prove boisterous, or unfavourable, in any of these cases the going to the Eastward of Staten land is the most adviseable. And next, as to the runing into the Latitude of 61° or 62° South before any endeavour is made to get to the westward, is what I think no man will ever do that can avoide it, for it cannot be suppose'd that any one will Stear South mearly to get into a high Latitude when at the same time he can Steer West, for it is not Southing but Westing thats wanting, but this way you cannot steer because the winds blow almost constantly from that quarter, so that you have no other choise but to stand to the Southward close upon a wind, and by keeping upon that Tack you not only make southing but westing also and sometimes not a little when the wind Varies to the northward of west, and the farther you advance to the South[rd] the better chance you have of having the winds from that quarter or easterly and likewise of meeting with finer weather, both of which we ourselves experence'd. Prudence will direct every man when in these high Latitudes to make sure of Sufficient westing to double all the lands before he thinks of Standing to the Northward.

While ships were groping about the ends of the earth more or less individually, the accumulation of sailing knowledge was bound to be a slow process. But trade followed the discoverers, and soon fleets of whalers and traders were both adding to knowledge and experiencing the need for more. There were books of sailing directions for the Atlantic Ocean first, then for the other oceans. Blunt's epitome of instructions on the sailing of ships along the eastern seaboard of the United States is a classic. Captain Becher's *Navigation of the Atlantic Ocean,* and Captain Kerhallet's similar work before that, and Findlay's Directories of the various oceans, followed one another, each apologising that its information was sadly incomplete. "Any information with which the Editor may be favoured relating to Winds, Currents, and the Mode of Navigating the Seas . . . will be thankfully appreciated," writes the hydrographer who pro-

Calm was the most-hated condition in a Cape Horn ship. Here the *Herzogin Cecilie* lies becalmed in the South Atlantic Horse Latitudes.

They loved to run before strong winds—the stronger the better!

duced Mr. Potter's *Navigation of the Indian Ocean, China and Australian Seas* in 1864 (third edition). It was a slim book with many gaps in its contents.

Other American hydrographers besides Blunt made notable contributions, especially Lieutenant Maury. Maury made a scientific study of ocean winds as they could be applied to the making of better sailing-ship voyages, and his researches were thorough, his observations sound, and his contribution to the science of passage-making was considerable. Maury's work, indeed, formed the basis of most sailing directions for many years. Maury concentrated on establishing which were the best routes for sailing-ships to follow at various times of the year, on all the standard voyages. He showed that even the maligned North Atlantic, whose winds and weather are notoriously so often vile, offered defined sailing routes which shipmasters could use with the certainty that, by so doing, they stood the best chance of making reasonable passages. This is not to say that there was one sailing route, and one only: but at each season of the year, there was very definitely a *best* way for the sailing-ship, say, to reach Liverpool from New York or New York from Liverpool (which was much more difficult), or to sail from New York to Rio, the Cape of Good Hope, or anywhere else. Of course there would be daily variations in the weather. It was the best routes for average conditions that Maury established and, by and large, a shipmaster could be assured that if he followed these directions his ship (provided she could sail at all) would make a better and faster passage, on the average, than she would if he went by any other way.

Consider, for example, the passage from New York towards Rio de Janeiro, which is a straightforward run. A glance at the map shows a nice direct route, which the powered vessels of today are able to follow. But if a sailing-ship tried to sail along the direct route it would take months to reach even the equator, and then she would be jammed behind Cape San Roque with the wind in her face, and have to beat out. No, the way to go was first to run east or a little south of east for at least a thousand or 1500 miles into the North Atlantic, to get right away from the land

and to pick up the north-east Trade winds. These would bring
a ship quickly to the equator, where after working through the
doldrums—Maury gave the best longitudes to try to cross where
the doldrums belt would be narrowest at various times of the
year—the south-east Trade would take her practically to her
destination. This increased the distance sailed by perhaps a
thousand miles, but it shortened the time taken by weeks. It was of
no use for a ship to be stopped in calm or fighting a head wind in
her face, on the most direct route. The whole art of voyage-
making was to keep going, making progress somewhere in the
right direction. The principles of passage-making under sail are,
indeed, laid down by Captain Becher as follows:

1. Never hug the wind when it is foul, but let the ship go at least a point
   free through the water.
2. Profit as much as possible by the well-known prevailing winds and currents.
3. Lay the ship's head on that tack, with a foul wind, that will enable her
   to look best up for her port.

   In other words, use the wind to sail with and do not jam the
ship into it; make maximum use of the known permanent winds
and currents; study which way the wind is going to shift on you,
and put the ship on the tack which will allow her to benefit
most from any shift the wind might make. Be sufficient of a meteorologist to be able to observe which semicircle of the wind-
cycle the ship is in.
   "The extensive space between the tropics and either pole
is the region of variable winds, generally assuming a contrary
direction to the Trade winds, to contribute, perhaps, with other
phenomena to preserve the atmospheric equilibrium or counterpoise that is found in all the operations of nature," writes the
captain, discussing sailing routes (based on Maury) in the North
Atlantic. "But the whole subject of atmospheric changes, like
that of natural history generally, is replete with these beneficial
arrangements of an all-wise Creator in anticipation of the wants
of his creature man to reach readily the different parts of the

globe which he inhabits, by the aid of navigation, so that he may turn to his account the winds and the currents which again and again change their directions with the seasons of the year. All is ceaseless change, perpetually working to his good"—provided he had the knowledge to profit by the changes, of course.

I have been with sailing-ship masters who would have quarrelled with some of this. But broadly speaking, it was true. The Lord had provided sailing mankind with good winds for passage-making, so long as he knew how to use them, and they could be made to blow him where he wished to go. There was method even in the vagaries of the Atlantic gales, and a courageous master-mariner, in a good ship, could make use of them. So also could he defeat Cape Horn, as Hilgendorf did so consistently, and Boye Petersen and Nissen, and Learmont and Jarvis and many more. Westward crossings of the North Atlantic in winter and westward roundings of the Horn at any season were the classic challenges of the sailing-ship. Yet the sailing packets (most of them American) learned how to take the North Atlantic in their stride, west-bound or east-bound at all seasons of the year, and suffered little mortality, too, in their consistently good passage-making. Their masters had acquired the necessary knowledge, usually by painful and long-continued application to the subject. The ships were good ships. The crews were fearless, competent seamen. And so for more than a quarter of a century after the steamships came, the Atlantic sailing packets were able not only to fight back at the increasing competition, but to hold their own.

Rounding the Horn was a different matter. There is no doubt that the dread of Cape Horn had an effect on the nerves of far too many masters. As soon as they got near 50 South in the Atlantic they feared the worst, and shortened their ships down to wait for it. Of course they got it, then. If they had fought back, if they had sailed (as many did) with the quiet confidence born of courage and ability, then getting past Cape Horn was no worse than a winter rounding of Hatteras or Flattery, or a beat down-Channel against the November gales. The broad principles of getting round were well established. It was a fight,

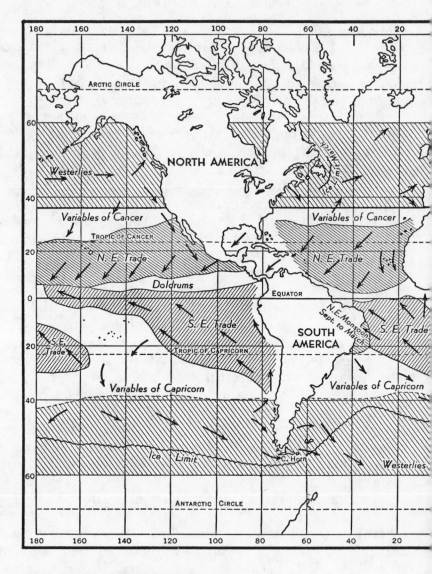

THE SAILING-SHIP'S WORLD

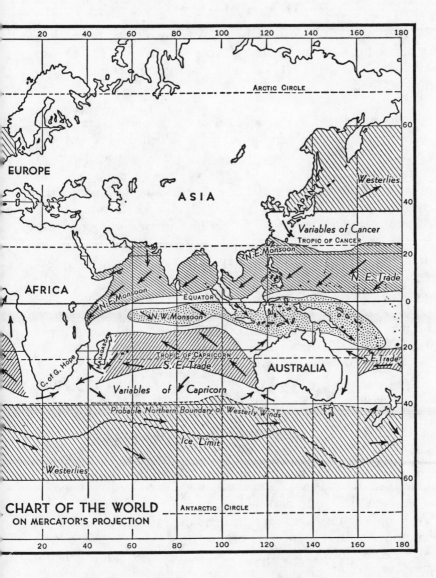

The chart shows general wind conditions for the first quarter of the year.

and a hard one. In the last analysis it was the quality and endurance of the fighter which counted. In a long-voyage sailing-ship the fighter was the master, far more than the ship. But the ship had to be good, too.

By the middle of the nineteenth century, there were plenty of publications, official and otherwise, which laid down the principles of passage-making under sail. Of course a master in any trade would build up his own knowledge of winds and weather, and this could be of the greatest value to him. In the later days of the sailing-ship most sailers were tramps, going anywhere. A typical voyage for a big four-masted barque in the 1890's or early 1900's, for example, would be from the Bristol Channel to a Chilean port with patent fuel, hoping to get a cargo of nitrate back to Europe. But there might be no nitrate available for her, so she would go up to San Francisco for grain, or perhaps across to Newcastle in Australia for a coal cargo to take back to Chile (she might make the Pacific round two or three times). Then finally she would pick up grain at San Francisco, or guano or nitrates somewhere along the West Coast, and sail back to Europe with that. (A *voyage* was a round trip from home port—or some port on the same coast—back to home port: a run between any two ports was a *passage*, not a voyage.) Masters called on to make voyages of this sort covered the world, and they were glad to have volumes of sailing directions even though they had to pay for them. British owners did not usually provide them, nor even such necessities as charts and chronometers. Shipmasters had to find their own.

Although British and American hydrographers appealed to shipmasters to send in reports of the winds and weather they experienced on all their voyages, few bothered to send such information in. Only a very few British sailing-ship owners required their masters to furnish such information, even to themselves. Masters and owners took a great interest in passages as they were made, but few ever considered the subject scientifically. A good passage was good luck, coupled with a good driver, perhaps. A bad passage was bad luck. The Germans, on the other hand, required *all* masters to send in passage-information, properly kept and collated. In this way the German hydrographic office was able to issue carefully thought-out sailing directions for any time of the year, for any square-rigged ship bound almost anywhere between 75 North and 60 South latitude. If a master of a Hamburg ship, for example, was ordered to take his ship in ballast to Philadelphia, sailing in October, to load case oil there for Yokohama, and, when that was discharged, to move down to Saigon in Indo-China to load rice for the return voyage, then the information furnished by the Deutsche Seewarte would be invaluable. The best way to make for Philadelphia in ballast might be north-about—towards Greenland first—and it might be south-about—the Trade wind way. The hydrographers would know, using all the information they had built up, and the master would be informed.

Having loaded his case oil he virtually had the oceans of the world before him, thousands upon thousands of miles of them. The long-voyage sailing-ship had tremendous endurance and could keep the seas while her people had water to drink and good food enough to keep the scurvy away. He could sail down both Atlantics (the Maury way, with such variations as the season might suggest) and then run his easting down past all Australia, if that were best, and not turn northwards until past Tasmania. Then he could run northwards with the south-east Trade of the South Pacific a favouring wind, and the north-east Trades of the North Pacific would follow. This route would avoid all the confusing channels among the Indonesian islands and the reefs of the China Sea. It might be best at certain times of the year, and a good many shipmasters tried it. (Most of these were not briefed by Deutsche Seewarte. Their decision was based on a healthy dread of pilotage among the islands and the reefs, and a general safety first policy.) Or the ship could turn north from the west winds before reaching the west coast of Australia and, standing north there in the Indian Ocean Trades, sail to her destination through Sunda and Carimata Straits and onwards, west of Borneo, through the length of the China Sea; or through Bali or Lombok Straits and then Macassar Straits, between Borneo and the Celebes, and then to the eastwards of the Philippines; or through the Ombai passage by Timor and thence past Gilolo, and northwards in open sea. There was a wide variation with differences of many hundreds of miles in distance and weeks of sailing. Choosing the best way to go was a skilled hydrographer's business, and the shipmaster who was able to go off properly briefed had a great advantage.

His short passage to Saigon and his homeward passage offered wide variations, too. No shipmaster could possibly be as expert at all this sort of passage-planning as an hydrographer ashore, working with the accumulated lore of all the ships to assist him, and his full-time occupation the discovery of the best way to find favouring winds and currents at all seasons. The hydrographer planned the passage. The shipmaster made it.

In Britain, the Admiralty had a department to do this sort of thing, though it had no officers to brief merchant shipmasters and did not get many reports. Its function in this sphere was to issue printed Sailing Directions and weather charts. The United States Hydrographic Office in Washington worked along the same lines. Its weather charts were invaluable. They are still, for winds and weather affect powered vessels to a considerable extent. The U. S. monthly weather charts, which are issued for all the major oceans, are extremely good. Using the information which the monthly North Atlantic pilot charts give, for example, together with the weather reports which may now be heard on the radio, a sailing ship would at all times know how best to make an Atlantic passage, whether she was going west or east. The tracks of hurricanes are shown in distinctive red. Average winds are shown for every five degrees of latitude and longitude. The best sailing routes are shown, over-printed in black. But, unfortunately, there are only a few yachts to use such information now. The Cape Horn shipmasters had to do without radio, except in the very last days: even then there were no weather reports which were of use to them, once they were away from the immediate vicinities of a place like the eastern seaboard of the United States, the North Sea, and the English Channel. Apart from the Germans, they made their ocean passages on their Sailing

Directions and their personal knowledge. The personal knowledge of a shipmaster like Hilgendorf, in the Chilean trade, could be very extensive. There were also plenty of fools who never acquired any. Some ships made good passages because they were blessed with hulls which moved easily through the water, even under poor conditions, and they were lucky with their winds. But most ships which consistently made better-than-average passages did so because they were handled by masters who always made the utmost use of the winds, and had the knowledge—and took the trouble—to place their vessels advantageously to benefit by every wind-change in their favour. These were the Woodgets, the Hilgendorfs, the Learmonts, the de Cloux's of the sailing-ship world. A poor master could spoil the best ship, and a good master could do surprising things even with a very poor vessel. There were, unfortunately, always more good ships than good masters, by a very wide margin.

The British Admiralty publication *Ocean Passages for the World* is a most useful work for planning passages under sail. I had a copy of the edition of 1933 when I was planning the voyage of the full-rigged ship *Joseph Conrad* round the world, in 1934. An earlier edition brought out in 1896 was just as good, from the sailing-ships' point of view. The 1933 edition devoted over 400 of its 600 pages to routes for steamships, for there were then—and there still are—many low-powered steamers and motorships on the sea routes which did not want to buck head-winds any more than they could help.

I planned to begin my circumnavigation from Ipswich on the east coast of England, and to go first to New York. I would have to sail in October, so there was no help as far as the Channel was concerned. I must expect westerly gales and many of them, and I would have to slog against them, using the tides, the contour of the land, and every favouring slant to help me. The *Joseph Conrad* was a small full-rigged ship of only some 400 tons dead-weight. She was built of iron, very strongly, and her rigging was good. Her masts and yards were wooden, and I had been used to steel. She had the old-fashioned very deep single tops'ls which required reefing: I had been used to the double topsails of later-day square-riggers, which were never reefed. She could set studding-sails, if I wanted them. She was designed as a school-ship with accommodation in her tween-decks, which meant that companion-ways and skylights broke the main-deck to give access below. This made the ship more vulnerable than an ordinary cargo-carrier, which caulked and secured her hatches until she was virtually as unassailable as a half-tide rock (so long as the hatches were intact) for all her people lived on deck, either beneath the poop right aft or in a house on the fore deck. On the other hand, having no cargo to carry, the *Joseph Conrad* was always in the best possible sailing trim. She was a weatherly and able little vessel and her whole business was sailing and training. In 1934 she was 52 years old, and she had not pre-viously been beyond the confines of the Baltic and the North Sea. She had laid up during the winters when ice conditions made Baltic sailing impracticable. Now, just how was I going to get this ship to the westward across the North Atlantic in the Fall of the year? And afterwards where should I go? And how?

Here the section covering sailing-ship routes in my *Ocean Passages of the World* was of great value. It began with a list of the average number of days taken by big sailing-ships on the passages they were still being called upon to make. There were over fifty of these, ranging from Melbourne to Hampton Roads (80 to 100 days) to the Channel to San Francisco (125 to 150). These figures were compiled, in the main, from the records of Messrs. Hardie and Company's square-riggers, from Glasgow. They were good ships but not clippers. Having obtained a general idea of the length of time required for the various passages—I already knew the Australian trade well enough—I could calculate roughly where I would have time to go. Channel to New York, winter months, 35 to 40 days (I would be lucky to do it in that; these figures were from ships of an average 2000 tons): New York to Rio, 60 to 65 days: Rio to the Cape, 20 days: Cape Town to the Indies, 40 to 50 days: the Indies to Sydney, Australia, 60 days: Sydney to the Channel, 80 to 100 days, or to New York in approximately the same time. It was my intention

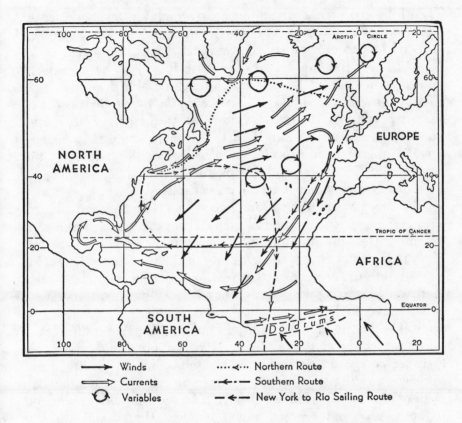

→ Winds	····◄··· Northern Route
⇒ Currents	·◄·◄·◄· Southern Route
↻ Variables	▬◄▬◄▬ New York to Rio Sailing Route

THE NORTH ATLANTIC, TO THE SAILING-SHIP SAILOR

to go to many islands once the Indian Ocean and the Pacific had been reached, and that would add many days.

First there was that winter passage towards New York. Thirty-five to 40 days? That must have meant sailing by the northern passage, and those days must have been from outside the Channel —certainly not from the North Sea where I had to start. I looked up the directions for the passage Channel to Newfoundland, Canada, and Eastern Ports of the United States. First came the northern route. I read: "In this route, although heavy weather is frequently experienced, the winds are generally more favourable, and the Arctic current assists in the latter part."

Then followed precise directions as to which latitudes and longitudes to make for. But that heavy weather threat did not appeal to me. I *had* to beat out of the Channel. I had an untried crew. No one knew just how kindly the little full-rigger was going to take to winter sailing. There were those vulnerable deck-openings. I had a lot of boys. No, no: I didn't care for that sullen threat of the great wind-tormented seas north of 55 in the grey Atlantic, nor for the idea of pressing a little ship with wooden yards and single tops'ls against a succession of westerly gales, with only the help of the Arctic current to look for as a change, at the end. It would be December before I was near New York. Ugh!

But there was another route. I read on. "The Southern Route. This is the best route to be followed during the whole of the year excepting the autumn months, on account of the better weather likely to be experienced, the certainty of the wind, and the avoidance of both fog and ice off the Newfoundland Banks . . ." That read well. I was against both fog and ice. But, unfortunately, it would have to be the autumn when I sailed. I continued to read. The instructions were brief enough. "By this route," they said, "vessels leaving the Channel with a fair wind may steer a direct course as long as it lasts, and should at least ensure sufficient westing to avoid the danger of being set into the Bay of Biscay. When the fair wind fails, take the Madeira route, and if the wind permits, pass midway between that island and the Azores into the N.E. trade wind, but if the wind does not favour, the trade wind will usually be gained sooner by passing nearer to Madeira. In that neighbourhood, it is usually found in the summer season between lats. 32 and 31 N; in winter, a degree or so farther south. When well into the trade wind limits, run westward, keeping southward of lat. 25 N until in long. 65 W, then steer northwestwards. . . ."

There were also directions for the direct route, which was not recommended, although it was about a thousand miles shorter than the southern route. "It is seldom possible to be taken on account of the prevailing westerly winds, and of the Atlantic Drift Stream and the Gulf Stream combined, running contrary to the desired track." It was however "recommended by some navigators," I suppose of the old hard-bitten sailing packets which cared nothing for sunshine or mild winds.

My choice was made. It was the southern route for me. Nor did I regret it. It took upwards of a week to beat out of the Channel and another week to get across the mouth of the Bay of Biscay. I looked in at Madeira and at Nassau in the Bahamas, and the whole passage to New York took 56 days—a little longer than Messrs. Hardies' average, but Glasgow barques made no wayside stops.

And after New York? Well, first to Rio. "On leaving New York," said my *Ocean Passages*, "make for the intersection of 35 N with long. 45 W," which is not far short of half-way across the Atlantic. From this position (or a little south of it in the winter months) the recommended course was to run south more or less direct through the north-east trades and to cross the equator somewhere between 24 W and 29 W, where the zone of calms would be narrowest. Thence the South American coast could be approached (with the south-east trades) "to a prudent distance, and the port steered for direct." This was all right. It took me 36 days to reach the equator and I logged 4283 miles (the direct distance is about 3000). But the directions were good: I was only three days in the doldrums though the south-east trade put me very close to the Brazilian coast, later on. The whole passage from New York to Rio took the *Joseph Conrad* 57 days. Then I sailed on to Cape Town in a month. This was largely a west winds passage, spoiled by calms and light winds at the outset and further delayed a little by a call at Tristan da Cunha.

From the Cape I was bound for Bali and the islands. This was another west winds passage at the beginning. "Should a south-easterly wind be blowing on leaving Table Bay," said my *Ocean Passages* (it was), "stand boldly to the south-westward until the westerly winds are reached . . ." I did. After that my good book became a little vague—"the best latitude to cross the ocean must to some extent depend on circumstances"—but I knew that road. It was the high road to Australia, part of the great watery way which, with the trade winds, really made sailing-ship voyages practical. *Ocean Passages* even became optimistic on this. "The Great Southern Ocean, which offers the only direct water-route right round the globe, may be considered as the Main Track of Sailing-Ships and traffic, on account of the strong westerly winds which there prevail, and may be depended upon at all seasons of the year to afford a swift passage, unimpeded by dangers". I don't know about that "unimpeded by dangers". There were icebergs and there were islands to keep away from, to say nothing of the danger of being overwhelmed in a small and vulnerable ship, or being dismasted. A good many ships were missing along that road, and I knew that. But the westerly gales were reliable; all I had to do was to haul out of their area in good time, before reaching the longitude of the south-western tip of Australia. Then I had a brief zone of variable winds to work through before reaching the south-east trades which blew me to the Straits of Bali. I meant to use Lombok Straits, but there was a strong set towards the west. In the end, I just managed to weather the south-eastern tip of Java and get into Bali Straits.

After that, my passages round Indonesia, to Singapore, over the China Sea, through the Sulu Sea and so on, were local, made with a favouring monsoon (as I had planned). The next passage which really bothered me was from that area towards Sydney. The sensible way—and the way my *Ocean Passages* recommended—was to get out of Indonesian waters altogether, making southing to the west of Australia, and then run south of all the Australian continent in the great west winds again, the "Roaring Forties", and head up for Sydney from off Tasmania. This was a long way round. *Ocean Passages* gave another route north-about from Singapore towards Darwin, but not for Sydney. However, I intended to go north-about. I had, after all, a fairly long experience of those wild west winds. I had not had a ship of my own before, which I could take anywhere. The route north-about would take me by the Celebes, north of New Guinea, and I could go among the Solomon Islands. It might also take me six months. Well, I had six months. The north-east trade wind was a head wind, as soon as I emerged from the Sulu Sea. The equatorial current would be against me. But—and it was a very big 'but'—

there was also the counter-equatorial current, setting the way I wanted to go. If I could get in that—it worked, very kindly, in the area where the trade wind was lightest—and ghost along, then in due course I should make sufficient easting to be to wind-ward of New Guinea, and so able to stand down towards Sydney. The alternative, if I found I could make no satisfactory easting at all, was to take the north-east trade on my starboard beam and sail boldly to the northwards out of it altogether, making east then in the west winds of the North Pacific and southwards again when I had come east far enough to make Sydney on a sort of great horse-shoe course—a long way round! But sailing-ships sometimes *had* to make passages like that.

I was lucky. The counter-equatorial current was there, all right—its position was a little vague—and it was working well. The north-east trade was light. The *Conrad* was good at ghosting. I could make easting, after a fashion, and in due course I passed north of New Guinea, and came among the Trobriands, and the Solomons, and went on down to Sydney when the spirit moved me. But the *Ocean Passages* were definitely not for this kind of voyaging. Their directions were purposeful, clear, concise. I had good precedent for sometimes not holding to them. Conrad him-self, when he commanded the iron barque *Otago*—a sweet-hulled little sailing beauty—once determined to go north-about through Torres Straits on some passage which should not have taken him that way at all—Melbourne towards Mauritius, I think it was. To go the Torres Straits way he had to negotiate the Coral Sea, then very poorly charted, and the Torres Strait itself was a maze of sand-banks and ill-defined reefs. But he made it.

I had to sail through the Coral Sea, too: but it was not by choice. The Coral Sea receives scant mention in the Admiralty volume, which obviously and very properly regards it as a place prudent ship-masters would do well to avoid. After that, I sailed among the South Seas Islands for a while—six months or so—and my book was of little value there, though the *Pacific Islands Pilot* (three volumes) was most useful. The U.S. pilot charts were invaluable, as they had been, indeed, over the rest of the voyage. I picked up my regular sailing routes again when I reached

Tahiti, and was bound back towards New York from that pleasant island.

As far as sailing among the islands went, the *Ocean Passages* had little to offer. "For all practical purposes of navigation between the various groups of islands, it is important to draw attention to the fact," it points out, "that they lie within the limits of the SE trade wind and of the equatorial current. For sailing vessels this means a favourable wind and current when proceeding from eastward to westward . . . and a beat to windward against the current and a choppy sea, when bound in the opposite direction," as I was, of course. The sensible thing to do was to use the trade wind for making latitude only, and to make my easting out of the trade wind zone altogether and back in the westerlies. This I did, though it meant covering tremendous distances. I was 77 days from Samarai by way of Lord Howe Island and Cook Straits to Papeete.

As for my last long run, the *Ocean Passages* was almost laconic. "Route 781: Islands to Cape Horn, or South American Ports," it said. "From any of the Pacific Islands stand through the trades to the southward and then into the westerly winds of the southern hemisphere; from thence, proceed by great circle to Cape Horn." And once there, pick up the old familiar road, varying a little according to the season and the conditions one chanced to meet off the Falkland Islands. There was drift-ice to be guarded against (the limits were clearly marked on the pilot charts) and there were the sudden storms called pamperos to be watched, even hundreds of miles out from the coast of the Argentine. That sort of sailing was familiar and the routes well known. I might have been able to get from Deutsche Seewarte precise information as to where to find the strongest trade winds, where best to cross the equator, and so forth. For my purposes, the American pilot charts and the British volume were sufficient. From Tahiti to New York I was 105 days.

Messrs. Hardies' barques had made no passage between Tahiti and New York, or at any rate none was listed. Tahiti has few cargoes to offer. I saw that the nearest similar passage, that from Valparaiso round the Horn to New York, was listed as

↑ In a fresh trade wind

↓ Cape Horn. The photograph was taken from the *Parma* in 1933.

↑ A great white wake was a sign of a poor hull-form,
a bluff cargo-carrier. This was the ship *Grace Harwar*.

↓ The cutwater must cut the water cleanly, without fuss.

taking an average 75 to 85 days. It was perhaps a thousand miles the shorter journey, but I wondered just how many big-carrying Glasgow barques *had* made that run in 75 days. The average for the passage Valparaiso to the Channel was given as 80 to 90 days.

The point is that I had no real difficulty in planning and in making my sailing voyage round the world. There was ample information and had been, then, for well over a century. It was only in the truly pioneering days that sailing-ships had had to grope. Even by the 1800's, the principal sailing routes were well established and thoroughly well known. Long before the end of the sailing era the accumulated knowledge was adequate for any calls that could be made upon it. The making of long voyages was far from being a hit-or-miss affair of hoping for the best. The average number of days required by the average well-found vessel, to sail at any time of the year between any ports which ordinarily offered trade, was well-known to shipowners, masters, charterers, underwriters and hydrographers alike. Here and there, steady progress was being made to cut down the time required for the more important passages, but the rapidly encroaching competition of powered vessels brought the quest of such knowledge to an end.

Chapter five

HANDLING SQUARE SAILS

Looking in a museum at a scale model of the five-masted full-rigged ship *Preussen,* or any steel four-masted barque or full-rigged ship, the array of masts, yards, and wire, chain, and cordage of all sorts looks complicated almost beyond comprehension. How could such a vessel be controlled? Where, indeed, could the sails be set, in all that puzzle? How were they set, manipulated, taken in? The text books give plenty of *descriptions* of sails and rigging, but just how was the great ship under sail *worked*?

To understand something of that, it is first necessary to master the general principles of her rigging. But first let us have a look at a simpler vessel, say, a typical Chinese junk. The junk does not look complicated, nor is it. The standard junk has three masts, a squat mast jutting out at an angle in or near the bows, a great tree of a mainmast growing from the centre of the vessel, and a small aftermast, like the foremast, sprouting from somewhere near the stern. With the sails set on these three masts, and a large balanced rudder, the junk is handled with skill and precision by its sailors. It can be swung in any direction, made to go sideways or ahead, put into a snug anchorage, tacked in a congested roadstead, and can safely prosecute such ocean voyages as are still open to it.

Its masts are simple trees chosen for their solidity and strength, and even the mainmast (in all types of junk that I have seen) is so solid that it carries its huge single sail without any complications of standing rigging to support it. On each of the masts,

97

JUNK

a single sail is hoisted, like a balanced-lug on a ship's lifeboat.
Each of the sails is extended and kept in good pulling shape by
a series of battens, and each batten, where it emerges at the
after edge of the sail, is secured by a piece of cordage—a sheet
and brace combined—which leads more or less directly to the
deck. The large number of battens—they pass right through or
across the width of the sail—in big junks sometimes makes the
cordage controlling them look like a spider's web. But their purpose is clear enough. The whole working of a junk's sails and scant
rigging is obvious at a glance. The battens are laced to the mast,
loosely but effectively, and the sail rides up and down on them.
Roughly a fifth of the sail's area is on the fore part of the mast,
and the rest abaft it—just as in the ordinary European balanced-
lug rig. This means in effect that the junk sails combine the
advantages of the square with the fore-and-aft rig. They will lie
almost flat into the wind, and give the vessel good headway (for
the Chinese know how to build hulls, too) : and they will square
off before a favouring breeze and let the junk boom along. They
can be shifted to the other side of the mast by being dipped
behind it. Each section of the sail between the battens is individually controllable, so the sail may always be extended with
perfection. Each section, too, can be taken in easily, by the

Mainsail of a junk
(simplified)

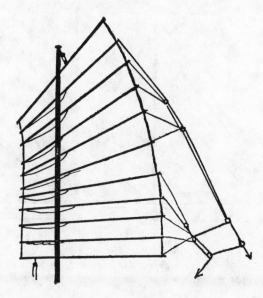

simple process of lowering the battens, which act more or less like the pieces of a Venetian blind. There is no need to go aloft in ordinary weather.

True, the great mainsail *looks* unwieldy, but in fact it is not. As for the handiness of the junk herself, the placing of the masts is ideal. She will swing on a piece of seaweed, for the smaller sails in the bows and stern are carefully placed to exert the maximum pivotage whenever it might be required. Either can be lowered in a matter of seconds. The sail on the aftermast will bring the junk up into the wind whenever that may be thought necessary, and the sail on the raking foremast will blow her bows round from the wind in the same way. When the junk is just sailing along, the two sails nicely balance one another—their placing assures that, too—and both, together with the mainsail, then assist the vessel's headway.

Junks were sailing in that manner long before there was any seagoing European sailing-ship, and they are still sailing now that all the European square-rigged sailing-ships are gone. Looked at broadly, the principles of square-rigged sailing are the same. In

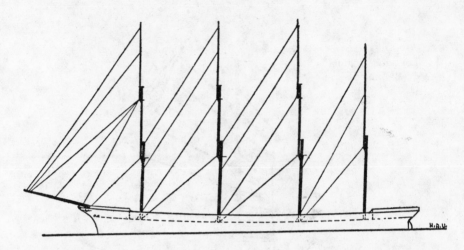

European sailing-ships often had four masts—fore, main, mizzen, and jigger. The bowsprit protrudes from the cutwater, and the system of fore-and-aft staying depends to considerable degree on the security of the bowsprit. Here, the fore-and-aft stays only are shown.

European ships the bowsprit takes the place of the junk's raked foremast, and there are two, three, or even four 'main'-masts instead of one, and the aftermast which always carries a fore-and-aft sail (though it may carry square sails as well) is the counterpart of the little mast jutting out at the junk's stern. The European masts have become much higher and more complicated in order to spread sail area sufficient to move the larger, deeper hull, and they require the support of what looks like a maze of heavy wire stays. The battens have become yards—at first made of wood but later, as ships became larger and larger, made of tubular steel. The battens in the junk keep the shape and ensure the good pulling qualities of a single sail. They are part of the sail. But in the European square-rigger they were quite separate. The sails were suspended or set from the yards, and there were as many quite different sails as there were yards. The angle of the sail to the wind was controlled in both types of ship alike—by swinging the battens-yards by means of the braces. The European ship reduced sail in the same way—by lowering

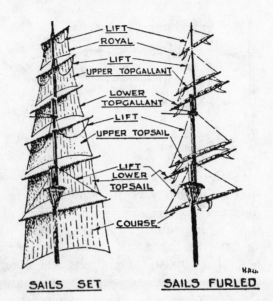

LIFT
ROYAL
LIFT
UPPER TOPGALLANT
LOWER
TOPGALLANT
LIFT
UPPER TOPSAIL
LIFT
LOWER
TOPSAIL
COURSE

What happens to the rigging
when sails are set, or furled.
Only some of the rigging is
shown, for the sake of clarity.

SAILS SET   **SAILS FURLED**

her 'batten', her yards. The only difference was that she hauled
some sails right up to the yards, which became fixed (because
they were so heavy) and the sailors had to climb aloft to secure
the canvas to prevent it being blown away. As the ship's source
of motive power, the canvas had to be conserved.

The necessity to climb aloft introduced further complications,
and the Europeans laced ladders in their standing rigging. (The
standing rigging is that which stands—is rigid in its work of supporting the masts. The *running* rigging runs—its function is to
control the movement of the sails and yards, though much of it
helps also to support them.)

What appears so complicated both on the actual ships and
on models is the tremendous construction of standing rigging and
running rigging, most skilfully contrived through the centuries
each to perform its own function without getting in the way of
the other, chafing itself to pieces, or preventing the proper setting
of the sails. The standing rigging must support many tons of masts
and yards, and it must do this in such a way as never to interfere

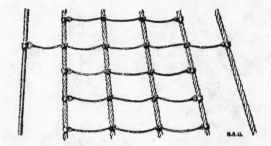

Ratlines were attached to the shrouds to help the sailors to climb aloft. These were often wooden battens, or steel rods.

with the necessary movement of the yards. 'Square' rig means that a ship has yards which can be used square across the ship: 'fore-and-aft' rig means that instead of the mast carrying yards from which square or rectangular sails are spread, there are no yards across the mast and the sails are hoisted on gaffs and booms behind the mast. These gaffs and booms can be made to lie in the fore-and-aft line of the vessel—along her keel. Square sails can never be manipulated as close to the wind as that, for the standing rigging supporting the masts that carry them must, to some extent, prevent the free swinging of the yards. In order to allow the yards to swing as near to fore-and-aft as possible (and so bring the sails as close to the direction of the wind as can be contrived), the standing rigging never extends forward of the masts, except of course the fore-and-aft stays, which are comparatively few. The first heavy stay on either side goes down to the hull directly beside the centre of the mast it is supporting, and all the other stays—those to the lower masts are called shrouds, the others backstays—in turn go down behind it. (A glance at the diagrams illustrating this chapter will show this clearly.) In this way, the yards can be swung in such a manner that sails set from them will usefully convert the wind into motive power even if the wind is blowing from a couple of compass points for'ard of the beam—that is, almost in the ship's face.

Hull-form comes into this too, of course. The sailing-ship must have a hull-form which will go easily through the water, setting up the minimum resistance and at the same time, it must grip the water well enough to permit motive power applied from

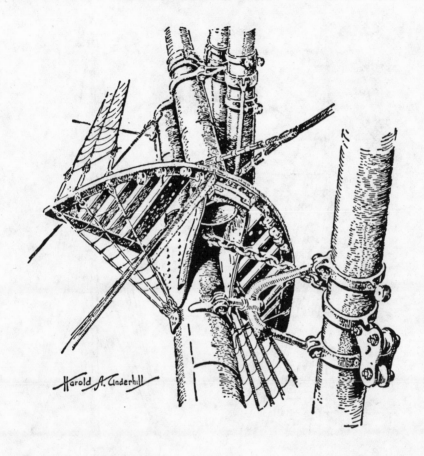

Massive strength was the keystone of a square-rigger's masts and yards. Here can be seen the maintop of a full-rigged ship, with part of the mainyard (lowest) and parts of the lower and upper topsail yards, showing the manner in which they are supported and, at the same time, held clear of the masts and standing rigging, in order to allow the sails to be well set. The upper topsail yard hoists on a parral, which can be seen around the mast.

ahead to force the ship along. So the sailing-ship is deeper than the powered-vessel, and not so flat in the floors. She is deep to grip the water; beamy—but not too beamy—to support the enormous weight of her masts and yards and give a good spread to her standing rigging; long, to carry her way and run well even

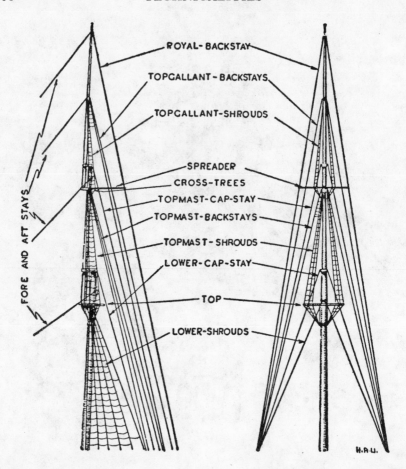

ROYAL-BACKSTAY

TOPGALLANT-BACKSTAYS

TOPGALLANT-SHROUDS

SPREADER

CROSS-TREES

TOPMAST-CAP-STAY

TOPMAST-BACKSTAYS

TOPMAST-SHROUDS

LOWER-CAP-STAY

TOP

LOWER-SHROUDS

FORE AND AFT STAYS

H.A.U.

The standing rigging which supports the masts is skilfully led, in order to minimise interference with the yards and sails.

in the vilest weather; high-sided to afford some protection to her crew whose most dangerous work (in terms of peril to life and limb) is on her decks, not in her rigging. She must have reasonably fine ends, too, to part the water easily as she moves along and not to cause disturbances which her sails must waste power to overcome. She must have such a hull as will always go through the water, and not under it. Too fine a bow, too fine a stern spoil their own objects, for the very wet ship drowns hands and often drowns herself, sooner or later. Just as the bows must slip along and neither push the sea before them nor knife their way through, leaving the rest of the ship to follow in the best way she can, so the shape of the hull aft must be such that it causes the minimum disturbance in the sea, and yet there must be buoyancy enough to lift the stern out of menacing following seas. A sailing-ship which raced along with a great wake foaming white astern was a poor sailing-ship, but one which put her poop under was worse. What sailors called 'pooping' should be rarely experienced—very rarely. The lines of the hull and the manner of her sailing affected this. Sailors spoke of ships which pooped or which made hogs of themselves in the sea as 'wet' ships. If they were particularly bad they were known as vicious. The following sea, racing at the fleeing ship, had to find something to lift. Otherwise it would break right over the stern, smashing the wheel, washing the helmsman overboard, carrying the compasses away, flooding the accommodation. A ship might not survive such an onslaught.

So much for hull-form, which is a complicated subject not thoroughly understood even today. The most nearly perfect underwater bodies I know are those of some Arab dhows which can be seen hauled out at such ports as Aden, Mukalla, and Kuwait. But the hulls of the better European—and American—sailing-ships came very near to perfection, too. Such ships as the Donald Mackay clippers and the Scots-built *Cutty Sark*, and dozens of the semi-clippers which came after her, had lovely hulls. Though their towering midships superstructures spoiled their hulls above water to an older seaman's eye—while he granted their use—the under-water lines of such ships as the big 'P' four- and five-masters were extremely good. They were perfect for the job they were designed to do. They had to add another quality: they had to accommodate vast quantities of very heavy cargoes, and accept all the stresses which they could put on a long hull while it was being flung and rolled about, and furiously driven, in the highest and most dangerous seas in the watery world.

STEEL YARDS

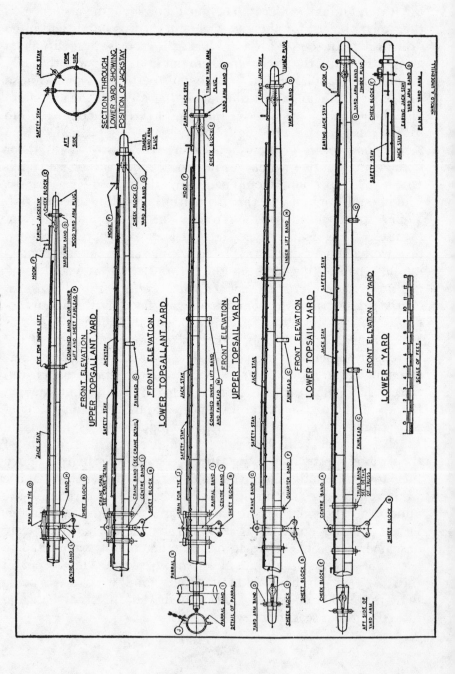

SAFETY STAY

JACK STAY

FORE
SIDE

AFT
SIDE

SECTION THROUGH
LOWER YARD SHOWING
POSITION OF JACKSTAY

FRONT ELEVATION
UPPER TOPGALLANT YARD

FRONT ELEVATION
LOWER TOPGALLANT YARD

FRONT ELEVATION
UPPER TOPSAIL YARD

FRONT ELEVATION
LOWER TOPSAIL YARD

FRONT ELEVATION OF YARD
LOWER YARD

SCALE OF FEET

0 1 2 3 4 5 6 7 8 9 10 11 12

PLAN OF YARD ARM

HAROLD A. UNDERHILL

The hull was something which no master could do much about, even if he were competent, but the masts and rigging were in his care and the sails were his only engines.

Another point of importance to bear in mind when looking at a model or a photograph of so apparently complicated a thing as a big square-rigged ship, is that everybody concerned with the working of such vessels lived aboard. More than that, the great majority had been living aboard such ships since they were children, and many of them knew no other life. The ships were always with them, and the ways of the ships were their ways. Nothing about the *Preussen* or the *Potosi,* or the *France* or the *Kjøbenhavn* would appear in the least complicated to them, except the *Kjøbenhavn's* engines. They were actively carrying on a profession, and traditions, which they had absorbed since childhood. They knew precisely where every piece of running rigging was, what it did and how it led, and they could find it on the blackest, wildest night. With minor variations, all big square-rigged ships were rigged in the same manner, and the variations were easily mastered by those accustomed to such things. Every single piece of wire, chain, and rope had its function, its name, and its place. The whole fabric of the rigging was orderly and organised. It was a man's world, a bachelors' world, run at sea (but not in port) very like a monastery. Any group of men living alone like monks, cooped up in a ship or anything, may be relied upon to organise whatever was organisable around them. Everything would have its place and nothing but its place, which would be known to all whose business it was to know it. So it was, at any rate, in big sailing-ships. The mariners not only knew the rigging with an all-embracing thoroughness. They comprehended immediately any and all orders which dealt with any of its functions. There were set orders for most manoeuvres, even the least important. There were certain fixed ways of doing the more important things. The ways of doing lesser things might vary from ship to ship and, at times, they might vary considerably; but the orders did not.

Another point of importance where merchant ships were concerned—I am dealing entirely with merchant sailing-ships—is that there never were any surplus people about, to get in the way. Apart from some masters' wives, there was usually no one in the ship who was not necessary. There was uniformity of orders but there was no drill. Drill was not necessary and would have been strongly resented. The sailing-ship man had absorbed his profession; he was never drilled into it. He did not understand doing things by numbers or by rota. He did them because they were necessary and he knew how to do them, and took a great pride in his competence and ability. What was drill for twenty bluejackets was a job of work for three sailing-ship sailors. The drill method was forced on ships which were crowded with men, of course, for it was the only way to organise things. It was the way to fight ships, when casualties might be suffered. It had had its place in the old East Indiamen which had to be fought, at times, and in crack ships manned by Lascar crews (who were very good seamen), and a little of it was retained in the passenger vessels, to impress the passengers. But it had no place in sail-handling aboard the big steel sailers. It was dangerous to have things organised to too settled a routine in a Cape Horn ship, for the wind knew no drill. Neither did the sea.

As for the names of the various masts, yards, sails, and so on, the diagrams show these clearly. They followed a strict pattern which had grown up through the centuries. Consider the masts, for a moment. The early European masts were made just like the Chinese junks' masts, from a single tree. So long as ships carried only one sail, this was adequate and could be supported by the minimum standing rigging. But then another mast was placed above the single mast, and this became the topmast simply because it was just that, and the mast below was then the lower mast. The lower mast carried one yard, which was fixed to it fairly near its head, and the topmast carried another yard which could be hoisted. The idea of hoisting the sail on the topmast—the topsail—was simply for convenience. It was easier for the sailors to work on the yard (as they had to do, to hand the sail)

Different types of masts in big square-rigged ships. Mast A, with a fidded royal mast, was unusual. B is the more usual type; the pole-mast C was used in many of the last of the big steel sailers.

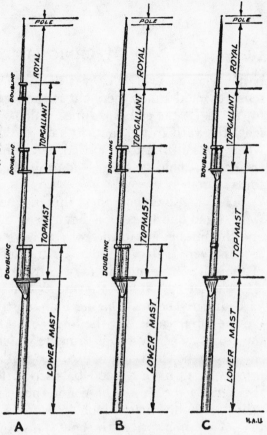

when it was lowered, and it was a much simpler matter to keep the yard rigid when it was down than up. To keep it hoisted put unnecessary strains on the mast, the gear, and the mariners. So the topsail yard required various pieces of running rigging—braces, to haul it round and so trim the sail to the wind; lifts, which were pieces of rope—later heavy wire as the yards became longer and were made of steel—going from near the masthead to the ends of the yard (the yardarms), and the lift's function was to support the weight of the yard so that it did not rest on its parral (the contrivance by which it was held to the mast); and halliards—haul-yards—to haul the yard up.

If a yard was hauled up it would also have to be hauled down again, in a breeze of wind, and so it must have down-hauls of some sort or other. And there must be some gear on the sail itself to make it controllable, for mariners could not climb aloft to do battle with a piece of canvas flapping wildly like half a circus tent. It would knock them out of the rigging and soon blow itself to pieces. So the sail had ropes which went over the front of it, from the yard to the foot, to haul the foot up snug to the yard when the sail had to be furled, and other ropes—or tackles, for their work could be heavy—led to the corners of the sail to pull them in, too.

The diagrams show these things. The lines going over the sail were called buntlines (for they passed over the bunt of the sail), and the lines going to the corners were clew-lines, for the lower corners were called the clews. Attached to each bottom corner of the sail were stout pieces of cordage called sheets, and a topsail was set by hauling the sheets out to the extremities of the yard directly below. On the mainmast, this was the mainyard. On the foremast, it was the fore-yard. On the mizzenmast it was the crojack, the cross-jack, a name which probably derived from the days when it was usual to sling a large lateen yard on the aftermast, to have a good balance of fore-and-aft canvas near the stern of the ship. The counterpoise for this was the sail—or sails—set from a mast which grew out of the bows and was called the bow-sprit, a sprit at the bow. This bowsprit, and an additional spar rigged out rather cumbrously beyond it, used to set all sorts of sails on awkward yards. These sails were called spritsails and sprit-topsails or spritsail-topsails, because they were set on the sprit. A sprit-topsail must have been the very devil to handle and its necessary gear must have been most awkward to rig. It was the first sail to go, and gradually the balancing canvas necessary forward was developed on the fore-and-aft stays leading from the foremast to the bowsprit. These stays—there was the necessary minimum of them between the masts as well—helped to support the masts. Sails on the stays to the bowsprit were jibs, and sails on the stays between the masts were stay-sails. (The diagram of a steel four-masted barque shows that there were quite a lot of these fore-and-aft sails in the big square-riggers.)

In the course of time, yet another sail had to be set above the topsail, and this required another extension of the mast. So a new piece of mast was secured to the head of the topmast. Since it was

The sails on a square-rigged mast were simple to understand. This is the foremast of the barque *Sagres*: the sails, from the lowest to the top, are the foresail (or fore course), fore lower topsail, upper topsail, lower topgallantsail, upper topgallantsail, and royal. Note the buntlines on all the sails.

The buntlines and clew-lines 'bunted' up the sails. They were operated from the deck, and the sail was well snugged up before the men went aloft.

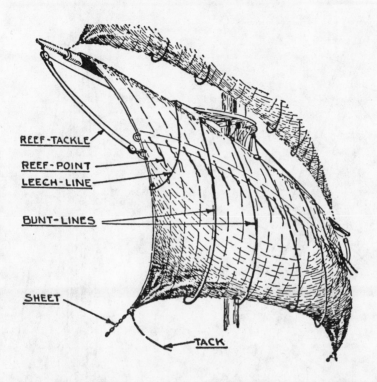

REEF-TACKLE

REEF-POINT

LEECH-LINE

BUNT-LINES

SHEET

TACK

Showing how the necessary gear was rove across and on the sails

above a mast which was already known as the topmast, there could be only one name for this mast. It was the topgallant, and the sail set on the yard it supported was the topgallant-sail. When yet another sail was used above the topgallantsail, it was of course the royal. Clippers sported sails above the royal, known as sky-sails and moonrakers, and so on, but these were not really worth their maintenance. They were morale-builders, a delight to the more bombastic masters and a source of wonder to the passengers, if any, and a curse to the crews. They were an endeavour to increase sail area upwards, for the strength of wooden yards and the length of spars available put limits on the extension of the breadth of sails, before the general use of steel. In the preclipper days the higher yards were very light—bits of broomsticks, fit

DETAIL OF
A BOWSPRIT

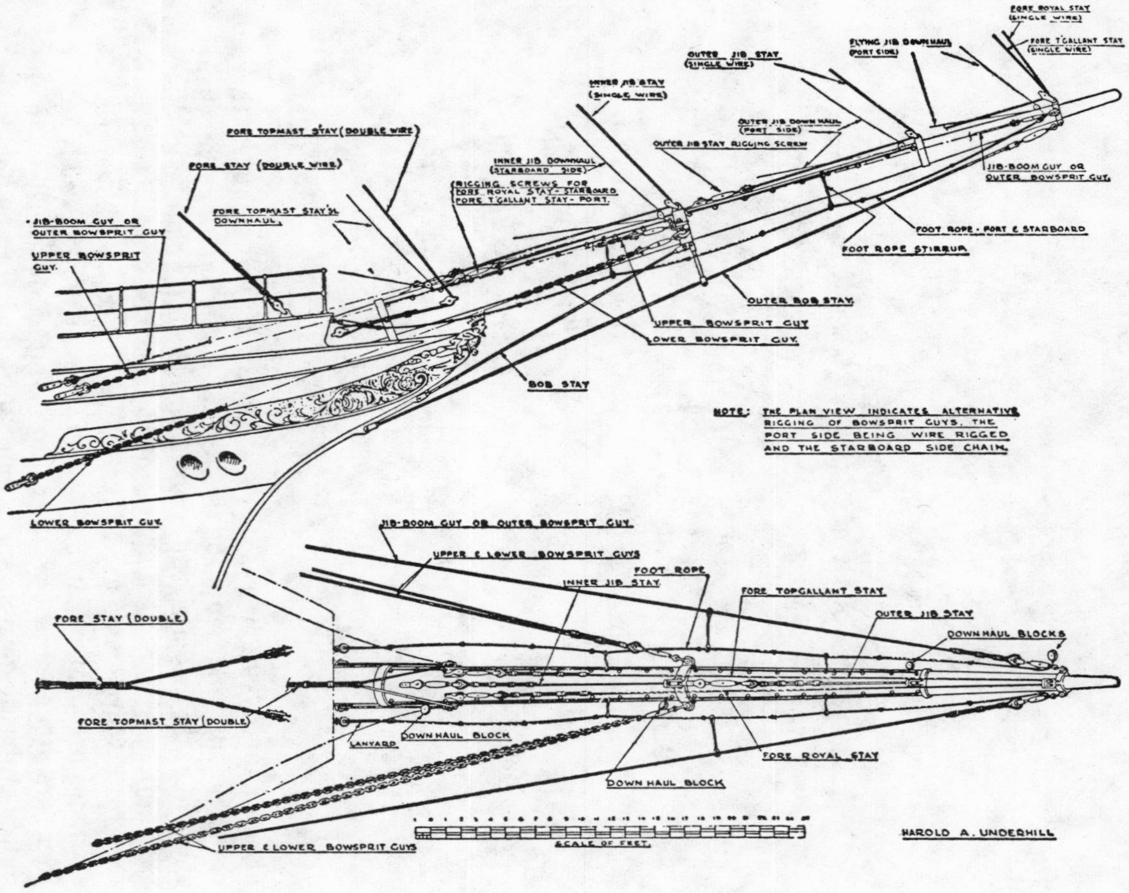

HAROLD A. UNDERHILL

NOTE: THE PLAN VIEW INDICATES ALTERNATIVE RIGGING OF BOWSPRIT GUYS. THE PORT SIDE BEING WIRE RIGGED AND THE STARBOARD SIDE CHAIN.

SCALE OF FEET

FORE ROYAL STAY (SINGLE WIRE)
FORE T'GALLANT STAY (SINGLE WIRE)
JIB-BOOM GUY or OUTER BOWSPRIT GUY
FOOT ROPE, PORT & STARBOARD
FLYING JIB DOWNHAUL (PORT SIDE)
FOOT ROPE STIRRUP
OUTER JIB STAY (SINGLE WIRE)
OUTER JIB STAY BOTTLE SCREW
OUTER JIB-BOOM HALYARD (PORT SIDE)
OUTER BOB STAY
UPPER BOWSPRIT GUY
LOWER BOWSPRIT GUY
INNER JIB STAY (SINGLE WIRE)
INNER JIB DOWNHAUL (STARBOARD SIDE)
RIGGING SCREWS FOR INNER JIB STAY AND FORE T'GALLANT STAY POINT
BOB STAY
FORE TOPMAST STAY (DOUBLE WIRE)
FORE STAY (DOUBLE WIRE)
FORE TOPMAST STAY DOWNHAUL
JIB-BOOM GUY or OUTER BOWSPRIT GUY
UPPER BOWSPRIT GUY
LOWER BOWSPRIT GUY

DOWN HAUL BLOCKS
OUTER JIB STAY
DOWN HAUL STAY
FORE TOP-GALLANT STAY
FORE ROYAL STAY
DOWN HAUL BLOCK
UPPER & LOWER BOWSPRIT GUYS
FOOT ROPE
INNER JIB STAY
JIB-BOOM GUY or OUTER BOWSPRIT GUY
DOWN HAUL BLOCK
LANYARD
UPPER & LOWER BOWSPRIT GUYS
FORE STAY (DOUBLE)
FORE TOPMAST STAY (DOUBLE)

only for the kindest breezes. The clippers extended their sail area sideways by the use of additional sails set from booms which could be rigged up temporarily beyond the yards. These were studding-sails and, though they could extend the sail area of a ship considerably and certainly were of real use in light winds, they were not really worth their maintenance either. The development of steel masts and yards, and the use of iron wire for standing rigging instead of the ancient hemp, made it possible to lengthen yards considerably, and splitting topsails first and later topgallant-sails into two sections—upper and lower—led to the use of much wider but shallower sails which incorporated the area of the studding-sails (or most of it) and were at the same time much

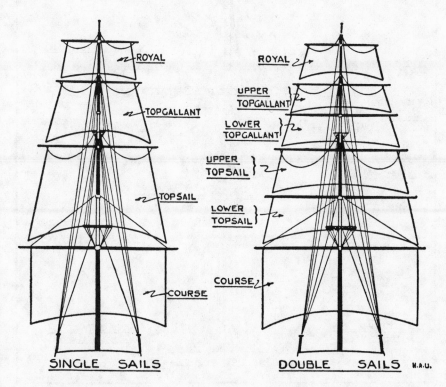

Single sails were common in the old clippers, and double sails in the more modern sailing-ships.

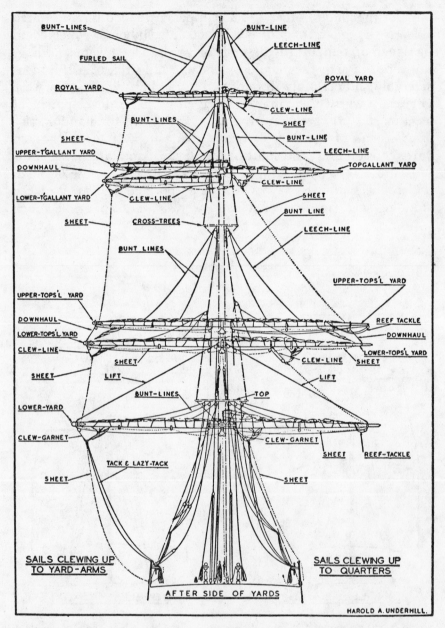

Looking at a square-rigged mast from abaft, with different types of sails clewed up in different fashions.

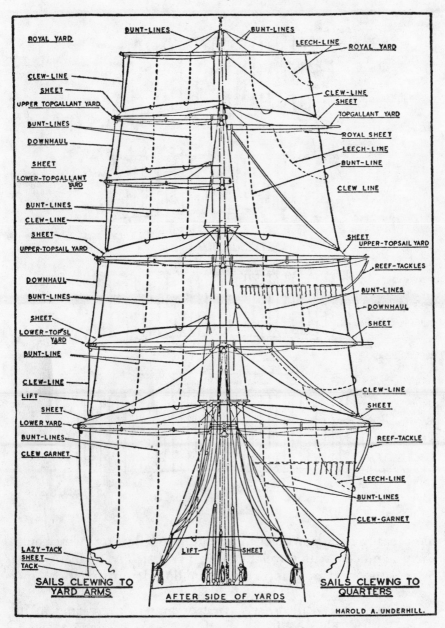

ROYAL YARD

BUNT-LINES

BUNT-LINES

LEECH-LINE

ROYAL YARD

CLEW-LINE

SHEET

UPPER TOPGALLANT YARD

CLEW-LINE

SHEET

TOPGALLANT YARD

BUNT-LINES

ROYAL SHEET

DOWNHAUL

LEECH-LINE

BUNT-LINE

SHEET

LOWER-TOPGALLANT YARD

CLEW LINE

BUNT-LINES

CLEW-LINE

SHEET

SHEET

UPPER-TOPSAIL YARD

UPPER-TOPSAIL YARD

REEF-TACKLES

DOWNHAUL

BUNT-LINES

BUNT-LINES

DOWNHAUL

SHEET

SHEET

LOWER-TOP'SL YARD

BUNT-LINE

CLEW-LINE

CLEW-LINE

LIFT

SHEET

SHEET

LOWER YARD

BUNT-LINES

CLEW GARNET

REEF-TACKLE

LEECH-LINE

BUNT-LINES

CLEW-GARNET

LAZY-TACK

SHEET

TACK

LIFT   SHEET

SAILS CLEWING TO
YARD ARMS

AFTER SIDE OF YARDS

SAILS CLEWING TO
QUARTERS

HAROLD A. UNDERHILL.

The same, with the sails set

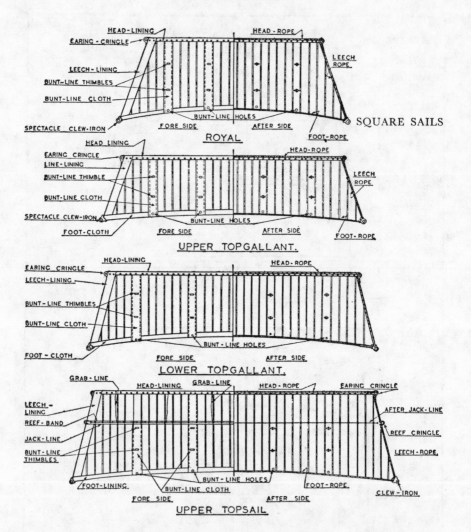

more easily handled. Steel masts supported by iron wire could carry a much greater weight aloft, permanently, than wooden masts supported by hemp could ever do. Hemp stretched, and was expendable.

So there it is—all orderly, well organised, everything in its place, and nothing confused at all. No maze of rigging, but a carefully contrived construction of masts and yards supported by

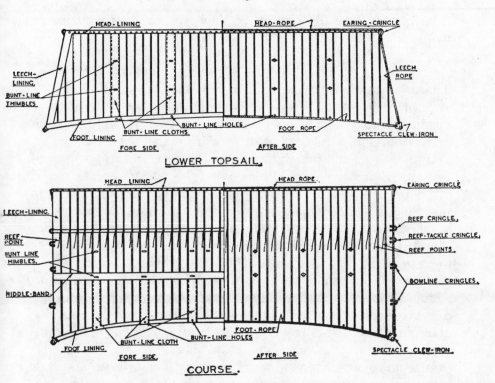

a network of necessary stays developed carefully through the
ages. No disorder of ropes of various sizes; no piled-up pyramid
of makeshift sails, set according to the whim of individual shipmasters; no wandering 'wind-jammer' with a spar stuck out at
an odd angle somewhere in front and a series of masts arising
from the hull—none of these things, but an able and magnificent
feat of practical engineering, a wonderful machine for harnessing
the ocean winds to the use of man. The haphazard strength of
the Chinese junk, adequate as it was in her own waters, would
not do for Cape Horn. The graceful lines of the swift Arab dhow,
unrivalled as they were in the Red Sea, the Persian Gulf, and the
whole western littoral of the Indian Ocean, had to be modified
to bring nitrate cargoes from Chilean roadsteads to the ports of
Europe. The triangular sail-plan of an easy-going East Indiaman
had to be extended when a Hilgendorf was driving the *Potosi*

from the Horn to the Line in 18 days, with a Learmont in the *Bengairn* not far behind him.

How near to perfect did the big square-rigged ship become? That is a question. So long as men remained who could man her and the tradition of her sailing was unbroken, in my opinion— for what it may be worth—I think at her best she did approach perfection. The achievement of such a ship as the *Preussen,* for example, was astonishingly good. With a crew of little over two-score men, she moved 8000 tons of cargo under sail alone, regularly, at the speed of a contemporary tramp steamer which, to shift such a cargo, would require the same number of crew, a large quantity of bunkers, and earnings enough to cover the depreciation of her engines and the cost of the extra space necessary to house them. The steamer's range was dominated by her bunker capacity and the sailer's was unlimited. The sailing-ship's maintenance, to a considerable extent, was in her own hands, and her own crew could look after her rigging, and cut her sails. Engine maintenance could be a very different affair, calling for the intervention of expensive technicians from the shore. The sailing-ship could voyage while she kept her strength and the ocean winds blew, but the steamship was of use only while her boilers and engines lasted, and good bunker coal was freely available to her. The steamship's manning and economics were much more complicated than the sailing-ship's, and she was still vulnerable in the sea. Even in 1953, the Lutine bell at Lloyd's in London can toll for the bad news of a missing steamship, swallowed into the wintry maw of the dreadful North Atlantic, such as the German *Melanie Schulte,* of nearly 7000 tons, a new ship on her first voyage. The *Melanie Schulte* sailed from Narvik in December 1952 for U.S.A., and disappeared.

Be these things as they may, it is certain that bringing the square-rigged ship to such perfection as she achieved was a long and often a painful process, and it was a process in which the great majority of shipmasters had—and wanted—very little say. With few exceptions, they were the most conservative men on earth. Nine hundred and ninety-nine in every thousand of them took things as they found them, and abhorred the idea of change. But there was the thousandth. One of these was a certain Captain Jarvis—Captain J. C. B. Jarvis, from Tayport in Fife, a man who commanded ocean-going square-rigged ships for over thirty years, and did *not* leave them as he found them. Some of Jarvis' ideas were used in the *Preussen* and the other 'P' ships, and helped to make them the splendid sailers they were.

I knew Captain Jarvis well. He was a fine old Scots ship-master with an independent outlook. He was a very tall man, well over six feet, with mild blue eyes and a gentle voice, in ordinary conversation, though he could make noise enough aboard a ship. When I knew him he was living ashore in Brooklyn, New York, not far from the Narrows. He had served the Anglo-American Oil Company for many years, mostly in command of its big sailers in the case oil trade. We used to walk down on the Shore Road together by the side of New York harbour, looking for sailing-ships. Like Hilgendorf and Learmont and other outstanding masters, Jarvis was not interested only in sailing-ships. He was not just a die-hard, an ultra-conservative with his eyes glancing back-wards all the time, crying for what was gone. His view was that the sailing-ship, in some form or other, need not go, that there was work for her to do, and that the wind was too good a source of motive power—and the science of its use too well developed—just to be thrown away.

When Jarvis was in Cape Horn sailing-ships (he commanded half a dozen of them) he was always seeking to introduce im-provements, especially in sail-handling methods. It was he who thought of the brace-winch, and perfected that, and many other improvements great and small, all designed to lighten the work and to make the big sailing-ship handle better. Many ships had gear which was *too* heavy for the work it had to do. For example, to the end of the days of sail it was customary to use great chain sheets for the lower tops'ls. These sheets led right down to the maindeck. They were heavy, cumbrous, awkward, and dangerous. When the sail had to be taken in these great chains also had to be hauled aloft far enough to allow the clews of the topsail to come snug—more or less—up to the yardarms. A lower topsail

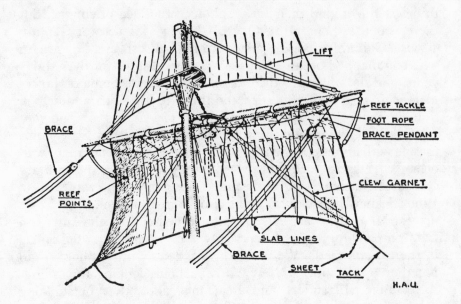

Detail of a course, and the manner of setting. Clew garnets are also called clewlines.

was the last sail touched and, by the time sailors were ordered to take it in, a very heavy gale would be blowing. Then there was a great danger that the chain sheets would take charge as soon as they were started, and they would flail about, setting up a wild shower of sparks and braining any unfortunate who got in their way, while the sail would thrash about and rip itself in pieces in a second or two.

These too-heavy sheets were one of the first things Captain Jarvis turned his attention to. Chain was undoubtedly the strongest form of sheet and it would stand up much longer than wire would, but those sheets did not need to be made of chain right to the deck. So long as there was a piece of chain passing through the iron blocks at the yardarms, then the sheets would stand up to their heavy work for years. The rest of the sheet could be of wire, which was much more easily handled. So Jarvis rove his sheets off that way, and even his mates looked askance at him. What, *changing* things? For countless centuries all improvements were thoroughly scorned. Jarvis went one better and made the sheets wholly of wire, putting some wire service along those sections of the sheet which took the greatest wear, where they actually passed through the blocks. This was excellent and the chain could be done away with altogether. At first everyone was horrified, but it worked. Then they were astonished.

If sheets were too heavy so often were halliards, especially on the upper topsails. The custom was to reeve an enormous section of very heavy wire through the topmast (over an iron block) and to convert this by means of a very heavy tackle, rove off with best rope, which brought the halliard-end actually to the maindeck. Jarvis worked out a halliard winch, and he worked out also better tackles which much lightened the job of hoisting the yards without taking any further time over it. There were many inefficiencies in the square-rigged ship's rigging and manner of working sails, which were tolerable in the days of lighter gear when hemp was used for running rigging, but were very bad in the big steel ships when things could become impossibly heavy and crews were very small. Clew-lines, for instance, could never hope to haul a great clew-iron and its length of shackled chain to the bunt of the yard or even to the yardarm, and so it was impossible to haul sails up snugly to their yards. The whole art of sail-management depended upon doing just that—getting the sail up snug to the yard from the deck *first*, with the sail's own gear, before the men ever went aloft. Yet it was made deliberately impossible.

Jarvis changed all that. He observed that the big clew-lines and the clew-irons and the rest of the necessary paraphernalia got in their own way, so long as the clew-line was rove off along the yard of its own sail. So he gave it a clear lead by taking it to the yardarm *above*, and in to the mast along that yard. In that way, his sailors could get the clews up really snug to the yardarms, and this helped very much to smother the blowing-out of the canvas as it was being taken in.

His brother ship-masters scorned all these ideas. Most of them spread the idea about that old Jarvis was slightly 'touched.' They scorned his brace-winches, too, and his improved buntlines, and all his other ideas. If sails blew out, they let them do so. If men were ruptured trying to hand a recalcitrant tops'l in a gale of wind, or knocked out of the rigging by a furiously flapping leach which should have been under control, they ascribed these things to Acts of God and never dreamt that anything could be done about them. But not Jarvis. He went blithely on. He sailed the *Lawhill*—a big lump of a four-masted barque which looked most awkward and unhandy—for many years and he handled her with a crew of eighteen, all boys and young men, and he got excellent passages out of that wall-sided carrier. His owners began to notice that his ships carried their sails longer and wore them out much later than any other ships in the case oil business, or any other trade. They were impressed. There were no reports of crew troubles in the Jarvis ships, and their maintenance costs were the lowest in the fleet. The oil companies then had considerable fleets of big sailing-ships and kept them right up to the first World War. So they had a good standard of comparison. Jarvis might have had Anglo-American support to try out others of his ideas for a really labour-saving and aerodynamically perfect square-rigger,

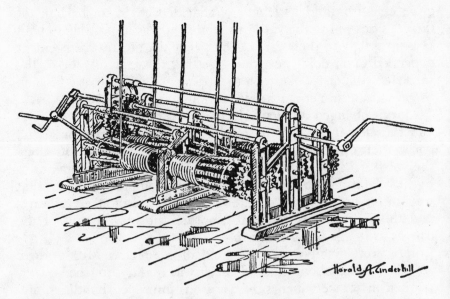

The Jarvis brace-winch, as used in the big 'P' ships. It was hand-operated.

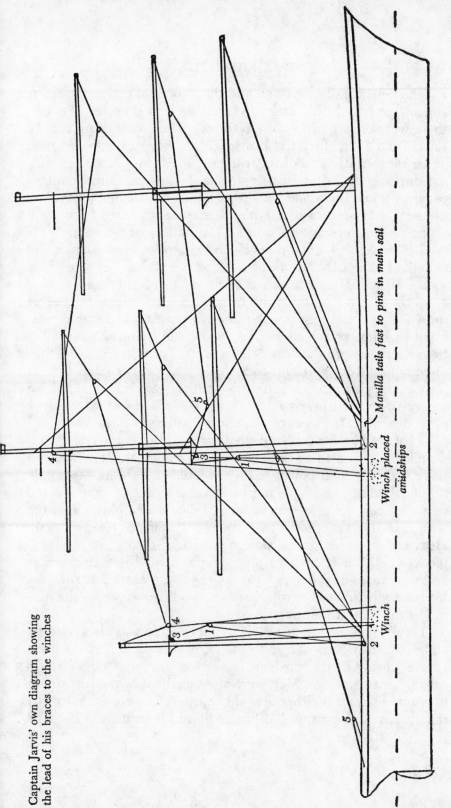

Captain Jarvis' own diagram showing the lead of his braces to the winches

Manilla tails fast to pins in main sail

Winch placed amidships

Winch

SKETCH SHOWING STARBOARD BRACES

BLOCKS

1. Formerly lower pendant of lower brace
2. Formerly leading blocks of lower brace
3. Formerly leading blocks of lower topsail brace
4. Formerly leading blocks of upper topsail brace
5. Formerly whip blocks of upper topsail brace

Port braces are rove the same but led to opposite side of drums. Braces all 2 in. or 2¼ in. flexible wire.

but the bulk installation of oil and the growth of powered tankers caused the sailing-ship to be given up, in the oil trade. (Though there were one or two sailing tankers.) The enterprising firm of Laeisz noted the Jarvis improvements. They might be scorned under his own flag and disregarded by British and American sailing-ship owners. The Laeisz masters knew real improvements when they saw them and they were not so hidebound. They took up the Jarvis brace-winch, which became a standard fitting first in the Laeisz ships and then in all German square-riggers.

Just what was this brace-winch, and what contribution did it make to the easier working of heavy ships? Every yard in a square-rigged ship, since it must be moveable in a horizontal plane at all times to allow the sail to be set in such a way as to convert the wind into the best possible motive power for the ship, was fitted with braces, which are lines which led from both yardarms to the deck, where they could be hauled. These braces led either directly to the deck, or first back to the mast immediately behind the yard they controlled, and thence to the deck. Hauling on these braces was called bracing the yards, and there was naturally a great deal of it. It was extremely heavy work when the yards had to be squared in, for then the whole area of the sails the ship had set had to be pulled back against the strength of the wind, and there was only man-power to do the job. Braces were essentially simple tackles, and it was not practicable to set up complicated sets of blocks and gear which, though they might have eased the weight of the work, were more nuisance than they were worth. Heavier braces led to the sides of the ship, through large lead-blocks (both diagrams and photographs show these very well), and the braces of the upper yards—the topgallants and royals— led generally first to the topmast-head and then down to the fife-rail at the foot of the mast.

Hauling on the braces at the side of the ship was always heavy and frequently also dangerous work, especially when the men were squaring in the yards in heavy weather and the ship was rolling her rails under. Men were often washed away while trying to brace. They went either over the side or they were spilled about the deck, to grave danger of life and limb. If men were knocked down, the brace-ends might be let go, and the yards would then take charge. Yards swinging loosely were a considerable danger. They could damage the rigging, dismast the ship, or at least rip the sails, and sails in those big ships were quite expensive even when made aboard.

For centuries things had been more or less like this, and everyone put up with it. It was part of the profession. Braces were awkward, bracing was heavy, and loss of life had to be accepted. But then along came Captain Jarvis and put an end to all this by the simple means of designing, and perfecting, a contrivance of six steel barrels, grooved for wire braces and cone-shaped with the points of the cones inboard, the six of them geared together by simple cogs to be controlled by a few men on a couple of winch-handles (there was no power, of course: they were not power winches) and placed one abaft each mast except the foremast (which had no braces leading to it). Then, instead of the tradi-tional long whips and tackles and the enormous coils of hemp and manila at the side of the ship, he made his braces almost entirely of wire and led them in such a manner that the six heaviest from each mast led to these steel barrels—the two from the course, the lower and the upper topsail yardarms—and then, as a couple of men turned the winch handles, each pair of cone-shaped barrels paid out on the one side and took in on the other, and the three yards were braced together. What a dozen men were required for on the old-fashioned long braces, two or three could do with the winch.

Jarvis first tried these winches of his in the ship *Duntrune,* and they worked so well that he took a patent out for them, and put them in each other ship he commanded. But he had to put them in himself. Apart from earning him the name of Brace-winch Jarvis and, in due course, much lightening the work of bracing the big German ships (with no profit to the inventor, for there was a flaw in the patent rights) the brace-winches did neither Captain Jarvis nor British sailing-ships any real service. They were all the inventor claimed for them—labour-saving, time-saving, economical in gear and upkeep, and life-saving as well. But the very great majority of his brother ship-masters would not have them, and it was not until German prize-ships were brought back under the British flag during the first World War that they learned at last how wrong they had been.

By that time it was too late. Jarvis was in steam. The British sailing-ships were on the discard, and so were the ship-masters as soon as the war was over. There is no shadow of doubt that the Jarvis ideas, properly applied as they were in the Laeisz Cape Horners, very much simplified the working of these ships and made no small contribution to their oustanding success. Laeisz ships rarely lost men overboard, and their handling was a byword in all the ports they visited. Yet the die-hards had objected that brace-winches would be unmanageable, and that they would 'take charge' when a big square-rigger was being put about. I have myself sailed in a British four-masted barque—the *Bellands,* ex-*Werner Vinnen,* ex-*Forteviot*—which had been fitted with brace-winches by the Vinnens and later taken as a British prize, and the British master was so afraid of the brace-winches that he never dared to tack the ship at all, but always wore her round. So we were five months at sea on a summer's run from Melbourne with a load of grain for France, and when the war freights dropped the ship lost money and was sold.

Captain Jarvis gave me a copy of his pamphlet on rigging improvements. He called it *"Wrinkles and Suggestions for Sailing Vessels,* by J. C. B. Jarvis, Extra Master," and it was published by William Kidd at Dundee, in the early 1890's, for threepence.

"Twenty years ago," it began, "steamers could not compete with sailing vessels on long voyages. But today steamers are found in every port, no matter how distant. During that time steamers have advanced, but sailing vessels have remained almost stationary. By improvements, the running expenses of the steamship have been enormously reduced. Could not sailing vessels have been proportionately improved, or have we arrived at so perfect a type that improvement is impossible? The writer ventures to suggest that we have not yet reached perfection, and will endeavour to point out a few improvements that have been proved practicable but are not yet generally adopted. . ."

But, unfortunately, the Captain Jarvises of this world have

Footropes, double jackstays, beckets, and their purpose can clearly be made out here. →

Here the parral on the topsail yard—the hollow cylinder on the mast—can be seen clearly. The sail is bunted up. ↓

The yards of a square-rigger could be made to lie near enough to fore-and-aft—
as near as the efficiency of the rigging would permit. Looking down on the fore.

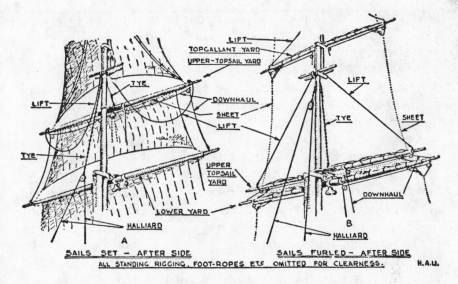

THE SET OF THE SAILS

It was essentially simple. The square yards acted like battens in the sail of a junk.

always been in the minority. While Jarvis was perfecting his brace-winches, a horde of ingenious men in cloth caps were busy improving steamships, and big steel tramps could be turned out at shipyards along the Scots and North of England rivers almost literally by the mile, and cut off in lengths as they were required. It was easier to use these steamships, and the sailing-ship was left to languish.

Another matter which engaged Captain Jarvis' close attention throughout his time in sail was handling the sails—getting them in without losing them. He had his own patent methods for doing this, but the secret was always the same—good gear on the sails and plenty of it, led correctly. By the very nature of their business, sailing-ships had to keep some sails set even in winds of near-hurricane strength. They could not just roll up their sails, as a tent may be rolled up and put away. Almost invariably—except in ships which were handled by the chicken-hearted—the sailors were called upon to perform prodigious feats of fighting the canvas, and securing it, under the most appalling conditions, and the worse were the conditions the more surely must they accomplish whatever they set out to do.

The six square sails which were set upon the square-rigged masts of most later-day sailing-ships were simple enough to put on the ship. Getting them off again was the difficulty. Speaking in unseamanlike terms, the sails were set like this—from the lowest yard on the mast, a large sail was pulled *down*, to the deck, and kept in position by wires at each side of it—from each clew—and these wires were called the tack and the sheet. The sheet led aft and the tack led for'ard, and they could be interchangeable. Since the strain on them was heavy, these tacks and sheets generally were led directly to strong capstans where they could be manipulated more easily. (They could not be controlled by hand at all in a big ship.) The foot of the sail had a large curve in it in order to clear protuberances on the deck, and its head was secured to a steel bar, called a jackstay, on the upper part of the yard. From the next yard above this—the lower topsail yard—the sail was set in the same manner, except that the corners were pulled out to the yardarms—the ends of the yard—immediately below them. The next sail was the upper topsail, and this was the first of the sails which was set by hoisting. It was literally *stretched*. "Stretch the tops'ls, lads", was often the order given by the mate, and the watch would then hoist the upper topsail yard as far as the depth of the sail would allow it to go, the corners of the sail either being fixed to the yardarms of the yard immediately below, or *sheeted* out to them. (The diagrams show this.)

Then, next above, come the two topgallantsails, lower and upper. They are set in the same manner as the two topsails, the lower having its clews pulled *down* while the yard remains fixed, and the upper yard being hoisted to stretch the sail. The royal yard is last, and from this a sail, with a deep curve on its foot to clear the fore-and-aft stay below it, is half pulled down, and half hauled up, until it is properly set. Three sails are pulled *down* from their yards and three sails are hoisted *up* on their yards: three yards stand (secured by various heavy pieces of ironwork to the mast) and three yards hoist. The lower topsails and the lower topgallantsails also had deeply curving lower edges in order to clear fore-and-aft stays leading forward from their mast, but the upper topsails and upper topgallants were not so impeded, and so had shallower curves on their lower edges.

Setting these six sails on one mast, or the eighteen on three masts in a four-masted barque, was a lot of work, and it was usually done only once each passage—at the setting out. Most sailing-ships had a donkey-boiler and one steam winch, and this was rigged up for sailing-day and rigged down again as soon as they were under way. It was never used on passage because there was neither coal nor fresh water to spare for it, and because there were men enough (or should be) to do all the usual sail-handling. When reducing sail, the royals and upper topgallantsails came in first, but after that, many masters preferred to keep the lower topgallantsails set even after they had taken the crojack in, and the upper topsails would be carried long after the mainsail was off. The reason for this is that the crojack, being set on the mizzen, was so far aft that if carried too long it would adversely affect the sailing balance of the ship and could make the steering difficult, and both the crojack and mainsail were very large sails. It was not customary to reef them or any other sails, in the last square-riggers. Reefing was almost unknown. It had been discarded as a waste of time. The custom was either to carry the full sail or to make it fast altogether, and the majority of the big steel square-riggers I knew usually had no reef-points on their sails. If there were any, they were only on the foresail. An easier way to take the strain off the upper topsails, if this was considered desirable and it was not thought necessary to take them in, was to ease the halliards down a little, and so put more belly on the sails. They did not pull quite so hard then and so did not strain the rigging so much.

In ships like the *Potosi* and the *Preussen,* even the lower topgallantsails were almost never taken in at sea. When they were secured (under Hilgendorf at any rate) it was not such a difficult business as it was in many a worse-sailed though less-driven ship. Hilgendorf had that sort of thing down to a fine art. On a wind,

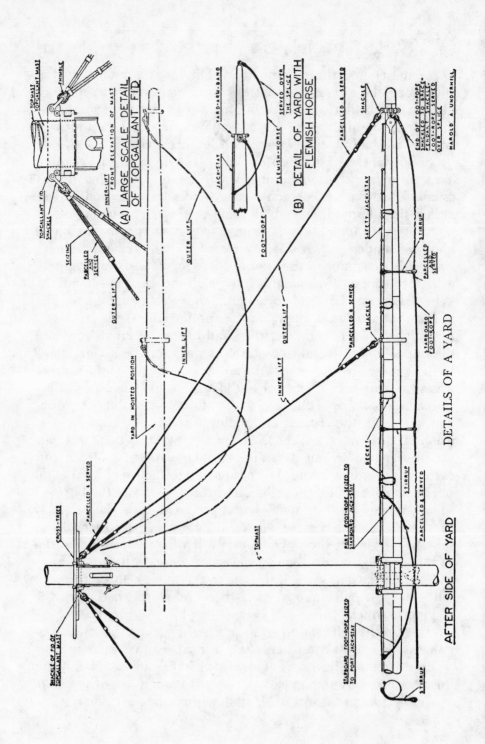

(A) LARGE SCALE DETAIL OF TOPGALLANT FID

(B) DETAIL OF YARD WITH FLEMISH HORSE

DETAILS OF A YARD

AFTER SIDE OF YARD

HAROLD A. UNDERHILL

of course—which is to say with the wind blowing more or less
along the yard—getting sail off could be a very heavy business,
to be managed by sheer brute strength on buntlines and clew-
lines (but there were tricks and knacks even in that). Before the
wind, if he *had* to get a lower topgallantsail in, Hilgendorf's practice was to have the various buntlines and clew-lines manned ade-
quately, with the bosun of the watch and another experienced
man at the sheets, and then, when all were ready, both sheets were
let go at once and all the gear hauled on hand-over-hand with
the utmost strength and celerity, so that the sail was snug up to
the yard before it had a chance to shake. The actual job was
superintended by the officer of the watch—never the master. The
master trained the mates or, rather, saw that they did things to
his satisfaction. The mates supervised the actual work of the
crew.

To get a sail off in this manner in a gale of wind meant perfect
team-work, and perfect confidence, too—each in all the others.
If the sheets took charge or if the sail took charge, it could be
extremely dangerous. But fooling about with one sheet eased at
a time, and a haul on this buntline and then that, made much
more labour of it and could be an even greater risk. The Hilgendorf method was not that laid down in the text-books, but it
worked, and it worked magnificently. It was used by most Laeisz
masters. One of the last to profit by it was probably Herman
Piening, who commanded three of the Laeisz four-masters before
he became marine superintendent ashore in Hamburg, after
Boye Petersen. Captain Piening was in the true line of descent
from his great predecessors.

Taking sails in by the Hilgendorf manner implied perfect
confidence in the gear and in the crew. One bungling fool and
one stranded wire, one too-chafed piece of service, could ruin the
manoeuvre and lose the sail. Other masters had other methods,
and so had mates. Some hauled up the lee side of a sail first, some
the weather. Some put their faith in extra buntlines across the
middle of the sail, or right round it. Some took in their courses
by means of the buntlines and leachlines first, not touching the

clew-lines until the foot of the sail was up. Most liked to spill the wind out of the upper sails before trying to get them in, and they did this by pointing the yard to the wind. Jarvis liked to get his lighter sails in by letting the lee sheet fly, pointing the yard, and then immediately easing the weather sheet (weather—that which is to windward, on the *weather* side) and hauling away on all buntlines and clew-lines. In the case of all hoisting yards, the yards were always brought down on their lifts before the sheets were let go and, to do this, the clew-lines were used as down-hauls, which they were. The sheets were not touched until the yard was properly down, supported by its lifts.

It was only when the sails were properly hauled up to the yards that the men went aloft. They always climbed aloft on the weather side of the rigging, so the wind was blowing them *on* to the rigging and not *out* of it, into the sea. They went up steadily but swiftly. It was a long climb up the steel or wooden battens in the lower rigging, over the top like spiders hanging on to a turbulent ceiling, up the hempen ratlines of the topmast rigging, over the crosstrees at the topmast head where the topgallant mast was stepped, and then onwards and upwards to whichever sail they had to deal with. No more men went aloft on any mast than were strictly necessary for the job, for there was plenty to be done on deck and there were other masts and yards. Once the yard was reached they swung on to the footropes, no matter what the conditions were like—day or night, pitch-black or moonlight, raining or hailing, ship rolling furiously and the mast jumping about, the sea boiling nearly 200 feet below them and nothing between them and an awful pitch to death but a wire or two, their own strong arms and their stronger nerves. They would leap for the footrope, which was a wire running below the yard just at the right place for them to stand on, and work on the yard. Then two or three, or perhaps four at the most, would pick up the sail, methodically, thoroughly, getting the securing ropes (called gaskets) round the properly stowed canvas with the utmost speed. They usually got a gasket round the middle of the sail temporarily first, and then moved out to the weather leach—the windward extremity of the sail, where it was most recalcitrant. Fisting the hard canvas, wet with the sea spray and the rain (for spray would drive that high) was difficult work, but sailing-ship sailors were used to it. They got on with the job and their bodies automatically balanced on the footrope. Unless the sail knocked them back from the yard, they were all right. Some ships had backropes fitted, which the men slipped under in order to ensure that they could not be knocked down. But most ships were not fitted with such things.

As the sail was muzzled the canvas was given a good skin (in order that it would not blow out again) and rolled up on the top of the yard, where it was secured with gaskets. These used to be very long and very awkward to use on big yards, for they had to be passed round and round yard and sail, and the men were forced to assume grotesque positions in order to pass them. But Jarvis had changed that. He thought of using what was called a double jackstay. Instead of yards carrying only the one jackstay to which the head of the sail was secured, there was a second abaft this and parallel with it, with just sufficient space between the two jackstays to allow the sail to be rolled up properly. Then short gaskets were immediately passed over the sail from the for'ard jackstay to the after jackstay, where they were made fast with hitches which would neither jam nor work loose. The sailor had always to use foresight in his work, to think of the next process beyond that which was the immediate concern. The next process after making fast the sails, he hoped, would be to loose them. The gaskets must be ready for this, too.

No matter how the sails might be handled, it was always a test of strength and nerve. Like so many of the sailing-ships' jobs it was a challenge, and it was a challenge which required perfection as an answer. It did not always get the proper answer, for there were many indifferently qualified mates as time went on, and poor masters. To handle sails properly crews had to be well treated, for there was always that extra bit of effort which the willing man could give, or withhold. Unfortunately, there were a good many masters in the last days of the big sailing-ship who did not treat their crews well at all, and the ships suffered for it. There were also owners who did not keep their ships supplied with adequate quantities of cordage, wire, and so on, in a false idea of economy. Ships without good gear could not be sailed properly, and they suffered, too.

Chapter six

SHIPHANDLING UNDER SAIL

THIS IS not a text-book, purporting to furnish the only correct manner in which things were done in the big square-rigged ships. Different ships, different long-splices, is an old saying of the sea, and the meaning of that was simply that things could be done differently in different vessels, even of the same rig. Oddities in the placing of masts causing one vessel to balance differently from another, inexplicable idiosyncrasies in the ships themselves (and much more often in the masters), and odd quirks of grace or viciousness in various vessels caused them to be put differently through the same manoeuvres. A sailing-ship responded to handling almost like a living thing. On the whole, good ships did what was asked of them by competent master-mariners and did it superbly, but there is no doubt that there could be different characteristics even in a pair of sister-ships, built from the same plans at the same yard at the same time. What I have set out to do is to explain, clearly and comprehensively, how I saw Cape Horn ships handled and handled them myself, in order that any interested reader will understand how such ships were sailed about the world, in fair weather and foul.

The best way to go about that is first to consider the handling of a simple sailing vessel such as a cutter, with a mainsail and a jib, or a sailing dinghy with the same rig. The cutter must be got under way, must sail with the wind and against the wind, survive such bad weather as it may experience, make the place to which it is bound, and be brought back to anchorage or to moorings again. So it was—speaking broadly—with the big four-masted

135

barque, or full-rigged ship. Any yachtsman comprehends clearly what he is doing when he is asking his own vessel to do things for him, and he knows how to get them done. Very often he has to contend with tide, which was something the big sea-going sailer removed herself from as quickly as possible. The yachtsman knows that he must use the tide to help him to do what he wants with his cutter, or his dinghy, or his sloop. What he has to do is to make use of the natural forces available to him, in order to make his vessel go where he wants her to go.

To get under way from a buoy, for example (or from an anchorage, or from any moorings), he has to get way on his ship and make her go under control where he wants her to go, which is to get away from a place of congestion without doing damage by colliding with other craft there and, using the proper navigable channels, reach the sea or at any rate open water, as soon as possible. The wind might be ahead and the tide favourable. The wind might be fair and the tide against him. Disregarding the use of auxiliary engines (which take the sense of achievement and so the skill out of the whole business, whatever their advantages might be), he understands quite well how to set and use his simple sails, in order that the motive power they impart to his vessel may be brought under control by his manipulation of the rudder and his main and jib sheets, and the ship may go where he wishes. If the wind is fair, it is a simple matter of running, steering the course he wishes to make and keeping the sails set as well as possible. In his fore-and-aft vessel he has the disadvantage that, if he must alter course and bring the wind on the other quarter or beam, then he has to let his main-boom swing across the vessel and 'gybe' her. In a seaway this can be dangerous, and it is always a strain on the gear in anything of a breeze. He has the further disadvantage that his sail, when the wind is free (or 'large' as the old mariners used to call it—'sailing large' was running free) cannot be so rigidly kept in the best position for it as the square-rigger's can be, for his mainsail sets on a gaff and boom abaft the mast, and the boom is freer than a yard and a gaff much too free in a seaway altogether.

However, he has many advantages. His craft is simple and so is his ship-handling. His sails are simple planes which he can control as he wishes by hauling in or slacking away on the sheets restraining them. He can bring the wind further aft by easing more out on the sheets until his boom (and his mainsail) are chafing his lee standing-rigging. He can point his yacht further up into the wind by flattening in his sheets until the main boom lies nearly along the line of the keel, and then he must take care not to nip the vessel too closely into the eyes of the wind, or she will not sail. If she is a good vessel with a nice wedge-like grip of the water, she will sail along very well just three-and-a-half or four points from the wind—that is to say, at 35 to 40-odd degrees from the wind's direction. If the wind is ahead, the yachtsman beats, tacks, advances in a zigzag manner first this way and then that, biting to windward the best way he can, using the tide under his lee bow (if he can), seizing every opportunity to advance. On one tack—one leg of the zigzag—his vessel will probably lie much nearer to the direction he wishes to go than she will on the other. Therefore the yachtsman will keep her on that tack—the *making* tack—as long as he can, making long 'boards' that way and short boards the other. (I do not know where that word board comes from. All I know is it is a very ancient term in sailing.*)

He tacks his ship—puts her about, changes from one board to the other—by bringing the wind on the other side of the sails by the simple process of swinging the jib and mainsail across the vessel while the hull, swung by the rudder, pivots across the face of the wind. A sloop, cutter, dinghy, or any other fore-and-aft rigged vessel is much more convenient to tack than any square-rigger because, since the sails are entirely abaft the mast or the stays from which they are set, they swing over very easily. They shake a lot but are not taken aback in the same sense that a square

---

* "Board, in Navigation, the space comprehended between any two places where the ship changes her course by tacking; or the line over which she runs between tack and tack, when she is turning to windward, or sailing against the direction of the wind," says William Falconer's *Universal Dictionary of the Marine* (London, 1789).

sail is. They practically look after themselves, and it is a very
indifferent yachtsman or a very poor yacht which does not tack—
in any good sailing conditions—with a minimum of trouble.

This fundamental difference between handling square-riggers
and fore-and-afters is shown very clearly in the steps taken aboard
to ease the ship when on a wind—close-hauled is the term: hauled
close to the wind—in squally weather. The yachtsman pinches the
yacht up into the wind in a squall, because he knows that will
shake the sails a little, take his way off, let the yacht stand more
upright, and generally ease the strain. But the square-rigged
helmsman lets his ship go off—away from the wind—when a
squall hits her, because he knows very well (and the officer of the
watch knows even better) that to shake her is the worst thing he
can do. Shaking square sails is not good for them or for the
rigging and, if the square-rigger is caught aback in a heavy squall,
she may be dismasted. If the yachtsman makes a serious error of
judgement and pinches his yacht into the wind too much, she
may fly round on the other tack (he will have to look smartly
after the jib-sheet, in that case). He can pay out on the main-
sheet, and his vessel ought to suffer no damage.

Let us look a moment longer at this business of tacking, of
going about, since that is the manoeuvre which most yachtsmen
find most difficult to comprehend in a square-rigger. They know
well enough how to go about in their own vessels. They know the
orders to the crew (if they have any crew)—"Ready about!"
"Lee oh!" They keep good way on the yacht before she goes
about, let the helm down easily—to bring her across the wind—
push her head round with the backed jib, if necessary, and the
mainsail takes care of itself. *Tacking* is to put the ship across the
wind in the wind's face: *wearing* is to put the ship across the
wind keeping the wind behind the ship—running right off and
coming up again with the wind on the other side. To do this, a
yacht has to. *gybe*—allow the main boom to swing across the
vessel.

A square-rigger tacks head to wind, too, and wears round
before the wind, exactly as a yacht does. But she does not ever
gybe. That risky manoeuvre is spared her, because the braces

always keep the yards rigidly controlled—or should do so and will, if there be no accidents. She has to haul her courses up before going about, though in good weather she may keep her foresail set. She can keep it set, too, to wear round even in bad weather, if she has a very good crew.

So the yacht beats, runs, sails with the wind abeam (which is exactly the same process as sailing close-hauled except that the sheet can be a little more free, and the vessel's way through the water correspondingly improved). She gets under way with easy sail, picking her way through the anchorage by her helmsman's good judgement and judicious use of the forces exerted on the ship by the planes of her sails, assisted by the rudder. She comes back to her moorings or her anchorage under easy sail, too—though not too little, for then she may not be sufficiently manoeuvrable—and again, the judgement of the helmsman is the important thing. He must know his own ship—how best to keep sufficient way on her and adequate control over her, and the best manner of approaching his moorings or his berth. If the wind dies or the conditions are poor, he can get out in his pram or rowing dinghy and tow her to the buoy, if he must. If the wind is fresh the manoeuvre of recovering the buoy will call for nicety of judgement. Compared with the square-rigger, he will be at a disadvantage in that the square sails can be thrown aback (by manipulating the braces) and so act as very effective brakes, and fore-and-aft sails with the wind on the wrong side of them will only push the yacht awkwardly around. Square sails will stop her. Their use in this manner calls for much nicety of judgement, too, and a very good crew.

The Arab with his lateen-rigged dhow, the Malay with his prau, the Chinaman with his junk, the West Indies sponge-fisherman with his two-masted schooner—all handle their vessels in the same way, by skilful manipulation of sails assisted by the helm. The Arab, having one big sail only to set from his huge mast, often uses a sort of balloon jib to get under way, hoisting the head of the jib to the masthead and setting the lateen as soon as he is clear of other shipping. Or he will set only the fore part of the lateen sail to push his ship round from the wind, and then give her the full sail as soon as it is convenient. To tack, he has to shift his lateen yard round to the other side of the mast and shift the sail, too, end-for-end, which means that men have to run right round the deck carrying the sheet from one side to the other, taking the whole of it round the fore side of the mast. To swing their lateen yards the more easily, dhows have a mast raked forward, and the lateen-yard is always hung at the point of balance with just sufficient length on the fore part of the mast to clear the deck when the yard is swung upright. It has to be swung upright to get the sail to the other side. The dhow, too, cannot have any real standing rigging, for obviously this would get in the way of the sail. Just as the yacht always sets up her backstays to windward and slackens those alee (altering them each time she tacks or gybes), the dhow sets up her rigging to windward each time she goes round. She usually sets up six shrouds made of coir rope twisted from the husks of coconuts, each shroud being set up by means of a simple tackle, the lower block of which is hooked to a strop which is always kept rigged at the proper place on the bulwarks.

This is fine-weather sailing, of course. Dhows are not for Cape Horn. A ketch, a topsail schooner, a three, four, five or six-masted schooner all handle in essentially the same manner as the cutter, except that there are more booms to swing across, more sails to handle and to choose from, according to their manoeuvre value, for the finer points of moving in confined waters. The sails are reefed for bad weather and set full in good. Fore-and-aft sails in big ships suffer badly from slatting in light winds and calms, because of the weakness inherent in this rig, of not being able to keep the gaffs rigid. In such circumstances, the bigger sails have sometimes to be run down lest they bang themselves to pieces. This was one of the disadvantages of the big Cape Horn barquentines, and another was the risks they had to run when gybing. Barquentines were not a success in the Cape Horn trade for they had to rely too much on their one square-rigged mast, and so were often under-canvased.

So much for the more easily understood fore-and-afters. The best way, perhaps, to convey a clear impression of the handling

Getting a square-rigged ship under way. For explanation, see text. The backed head-yards are used to swing the ship and point her in the desired direction.

of a big square-rigger is to describe an ocean passage in one, from the handling point of view. Our vessel, a big four-masted barque, lies deep-loaded and cleared outwards for sea off a port, say, in Spencers Gulf in South Australia, bound towards Falmouth, Plymouth or Queenstown for orders. The master comes aboard with the last of her many papers, and the mate has the ship all ready to go to sea—hatches secured and battened down and breakwaters built up over the larger of them (to break the force of the seas which will soon be assailing them), all the gear clear for running, sails held by a few gaskets, steam up on the donkey-boiler and some of the cable already shortened in. The vessel has loaded at anchor and she will sail from the anchorage, and tugs will not be used. If she had loaded up-river or at a wharf, a tug would have brought her to her anchorage, though some ships did sail from wharves.

The first problem is to get the ship under way. The course down-gulf is approximately south. The wind is from the west, moderate. The ship lies at her anchor head-to-wind. Her first compass course, then, will be south, and she will have the wind on her starboard beam. The mate has already trimmed the main and mizzen yards for this. He has braced the foreyards on the other tack. The master takes all this in with one quick look that misses nothing. Though his ship is considerably more than 300 feet long and she is drawing 26 feet of water, he is well used to her. He can spot the slightest detail out of order. The mate knows the ship, too. Nothing is out of order. Everything is as it should be.

"Heave short," is the first order. In some ships, the anchor was worked by means of the hand-operated capstan on the fore-castle-head, which could be geared to the windlass below, but this was laborious and slow. Most big sailing-ships could operate the windlass by steam, if they had a steam winch, or by means of an endless chain traveller from an oil winch. The windlass itself was not power-operated, except in a few of the very largest ships. So the chain traveller would grind around and the cable would come in very slowly, but much faster than by hand-power however applied. The master's problem was to have his ship under control by the time the anchor was off the bottom but, if

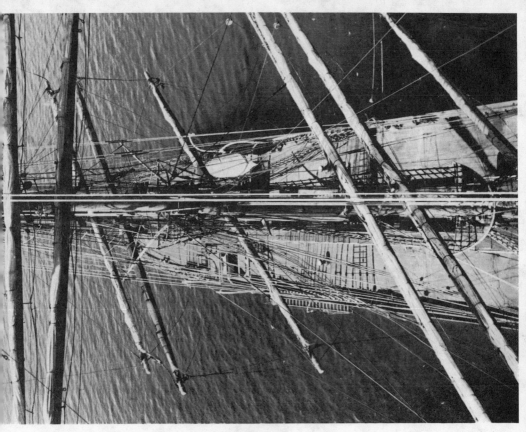

↑ The graceful square-rigger lies at her anchor, head to wind.

The sails are ready, and everything clear for running. ↑

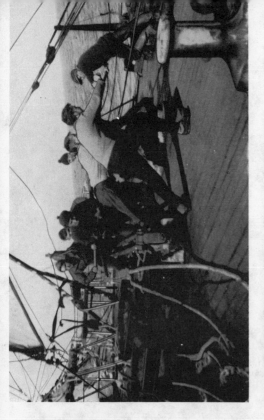

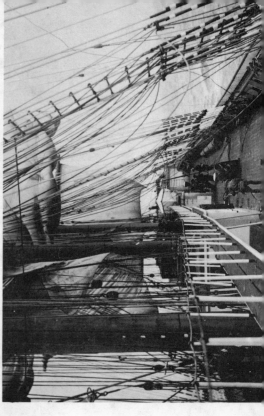

↑ Man the capstan! This is aboard the *Sagres*, with a big crew.

ABOVE RIGHT
Manning the capstan in a short-handed Finn.

Going about! Head to wind and sails aback. →

he set his sails while the anchor was still down, then the ship would barge about in all directions, and the windage of her sails could make the anchor almost impossible to dislodge from the bottom. If he did not have the sails set and under proper control when the anchor was free, then the ship would be drifting helplessly. So first he hove short—hove in so much of the cable that there were only the last few fathoms to bring in. Then all sail was loosed, and boys were stationed aloft to overhaul the running gear while the sails were set. The buntlines and clew-lines were heavy and required lightening, and this was done by hauling up slack from the deck and paying it out over the sails as they were set. It was usual to leave the big sails—the courses—until last, and these were generally held by a few gaskets and their own buntlines until the decks were clear.

The port watch works the for'ard end of the ship and the foremast, and the starboard watch works the main and mizzen masts. The man standing by to take the wheel as soon as the ship can be steered helps to look after the jigger-mast. The mate has charge of his watch and the anchor-work, while the second mate superintends the work of his watch.

"Set the tops'ls!" was the next order, and the six topsails would be set as quickly as possible. By the manner of bracing the yards, the sails on the main and mizzen masts would be just filling and so giving the ship a little way, and the sails on the foremast were aback giving her sternway. So she stood more or less where she was.

Then the windlass was manned again and the anchor hove up. In a moment or two the mate would shout "Up and down!" to indicate that the anchor was held merely by a length of cable equal to the depth of water.

"Break her out!" and up came the anchor. Immediately the ship was free of her ground tackle she began to move, pivoting first, with the backed foreyards canting her head round until she was headed in the right direction. If necessary, the jibs could be hoisted and sheeted to windward—set aback—to help swing the ship. As soon as the ship was canting nicely round to her course (with a man at the wheel to look after her) the foreyards were

hauled round until the sails on that mast filled on the starboard
tack, like those on the other two masts, and the ship was properly
under way. Then all sail was set as quickly as possible, the watches
looking after their own masts and the port watch, as soon as their
one mast was clothed, going at once to get the heavy anchor
inboard and secured on the forecastle-head. They would not
secure it too well as it might be needed again, for the Gulf was
a long one and the wind might come ahead, or drop to a calm.
Many masters left their anchors cockbilled until they were clear
of the land—that is, not stowed on the forecastle-head at all but
secured at the cathead, whence they could be let go as needed.
When the ship was outside the anchor would be taken inboard
and the cables unshipped until the vessel was approaching her
landfall, perhaps at the other side of the world.

All hands always worked until the anchors were secured (the
starboard watch helping as soon as their masts were looked after
properly) and all the sails set, the gear cleared up and everything
shipshape, and the watch-and-watch routine did not generally
begin before the evening of sailing day—late on the evening,
more often than not.

Getting under way from anchorage was always managed in
the manner described or by some variation of it, for the vessel—
except when tide-rode—would always lie head-to-wind and have
to be canted round. Strong tides would make a difference, of
course, but the master would simply use the tide as an additional
force to act for the good of his vessel and his control of her. If
the wind was very fresh he would set fewer sails at first: if there
was no wind at all he couldn't do anything and it was better to
wait for a bit of a breeze. In flat water, a sailing-ship did not
need much movement of the air to be manoeuvrable. As much
as could be felt on the weather side of a moistened finger would
suffice, though not for all ships.

A good many ships got themselves under way by towing outside to a good offing—well clear of the land—and then giving the
ship her sails easily as they followed behind the tug. This was
forced on ships leaving big ports well inland, up rivers or on
land-locked bays, but from open roadsteads and the like, it was

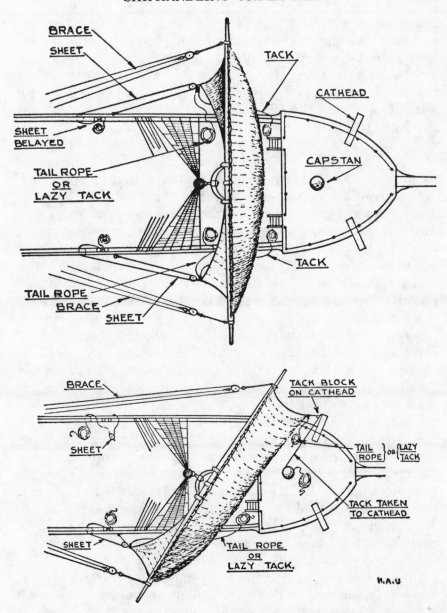

The set of a fore-course (foresail). Above, with the wind right aft; below, with the wind on the quarter. The gear is minimised in order to show the sail more clearly.

a lazy man's way. Tugs cost money and square-riggers were run on a very tight purse—so tight that many owners, buying a ship with a double-barrelled name, would shorten the name to one word in order to save cable costs, though they might not send or receive three cablegrams a year. I remember this being done with a lovely ship named the *Thomasina Maclellan,* whose name was shortened to *Thomasina* when she became a Finn.

Well, there is our big four-master, under way. The sun is shining and the weather good. A leadsman is ready. The carpenter has oiled and greased all the working parts of the masts and blocks and steering-gear—a prodigious job, which was usually done each Saturday morning. The patent log is ready to set going from the rail aft as soon as the ship is outside and her position fixed accurately for her 'departure'. The binnacle lamps and the sidelights are trimmed and ready. These are oil lamps, and the ship has no other lights except a minimum in the forecastle and cabins. Half a dozen small hogs grunt in a sty beneath the forecastle-head, unworried about the coming run towards Cape Horn and the certainty of the fate awaiting them. A hutch of chickens cackles aft: perhaps a sheep or two, bewildered and resentful, staggers on the maindeck, seasick already. These animals were carried for fresh food.

Evening comes and the lights are lit, and the master puts some flares handy in the charthouse to burn in case any steamers come too close, failing to notice a ship which burns no white masthead lights. (Sailing-ships carried red and green sidelights only, to comply with the International Rule of the Road, the idea being that this would distinguish them from powered vessels which were required to burn bright white masthead lights, and to keep out of the sailer's way. But young watchkeepers in steamers soon looked only for other masthead lights and failed to see the sailing ship's sidelights. Only one sidelight could be seen, at a time, usually, and the oil lamps shining behind thick coloured glass could be seen only two or three miles. They were sometimes not at all easy to see, even when they were being looked for. So prudent masters kept brilliant flares handy and, if they saw a steamer not altering course to give them right of way, they burned a flare. This lit the sails and the steamer would sheer away.)

The night passes. But in the morning the westerly wind has gone to the south-west, fresh. This is a head wind. What to do now? Anchor and wait? It is best to keep the ship under way. There is room to beat. In flat water any ship handles better, when there is no sea to slap her about. Our master beats. To do this, he has to tack ship just as a yachtsman would have to do. With the wind at south-west and the water flat, his ship will point up six points and make a very good course at six and half from the wind, which means that when she is on the starboard tack, she can steer a little to the eastwards of SSE, and on the port tack, a little to the nor'rard of WNW. South-southeast is nearest the ship's course, so the master (other things such as the proximity of dangers being equal) will try to keep the ship longest on that tack. The ship steers a good course when close-hauled because the yards are skilfully trimmed to have the mizzen royal pointed up highest, and the helmsman watches the weather clew of the mizzen royal and the officer of the watch watches him. If he brings the ship too close to the wind, the clew will shake, and perhaps the whole weather leech: the ideal is to keep the clew just lifting, and then all the other sails are full. Each yard, beginning at the lower topsail yard, is checked in just a little more than the yard below it, the course yard being laid along the backstays of the standing rigging as hard as it will go but not so hard that there is undue chafe. The fore-and-afters are all pulling well, as they always did when the ship was on the wind. They help both the balance and the speed. A well-designed ship, in good trim, would practically steer herself under such conditions. If she required much steering then there was something seriously wrong, either with the set of the sails or the stowage of the cargo.

Our four-master is properly stowed and the sails are well set. She hums along with a bone in her teeth and the sun glinting white on the sails. Beating in confined waters is all-hands work, though the full crew is required only for the actual going round. The watch can handle her otherwise, although it is only nine men strong and the 'men' are youths and boys.

The brace-winches are in perfect order, and the other braces are coiled down on the deck clear for running. Since the mainsail and crojack will both have to be hauled up each time the ship is put about, their gear is all clear and the buntline stops broken. (It was customary to haul a little slack of the buntlines over the sail and to put a light piece of twine across buntline and jackstay to hold the buntline in position. This was done to minimise chafe, which wore out canvas.) The lifts on the fore, main, and crojack yards—the only lifts which lead to the deck—are slacked off. The mates station their men. The master puts the ship about whether she be tacked or worn round: it is only in doldrums catspaws that the officer of the watch may haul the yards round without first calling the master. The mates supervise the work on deck. The master stands on the poop, by the helmsman. Four hands are told off to each brace-winch, except that controlling the fore braces—two to each handle. The carpenter and perhaps the sailmaker go to the forecastle-head to tend the jib-sheets, under the mate's eye. A couple of hands are on the poop to handle the spanker. The sailmaker might be stationed here. A boy to each mast will take care of the slack of the topgallant and royal braces. The cook must see to the foresheet, which traditionally is his post because the galley is usually close by it.

Everything is now ready and it *must* be ready—no oversights, no stupidity. The whole success of the manoeuvre rests on foresight and organisation beforehand, as in so much of the square-rigger's work.

The master is satisfied.

"Keep her clean full," he orders the helmsman, or he might say "Keep her full for stays." This to get good way on the ship in order that she may slam across the wind with her sails aback, and yet not gather sternway.

The crojack and mainsail are hauled up in their gear.

"Ready about!" is the next order. The tacks and sheets of the courses are clear for the yards to swing, and nothing is left where it can inconvenience the free swinging of the sails and yards. The cook stands by the fore-sheet, at its capstan. The carpenter stands by the jib-sheets.

"Lee-oh!" shouts the master, and to the helmsman, "Down helm!"

The wheel is spun down—that is, towards the direction of the wind: *up* is away from it. The rudder kicks the ship to windward, the fore-sheet and the jib-sheets are eased to take the weight out of the head sails, the spanker is hauled to windward to cause the ship to fly up into the wind's eye more quickly. There is a great shaking for a moment or so and then, as all the sails are taken aback with the wind blowing upon their fore sides, the ship's way slackens greatly while she swings across the wind. Swing she must though stop she may, for the moment, and the quicker she can be made to swing the better. With the force exerted by the sails for'ard considerably lessened, the after sails push her round like a weather-cock. Within a few seconds the ship lies almost head to wind, still swinging. At the precise second that the ship is pushing her bowsprit across the direction of the wind, when the weather sides of the sails on the main and mizzen masts are aback and the lee sides becalmed by the sails ahead of them, the master gives the next order.

"Mainsail-haul!"

He says mainsail (because this is the traditional order) but of course he means the crojack as well—all the yards on the main and mizzen masts. If he has timed things rightly, the yards will come round of themselves and all the hands have to do is to wind the brace-winches furiously and keep things clear, while the boys take in the slack of the lighter braces, hand-over-hand. The yards are trimmed hastily, the after fore-and-aft sails are sheeted to the new lee side, and the hands dash along the deck to the fore braces. Meanwhile the carpenter has looked after the jib-sheets. If the ship is reluctant to cant the right way, the jib-sheets may have to be hauled aft aback to help push her round but, under good conditions, this should not be necessary. All being well, the ship is still swinging, though much more slowly; the sails on main and mizzen begin to fill on the new tack, while the sails on the foremast, being still on the other tack, are aback and holding the ship.

"Let go and haul!"

At once the brake is taken off the fore brace-winch, the ends of the lighter braces let go, and the hands grind the fore-yards round on winch and by hand as quickly as they can, while the cook and the second cook (with the steward as well, very likely) gather in the slack of the fore-sheet, and the carpenter and a few good men, having looked after the jib-sheets, take the new fore tack, on the other side of the ship, down to the capstan. The spanker (being a fore-and-aft sail like a yacht's mainsail) has more or less taken care of itself. The mainsail and crojack are set again as quickly as possible, on the new tack, the trim of the yards is perfected and the bracewhips and tackles set up, the buntlines are overhauled again (for things must always be done correctly), and away bounds the ship full-and-by on the other tack. Full-and-by means that though she is steering by-the-wind, she is not kept so close that anything shakes. The sails are full and the ship is by-the-wind. Again the gear is coiled down clear for running, the longer gear being flaked down on the deck to ensure that the lines will run out clean through the blocks, and not pick up a snarl.

Making short tacks, as in the narrow waters of the Gulf, possibly the crojack would not be set except for the longer boards.

You will observe that the orders are the same as those used in a small yacht. The ship has gone through precisely the same manoeuvre, with complications.

Sometimes things do not go so smoothly. Perhaps the wind shifts just at the vital moment the ship is swinging across it, or for some other reason things go wrong. Then the ship will gather stern-way and the helm must be shifted, or the ship may get 'in irons', as the sailors say. If she is taken in irons then there is a mess, for she won't sail and won't fall off in either direction. She may be brought back under control by taking the spanker in, running down the jigger and the mizzen topmast stay-sails, and squaring the main and crojack yards. The ship will then back on her heel and gradually fill the after-sails, and so gather headway again. Headway is her lifeblood: with that, she can be fully clothed and tacked again, or put about by wearing, if that is the best thing to do.

Tacking ship in a full-rigger. For explanation, see text. To tack ship is to change tacks by putting the ship about *across* the wind, letting the sails be aback.

Under good conditions there should be no trouble about getting in irons, and our ship beats on until she is out of the Gulf. Outside and clear of the land the south-west wind is a fair wind, and the welcome order is heard to "Check the weather crojack brace," or simply, "Weather crojack brace." Everyone aboard knows that if the wind hauls fair the yards are checked in, and as the wind heads the ship, the yards go for'ard. So the squaring-in order is "Weather main brace" (in a barque or ship) and "weather crojack brace" in a four-master, and the order for further pointing the yards is "Lee fore brace", for the yards on .he foremast are pointed first.

Reference to the diagrams accompanying this chapter will help to make clear the manoeuvre of tacking-ship. The whole point is to swing the ship across the direction of the wind in her stride, if you can do it. There was always a windsock—a miniature copy of that at flying-fields—to assist the master, if he required such assistance, to gauge the direction of the wind. For light winds, some ships flew little feather streamers from a stanchion on the 'weather side of the poop, a couple of feathers on a few feet of very light marline.

Five-masted barques and five-masted full-rigged ships handled in the same way as their smaller sisters. The headyards boxed the ship around, and the yards on all the other masts were swung together. These big ships, being much longer, were actually the more easily handled by a self-confident master-mariner, for their head-yards and after canvas exerted much more effective leverage. A full-rigged ship with the standard three masts was usually the most awkward rig to handle, especially if she were a big ship.

Once outside, our master does his best to put every possible mile behind him. The sails are always perfectly set, the yards well trimmed, the maximum useful canvas kept aloft to help the ship along. Eternal vigilance was the way of it, night and day, day after day, week after week, always getting the best run from every possible chance. As the wind and sea increased sail must be shortened. If a hurricane blew, the ship might have to be hove-to. (This was most unusual in the big steel sailers, though common enough in smaller vessels. I had to heave-to in the *Joseph*

Conrad four or five times on the way to Cape Horn, even with a fair wind. There was too much sea for the ship to run in without grave danger of running under.) The square-rigger knew two kinds of heaving-to. One was in bad weather, when she hove-to like an albatross asleep on the sea with her head tucked under her wing, shortened down and no longer fighting to make headway but giving slowly to the seas, coming up a little, falling off a little, drifting to leeward under minimum canvas. I hove-to in the *Conrad* under a goose-winged fore tops'l, which means that one corner only of the close-reefed sail was set, and a weather-cloth was lashed in the mizzen rigging, with the helm eased down. She would lie like that quite safely through the strongest gale.

The other kind of heaving-to was for fine weather and was achieved by simply throwing the mainyards aback while the fore and mizzen sails were still full. The efforts of these sails to give the vessel headway were counterbalanced very nicely by the brake of the backed main sails, and so the ship would lie quietly, practically still. In this way pilots were taken aboard or dropped, or a boat might be put out for any reason.

If our master finds he must put the ship about in bad weather, then he has to wear. For that he needs room, for the vessel must lose some ground. Again, foresight and organisation are the keystones but, since the manoeuvre is required only in bad weather under short canvas, greater care is needed to prevent damage to sails and rigging, and loss of life. The ship running off before the wind falls into the trough of the sea, which means that she will roll unmercifully and the seas might make a clean sweep of her. Having run off, she must be brought up again, and here, too, she may suffer severe damage and the seas might wash some of the crew overboard. Squaring the yards was always much heavier work, naturally, than letting them go for'ard, and the men were necessarily kept on the maindeck longer and so were more exposed to the fury of the sea.

The first step when it is intended to wear ship—the old expression was to *veer*, not wear—is to reduce the after canvas by hauling down whatever stay-sails are set aft, and brailing in the spanker. (A square-rigger's gaff was permanently fixed abaft the

mast and did not travel up and down on jaws, as a schooner's
does. Consequently the sail was hauled in—*brailed* in—to the
mast by a series of lines called brails, running from the luff to the
leech, right across it.) The crojack would certainly be fast and,
most likely, so would the mainsail be. The ship would be unlikely
to be showing any canvas above the lower topgallantsails unless
she was a 'P' ship or some other exceptionally able and hard-
driven vessel. The braces, course tacks, sheets and so forth would
all be clear. The foresail might be in, too. If not, it could be
hauled up in its gear or possibly left set, though in that case shifting the tacks and sheets without shaking the sail or letting the
heavy wires take charge and kill somebody would call for good
judgement and the very best seamanship. It *could* be done but,
in really heavy weather, most masters preferred not to take the
chance.

The ship being ready, a good man at the wheel (and possibly
a couple of very oily wads of oakum put in the lavatory pipes
forward to drip a little oil upon the sea, and so make a slick for
the ship to live in), and all hands at or very near their stations,
ready to do their work the instant they were called on, the master's first order would be "Put the helm up! Up helm!"

"Up helm!" repeats the man at the wheel, shoving the spokes
of that heavy structure away from him for his life.

"Stand by to square the crojack yard!" came next.

As the ship fell off from the wind, which she would do the
more rapidly because the pressure of the after-sails had been
relieved, the yards on the mizzen and main masts would be
squared in as quickly as possible, keeping the sails almost shiver-
ing, in order to keep the weight of the gale out of them and so
lighten the bracing. The main and mizzen yards, being square,
and the ship, meanwhile turning on her heel, now scudding before the wind (in the wrong direction), the fore-yards are next
hauled right round, though the wind is then out on the other
quarter. The fore topmast stay-sail and whatever jibs might be
set are shifted over, and the hands make the best of their way
then to the main and mizzen braces. These are worked until the
yards on those masts are brought up to the wind again on the

FIG 1: ON PORT TACK   FIG 2: RUNNING OFF.

WIND   WIND

FIG 3: BRACING YARDS   FIG 4: ON STARBOARD TACK.

WIND   WIND

HAROLD A. UNDERHILL.

Wearing ship. For explanation see text. Wearing ship is to change tacks by running off before the wind and coming up again.

new tack, and properly trimmed. The helm is eased long before this, for the ship must come up to the wind again now. (The diagram shows what happens.) Coming up to the wind is done most carefully. The master watches for a lull, watches his oil-slick doing its work, nurses the ship up to the wind when the best chance presents itself, when the ugly crest of no great menacing sea is roaring upon her.

When the ship is brought up to the wind again on the new tack, the perfect set of all the sails is attended to and the gear cleared again, ready for the next manoeuvre. Instead of a full spanker, only the foot of that sail might be set or, more probably, a three-cornered trysail made of the stoutest canvas. Some ships used three-cornered crojacks and even three-cornered mainsails, for such sails could be kept set much longer than the usual rectangular sails could be, and could be kept set when she was put about. I put such a triangular main on the *Conrad* for Cape Horn, and was very pleased with it. She was rather an over-canvased ship, being a full-rigger and so small.

Our master wears his ship around only when he must, and then usually it is not to beat her but to put the ship on that tack which will bring her up to her course as the wind continues to back or to veer. He does not usually beat in the great open spaces of the South Pacific. He backs his judgement of what the wind will do next, and acts accordingly. But sometimes he may be wrong. A cyclonic movement of the wind may pass over his ship more quickly than he expected it to, and another catch him up, beginning from a different quarter altogether. It is all a matter of skill and vigilance and good courageous sailing. For all wind changes except when the ship is by-the-wind, the trim of the sails may be altered a little, but the great aim is to keep the yards off the backstays and so let the ship sail at least a little free. As soon as the wind hauls free at all, the course yards are checked in from the backstays. With the wind abeam, or well out on the quarter, is the best sailing-point. With the wind right aft, the spanker and perhaps all the fore-and-aft sails come in, and the crojack and mainsail are hauled up to let the wind get through to the foresail and so help the steering. The square-rigged ship is never gybed as the fore-and-after is. If the wind changes from one quarter to the other, the yards are swung to adjust the trim of the sails, and the ship can run off course a little while this is being done. She must take no chance of being caught aback.

Our ship runs bravely on. She is difficult to steer when running heavily, as all square-riggers are, and the work at the big open wheel—or pair of wheels—is very heavy, so heavy that the boys sweat there though there is ice along the yards and in the service covering the wire footropes. Big jobs such as wearing ship or making the mainsail fast, or handing one of the upper topsails, are left if possible to the change of the watch, so that all hands can attend to them without either watch being called out from its watch below. That is necessary quite often enough: an intelligent master will look after his crew in every way he can. He will see that they are fed as well as possible and that their quarters are dry, if this can be contrived. In a good ship they have a place to hang their oilskins and their wet clothes. There may be stoves burning in the forecastle, though some masters forbade this not because they were opposed to the idea but because they held that it was healthier for the mariners not to live in a fug. Mariners loved fugs and stoves encouraged them. Many ships, of course, would not spend the money either to buy stoves or coal to burn in them.

The trim of the gear and the set of the sails are the constant care of the watch-officers. Gear works loose and must be set up again. Buntlines must not chafe the sails. Braces must be taut. Nothing can be slovenly. The ends of the gear on deck must be triced up in order that they will not go out through the wash-ports as the ship rolls in the sea, and get snarled up, or chafed. Rope is expensive and must be looked after. Sails are expensive and they must be looked after. Men are valuable, and they must be looked after too.

Sometimes there are calms even on the road towards the Horn. Usually they do not last long. If they do, everyone becomes very fretful. Under such conditions masters might be known to turn into surly, cross-tempered morons, raving about the poop and finding fault unnecessarily, or jumping on their so'westers in a fury. Some took to the bottle. I remember one such who was cursed—in winter, too—by almost a week of continuous calm, during which the empty whisky bottles went plop-plop over the side and the cases after them and, in the end, the master took delirium tremens so badly that he had to be lashed in his bunk a day or two lest he go over the side after his bottles. It wouldn't have been much harm done if he had followed them. Command of a Cape Horner was a severe test of character which not everybody passed, by any means.

In due course our ship is past the Horn, generally within a month of leaving Australia. (I have been two months.) Then she swings out past the Falkland Islands and up towards the southeast trades, again making the best use of every breeze, keeping the ship moving, endeavouring so to shape the course that she will always find good sailing conditions and not drift into hopeless zones of calm, and getting maximum value out of every shift of the wind. In the Horse Latitudes the hard-weather sails—the best suit—come down from aloft and the oldest suit is bent in its stead. There will inevitably be some calm, and square sails bang and slat against the masts and the fore-and-aft stays when they hang lifeless and the ship rolls uneasily about. Alternating rain-squalls and blinding sunshine are very hard on canvas, and this is another reason for having old sails aloft. Meanwhile the good sails are being repaired, for they will be bent again for the run towards the Channel from off the Azores. This run, if made at any time other than high summer, could be hard—as hard almost as Cape Horn, with the added risk of a dangerous landfall at the end. It was one thing to run for the Horn without a very accurate idea of where the ship might be and without any strict check on her course, but it was quite another to try to thread the ship nicely past Land's End and take no chance of running into the Bristol Channel instead, or hitting the land. (Quite enough ships did hit the coast of England. Few came off intact.)

ABOVE   Hauling on the braces

BELOW   Arab dhows must set up their rigging to windward again, each time they go about.   →

Navigation in many sailing-ships was not their strong point—
no sun, no fix, was the fairly general rule. There often was no
sun to be seen near the chops of the Channel. Nor were the old-
timers well off for charts, since the masters had to buy their own.
It was usual to have a very few and those few small-scale—one
for the whole of the South Pacific (including Australia), one for
the South Atlantic, one for the North Atlantic, and a general
chart of the English Channel. Chronometer rates were kept as
carefully as possible but, even with two or three chronometers,
there was an element of chance in this. All three could be out,
over a four-month passage. Herman Piening, on his first voyage to
sea, was 99 days beating off the Horn in a big full-rigged ship—
the *Susanna*—partly because the master was afraid of the place
(having been dismasted there on an earlier voyage) and partly
because his one chronometer was so far out that, when he came
to run in for his destination, he found that he had sailed 500
miles further to the west'ard off the Chilean coast than he need
have done.

In our hypothetical case we will suppose our master's chronometer to be accurate, his navigation good, and his landfall
perfect. But the wind heads him—blows in his face—just as he
gets off the Lizard. He has called Lloyd's signal station and there
are no orders for his ship. So he has to beat into the roads to
anchor. He has the strong tides of the Channel to help or hinder
him. (Perhaps he has tide tables aboard, perhaps not. He *should*
have them.) At any rate he can see what the tide is doing and,
when he makes a board near the land, some Falmouth boatman
is sure to approach him seeking business and offering advice,
which may or may not be reliable. Now the big ship is tacked,
for there is not room to wear her, and no ground is to be lost.
Should the wind hang in the east the master may decide to make
for Queenstown, but being so close to Falmouth he will probably
beat on. He does not wish to be beating about that busy corner
of England by night, if he can help it, for far too many steamers
are to be met there and they are a source of danger. Again he

The sails on the fore are aback to cant the ship's head round.
(Note here the chain lower topsail sheets in the right foreground.)
←

has the flares ready, and the sidelights are burning as brightly as they can be induced to burn. (One four-masted barque was actually hit twice by the same steamer, beating out from the Channel. She was struck in the bows by a little steamer bound in towards the Bristol channel and not keeping a proper lookout, and then she returned to port, was repaired, sailed again, had to beat again in the same place, and the little steamer—which meanwhile had made another short voyage—came up again and hit her in the bows a second time. So again she had to be repaired, but the third time she was lucky. When the last four-masted barque was coming up-Channel from New Zealand in 1949, the British Broadcasting Corporation broadcast a warning to all steamers in the area to be on the lookout for a vessel carrying no masthead lights. By that time, such vessels were so rare that the risk of collision was much graver.)

At last the wind hauls fair for our master to make in for his anchorage in Falmouth Bay, with a nice whole-sail breeze. Two other square-riggers are already lying there. He comes bounding in under a nice press of sail, well aware that with his good gear and well-trained crew he can clew up all he needs very quickly and brake the ship most effectively by simply backing his main yards—at the proper time. In he comes, a great bone in the old ship's mouth and her sides rust-streaked from her long battle with the sea, but everything else about her in perfect order. (Those rust-streaks are honourable scars.) He shortens her down as he comes—first the lighter fore-and-afters, then the royals and upper topgallantsails. Then the courses are hauled up, the mainsail and crojack because they are so big and awkward and need so many of the crew to handle them, and the foresail in order to leave the forecastle-head clear for working anchors, and to give the master an unimpeded view along the decks. Then come the lower topgallantsails, and after them, the three *lower* topsails—not the upper topsails. The reason is that it is more difficult and therefore slower to haul *up* lower tops'ls than to run *down* uppers, and speed is the essence of the problem in good seamanship when coming smartly to the selected anchorage.

At last the big vessel approaches her anchorage under the three

Coming to anchorage under sail. The backed sails act as brakes. For full explanation, see text.

upper tops'ls, fore topmast stay-sail, and the jigger stay-sail and spanker. The wind has freshened and hauled more free and she still has a good speed, for the other sails have been clewed up only—bunted up to the yards—and not made fast. There has not been time for that. The fore and mizzen upper topsails are lowered, leaving only the main upper topsail set.

The anchor hangs at the cathead, ready for letting go, with the carpenter standing by with a maul and the mate in charge. The mate's traditional place is for'ard, when the ship is entering and leaving port. The second mate is working the deck. The master is aft by the wheel, conning the helmsman. There is no pilot, for the ship is not going inside. (She would have to hire a tug to pull her out again, and she is touching at the port only for orders as to the destination of her grain.) Her ensign flies bravely at the peak—the end of the gaff. She shows no other flags except perhaps a house-flag at the main truck, if the master has made a good passage and is feeling pleased with himself, and he has such a flag.

Now the ship nears the appointed anchorage.

"Down helm! Haul down the fore topmast stay-sail!"

The wheel spins down and the ship, lightened of all leverage for'ard, turns on her heel. The spanker is hauled to wind'ard to turn her the faster. The main tops'l begins to shake and then is caught aback, as the ship swings into the wind. She begins to lose way—slowly at first, then quickly. Then she stops. Just at that precise moment she must be at the place where the anchor is to be dropped.

"Let go!"

Let go it is; the carpenter takes a mighty blow at the one pin holding the chain stopper round the anchor at the cathead, and the windlass is free. Down goes the anchor with a great splash, and out rattles the cable with a bit of rust flying. The backed tops'l now gives the ship sternway and she pulls the cable out, for she must not sit upon a bight of it coiled on the anchor. The cable must ride clear and the flukes have a good bite of the ground, for a turn of cable under the stock will prevent the anchor from holding properly and the ship may drag. Things must be done *properly.* The mate pays out cable nicely as the ship takes it, signalling with his arm to show the master how the cable 'grows'—at what angle it lies from the ship. The anchor ball is hoisted to show other ships that the ship is at anchor. Two shackles, three shackles, maybe five shackles run out—a 'shackle' is fifteen fathoms of cable—and meanwhile, the main tops'l is lowered, and the hands run aloft to get a good harbour stow on all the sails.

The ship has arrived.

Picking up a mooring in a crowded anchorage or taking the ship's allotted place in a tier of other shipping, called for skill and nerve, and the sailing-ship master showed the stuff he was made of on such occasions. But he knew his ship, if he was worth his salt at all, and he knew quite well how to manipulate the forces controlling her in order to make her do what he wanted her to do, and go where she must. It was a nice skill, and its exercise gave not only the master but the whole crew a feeling of achievement.

Part III

——◆—◆——

THE MEN

Chapter seven

PERSONNEL—THE SAILORS

THERE WAS one factor which mattered far more than ships and that was the men who served them; yet it is curious how many owners and masters overlooked this commonsense truism. On the whole the men who went to sea in sailing-ships as professional seamen were splendid men, at any rate at sea. They were men who took a fierce pride in their competence, which had been developed down the ages. It was groups of the seamen themselves who insisted on the maintenance of strict standards, for example, in such ships as the North Sea collier brigs, and no man was rated able seaman in them until he had satisfied a committee of his peers that he was really a thoroughly competent and experienced man. The square-rigged ship was a hard and exacting taskmaster which never bore fools gladly. A fool at the wheel could broach a ship to, or by coming up too close to the wind, shake a sail and knock a man from the yard. A fool aloft would lose his own life and there was no objection to that. But work ill done would kill others, too. Men who were well aware how much their lives depended on the good teamwork of their fellow seamen set high standards, and saw that there was no departure from them. The same thing applied in the Baltic, in Aveiro on the coast of Portugal, in the once-busy ports of Wales. Boys were apprenticed to the trade of seafaring in the merchant service and learned to become real able seamen, before there was any selection as officers, and promotion was by selection on the grounds of proved leadership and ability, as shown in ships at sea. No qualifications granted by an establishment ashore came into it at all, though of course family influence might do so, for the favoured. There were always two roads to command. One was through the fore-castle—through the hawsepipe, as sailors said—and the other by family influence, and that was called coming in at the stern windows.

The big ships of the East India Company had their own apprenticeship system but they were a class apart, a private navy. Speaking broadly, it was the small ships which bred the real seamen, the backbone of any country's merchant marine, and an assured flow of good recruits with a thorough training in that school meant that there was an abundance of good officer material, too. James Cook began his great career as an apprentice-seaman in a Whitby collier-brig and served in such ships for eight years or more. Cook was a seaman *first,* and an officer and a master afterwards. Cook was outstanding for his leadership, his far-sightedness, and his humanity, but there were many others like him, as far as their seamanship was concerned. The coming of powered vessels lowered the standard of seamanship and, though at first the old hands derided the steamships seafarers as no sailors at all, before very long it was the sailing-ship men who were on the discard. The traditional high standards they had set up had no place in a short-handed steamer, and so the stand-ards went. Many old die-hards stuck to the sailing-ship but, on the whole, the men with family responsibilities went into steam, and stayed there. I am speaking of the coastal and short-sea trades, of course, but these were the nursery of the deepwater men. Before long, British sailing-ships were manned very largely by foreigners. So were Americans, though for quite different reasons.

There had always been a good many foreigners in the deep-sea trades, for the long-voyage sailing-ship was perhaps the best really international instrument there has ever been. In her, men had long learned to live and work amicably together regardless of nationality or any other consideration save the common con-tribution to the working of the ship, the good of all. One reason perhaps for this was that the long-voyage sailing-ship drew adventurous spirits together. On the whole, it is true to say that coastal ships recruited from seafaring families in the ports they served, but the deepwater ships drew their crews from everywhere. Youths from inland, fired by the spirit of adventure, preferred the long trades as more interesting; lads from the ports went in the ships their fathers knew, well aware that adventure was very much a sideline. They might go in deep-sea ships afterwards. They very often did, but they first learned their business in the smaller vessels. In the days of sail, the sailor had not become the documented, form-harassed product he is now. He could go anywhere, once he knew his business, with no documents at all. He was readily identifiable to his own kind. He bore a different stamp from the landsman. At the best, his discharge from a long voyage was a piece of paper which he could lose very easily, even if he wished to keep it. He usually had no discharge-book, no passport, no document of identity. While ships normally signed for a voyage out of their home ports (or some port at least in the same country, or on the same coast of the right continent) and the articles of agreement signified that the men should serve until the ship returned to the same neighbourhood, this was not strictly observed. The usual thing in European vessels was to sign from Europe back to Europe, to serve the ship wherever she might go between 60 South latitude and 75 North—in some ships it was 60 North—for a period of three years.

But desertion was commonplace, particularly in the colonies. In the big ports of North America, it was an organised industry. Whole crews were induced to desert in such ports as San Francisco or Seattle, and then they were shipped out again—with or without their consent—in any vessel which would pay the crimps' blood-money to secure them. This was called shanghai-ing, and it was a highly organised business. Naturally, no one asked for papers. They could have been supplied as easily as the men were, and by the same gentlemen. But they meant nothing. Of course shipping off in a sailing vessel like that was the ideal escape, and some wild spirits went to sea that way. Few such misled recruits stayed at sea. The sailing-ship profession *was* an adventurous life and a satisfying one, but its attractions were not for the late starter or the hasty convert. The great core of professional seamen were more solid citizens who had gone to sea when young, for one reason or another and, finding themselves cut off from the land whether they wished or not, they stayed at sea. It was the only life they knew.

A great factor in providing recruits for the sea was undoubtedly economic stress. The wages were poor, the life hard, and the reward at the end a piece of canvas for a shroud, if the mariner survived the hazards of death by drowning or disease. There was plenty of economic stress ashore, too, and conditions for the labouring man were very hard well after the turn of the twentieth century. The sailing-ship offered at least a clean life which knew considerable contentment, in a way few shore-bound occupations could do. Red-blooded men have always been adventurous, but it took more than a sense of adventure to keep a man in the Cape Horn trade. As for that, even the men who served in the greatest ships did not regard their calling as very adventurous. They did not see it in that light at all—not, at any rate, while they were actually in the ship. It was always old ships which had had adventures. A good many had gone to sea because it was about the only thing they could do. Most of them came from countries which were over-crowded and offered the poor boy little or nothing. The wild unfertile coast of Norway, the lovely but harsh Nevin peninsula of North Wales, the hard-bitten Friesian islands and the Western Isles off Scotland, the rockbound coast of Maine, the over-populated islands of Denmark, the bleak wastes of so much of old Russia's Baltic coast—these were the homes of seamen. The over-populated south-east corner of England, crowded Holland, the virile Irish exiled to Liverpool, the Breton-French, the islanders of Madeira, the Cape Verdes, and the Azores, provided large contingents of good seafaring men. So did the coast of India, for several British sailing-ship lines employed Lascar crews.

The sea was not 'escape' to all these people. It was first and foremost a source of employment, a means of livelihood. Their motives for choosing that life were perhaps as varied as the ships they served in but, by and large, it is landsmen who speak of the 'call of the sea'. A foremast hand stayed at sea because it was the only life he knew and because, having begun young, he found some satisfaction in serving good sailing-ships. He might love ships and indeed he did, but he hated the sea as a savage enemy. He was cut off from the land by his own first voyage, which might well last two or three years. After that he was content to identify himself with ships and the sea. The free roving life appealed to him, despite its hardships, and the poor money meant nothing. He often gambled or threw away the little money he earned as soon as he received it. He was notoriously an easy victim for shore sharks. The whole idea of 'bettering himself' was abhorrent to him, whether he was young or old. He did not think as a landsman did. The world was his and his marlinspike was the key to freedom. Generally, he died young. Fevers took far too many of his shipmates. The sea took others.

Such men, signing away voyage after voyage in deepwater ships, soon found themselves without a home, if ever they had known one. Many were orphans. Others were members of large families which could spare a boy or two. They went off from home as little more than children, and they rarely returned. I remember, for example, the bewilderment aboard a big British four-masted barque in which I was serving when, on the return to Europe at the end of a voyage, it was announced that the men must all be repatriated. Repatriated? What on earth was that? The ship had twenty-four able seamen and I think there were at least fifteen nationalities among them. Some older men no longer knew to which country they properly owed allegiance. This happened in France, not long after the end of the first World War. Some, born Russians, found themselves labelled as Estonians, or Lithuanians, or Finns. None had a birth certificate or anything like that. Somehow or other, the whole lot had to be documented and shipped across Europe. It was officialdom's decree and it had to be obeyed. The sailing-ship was paying off, but instead of the crew landing to seek other ships of their own choice, or putting up with some boarding-master who would find them a ship, they had to go back to their own countries and seek em-

ployment there. Some of them had not been home since they
first went to sea, and several were men over 70. Home? They had
no homes. The ships were enough for them, with an occasional
spell in a sailors' boarding-house or adrift in foreign parts. 'On
the beach', they called it, and it held no terrors for them. A man
was his own master and was supposed to take care of himself. They
knew how to do that over the length and breadth of the world,
but now that they had to accept compulsory repatriation and put
up with whatever officialdom thought was good for them, they
were utterly lost.

I never saw one of those good men again. God knows what
became of them. They dispersed from the little port, and that
was more than just the end of them. It was the end of sailing-
ship seamen. I was in several sailing-ships after that, but the
crews were boys. The men had gone and they did not return.
Bureaucracy killed them as it stifles all enterprise, in the long
run. Whatever the hardships of the life and regardless of the
amount of heartless exploitation they might have suffered, those
men were of a type which has now been destroyed—the truly
free, international seaman. They asked very little and they
were prepared to give a great deal, even their lives. The amount
of work they did and the degree of hardship they accepted,
in the movement of wind-propelled cargoes about the free
waters of the world, is now incredible. They responded magnificently to reasonable treatment, and a ship and her officers
had to be bad indeed before they thought of giving anything
but their best. They were fearless aloft and fearless on deck,
indefatigable and splendidly competent. They thought as little
of setting out for a Cape Horn rounding with no clothes at all
and no bedding as they did of jumping into the rigging to be
first aloft to hand a blown-out sail. The ordinary trapperies
of landbound life meant nothing to them, for they saw through
shams. They were a type apart, and they did not pretend to be
anything they were not. They were merchant sailors and they
looked like sailors: if they had a seabag to call their own, that
was the limit of their possessions. In that seabag there was certain
to be a little piece of sailcloth containing the tools of their calling,

whatever else might not be in it—a fid,* a palm, a spike, a few sail-needles, a good sharp knife. These things they treasured. The disciplined freedom of a well-run ship they valued, too; they knew the value of good team-work. A respected shipmate was a friend for life, not to be forgotten though they might never see him again. Good ships they swore by, and poor ships they cursed.

When I was trying to serve my time for a British second mate's certificate as a necessary step in the road towards command in sail, it was my privilege to know some of these men. I was lucky, for that was the last of them. They were the men who had chosen to remain in sailing-ships, though it was then after the first World War. They had been in sailing-ships all their lives. Many were older men, over 50 years old, and some were considerably more than that. There were men in the forecastles of those last square-riggers who had been in all sorts of ships, even the great clippers. I listened to them with interest, of course, for yarns about ships were the great dogwatch diversion. But I paid no particular attention to them. I took them for granted. I did not write anything down for, like them I suppose, I did not then appreciate how close to oblivion all this life was, nor, for that matter, was it any part of my ambition to become a writer. Most of those men were articulate only among their own kind. There are few genuine chronicles anywhere of the Cape Horn life as the real foremast hand saw it. I mean the plain seaman who was not on his way to the poop, who accepted his foremast status and was happy with that. Quite a number of such men could not read or write, and that was little loss to them. None wrote books.

But afterwards, when I found a few old men of that breed, I did record something of their experiences. I found one in Warren, Pennsylvania, for instance. He had left the sea long since and set himself up in business ashore, in which he had prospered. I met many around San Francisco, but most of these had deserted from British ships in which they had been apprentices for a brief while only, towards the end of the sailing era.

* A fid is a wooden spike used in sail-making and rope-work.

The men whose stories I wanted were those who really *had* been at sea, like that ex-mariner in the inland town in Pennsylvania. He wrote me a long letter. He is dead now, but he asked me not to give his name. Here is his document:

"The writer spent more than ten years at sea in sail. I have doubled both capes. Four times around Cape Horn, and six times around the Cape of Good Hope. Three voyages around Cape Horn I made in Lime-juicers, and one voyage in an American hell ship. Although an American by birth, most of my deep-water sailing was done in English ships for the very good reason that the 'Limeys' were always better manned, and although the food in American ships as a rule was better than in any others, American deep-water ships were usually sent to sea short-handed with a mixed crew of 'soldiers and dishwashers', and at the time of which I speak, in the early eighty's, we still had brutal, bucko mates on many American deep-water ships.

"I was an ordinary seaman on Dicky Green's famous Aberdeen clipper, *Thermopylae,* when she made her famous run from London to Melbourne in 60 days. In the *Thermopylae* we carried 30 before the mast. Six apprentices, 8 ordinary seamen, and 16 A.B.'s. Although she was only of about 1000 tons, we surely needed all we had because the old man would carry on until her lee rail was almost under water before he would take a stitch off her. As soon as it began to blow great guns, we would take in the kites and stow the head sails, except the foretopmast stays'l, and the rest of them had either to stand the gaff or blow out of the bolt ropes. She also had a steam winch, a great blessing to sailors, and the only ship I ever sailed in that had such a luxury.

"I can see her now in memory with her slender tapering tall masts and yards which many a time I helped to paint white, swinging in a bosun's chair. Her hull was painted a bright green as were all of Richard Green's ships, and she looked more like a yacht than a cargo carrier. One of my shipmates that was in her when she first came out, told me that she logged more than 300 knots many a day.

"Two voyages I made in another famous sailing ship, the *Sir Lancelot,* a famous tea clipper in her day, but she wasn't in the China trade when I was in her. I made one trip in her for wool from Melbourne, and one to Calcutta for jute. I left her in 1895, the year before she was lost, somewhere in the Indian Ocean, I believe. The two ships above mentioned were probably the fastest ships that ever sailed, with the possible exception of the *Flying Cloud, Sovereign of the Seas, Red Jacket,* and one or two others built by Donald McKay.

"Every red-blooded boy at some time feels the urge to go to sea, and it isn't a matter of geography either, as it don't make any difference whether he was raised inland or on the coast. I have been shipmates with men that were raised in the corn belt of the west that were excellent sailors. My first experience was in fishermen out of Boston to the Grand Banks, than which there is no better training for a man that intends to follow the sea. Next in 2, 3, and 4-masted schooners carrying ice from Rockland, Maine, to Cuba, lumber from Brunswick, Georgia, and coal from Norfolk to Boston and Providence.

"Any boy that makes the voyage around the Horn will have something to talk about for a long time afterwards, but there will be mighty few of his listeners that will know what he *is* talking about. Most of the men that have sailed on any of the old time clippers are, like myself, pretty well up in the sixties, and a considerable number are in Sailors' homes, and before many more years have passed most of these old 'Shellbacks' will have weighed anchor for their final voyage. [This was written in the 30's.]

"There has been a lot of controversy about what country produces the best sailors. I have sailed under four flags: American, British, Italian, and Spanish. I have had nearly all nationalities as shipmates, and I don't believe *any* country produces the best, as I have seen many excellent sailors of *all* nationalities.

"I have had experiences at sea that I would not care to live over again. I had some pretty good times also, but taking it as a whole it was mostly grief. Sailors, as a general rule, are a pretty good class of men. In the American ship referred to earlier, we had a hell afloat in our voyage from New York to San Francisco, via Rio Janeiro. As you know, sailors have a 'chantey' for every job aboard ship, but there were no 'chantey's' on her after we passed Sandy Hook. The third day out we went aft in a body and complained about the food which was the very worst any of us had ever had. The Captain told us the food was good enough for a bunch of wharf rats, and he said some other things that I cannot put on this page, ordered us forward, and as we did not move fast enough to suit the mates they waded into us with belaying pins and beat us up plenty. If we hit back, that would be mutiny, of course.

"However, in the second dog watch that evening we passed the word that we would teach that Skipper a valuable lesson. A sailor usually loves his ship because it's his home. But we said: 'To hell with her. The first time we get into a gale and have to shorten sail, we will make a darned slow, sloppy job of it and let the rags blow out of the gaskets.' We got it about the 8th day out, off Hatteras. We passed the gaskets so loosely nearly half the sails were blown to ribbons. We bent new ones, and lost them before we got to Rio. Two days before we got to Rio we had another gale. The second mate struck the man at the wheel in the face because he was half a point off the course. The helmsman knew better than to do it, but he let go of the wheel and she came up 'all standing' and shook the fore and main to'gallant masts out of her. Hell broke loose, but we went about the work of cutting away the gear just as calmly as if she was tied to the dock. We tried to jump her in Rio, but could not get away as we lay out in the harbor. The Skipper disrated the second mate for striking the man at the wheel and the consequent loss of the upper sticks. The old man sent him forward, and when a couple of the boys got through with him he wasn't worth picking up. He never turned to with the watch he was in but was paid off in Rio.

"We sent new sticks aloft in Rio, bent new sails that we had made there, and before leaving port the Skipper called us to the break of the poop, threatened to put us in irons, said he would have us put in prison for insubordination and mutiny, threatened to shoot us, hang some of us from the yardarm as an example to the others; but as the grub did not get any better, neither did the crew. We had a hell of a time getting to the Horn, got off our course through compass error and came near piling up on Staten Island, about 60 miles east of Cape Horn on July 4th, 1886. Twelve days we 'laid to' off the Horn in a westerly gale that would blow the hair out of your head, lost a few more sails, and to make a long story short, we limped into Valparaiso 104 days from New York, with nine of the crew down with scurvy and the Skipper with a broken leg. We jumped * her in Valparaiso and glad of the chance to do so.

"Many a spar has been lost through the sullen response of a badly treated crew. Many a sail has been blown out of improperly tied gaskets. With a willing crew that jumps to it and knows their business, a ship may carry her royals and to'gallants'ls to the last moment. With a sullen, ill-treated half-starved crew it means take everything in and reef down as soon as the glass falls, or you will lose sails and spars. As in our case, this means longer, more expensive voyages lengthened by many weeks, without mentioning the added cost of the new sails and cordage, and the risk of losing the ship.

"In my experience I have found that deep-water sailors treated like *men* are the most loyal, active, dare-devil bunch in the wide world. They will put up an awful fight to save a ship they love, in which they get decent food and fair treatment. By this I do not mean that they must be coddled, because sea discipline must be maintained at all times. Treated as dogs, like we were, they can be sullen and unresponsive, caring less than nothing either for their own lives or for that of the ship. We had a *good* crew on the ship above mentioned, amongst which we had five Liverpool Irishmen that, to use a sailor's expression, 'were hard men to shave'. I really believe that after the Liverpool gang declared themselves that the remainder of the crew were more afraid of them than they were of the Skipper and the two mates. She was a 2100 ton ship. Her com-

* Deserted.

plement was 24 men before the mast. We sailed from New York with 17. Bad as she was, she sure was a beauty, and I still contend that the finest sight in the world is a full-rigged ship under sail."

There speaks the authentic voice of the foremast hand. I met the writer by chance, travelling in a train in the mid-west. He was a rugged man and he still looked what he was, a Cape Horn sailor, though he had become a large employer and a wealthy man when I knew him. His views, in my opinion, are wholly sound. The substance behind most stories of mutinies was the ill-treatment of the men, and this was more often stupid than intentional. Stupid officers made poor ships. The foremast hand, though he had the protection of merchant shipping acts of several nationalities, did not usually get a square deal from officials ashore. He could complain to his consul, if he could get ashore, but there was little hope of justice that way. It is fair to add that consuls had to listen to many frivolous complaints, and there were always sea-lawyers. The only real remedy a sailor had in a bad ship was to desert her, and he was always ready to do that. In some ships the crew were hazed deliberately in order to drive them to desertion to save their pay, perhaps, or because the ship had no charter in the port to which she was bound, and poor hope of getting any. So the men were driven out to save the expense of keeping them. This was a practice met more often in American ships than in others, and one of the reasons for that was that very few Americans served in their own ships. Others had no real redress.

Just as some crews were deliberately driven until they deserted when that suited the master's plans, others were kept compulsorily aboard, and even sent to jail for alleged mutiny in order that they would be delivered back to the ship on sailing-day, and so compelled to leave with her. This sort of thing happened, for example, in the famous clipper *Marco Polo* during the Australian gold-rush days. Sailors and everyone else cleared out when they could and went off to the gold-fields, but the master of the *Marco Polo* intended to keep his crew. So he had them arrested on a charge of mutiny and, though they were entirely innocent, the case was never heard. The ship sailed

before the trial came on, and the master withdrew the charge
on condition that the crew were returned aboard. Then he sailed.
Those men had no redress. Indeed, it was reported afterwards
that most of them had better quarters and better food in the
Melbourne jail than they had aboard the clipper. They had
all night in, and all they had to do was to pick some oakum.
They were treated quite well, and they responded by polishing
up the jail magnificently. The sailor was a born philosopher,
and they accepted their fate, going back to the *Marco Polo*
quite cheerfully.

When times were good, men were the more ready to desert.
Pay in British ships was about £2 or £3 a month, and in
others it was usually a little less. The practice was to give a
crew a month's advance of wages when they signed on, so that a
ship would arrive in Melbourne, say, after a three-month passage,
and the men would have a credit of £6 or so, at the most. This
was reduced by purchases from the slopchest, a shipboard store
run by the captain at sea prices. If wages were good ashore and
work was plentiful, then the loss of his few hard-earned pounds
did not deter any man from deserting. Apart from the sailing
liners, very few of the men had any family responsibilities or
ever intended to acquire them. When the ship was ready to
leave she had to get a crew together as best she could, and it
was usual to take men from sailors' boarding-houses. Then they
had to be paid the wages ruling in the port, or they would not sign
on, and it was no use hazing them, for the ship was bound home
for her pay-off anyway.

These sailors' boarding-houses served a useful purpose and
they were not all bad, by any means. In the great sailing-ship
ports away from the west coast of North America—places
like Sydney, Melbourne, Newcastle, Callao, Cape Town, Liverpool, Hamburg, Rotterdam, Antwerp—there were many such
boarding-houses. Sailors kept together ashore as well as afloat.
Many boarding-houses were kept by old sailors who had married
a barmaid or a publican's daughter, or set themselves up some
way or other. They offered cheap board, crowded quarters, a
thriving bar trade, no credit, and a quick ship out when the

sailor's funds were gone. A paid-off crew were good customers and it was worth catering for them.

Such establishments as Alec Townsend's in Callao, Rasmussen the Dane's place at St. Pauli in Hamburg, and Big Nellie's in Newcastle N.S.W. were known to sailors all round the world. Masters knew them, too, and went to them for crew. Of course, the seaman could go along to the shipping office whenever the spirit moved him, but it rarely did. He did not trust the world of petty bureaucrats. Men were signed on at the shipping office, before the shipping master, but usually only the confirmed indigent and the complete no-good were to be found there. Sailors had a fine sense of loyalty, even to boarding-house keepers, especially to those who were themselves sailors and treated them at all decently. A welcoming smile from Big Nellie as she operated the bar-room pumps was a lasting bond, though Nellie had a heart of solid marble. Nellie died a rich and respected citizen after a long and prosperous career. Here and there in old sailors' homes, she is still remembered. She had a tremendous memory and a remarkable flair for never forgetting a face and the name that went with it. Charlie Müller told me that whenever he showed himself in Nellie's she always knew him, though he might have been away for years. The same thing applied to all her other customers, though she numbered them by the thousand.

Charlie Müller is one of the few real old-timers still surviving, in the year 1953. He went to sea in 1890 in the barque *Luna* and he was at sea until 1939, always in sailing-ships—all sorts of sailing-ships, his own German, French, British, Australian, American, New Zealanders. He was in at least three of the 'P' ships besides the *Potosi*—the *Prompt*, *Parma*, and *Posen*. He was an able seaman in the American ship *John Currier*, in the French ship *Leon Blum*, in the Britishers *Fulwood*, *Lodore*, *Miltonburn*, in the Germans *Melete*, *Melpomene*, *Octavia*, and many more. He was in a dozen little South Seas barques and brigantines and schooners whose mellow-sounding names are now forgotten— the little *Silver Cloud* and the *Senorita*, the white barquentine *Handa Isle*, the barques *Aldebaran*, *Antiope*, and *Manurewa*,

the swift schooner *Huia*. Charlie was boatswain with the famous
Count Felix von Luckner (who himself had served for years
as a foremast hand in all sorts of sailing-ships, though the Count
is hardly to be considered as the usual type of seaman). At the
age of past 70, he escaped from the Russian zone of Germany
and got to Hamburg, where he was still ready to ship out
under sail. But Rasmussen the Dane's had gone and all the
other sailors' boarding-houses, and so had all the ships. When
I last saw Charlie he was waiting for a place in the Hamburg
Sailors' Home, and I hope he gets it.

   Charlie went to sea from a boarding-house. It was the way to
go. Here is his own account of his first voyage.

   "In April 1890 I left school, and although my father wanted me to
enter his business (he had a printing and paper box factory) and I
happened to be his only son, I did not want any of that life, but wanted
passionately to go to sea. I don't know where I got this notion from,
none of my folks had ever seen the ocean or a sailing ship, and we are
all South Germans, (Black Forest people). I kept pestering my parents
and at last they gave in and sent me to Hamburg, where my father had
a business friend. This man put me into a cab and we drove to Altona,
where he knew a boarding master and deposited me with a gentleman
who kept a sailors boarding house in the Grosse Bergostrasse and just left
me there. I had enough money to pay a couple of weeks board, and after
about 10 days stay in that house I was told to report on board the 800 ton
bark *Luna*.

   "Next day we signed on for a voyage, which should last more than
two years. We were at the shipping office punctually at 10 o'clock the
next day and there for the first time in my life I made the acquaintance
of real sailors.

   "The *Luna* was a small bark of 800 tons and had a total crew of
15 men all told: Captain (who was over 70), first and second mate, carpenter, cook, 6 able seamen, 2 ordinary seamen and 2 boys. She was a
composite ship, built 1885 by the Germania Werft at Kiel. We signed
articles for a voyage from Hamburg to Jaluit in the Marshall Islands,
which were a German possession at that time, and we were loaded with
general merchandise, tools and trade goods etc.

   "On May 10th 1890 the ship was ready for sea and all hands being
on board, the tug boat got a hold of us and towed us down the river Elbe
as far as Cuxhaven. The wind being out of the east, the Captain dismissed
the tug and we soon had all the canvas on her. I don't think I was much

of a help that first day making sail. But I remember being chased around plenty by either the master or by the sailors. Those six able seamen were the kind one don't meet nowadays any more. The youngest of them was 45 years of age and the others were all between 50 and 60. Four of them were Germans and they all came from Danzig or Memel. The other two were Danes and they had been in German ships for many years. The wages for an A.B. was 50 Marks a month in those days, that would be about $10 in American currency. The two ordinary seamen were second voyagers. They came out of one of those tobacco ships, which used to trade to New Orleans and brought tobacco back in heavy hogsheads. The ordinary seamen received 24 Marks and we boys got 10 Marks a month and no advance. There was of course a slopchest on board, but there was only tobacco to be got out of it, and as we boys were not allowed to smoke, we did not buy anything.

"Life in German ships was very hard for boys in those days. In port I had to get up at 4 in the morning and scrub the focs'l floor and the table, having to move all the seachests out on deck and make no noise so as not to wake the sailors. The focs'l was in a house abaft the foremast, and there was also the galley and the cook's room in the same house. The food could be reached through a hole in the bulkhead, which divided the galley from the focs'l, which was very handy in bad weather. The carpenter had his shop forward underneath the focs'l head and his room was aft, which he shared with the second mate. After I had scrubbed the floor and the table, I had to move all those chests back again and then it was time to rouse the sailors. Half past 5 the table had to be set for coffee and at six o'clock it was turn-to for all hands. The decks were washed down and at 8 all hands went in for breakfast, which lasted half an hour. Turn-to again till 12, then dinner till one, work again till 3.30 and take 20 minutes for afternoon coffee and all hands knock off at 6 o'clock. But there was no knock off for us boys. We had to sweep the decks, put all the gear away, set the table for supper and after supper wash the dishes and they were inspected by one of the A.B.'s. Then we could sit outside on the hatch till it was time to turn in. I was not allowed to smoke or join in the conversation with the men and generally at 8 sharp I was chased into my bunk. I was the boy for the focs'l and the other boy had the cabin. In between I had to help the cook peel potatoes, clean the pig sty (we had two grunters along) and do odd jobs around the decks and so by 8 o'clock I was good and ready for my bunk.

"As soon as the sails were all set, the watches were set. All hands mustered aft and the mate and second mate picked their men. I was in the mate's watch, the port watch. In German ships we had the following watches. Supposing the port watch had the morning watch from 4 to 8, then the Starboard watch relieved at 8 of course, but the Port watch was

not allowed to go below, but had to stay on deck till 10 o'clock. At 10
we went below till 12 o'clock when we had our dinner and came on deck
again at ½ past 12. Now the Starboard watch, who had the forenoon
watch, did not go below till 3 o'clock, they just went in for their dinner
and had to start work again at 1 o'clock. We called these watches 10
and 3, and they were a real nuisance to my way of thinking. The afternoon watch was relieved at 6 o'clock p.m. and the other watch took over
from 6 till midnight. Then came the watch from 12 to 4 a.m. and then
again from 4 till 8 a.m. The last time I had these watches was in the
Potosi in 1901, but they were done away with around 1902 I believe, and
I am sure nobody was sorry.

"We had a fairly good run through the North Sea and the Channel
and soon picked up the North East trades, and then I was introduced to
the wheel and learned steering. And in fine weather we boys often stood
4 hours at the wheel, because the men had to work and so it fell to us
boys to steer the ship. The able seamen of course taught me all about
seamanship, mostly in their spare time, and they were quite proud when
we picked up quickly whatever they showed us.

"I remember, we had quite a long time in the Doldrums, but had a
good South East Trade afterwards. Around the Cape of Good Hope we
went and then ran our Easting down until we shaped up for the Sunda
Strait, passed Anjer and then the Philippines and, after a slow but
uneventful passage of 169 days, dropped anchor at last in Jaluit. We laid
there about 3 weeks, discharging our cargo and took over a few tons
of copra for stiffening. Then we made sail for different islands in the
Carolines; I remember Ponape and we also called at Yap. In about 4
months time we had our little bark full of copra and made sail for
Sydney, where we arrived after a passage of 92 days from Yap. Sydney
made a great impression upon me, what with the beautiful harbour and
the port full of those stately tall sailing ships.

"We discharged our cargo of copra and got a few hundred tons of
coal for stiffening and then we went on to Newcastle, where we finished
loading the coal cargo and then we were bound for Guayaquil, in
Ecuador. We had a fairly good passage of 59 days, but it took us all
of a week to sail up the river to Guayaquil. This port had a bad name
that time on account of so much fever. We were lucky in so far as none
of our crowd was stricken. But we were told that a small German bark
from Elsfleth, which had been there before us, lost nearly half of her
crew with malaria. I don't remember much of our stay in that port,
because we were not allowed to go ashore. We got a cargo of stone nuts,
which are used to make buttons out of, and we also had some dried hides
and oxhorns and so on; after our cargo was all stowed, we drifted down
the river and started our long homeward bound passage around the Horn.

harlie Müller
→

↑ One hand for himself, one for the ship

↓ Cape Horn sailors—the port watch of the ship *Grace Harwar*. Mate on the right.

ABOVE LEFT
Some masters were tough—
the master of a Mariehamn
Cape Horner.

ABOVE RIGHT
Astronomical navigation
was not always a
strong point.

And others were just as
tough but didn't look it—
the master of the *Sagres*.
→

Working on deck could be really dangerous. Note the towering sea astern—that is not the horizon. ↑

He could wash clothes beautifully in a minimum of water, and without detergents.

e loved doing intricate ncy-work with cordage d line. →

He had a good head for heights.

He could climb anywhere: there was plenty of rigging to climb on.

A square-rigger's rigging offered many good spots to sit: when he could, the sailor sat.

We were bound for Antwerp and after a passage of 106 days, we picked up a tug off the river Schelde, which took us up to Antwerp. We were all paid off in Antwerp and I received the sum of about 250 Marks for this my first voyage, which lasted from May 1890 till July 1892, two years and three months. We all were sent back to Hamburg by train, our passage being paid, and I went back to the same Boarding Master and stayed 14 days in his house, till he got me another ship, which was a wooden bark of 1200 tons bound for New York to load case oil for Rangoon. But this is another story."

Charlie did his share of deserting. Once, after an 81-day run from Hamburg to Sydney in the heavy big ship *Melpomene*, he decided to clear out. He could not get on with the mate.

"I thought it best to pack my bag and clear out, which I did, before the ship was half discharged. I was the only one who cleared out, and as I very well knew the skipper would put the police on my tracks and of course would think I'd go to Newcastle to get another ship. I fooled them and went straight to the Sydney Railway Station, plunked down a 10-shilling gold piece, which left me with exactly 10 shillings cash, and asked the man at the ticket office to give me a ticket as far as I could go for 10 bob. So he gave me a ticket to a place called Tarana, N.S.W., just over the Blue Mountains and close to a town called Bathurst. Just before the train came to Tarana an elderly gentleman came into the compartment where I was sitting, and after he had scrutinised me for a while, he said: 'I am sure you are a runaway sailor.' So I told him yes, I had run away this very morning. It seems he took a liking to me, because before we came to Tarana, where he had a farm, he asked me whether I would work for him. So, having no money, I thought it best to say yes, and after our arrival in Tarana, I went with him to his place, which was about 10 miles from the station."

And there Charlie worked as a farm-hand for four months. He had no intention of changing the sea life for a farmer's and, when he considered his ship had sailed, he went down to Sydney and promptly shipped out as able seaman in the little *Silver Cloud*. That was the beginning of several years in the southwest Pacific, which he thoroughly enjoyed. The life in those small sailing-ships was usually a pleasant one. Those ships sailed under the Australian or New Zealand flags and the men were treated well in them. But Charlie was a born deepwater sailor and,

after a while, he was off again in a big Limejuicer round the
Horn, shipping from Nellie's place in Newcastle. Here are some
of Charlie's reflections on those boarding-houses:

"Three of us, an Englishman and two Germans, went into a boarding
house, which was kept at the time by a Negro and his white wife. Now
while I am about it, I may as well give a little talk about these boarding-
houses in Newcastle. This negro, a fellow with the name of Joe Hinds,
kept a so-called hard-up boarding house, and we should not have gone
there in the first place, as we had money, being regularly paid off. But
we thought we could get an American ship from there, and this Mr. Joe
Hinds promised us to get us the next ship bound for 'Frisco. The place
sure was a bit of a surprise. The house was crowded, every bed was taken,
in some of them slept two, and four or five men slept on the floor on
straw mattresses. After a week or ten days, no ship being forthcoming,
the three of us thought it best to clear out before our money had melted
away, and so we left the house and took passage to Melbourne in one
of the coasting steamers. There was another boarding house in Newcastle, kept by a very famous woman by the name of Big Nelly. Now
Nelly was known to every deep-water sailor; in fact she was known all
over the world. She used to be a barmaid in an equally famous pub in
Newcastle—the Black Diamond in Hunter Street, and then in the
Clarendon. What that woman did not know about a sailing-ship was not
worth learning."

Nellie shipped him in the barque *Lodore*, a hungry and poor
sailing-ship, according to Charlie. She was 68 days to the Horn
which is remarkably poor going, and a little while afterwards
the crew were reduced to grinding up wheat from the cargo to
get something to eat. 'Hunger and ease' was the slogan in the
Limejuice ships, meaning that they had big crews and not enough
to eat. The *Lodore* had a big crew and they were not worked
hard. Like all British ships, she had to comply with a manning
scale which was an imposition of bureaucracy that a few bad
owners had brought upon themselves. It was foolish to overman
sailing-ships, just as it was foolish to underman them. Most of
the able seamen in the *Lodore* were Welshmen, and Charlie
speaks very highly of them both as shipmates and as seamen.
The crew had to go hungry from off the Falkland Islands until

the ship touched at Flores in the Azores, and the whole passage to Queenstown took 154 days.

A voyage or two after that, in a very hard ship, Charlie felt compelled to desert again. This time he was in Guaymas, on the Gulf of California, in Mexico.

"The opportunity came one bright morning, when the captain wanted to go ashore to pay off the Finnish carpenter who had hurt himself. The lifeboat was alongside, mast stepped and sail ready for hoisting and so we slipped down, cut the painter and let the boat drift astern. No sooner we were clear of the ship than we hoisted our sail and before a spanking fair wind, we sailed the boat into a small bay and there and then sold the boat to a Mexican fisherman. And now started our long tramp through the State of Sonora towards Arizona in the U.S.A. We stuck together till we came to a place called Ortis. From there I jumped a freight train, which took me as far as Hermosillo, where I got a job picking oranges. Then I started to tramp again and after 16 days on the road I crossed the border at the town of Nogales and was happy to be in the U.S.A. The very same night I started as dishwasher in a small restaurant, where I stayed a couple of months and then went on further to Phoenix and Tucson, and from there made my way back again to Guaymas and Santa Rosalia."

In Santa Rosalia he soon got a deepwater ship again, bound back to Europe. So it went, year after year. It was a colourful and an adventurous life. Charlie Müller's experience differed from many only in that he survived longer and was more sober than most. His story would make a most interesting book, and so would those of any other of the real old-timers.

Charlie Müller was never shanghaied. He had too much sense for that, though it was commonplace for whole crews to be taken boldly away from ships in ports like San Francisco, Port Townsend, Portland, and Seattle. The men went as free agents, going off with the crimps' runners. Masters dared not prevent these louts from boarding their ships because they knew they would be compelled to go to them for crew, when the time came to leave again. They did not dare to antagonise them. The crimps were powerful, and they were a recognised institution. As soon as the anchor of an outward-bounder was

down, the crimps' runners would come over the side bringing
bad whisky and worse promises. Within half-an-hour the ship
which had come in with a fine band of clean-living men was trans-
formed into a bedlam, and the sailors, their minds besotted with
drink, were going off with the runners in boats to the shore,
shouting and cursing and looking forward to a job with unlimited dollars. Anything did as the promised source of riches,
even picking oranges, or serving in a steam-schooner on the
coast. The very same night, if there were a homeward-bounder
stuck for crew, those men might well find themselves, still stupid
with drink, shipped away for a Cape Horn voyage. The boarding-
master would pocket their advance of wages—generally two or
three months in San Francisco—and charge the ship whatever
he could get for providing her with a crew, usually $100 a head.

Time and time again the same men would submit to this
kind of treatment. Why? The answer was in part that no one else
welcomed them into those ports (or most others) and, coming
in after a long voyage, the sailor was not quite as other men. He
was not his normal self. He might be a man who had known
no home life since he was 10 or 12 years old, a confirmed wan-
derer; yet the smell of the land after a long voyage was exciting
to him, that first day, and put him off his balance. He became
a little light-headed, perhaps, just for that day. The runners
came quickly and took advantage of his vulnerability, at once.
Some men resisted all blandishments and stuck by their ships,
but they were very much in the minority. Many masters tried
to fight the racket, but it took a Jarvis or a Learmont to defeat
such scoundrels as the notorious McLevy and his kind. Jarvis
did it by daring to sail a great four-master with only his tradesmen and apprentices as crew, and so reached another port where
he could sign men in the proper way. Learmont did it by treat-
ing his crews so well that they refused to desert him. Jarvis
treated them well, too, but Learmont made a study of it. He
was curiously alone in that intelligent proceeding.

A milder form of shanghai tactics could be employed almost
anywhere, if a big Cape Horner was short-handed and knew
where to look for men, as she generally did. The Norwegian full-

rigged ship *Hovding*, for example—which was anything but a hell-ship—was not above man-stealing even in a port as sedate and law-abiding as Hobart in Tasmania. The *Hovding* loaded a cargo of blue-gum piles in the Huon river for Hull and required three men to complete her crew. The mate had become friendly with a Dane who was master of the schooner *Hawk*, an ex-pilot schooner which was in the trade between Tasmania and Melbourne. In addition to the master, the *Hawk* had a crew of two men, a Swede and an Italian. So when the *Hovding* was ready for sea, the mate went on a drinking spree with the crew of the *Hawk*, but he saw that they drank a good deal more than he did. At the end of the spree the mate very obligingly bundled the three into a cab and drove them back to their ship. They were too far gone to know what ship it was. Next morning they awoke in the *Hovding* far outside, bound for Cape Horn. The Dane was particularly angry and demanded that the Nor-wegian should return to Hobart to land him, but he might as well have saved his breath. All three had deserted other Cape Horners: there was a certain rough justice in the manner of their return. Within a day or two they had accepted their fate. They were good sailors and they worked well for the *Hovding*. All three swore that they would return to Tasmania and to the schooner *Hawk*, but of course they did not.

No matter how they might be treated, no matter how appall-ing the wastage, at no time was there a shortage of men or of boys to go in sailing-ships. There might be understandable local shortages of experienced men when times were good in some big port or other. There were man-created shortages as, for ex-ample, in ports where there was a callous exploitation of crews as saleable bodies, or in any port where a gold-rush might be in progress. But, on the whole, while the ships lasted, there were men and boys to go in them.

One other quality the sailing-ship sailor had, and that was an awareness of God. He did not talk about it. He abhorred what he called 'Bible-punching' in any form, and even seamen's missioners were apt to form a false impression of him. Yet he

was a man well aware of his tremendous debt to Providence.
Most foremast hands responded to the beauty of the ships they
served, and part of their reward lay in the great evidence for
Eternity which was displayed before them. The life was a satisfying one spiritually, in a mechanical age. Your true deepwater
sailor knew real loftiness of mind in his ship at sea, though he
was rarely if ever articulate about it, and he might be the
despair of the port authorities and the harbour police of half
the big ports in the world. It was his privilege, once away from
the distracting land, to live a man's life—a *whole* man's life—
and he knew it.

Chapter eight

THE MASTERS

THE MASTER is the sailor of the ship. All serious working and sailing of the ship is done by him and by him alone, even to giving the minutest orders. For all manoeuvres of any importance the chief mate (called invariably the mate) has charge on the forecastle-head, under the master, and the second mate works the hands, and works with them, on the main deck. Even the largest sailing-ships usually carried only two watch officers, the mate and the second mate. If there was a third mate, he had no watch. He was a kind of senior boatswain in the mate's watch during bad weather, and he worked all day during the trade winds. A few ships when on long good-weather runs in ballast, or on other occasions when it was predictable that there would not be much working of the ship, put the crew on the three-watch system instead of the universal two-watches. But there were never three watch-keeping officers, except in one or two square-riggers extravagantly run by the Australian government for a year or two during the first World War. The idea of using three watches in a British sailing-ship was to keep two watches on deck all day, and to use the three-watch system at night. In that way, they got more work out of the men. Instead of half the crew being below at any time, only a third were during the day, and two-thirds during the night. Finnish ships and Scandinavians generally achieved the same result—or better—by taking men out of the watches altogether and making them day-men in the good weather. American sailing-ships went one better, for they were

accustomed to allow none of the hands an afternoon watch below
at all.

It must be remembered that in a sailing-ship there were at
all times two distinctly different functions for the crew. The one
was *working the ship*, and the other was *working in the ship*—
cleaning, chipping, painting, overhauling the gear, carrying on
the daily routine, getting up the galley coal, greasing down the
masts, tarring-down aloft, and so forth. This sort of thing was
endless, but there were long periods when there was very little
working of the ship to be done at all, as for example when she
was making a long board through the trade winds, or running
westwards across the South Pacific bound for Newcastle in ballast from, say, Callao. At such times the set of the sails was
attended to at break of day and in the evening's last light and,
for the rest, the ship sailed herself in the hands of the man at the
wheel while everybody else got on with maintenance. With
the ship in ballast, they might all be down the hold chipping rust
and cleaning, for then they could get at the inside of the plates
which were ordinarily buried under cargo. The inside of the ship
was just as much in need of care as the outside.

The master said what was to be done and when. The mate
superintended the doing of it and he was left to get on with
that. The master had complete control of the internal arrangements and the whole economy of the vessel. As R. H. Dana remarks in his classic *Seaman's Friend*: * "Upon his character
and upon the course of conduct he pursues, depend in great
measure the character of the ship and the conduct of both officers
and men. He has a power and an influence, both direct and
indirect, which may be the means of much good and much evil.
If he is profane, passionate, tyrannical, indecent, or intemperate,
more or less of the same qualities will spread themselves or
break out among officers and men. . . He may make the ship
almost anything he choose, and may render the lives and duties
of his officers and men pleasant and profitable to them, or may

---

* Dana's *Seaman's Friend*, called the *Seaman's Manual* in England. My edition (the
  13th) published by E. Moxon & Sons, London, 1873.

introduce disagreements, discontent, tyranny, resistance and, in fact, make the situation of all on board as uncomfortable as that in which any human beings can well be placed. Every master of a vessel who will lay this to heart and consider his great responsibility, may not only be a benefactor to the numbers whom the course of many years will bring under his command but may render a service to the whole class and do much to raise the character of the calling."

It is a long time since Dana wrote that, but it remained true to the end of the sailing era and still has some truth now. "Master under God," the old charter-parties and insurance policies had it. As soon as the sailing-ship left port the master was absolute monarch. That was the tradition of the sea. As a class, British and American merchant service masters were good men. Many of them were splendid sailors and some were outstanding, but when the sailing-ship was in decline it was a different story. While many good men remained in the only sort of ship they knew and loved, it was natural that many of the better men would go into steam, and so would practically all the younger officers. Moreover, as the octopus arms of bureaucracy extended into every phase of seafaring life there were many jobs ashore for master mariners to fill—port and harbour-masters, dockmasters, examiners, surveyors, advisors on the staffs of ministries, nautical assessors, marine claims adjudicators, marine superintendents and the like—and these absorbed many of the best men. There always had been a considerable wastage of good personnel from the sea, but bureaucracy put a premium on it. In the great sailing days along the eastern seaboard of the United States there was a splendid source of recruits for the command of American ships from the owning and the sailing families of such a state as Maine—the Carvers, the Colcords, the Blanchards, and the like. Ships were more personal then, and command came to a man young, when he was full of fire and life. Those ships were happy ships, not at all to be confused with the notorious American hell-ships of later days. All that came to an end when Maine shipbuilding was allowed to languish.

In Britain every seaport town and every country village
could produce its quota of master-mariners. There, too, command
came young in the days of sail. Instead of a comparatively few
large ships hogging all the cargoes, there were a great many small
ships. The North Atlantic trade was carried on to a great extent,
within living memory, in ships of incredible smallness, such as the
Portmadoc schooners from North Wales and the little Breton
ketches, and the host of small square-riggers out of Newfoundland, New Brunswick, and Nova Scotia. In the long-voyage
trades a thousand-ton ship was a big ship, even as late as 1890.
This meant that there were plenty of commands, and promotion
came quickly to the deserving. Looking up the careers of some
twenty representative British shipmasters, for example, I find
that the average sea service of the lot before reaching command
was seven years. They were 23 or 24 years old when first appointed master. British regulations required an officer-aspirant
to be 17 before he could sit for his certificate as second mate,
19 as mate, and 21 as master. In America, masters from New
England were often even younger, though there might be a
hoary old mate—a friend of the family—to keep an eye on the
excessively juvenile during his first voyage.

All this died fast with power. Britain, being the leader in
industrialisation, industrialised shipping, too, and no one can
deny that she has made a great success of it as far as the running
of a vast and efficient merchant marine is concerned. The conditions both for men and officers have changed out of all recog-
nition, as has the work. In the old days of the square-rigged ship,
even masters knew at the best only a dubious security, unless
they had the good fortune to be employed by an outstanding
line. Their financial rewards were poor. Pay for a master of a
big full-rigged ship was £13-10 a month, at a time when clerks
were paid £8. Pensions and paid leave were alike non-existent.
Far too often, the master was poorly received in the owners'
offices ashore (though this was never true of the really well-
run lines) and made to feel like the office-boy. His voyages meant
continuous and lengthy absences from home and all the amenities
of the shore, to say nothing of the severance of all family life.

The steamship offered better things, and very naturally he took them. In the last days of sail the only certainty a master could know was that his ship was on the way to a foreign flag or to the scrapheap. These were poor conditions to grant to men who were absolute monarchs!

It is not to be wondered at that some ships were poorly served. The remarkable thing is that so many of them were splendidly served, right up to the last. The traditions carried on so well by masters such as Richard Woodget of the *Cutty Sark,* Kemball of the *Thermopylae,* Fearon of the *Fitzjames* and half a dozen other ships, William Stuart of the *Lochs,* and many more, were not lightly to be discarded. These masters did their best for whatever ships they commanded, and they continued to do their best according to their lights. So it remained (with a few unfortunate exceptions) to the end of sail, despite the fact that there were far too many bad owners. If an owner was not worth his loyalty, what inducement was there for the master to do his best? Many owners were quite ruthless with the men who served them well. They could understand the upkeep of a ship but not that of men. One master equalled another, according to their way of thinking, and they wanted the last ounce of effort and the last cent of profit from whosoever had command in their ships.

Consider the example, for instance, of the ship *Araminta,* a Liverpool full-rigger in the Australian trade. The *Araminta,* which was a ship of only 800 tons though she carried 400 emigrants, found herself in the port of Geelong, near Melbourne, when a gold-rush was in progress. Of course the crew wanted to desert and be off to the gold-fields and, if they had done that, the ship would have had great difficulty in signing on men enough to form a crew when she left. More than that, such men as she did get would have been landsmen, mostly, and their wages were high. So the master of the *Araminta* called a conference of all hands the first night alongside at Geelong. The ship was to remain at Geelong for a couple of months, and then go up to Bombay to load for the homeward passage to Liverpool. The master told the men that he knew they intended to desert for

the gold-fields. He pointed out that, if they did, they would find
the gold-fields very hard, the cost of provisions and everything
else exorbitant, and nuggets and gold-dust difficult to come by. So
he made them a proposition, and that was that the whole ship's
company should go off together to the gold-fields as a unit,
still under his command—a couple of old ship-keepers being
appointed to look after the ship—and take their victuals with
them from the ship's supplies. They would remain on the
fields for two months, and then all come back together with
the profits from their prospecting, which would be shared among
them according to an agreed scale. In consideration of the fact
that they were taking the owners' victuals, they must agree to
the stoppage of all wages while they were away and to sub-
scribe to the payment of the ship-keepers, and they would allot
one third of all the gold they found as the owners' share.

The crew—there were thirty of them, though she was a
small ship—accepted this with pleasure, and off they all went, as
soon as the emigrants and their gear were landed. The master
of the *Araminta* must have been a good prospector, too, for seven
pounds' weight of gold-dust were brought back to the ship as the
owners' share, and that was worth a considerable sum of money.
Not all the crew kept their bargain, and half of them were missing
when it was time to return to the *Araminta*. It was impossible
to replace them in Geelong, and so the master put up another
sporting proposition. He told the loyal members of the crew that,
if they would work the ship to Bombay, he would share out the
deserters' pay between them, for they would earn it. This he did,
and the amount came to £8-10 for each of the loyal seamen.

The *Araminta* made a successful voyage and duly arrived
back in Liverpool with a contented crew, a good Indian freight,
and an excellent bonus of seven pounds of gold-dust for the
owners. The owners accepted the gold-dust, and promptly
brought an action against the master to recover the deserters'
wages which he had disbursed to the crew. Everything that
master had done, although perhaps unusual, had been in the
owners' best interests. He had prevented mass desertion in Melbourne and avoided the need to engage an expensive crew at that

port. The owners had lost nothing, and had gained a good deal. Their share of the gold-dust was worth a hundred times more than the cost of the victuals expended to earn it, and the victuals would have been used in any event. The case came before the Admiralty Court in due course, where the learned judges had no choice but to find for the owners. The master was absolute monarch of all he surveyed at sea, but not in port. He had exceeded his powers in making that sporting agreement. The senior judge left no one in doubt as to his own views, for he refused to grant the owners their costs which absorbed most of the money from the gold-dust. If they had had the common-sense to stand by their captain's very intelligent arrangements, they would have profited much.

How could an officer be loyal to owners who were so narrow-minded and stupid? There were many such owners, unfortunately, although there were also many good ones. It was the same poor owners who later developed the useless big cargo-carrier when they might have built a fleet of *Potosi's* and *Preussen's*.

What sort of man was the typical Cape Horn shipmaster, at his best? There was in truth no type. The public is familiar with tales of Bully this and Bucko that, braggarts who shouted "Hell or Melbourne in 60 days", exhibitionists who were accustomed to fling a bucket of salt water over themselves when leaving the land to signify that they washed themselves free of all its softening influences, and so on. There were such characters, undoubtedly, but they were very much in the minority. One quality most sailing shipmasters shared if they were worth their salt at all, and that was that they were natural gentlemen. The life made them that way. I have known a good many, though it was 1919 when I first went to sea. I met them ashore afterwards —men like Fearon, Jarvis, Learmont, the Murchison brothers Finlay and Murdo' (I sailed with Murdo'). These were all masters in sail of wide experience. They were quiet-spoken clean living men, though they could make noise enough when it was necessary. Though there was—and still is, in some cases—the undefinable stamp of the sea about them all, only another sailing-ship man would know it. Apart from that, there was nothing to distinguish them from their fellow citizens—no change of gait, no habit of speech, none of the alleged hall-marks of the Cape Horn seaman. They had the look of men accustomed to authority. Jarvis looked like a retired and benevolent old judge, when I knew him.

His career and his accomplishments are I think interesting, for Captain J. C. B. Jarvis was one of the small band of ship-masters who, serving sail in its extremity, did *not* leave things as he found them. There were many competent shipmasters who sailed ships well and looked after their crews, but the number who really made an important contribution to the science of sailing and the perfection of the square-rigged ship was always very small. On the whole, masters were an extremely conservative lot. I believe for instance that Jarvis was the first ship-master to clew sails to the yardarm. Before his time, they always clewed to the bunt of the yard which was all very well in the days when big crews were carried as a matter of course, because merchant ships had to be fought as well as sailed, and a high rate of mortality had to be allowed for from other causes. Square sails were clewed up to the quarters of the yard and always had been, with the result that an enormous tent of canvas had to be rolled up at a place where comparatively few men could get at it. It made a good stow. Ships with their sails rolled up in that manner with the clews poking out like dogs' ears and every gasket in its place, bound round and round the yard, looked all "shipshape and Bristol fashion" to the old-time masters, though they knew quite well that the great bunt of sails could—and often did—knock men from the yard, that it was brutal, unwieldy, and dangerous, and that it need not be tolerated for a moment. Jarvis found the cure. He simply shifted the clewlines out to the yardarms. Sails then could be clewed up much more easily and could be man-handled aloft with far greater speed and safety, for as many men as could fit along the yard could work at the canvas. Yet for hundreds of years no one had dared even to suggest such an improvement.

Jarvis was a man with an unusual mind. He was a Scot from Tayport, in Fife. His father was a shipmaster before him, but he had to begin as a boy and ordinary seaman. His first ship was a 250-ton wooden barque named the *Grecian*, in which he served for two years in the Western Ocean trade. (The North Atlantic was the sailors' 'Western Ocean'.) After a year in another old-timer named the *Premier*, he was a long time in the wooden *Earl Dalhousie*, a ship which was carrying emigrants to Australia. He was in that ship a total of eight years—two voyages as third mate, two voyages as second mate, one voyage as mate, and two voyages as master. Next he was master of the *Cicero*, a barque, and then of a big steel ship, the *Earl of Dalhousie*, which replaced the old wooden ship. After that he commanded the well-known ship *Duntrune*, and the four-masted barques *Lawhill* and *Alcides* in the case oil trade. He retired from the sea in 1921 after having been 49 years at sea and in command since he was 23, for 43 years.

The *Earl Dalhousie*, although a small ship, spent most of her time in the passenger trade. When there was a shortage of emigrants for Australia she took Azoreans from St. Michael's to Honolulu at £13-10 a head out round the Horn, and paid quite well at it. The Azoreans were imported as labour for the sugar-cane plantations; when I was in the Hawaiian Islands a year ago some of them were still there. They were tough stock. Some of them, even then, still remembered Captain Jarvis, who was a youth of 24 when they knew him. The *Earl of Dalhousie* was a steel tramp of no particular merit, but Jarvis soon made a name for her. On one occasion, arriving under his command at San Francisco with her coal cargo afire, Jarvis succeeded in keeping the burned and scorching side away from the tug and so was towed in at proper towage rates, instead of salvage. Jarvis loved doing things like that. The quest for 'salvage' was one of the curses of the sailing-ship life, for a lame duck injured through any cause was regarded as fair plunder by any and all tugboats and other shore-based organisations. Far too many of them were interested not in succouring the damaged vessel but in extracting the utmost profit from her plight.

They made no profits out of Jarvis, even when later the same towboat pulled the ship over in San Francisco Bay, and capsized her. She was very lightly ballasted at the time and Jarvis was rescued from her upturned keel just before she went down. Even then, the Scots shipmaster turned the occasion to one of considerable profit for his owners, for the underwriters agreed to pay a compromise £16,000 on the ship from her total insured value, which was £23,000. The *Earl of Dalhousie* lay for three months on the bottom of San Francisco Bay. Then Jarvis raised her, rigged her again for less than £5,000, and sailed her away. The crimps would not give him a crew except for an extortionate sum. As the ship was bound for Iquique to load nitrates there for Europe and the run from San Francisco to the Chilean port was a fine-weather one, Jarvis sailed with his officers, petty officers, and apprentices—twelve hands all told. They were 63 days without incident to Iquique, where good crews were to be had cheaply. Ship repairs were expensive in San Francisco, by comparison with the Scots charges. The *Earl of Dalhousie* belonged to a Dundee shipbuilder, and Jarvis brought her home with the saloon and all the after accommmodation gutted because he thought the prices asked for the job in California were too high. The afterguard camped in the washed-out poop for the whole long way home. Even then, the ship made a day's run that voyage of 346 miles—"The best I ever had out of her or any other ship", Captain Jarvis told me, "and the best week's sailing I ever had was 2150 miles."

Jarvis thought nothing of spending eight months in a ship without even a proper bunk to sleep in, and driving the ship along with or without a crew at a furious rate whenever he got the chance. The *Earl of Dalhousie* earned her owner £10,000, he told me, from that voyage on the bottom of San Francisco Bay, but Jarvis didn't try any more voyages of that kind.

The *Earl of Dalhousie* could sail quite well and so could Jarvis's next ship, the *Duntrune*. She was built in 1875 for the Dundee Clipper Line, and was intended for the passenger trade to Australia. Jarvis commanded her for six successful years, during which he raced her across from South Australia once to Valparaiso in 31 days at an average nine knots for the whole 6930 miles. There were no passengers aboard at the time. The emigrant trade was popular with masters, for they were paid a bonus of two shillings a head on all who were safely landed. The emigrants had to look after their own quarters and, indeed, look after themselves generally. They had time enough. A passage out in less than 90 days was reckoned good. The Dundee clippers took them for £15 a head second class and as little as £5 steerage, which could not have shown much profit even to a Scotsman.

On another occasion, Jarvis got among icebergs on the run towards the Horn and the *Duntrune* struck a large ice-island by night, and stove in her bows. Though the ship was floating on her collision bulkhead he brought her home, sailing the handi-capped ship from the wrong side of Cape Horn for another seven thousand miles. Her bowsprit had been knocked away by the ice and her fore topmast came down, but he rigged jury spars and restored the ship to reasonable trim. He could have run for the Falkland Islands or for Montevideo in distress, but Jarvis was not the man for that. In the Falklands were some brother Scots who were notorious for the prices they liked to charge ships driven into their haven by Cape Horn damage, and Montevideo was worse. The *Duntrune* was still afloat and seaworthy enough, and Jarvis sailed her on. After all, by the time he was in the latitude of Montevideo the ship had come through the worst weather. If she survived that far she might as well sail on, for the trade wind zone was before her and it would be summer when she came up to the North Atlantic.

It was in the *Duntrune*, too, that Jarvis brought his brace-winch experiments to perfection, and she was the first vessel fitted with them. She was a handy ship and, with the brace-winches, one small apprentice could swing all the main yards in good weather. Jarvis set about improving the working rigging of the *Duntrune* in every possible way which occurred to his fertile mind. Some of these improvements have already been mentioned. Apart from the brace-winches they were all small, but their

cumulative effect was to save the owner at least £1 a day and
to enable the crew to be safely reduced. £1 a day was money,
then.

"Previous to being improved," Jarvis pointed out in a report
to his owners, "the vessel was none too well manned with 28
hands, only four of whom were apprentices. With any wind the
courses were always an all-hands job, and it was only in very fine
weather that the ship could be worked by the watch. After being
improved the average complement was 22 hands all told, and the
ship was thoroughly well manned. During long spells of bad
weather the ship was entirely worked by the watch on deck. No
matter what the weather was, even working short tacks, the watch
below was never required to work ship. Sail could always be
shortened and the ship has even been rounded to in a heavy gale
by the watch on deck.

"Although not a particularly fast ship, the season's record
passage was made in more than one instance which proved that
she was sailed for all she was worth. . . No tradesmen's bills were
incurred for repairs, either at home or abroad. All new sails
required were made aboard and all repairs of every kind were
executed by the crew."

A saving on maintenance costs of £1 a day and a saving of
six men in the crew were big items, in the sailing-ship days. Jarvis
had had to learn how to economise in man-power when he was
sailing the *Earl of Dalhousie* with a twelve-man crew. Saving the
underwriters the repair bill in Port Stanley or Montevideo for
the *Duntrune*'s ice damage was a much bigger item.

In the big *Lawhill* Jarvis had a ship after his own heart, for
she was full of 'gadgets'. She was a clumsy-looking ship with a
very square rig, without royals, and her steel topmasts were built
in one piece with the lower masts. Her topgallant-masts were
stepped abaft the topmast-heads instead of on the fore part
of them, and this, coupled with her rather squat rig, gave her an
ungainly appearance. Her wall sides and not too fine ends made
her look a poor sailer, too, and her big midships superstructure
(which was the same sort of thing the 'P' ships had) further
spoiled her appearance, in the estimation of sailing-ship sailors.

Yet she was in fact an excellent ship, a good carrier and a good sailer, and most economical of crew and gear.

Those queerly placed topgallant-masts were an American invention which had been developed by a Bostonian named Forbes to give MacKay's *Great Republic* double topsails. The idea was that the lower yard was supported from very near the topmast-head and the upper yard, which was supported by a long truss mounted on a strong parral, was hoisted on the topgallant-mast. This kept the two yards well apart, which was an advantage. It meant, too, that there was only one yard on the topgallant-mast, and so it could very easily be sent up and down without sending any yards down at all. The *Lawhill* traded a lot to New York, and this handiness was of great value when she was called upon to pass under the East River bridges. Much later, I was in the *Lawhill* myself (it was there I first heard of Captain Jarvis) and I can give my personal testimony that the queer rig, together with all the innovations the redoubtable Jarvis introduced, made her the handiest big ship I was ever in, or heard of. We sailed her to Australia with a crew of seventeen boys. At 17, I was one of her few able seamen.

Jarvis made bad passages as well as good. In the ancient *Cicero* he was once 168 days from San Francisco to the Channel, and he once had to wander three times across the greater part of the Pacific trying to induce the *Lawhill* to sail from Hongkong in ballast to New York, and took 176 days to make the passage. First he ran towards Hawaii, driven by a great gale. He sighted the Hawaiian Islands and, after that—some time after—the *Lawhill* was among the Solomons. Then the south-east trade forced her on the Australian coast. Out of that, she crossed the Tasman Sea and at last was able to run for the Horn. That passage she logged 26,000 miles, but there was no scurvy. Jarvis looked after his crew, who consisted on that run of nine young Japanese cadets, nine British boys, and three Japanese shoe-makers going to America for experience. All the Japanese were excellent sailors, said Jarvis. He put them in three watches, keeping two watches on deck by day and one by night, in the Scots fashion. The *Lawhill* took so long because her rigging had been

weakened when she was on her beam ends in a typhoon before
reaching Hongkong, and Jarvis was determined to put things to
rights himself. He did, but it took some time, and the weakened
ship could not be sailed properly. By the time she was on her
third crossing of the Pacific, she was in first-class order.

This passage in the *Lawhill* was a fast one compared with
her sister-ship, the *Juteopolis*, which was 287 days at sea on a
somewhat similar run. The *Juteopolis* (which ended her days as
the *Garthpool*, registered in Montreal and the last big square-
rigger to fly the Red Ensign) sailed from Ilo Ilo towards New
York with a cargo of sugar on April 30, 1903. She lay becalmed
in sight of the Carolines for two solid months. Over five months
out, she finally drifted into Honolulu, where her fresh water and
provisions had to be replenished. Setting off again with her bottom covered with barnacles, she made a painfully slow passage
to the regions of the Horn, and it was not until the middle of
the following February that she finally arrived at New York.
There was nothing wrong with the rigging of the *Juteopolis*.
Rather is that passage an example of what could happen to masters who did not bother to sail properly briefed. Any hydrographer could have routed the ship to avoid those zones of calms,
which were well-known. Some masters were notoriously pig-
headed, and the *Juteopolis* suffered her share of them. It is probable that the master chose that way to sail because it avoided
more land than the route through the Sulu and Celebes seas and
among the Indonesian islands, which he should have taken.

Jarvis had many a famous passage, too, though his ships were
not clippers—far from it. Once he sailed the *Duntrune* from the
Thames to the Equator in 17 days—"Luck," he said; "luck and
the brace-winches"—and on another occasion, he was 22 days
from the Cape to Sydney. But it is not as a driver that Jarvis
deserves to be remembered. There were many drivers. His
brother-shipmasters refused to have anything to do with most of
his innovations and looked upon him, indeed, as slightly mental,
but if they had exercised one-tenth of his ingenuity and rich
resource the British sailing-ship would have lasted many years
longer than she did. Jarvis could have produced an improved

Preussen, a six-masted barque carrying 10,000 tons. And he could have sailed her.

Captain James S. Learmont, like Captain Jarvis, was a Scot. He spent his boyhood in Port William in Wigtownshire, and his father had command of a coastal schooner. Learmont was off to sea at 12, too, though not in a deep-waterman. He spent his early youth in coastal vessels, and never regretted it. When he first went into deepsea vessels he was horrified at the standards prevailing. His training on the coast was in pure seamanship, for the schooners were *sailed,* but in one or two of the deepsea ships he served in as able seaman he learned more about how things should *not* be done than how to do them. For example, it was customary in many ships which were poorly commanded that the officers should give their attention almost exclusively to the work about the decks, to maintenance. They were not so much watch officers as deck foremen, and the trim of the yards in working hours—6 a.m. to 6 p.m—had to take care of itself.

Some masters, too, rarely showed themselves on deck from week's end to week's end, though the Lord alone knows what they found to do. They had spacious quarters below, for deepsea sailing-ships kept the big saloons of the old passenger-carrying days right up to the last, and the mates went in there rarely and then only by invitation. There was usually a small mess-room where they took their meals. The master had a three-room suite at least, to himself, and this almost always included a large saloon. So he could disport himself quite well, or drink himself to death if he wanted to. Learmont hated to see the sailing neglected. Sloppily set sails, untended gear, poor and unsupervised steering meant poor passages, and it was of little use to bring in a beautifully cleaned and painted ship if she arrived too late to keep her charter because she had not been sailed properly. Learmont was a bright youth, and he took due note of things. He determined that when he commanded a Cape Horn ship—which he was sure he would do—his officers would be watch-keepers *first,* and running the work would be left to the boatswain under their supervision as necessary.

Learmont was determined to serve sailing-ships, though he knew quite well that most officers were going into steam. When he was at sea and, indeed, to this day, it was possible for the embryo officer to present himself for examination without ever having been an indentured apprentice. So long as he could prove that he had served in deepsea ships for a minimum of four years and had references of good conduct covering that period, he could sit as a candidate for the second mate's certificate. The requirements in the 90's were nothing like as complicated or as academic as they have since become. The essence of the thing was practical and, so long as a reasonably intelligent youth, having mastered his seamanship, devoted sufficient attention to elementary navigation, signals (not so much of that) and the Rule of the Road, he should qualify. Learmont qualified in this manner as soon as he had his time served, and he was fortunate in meeting, in the forecastles of some of his ships, able men who were both competent and happy to tutor him in such navigation as he required. This was especially so in a lovely barque named the *Strathdon,* which was commanded by an outstanding master named Philip who had previously been in command of the beautiful clipper *Salamis.*

In most British sailing-ships in those days—and indeed until the end of the era—it was the practice to carry a number of apprentices, boys who were indentured to the owner to serve their qualifying sea time before sitting for their junior officers' certificates. As a general rule these were exploited shamelessly as misguided cheap labour and, even at the best, little interest was taken in them while the ship was at sea and none at all when she came to port. Masters and mates who had been reared in a tough school themselves were not inclined to offer better conditions to the youths coming after them. Many such apprentices profited splendidly from their sailing-ship experience, for the ships themselves offered infinite opportunities for character-building and the development of initiative, and other desirable qualities. There were, in later days, a few training ships, like Devitt and Moore's. These were excellent. In a few other ships, which were good sailers and well sailed and blessed by good commanders who took a real interest in their boys, conditions for the apprentices, too, were nearly ideal. Such a ship was the *Strathdon,* and Captain Philip's interest in youth extended to those in the forecastle who were anxious to improve themselves, as well as to his fortunate apprentices. Learmont profited greatly, and he resolved, too, that when he was in command, his apprentices would be treated as Captain Philip treated them.

The resolutions he made when he was before the mast were never forgotten. Learmont rose rapidly in his chosen profession. He was second mate of a Nova Scotiaman, a full-rigged ship with a deadweight capacity of 3000 tons, before he was 19, and in command of a big Cape Horner when he was 25. He might have had command earlier but he had wasted some time, for family reasons, by spending a trial year or so in steam, serving as an officer with the Union Castle company in the trade between the United Kingdom and Durban. The monotony and the poor prospects of promotion very soon sickened him of powered vessels.

His first command was a fine barque named the *Brenhilda* which carried 1800 tons of cargo and was handled by a crew of seventeen. The *Brenhilda* belonged to J. and J. Rae, of Liverpool and, like most sailing-ships of the late 90's and first decade of the twentieth century, tramped wherever she could get a cargo. A typical voyage was from Liverpool to Melbourne, thence to Newcastle N.S.W. for coal to Chile, and back round the Horn to Europe with nitrates. Learmont got good passages out of the *Brenhilda* with her somewhat small crew. From her he moved on to larger ships, the *Brenda* and the *Bengairn*. The *Bengairn* had begun life with another name as one of the Lyle sugar company's fleet, the *Pass of Brander*. She was a powerful big four-masted barque and Learmont handled her splendidly. These three ships tramped about the world, generally to Australia, the west coast of South America, and to San Francisco. Learmont soon made a name for himself as a consistent shipmaster, a good sailor, and above all, a man who looked after his forecastle hands and his apprentices.

He was in command of the *Bengairn* until 1910. It was then becoming increasingly difficult to get officers for British sailing-

ships, though there was a proportion of good old die-hards in
them until the last. It was almost impossible to get British crews:
most of Learmont's crews were young Finns who, like him, had
begun in small coasting schooners and barquentines. They were
excellent seamen. The difficulty of recruiting officers was not
made any easier by the stupid rule—made by the bureaucrats
ashore—that any man could qualify for what was called a 'Sail
endorsement' on his certificate if he could prove just twelve
months' service on deck in a sailing-ship. Such an endorsement,
once gained, could be carried right through the various grades
until the officer would be allegedly qualified to act as master of a
Cape Horn ship, though he had in fact never been a watch-
keeper in such a ship and his whole experience under sail was a
year as apprentice or as deckboy.

After suffering a few mates with such 'qualifications', Learmont ran his great four-master with senior apprentices as his
watch-keepers. He sailed the *Bengairn* a long voyage without a cer-
tificated mate at all, to the horror of his fellow-shipmasters. But
Learmont had brought up his apprentices himself, and he had
confidence in them. A promising lad who had been three years
under his care was as good an acting third mate as it was possible
to find, and the best of these could graduate easily to watch-keeping second mate. It was only when a mate sent by the owner
proved grossly incompetent that Learmont had to promote his
apprentice second mate to be acting mate. The boy was 18, the
second mate was 17½, and there was no third mate at all. The
ship was sailed and maintained splendidly. Learmont had the
sense to know that young officers were good officers, and he had
the confidence to give them their chance.

The significance of Learmont's contribution to the whole science of deepsea sailing lies in that act, I think. He showed that
masters and officers belonged to no high priesthood, as some of
them liked to think they did. There was no mystery about their
ancient calling. A boy of 18 could be an excellent officer, so long
as there was an intelligent master to bring him along and have
confidence in him. So long as the tradition of the sailing art remained unbroken, youth would provide the officers for such ships

The *Lawhill*, Captain J. C. B. Jarvis' famous command

A fate to be avoided. The ship is one of the queer
Vinnen five-masters. They were not a success.

The sails were their engines.

as had the good sense to train them properly and to employ them.

But Learmont's brother shipmasters frowned. So, of course, would the Officers' Federation (if it had been formed then), fearing exploitation on the part of the less scrupulous owners. Learmont went about his way and the *Bengairn* prospered. She was dismasted, and he rigged her again—*he* rigged her, with his boy mates. He did not pay the extortionate sums demanded by the waterfront repairers. She got upon her beam ends, bound from Newcastle with coal towards Chile—a road on which many, many a fine ship has gone missing—and he righted her and brought her back, the *only* ship to sail back in from that stormy road after her cargo had shifted.

One other great quality Learmont had. It was, unfortunately, a quality far more rare among shipmasters than it should have been. He set his face against dishonesty in any form, and would not tolerate it. A master of a Cape Horn ship with disbursements of all kinds to make on behalf of the ship, in all parts of the globe, had many temptations. There were established dishonesties which were winked at—'making' something on the shipchandlery by connivance with suppliers, 'winning' a little cargo at one port and selling it at the next, stealing by short deliveries, in league with dishonest agents, or by knowingly accepting less ballast than was charged, and so on. This business of ballast was a serious one. Sailing-ships had to buy ballast in order to remain upright and to sail and, if they had insufficient or what they had was not properly secured, they were running grave risks. There was an especial need of ballast when shifting from one port to another on the west coast of South America. The weather there was generally good and the light winds and currents reliable, at any rate during the greater part of the year. So shipmasters developed the pernicious habit (seeing that they were paid about £13 or £14 a month) of sailing with dangerously little ballast, much less than the owners thought they were paying for.

It was too easy. The proper number of tubs or baskets of ballast were put aboard, but each was far from being fully laden, and the net total of the amount short-loaded in a biggish ship

would be several hundred tons. The master signed for the full
quantity and the owner paid for it, the master and the rascally
agent sharing a considerable commission on the cost of the difference. This sort of thing was particularly dangerous when the ballast was poor stuff to begin with, as it was at Callao—runny
shingle dredged up from the bay, which was inclined to break
out of any box built for it, and roll with the ship.

Many ships succeeded in making short ballast runs with im-
proper ballast, of course, but a good many did not. Several fine
sailing-ships had gone mysteriously missing after loading ballast
in Callao, when Learmont came along. By that time the tradition
of short-loading was so thoroughly established that no bucket or
basket of ballast ever contained the correct weight, whether the
master was a party to the fraud or not. Learmont, having a good
idea what had happened to those missing ships (one of them, the
clumsy great full-rigger *Dalgonar,* had refused to sink and had
drifted 5,000 miles with her shifted and insufficient ballast, and
had fetched up on a reef in the Tuamotus) demanded that any
bucket he selected should be weighed, as his ballast was being
put aboard. He was within his rights, but the uproar was terrific.
He had, in the end, to take his fight to the Minister at Lima
before he won, for some of the port authorities had been doing
quite well out of it. But Learmont *did* win, and his ship *was* properly ballasted. After that, no other sailing-ship was posted missing
out of Callao, through that cause.

Learmont always gave his crew sufficient to eat and went to
pains to buy them good fresh food in any port where it was available. There was a very ancient 'racket' in supplying seamen's
food, so thoroughly rooted in seafaring that ships' butchers and
shipchandlers found it difficult to believe that they had really
come upon an honest man. Learmont sometimes had to get some
apprentices together and land to do the ship's shopping in the
markets himself. He did not mind that. One reason why dishonesty flourished was that masters had to have receipts for their disbursements. It did not matter how dishonest the receipts might
be (so long as they were apparently reasonable). Learmont knew

his owner well enough, and was trusted by him. He could buy in
the market from illiterates who supplied no receipts: his expendi-
ture was sufficiently vouched for by the contentment of his crews.
They worked splendidly for him, and they did not desert. The
owner knew that quite well. So did other owners, but many of
them did not implicitly trust their masters.

Learmont was 35 years old when he left the sea and entered
the pilotage service. I knew him well. He piloted the *Joseph
Conrad* for me out of Harwich as far as the Straits of Dover, and
I was glad to have him aboard. He was a big man, always cheerful, and full of energy. He retained in full measure his enthusiasm
for sail and for doing things properly. In 1953 he is still hale and
hearty. He has recently written a book which is a most excellent
piece of work, well worth not only reading but studying. *Master
in Sail*,* he calls it, and that is just what he was—a *master* in sail.
It is a great pity there were not more like him.

I have given a picture of two excellent shipmasters. I have
written of them at some length, perhaps, but it is because I know
them. There were many others, of all nationalities. Elsewhere in
this book I have written something of the career of Robert Hilgendorf and Richard Woodget of the *Cutty Sark,* and Boye Petersen and Nissen, of the great German five-masters. Good seamanship knew no national bias and it is absurd to pretend that it did.
A 22-year-older from Bath, Maine, a braw tall Scot from Fife
or the Western Islands, a German from the Friesians or the cold
Baltic coast, a Dane from Marstal, a Norwegian, a Welshman,
a Portuguese from Ilhavo, a Finn from Åland, an Australian, a
New Zealander, a Frenchman, an Italian, a Nova Scotian, New-
foundlander, a man of Devon or of Kent—all these provided
material for the making of splendid Cape Horn shipmasters.
Command in sail was exacting and its demands were immense
and endless. They were not always met by any means, for they
were, above all, demands upon *character,* and the man without
real integrity of spirit had no hope of lasting success. But, granted

* Percival Marshall, London, 1950.

that, and good qualities of leadership, and indefatigable energy, skill, and determination, the rewards for the true spirit were immense and endless, too. If many were called and few were chosen, those few had a glimpse of glory. There was no other career comparable with it, nor is there likely to be again.

Part IV

———•◆•———

THE LIFE

Chapter nine

ECONOMICS

THE square-rigged ship, if she were to keep going at all, had to be made to pay her way. She had to earn a reasonable dividend on the capital invested in her, provide a livelihood for those who worked her, and earn the costs of a ship to replace her. Unless she did these things she must fail. Looking back on the capital costs of even the largest steel Cape Horners, in the 1950's, when a ship-owner thinks he is doing well to get a good tramp for half-a-million pounds and cannot get a firm price out of a shipbuilder at all (through no fault of the builders), they seem very low. £30,000 to £45,000 would build a good Cape Horner in the 1890's, with the very large four-masted barques costing perhaps a little more. The average investment was about £35,000 a ship, or something less.

I am speaking of new British ships. By the first decade of the twentieth century such ships were to be had, second-hand, at any-thing from £5,000 to £10,000, and £10,000 was considered a great deal of money to have invested in a sailing-ship. In 1910, big British sailers in good order were selling at the average rate of £2–2–6 (about $10) a register ton, and the reason for this was that, because of the competition from large cheap tramps, a properly capitalised deepsea sailing-ship, run in the ordinary way, could no longer earn her replacement cost. The top price paid for a second-hand Cape Horner a few years earlier was £4–7 a ton, which was paid by the French sailing-ship firm of A. D. Bordes for the ten-year-old steel four-masted barque *Achnasie* in 1907.

213

They had a bargain, for the first World War sent all freights spiralling up.

By no means all sailing-ships were sold to foreign flags when the big lines were forced or decided to give them up. A good many owners in Liverpool and at least one in London kept considerable fleets of square-rigged ships going for twenty years or more, though at no time did they contemplate building new ships. They bought second-hand ships cheaply, and they did not have to cover much capital depreciation or to consider the cost of replacement by new ships. They were simply running old ships to death. This was all very well while a sufficiency of second-hand tonnage was on the market to replenish their fleets but, very obviously, that state of affairs would soon come to an end. Ship-owning of that kind was not the backbone of a country's shipping, and could never be. Ships had to earn their replacement costs within their own earning lifetimes or, sooner or later, there must be no ships at all.

Sailing-ships, so to speak, grew up on a tradition of ventures and, to the very last, their voyages still remained ventures in a very real sense, though they were earning freights and no longer belonged to merchant-shipowners who sent them off with 'ventures' of their own. All this past way of voyaging was demonstrated very clearly to me when, after many years in European sailing-ships, I once had time to spend a year or so sailing with the Arabs in their big Indian Ocean dhows. At first all this dhow-sailing seemed remarkably complicated, from the economic point of view, until I began to realise that the Arab merchants and mariners were really still doing what our shipowners and seafarers had done for many centuries. There were some dhows which earned freights in the ordinary manner, which is to say that they carried merchant's goods to markets and the merchants paid them a fixed rate of hire for this service. The dhows I saw in this kind of trading were in the Red Sea, operating out of Aden. Others carried some goods for merchants and some ventures of their own.

But the really interesting dhows were those still carrying on in the traditional Arab manner, making the annual trading voyages from the Persian Gulf down to the western coast of India, or the Benadir coast and Zanzibar. There were over a hundred big ocean-going dhows in these trades operating out of Kuwait in the Persian Gulf, and I was able to make a voyage in one of these. There were also many more—I do not know how many—from Sur, near Ras al Hadd on the Gulf of Oman, and others from Trucial Oman and from the Hadhramaut ports also engaged in long-voyage ventures. These were all small dhows, and many of those from Trucial Oman were former Kuwait dhows which were both small and old. Their mainstay appeared to be the ancient migrant business down the east coast of Africa, with whatever ventures the captain, the merchants travelling with him, and his crew cared to bring along and had the funds—or the credit—to finance. The dhows were unbelievably crowded with passengers who came, I think, on the general principle that they could not be worse off than they had been at home, and the fare for the voyage to Africa was only a dollar or so, no matter how long they might be aboard. I was told that there were perhaps as many as two thousand dhows still trading round the coasts of Arabia then—the year was 1938/39—and half of them made long voyages or were prepared to make such voyages if the spirit moved them. The dhows I saw ranged from about thirty tons to 300 tons. I saw three or four large Kuwaiti and Persians which were in the latter class. The average size of the big deepsea Suri and Kuwaiti dhows was from 80 to perhaps 120 tons, European measurement.

I joined a Kuwaiti dhow at Aden early in December, 1938, just as she finished loading a venture in salt and various trade goods and was about to set off along the coast of the Hadhramaut to pick up passengers for the migrant trade, and to buy whatever ventures might seem readily saleable in the markets to which she was bound. She had already brought a full cargo of dates in packages from the Basra river, which she had sold in lots to merchants ashore at various small roadsteads along the coast of South Arabia and at Berbera, in British Somali-land. This distribution of Iraqi dates was the mainstay of the big deepsea dhow trade, and all the Kuwaiti and most of the Suri began their

annual voyages by shipping dates at Basra or near Fao, either for
Karachi, Bombay, or Cochin, or the East African round which
my dhow made. This trade was so important that the tonnage of
the ships was spoken of invariably in terms of their stowage-
capacities for the big packages of dates, never in European tons
or any other measurement.

On the economic side, the dhow I sailed with belonged nomi-
nally to the captain and, though she had a given name, she was
always spoken of as the *Boom* Nejdi—the *boom* (a double-ended
type of Kuwait dhow) belonging to the Captain from Nejd. In
fact, she belonged almost wholly to the merchants who also owned
the date plantations which gave her her initial cargo, but the
merchant financed the captain's family to build her—she cost
something less than £1,000 new, built on the beach at Kuwait—
because it suited him to control ships in this manner, since under
the rules of Islam there could be no insurance. To insure was to
fly in the face of Allah, but to hold the captain—and his family—
responsible financially for the ship was in keeping with tradition.
As far as I was ever able to find out (it was by no means easy to
know always what was going on, even though I was in the dhow
every day and night for about eight months) the merchant paid
the captain a fixed freight for the dates. They were the merchant's
venture, not the ship's, and he sent his younger brother to Berbera for the season to look after the sales and distribution ashore
there. Other brothers were stationed at Aden, Bombay, Basra,
and other strategic points, and there were close relatives at Mukalla, Jiddah, Calicut, and elsewhere. The brothers had financed
quite a fleet of big dhows—eight or ten of them, I think, using
various captains and their families as nominal owners. This
suited the captains quite well as they would not have had a ship
otherwise, and there were many avenues of profit open to them.
They had some of their own money in the ships, too.

With the money from the freight on the dates, the captain
bought a cargo of salt (there was plenty of that at Aden) and
cooking-stones, Hadhramaut honey, ghee in tins (imported from
Europe and not at all the genuine article), rice, and so forth. The
mariners, of whom there were about thirty, had each a chest of

his own of standard size, and these chests were kept in two rows on the raised poop where they were always in sight. A mariner could fill his chest with his own ventures, which were cheap perfumes, cigarettes, haberdashery, and so forth, with some Hadhramaut basketware bought in Mukalla. The dhow hawked her cargo—perhaps 'peddled' is the better word—down the east coast of Africa, putting in wherever there was a good bazaar and so a demand for her goods, and the Italian or British authorities had not made trade impossible. (Currency restrictions on the Benadir coast of Italian Somali-land and what the Arab regarded —justly, I thought—as over-regulation in the British ports, made trade difficult.) The ship sold what she could get rid of at any profit, and also carried whatever passengers she could induce to travel. The captain gave feasts and dances in order to establish the good name of the ship and to impress intending travellers. She carried probably two hundred or more—they lived on deck and were on no passenger-list that was ever furnished to any authorities: the number varied considerably in every port we touched at—from the Hadhramaut to various places in Italian Somali-land and Kenya Colony, and many others were embarked for shorter trips along the coast.

The last of the outward cargo was disposed of at Mombasa and Zanzibar, and then the dhow moved down to the delta of the Rufiji River, in Tanganyika, to load a cargo of mangrove poles for sale in the Persian Gulf. She also sold boats, and a shipwright was carried apparently for the sole purpose of boat-building during the course of the voyage He built a small dhow of about 15 tons, and this was also sold. The ship touched at Zanzibar before beginning the homeward passage, picking up further ventures there—an odd lot in cases of vermicelli, cases of soap, coconuts, and a group of Swahili passengers—and then she coasted up to Muscat and Bahrein. The mangrove poles and everything else were sold at Bahrein, at a good profit, and then the vessel ran home to Kuwait to lay up the few summer months while the south-west monsoon made the Indian Ocean untenable for her, and her mariners took up other temporary employment. Many of them were pearl-divers and tenders.

The gross profit on that voyage, as near as I could ever arrive at it, was not far short of 10,000 or 11,000 rupees, which was the approximate purchase price of the vessel. To gross this sum, the *boom* made a voyage of about nine months. She provided a livelihood for the thirty mariners, her captain, his brother, and both the captain and his brother's families, and a mate and his family as well. In addition to these earnings, each man had earnings of his own, and so had the captain. One of the captain's ventures was bringing 'Persian' carpets from Aden for sale to Italians in Mogadishu and the English at Mombasa, where there was no lack of clients. The carpets were almost all from Birmingham though some were made in Italy. Another venture was the purchase, in Zanzibar, of as many thousand newly minted Austrian thalers as he could afford to buy, for these handsome silver coins were in use in Oman and sold at a substantial premium in Muscat. He did very well on both these lines.

A complication in my studies of the economics of this ancient kind of sea-venturing was that nothing was quite straightforward. As far as I could gather, any or all the ventures rested on a vast and complicated structure of debt. No banking system was used, and in consequence there seemed always to be a shortage of ready cash, though all business was at least theoretically on a cash basis. The captain and the various merchants aboard (their ventures were quite apart from the ship's own) had to trade on credit, and had been doing that for years. The result was that they were always trying to collect debts owing from previous voyages. It was the custom to land an agent from the ship at the more important ports to collect her debts, and he would be left behind. When we finally sailed on the homeward passage from Zanzibar, the captain's brother did not come with us but shipped in another dhow which was going back to Mogadishu and a place called Haifun on the Benadir coast, where he was charged with collecting debts. It was not until the ship's debts were collected that there was a final accounting to the crew, who were paid on a shares system. If all the debts were not collected, then the sailors' accounts would run on until the following voyage, and meanwhile they would go out again in the same ship, with an advance. This advance they used to finance their own ventures, for which they themselves were also frequently in debt, and they had also creditors of their own in most of the bazaars along the coast of Kenya.

The manner of sharing out the proceeds, as far as I could understand, was something like this. First, the cost of the food was deducted. (This was not a large sum for the food was very simple. We ate a great deal of fish taken out of the sea, and a lot of rice.) Then the ship took half the sum remaining, as the ship's share. This was regarded as return on investment, and covering running costs, replacement of sails, and so on. The remaining half was then divided among all hands in accordance with a somewhat complicated system of shares. The money was divided into a number of standard shares. Exactly how many I did not know, but I think it was eighty. The sailors received one share each, with extra part-shares for such men as the quartermasters, serangs, cook, and so on. The captain received twenty-five shares, and the mate received I think five. A sailor's share on the voyage I made was 135 rupees, but there were many dhows in which the sailor's share that year (as reliably reported on the Kuwait waterfront) was less than 100 rupees. I heard of some dhows which paid only forty or fifty. The captain also distributed largesse fairly generously, giving good sums to such men as the ship's musician (who worked hard at the various feasts and entertainments and was an important man in building the ship's goodwill ashore) and a Persian sailor who acted as his personal steward, and the cook.

The share-out was accepted without demur. The sailors knew the captain and there was a bond of trust between them. When I saw the silver rupees being distributed, the sailors were obviously satisfied and even grateful. Many of them had no homes but lived in their cloaks on a bench in one of the seafarers' coffee shops, for the few days they were at Kuwait. Their clothes could be made up in a rather small handkerchief and their personal possessions consisted of one toothbrush, which was a piece of partially teased-out bamboo which they carried stuck in the after-end of their headropes. Kuwait was a big port and specialised in the Indian Ocean dhow-trading, and the captains were figures of importance. Most of the seafarers in my *boom* were Persians or the descendants of slaves.

The merchants and the captain were pleased with the result, for they were making immediate plans to furnish the captain's brother with another new *boom,* slightly smaller, to be built for a total cost of 10,500 rupees. The voyage was a sound economic proposition. The ship paid a handsome dividend, provided their customary living to her people, and earned a substantial share of the costs of her replacement. The life of such a dhow was at least fifteen years and, even then, she would have a fair resale value.

It is not so long since European and American ships were making voyages very much of this kind, but the big steel cargo-carriers of the nineties were too late for it—too late, too big, and too costly. They and their kind had to earn their livings by carrying freights, and to do this they had to compete against all comers on the open markets of the world. Ships were chartered—as indeed they still are—at exchanges such as the Baltic Exchange in London, where brokers, owners, and agents met to do business with one another, the one seeking to get a cargo shifted somewhere or other as cheaply as he possibly could, and the other to assure profitable employment for his vessel. Since it was rarely possible to define exactly how much cargo was to be put aboard any particular ship, the custom was to charter a vessel to load more or less to her capacity, plus ten percent. In a large four-masted barque, for example, known to be able to carry about 5200 tons, she would be chartered to load 4800 tons plus 10%, and then she would turn out 5230 tons, or 5260 tons, or some total near to that. She was then paid the total freight on the tonnage she turned out. Freight was hire-money for the use of the ship, and she had to meet all her expenses out of it. She had, normally, to pay for all the cargo-handling costs as well. In the dhow, the crew were stevedores and they did all the work. As far as was possible, big sailing vessels worked to the same rule. But it was far from always being possible. Big ports could not be efficiently worked without large gangs of shore-labour and it was not long before this labour, being organised effectively, was dictating to shipowners both that it must be employed and the terms of its employment. This was particularly so in the Australasian trades. Speaking broadly, it was only at the ports of the west coast of South America and odd guano islands here and there that crews could be used to reduce cargo-handling costs.

So a sailing-ship, out of the freight she was able to earn, had to pay all her outgoings and handle the cargo in and out as well. Her outgoings were considerable and they could easily be ruinous. She had to pay insurance costs, port costs, pilotage, towage, light dues, consular fees, wharfage, dry-docking costs (which should be annual) and survey costs as necessary, to say nothing of all her own maintenance and upkeep, victualling, and crew charges. Far too often, she was considered fair game for plunder by all who could do business with or for her and, in all ports, a master had to be alert to see that his owners were not robbed of any more than was the usual custom.

Consider the matter of insurance costs. In 1931, a small group of us bought the big four-masted barque *Parma* from Mr. Laeisz in Hamburg. The main members of the group were Captain de Cloux, who was then the late Gustaf Erikson's commodore master, a brother shipmaster of his in Åland who was a close relative, a London shipchandler, and myself. The first thing we decided was that we would insure against total loss and damage to other vessels only, and all other risks we would accept ourselves. These other risks were considerable. Indeed, there was no end to the various types of insurance we should have had, especially if we had tried to fly the British flag. The American flag was out of the question on the general score of costs. We flew the Finnish flag, and insured the vessel on the value of the little company we had formed to buy her—£3,000.

Only a year or two earlier, such a ship as the *Garthpool*, I knew, had had to pay 8% for one Australian round voyage and the lowest valuation underwriters would accept on her was £10,000. She was covered against accidents, too, but there was a saving clause by which the owner had to pay for any accidents the cost of which did not exceed 3% of the ship's insured value.

A good many accidents aboard a big sailing-ship cost less than
£300 but she could not stand many of them, on an Australian
round voyage, without losing all chance of profit. She went out
in ballast, loaded at an outport, and came straight back to the
United Kingdom, and earned only the one freight—that on the
grain in sacks which she carried back. She had other insurance
costs. As a British ship, she had to comply with the British Merchant Shipping and the Workmen's Compensation Acts, both of
which yawned with tremendous possible liabilities. All in all, the
Garthpool, which carried less than the *Parma,* was paying something like £1,000 more a year in insurance costs alone. That was
prohibitive. She had to comply with a manning scale, too. This
made her carry and feed a dozen more hands than we did, including a much higher proportion of expensive able seamen.
Claims for injuries, illnesses, repatriating seamen, damage to
cargo, and all that sort of thing could be enormous, under the
British flag. We looked after the cargo ourselves and took the risk
of accidents. The *Parma* was Scots built and a former Laeisz ship,
maintained under the eagle eye of Boye Petersen with Erich
Laeisz behind him. We knew there was not much risk of accidents which were not fatal; if they were fatal we were there,
too. Collecting the insurance would not be our worry.

In the *Parma,* our earnings were usually restricted to the one
freight of Australian grain a year. For this to pay, it had to be
loaded and discharged at ports which were as cheap as possible.
We had no say in that as far as Europe was concerned, for the
ship was chartered to discharge the wheat at any safe port between the Elbe and Brest to which she might be sent from Falmouth, Queenstown, or Plymouth, when she arrived for her
orders. Manchester only was excluded because of the cost of
sending down most of the masts and yards to get there. But we
took care we loaded at South Australian outports in the Spencer
Gulf. From the big Cape Horner's point of view these had many
advantages. Firstly, they could be made and left under sail, and
therefore towage costs were saved and so were some risks. Since
ships loaded at open anchorages there was no wharfage to be
paid. Most of the outports were unattractive little places and,

↑ Sailing-ships usually took a long time to load. Here Australian grain comes aboard in sacks.

Cape Horners carried pigs for fresh food.

↓ The famous *Herzogin Cecilie* cost only £4,250 to buy in 1921.

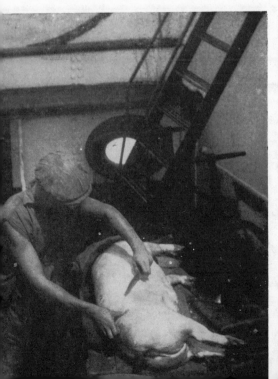

since the ships had to lie a long way out and it was difficult to get ashore, there was little desertion. (This was important. Ships are fined for leaving deserters behind them.) Again, because the ships were at an anchorage, their crews could work the ballast out. In a big four-master there might be 1500 tons of this, and paying shore labour to shift it was expensive. The weather was good in the South Australian summers, and major refit jobs could be safely undertaken during the six weeks or so it was necessary to wait while putting out the ballast and stowing the bags of grain. Like almost all Scandinavian deepwater ships we carried excellent tradesmen, though the forecastle was full of boys. We did all our own maintenance, and there was always plenty of that to be done in a big sailing-ship. We cut and sewed all our own sails, and the dry maindeck in the Australian sunshine was the ideal place for that.

We had other advantages under the Finnish flag, in such a ship as the *Parma*. Our wage costs were small, about what they were in the heyday of the British sailing-ship. In the 1930's, sailing-ship able seamen were paid £4 a month at the most, or perhaps £6 if they had to be signed on in Australia. Half the crew were cadets who had paid £50 apiece as premiums in order to come. This £50 was returned to them in wages (and in doing this we were well ahead of Scots ships, which were accustomed to return nothing. London and Liverpool ships usually gave apprentices 1/- a month). A good sailmaker could be had for as little as £8 a month, in the Åland Islands, and the supply of good sailing-ship men there was apparently limitless. (This was because of the large fleets of small sailing vessels which still plied the Baltic and Gulf of Bothnia up to the outbreak of the second World War. These ships trained good seamen and maintained the hard sailing tradition.) Our wage bill was about £100 a month for

HARLD A. UNDERHILL

The Parma

the whole crew, fore and aft, and our victualling costs worked out at between 1/1 and 1/3 a man a day. In the pre-war days—before 1910—these costs in the Laeisz ships were down to 10d a man a day, and the men were well fed.

The secret of keeping these costs down was very simple. It lay in good buying and the elimination of all dishonesty. For one shilling and threepence a day—about thirty cents a man at the rate of exchange then ruling—we fed quite well. All hands had the same sort of food out of the same pots, and there was no nonsense about cabin stores, with inferior qualities for the crew. This was one thing we set our faces firmly against. Above all else, the big sailing-ship depended upon a proper state of harmony aboard, if she were to make useful and profitable voyages, and the surest way to disharmony was by making stupid economies and by undemocratic differentiation in the food. There was a nice harmony in the Arab dhow. Our food was good food and the money spent on it bought food—it did not disappear into someone's pocket.

The food was plain, of course, for there was no help for that. Neither was there any harm in it. The sailing-ship staples remained much the same while the sailing era lasted—salt meat (called salt pork and salt beef, though badly bought salt pork could be really salt fat and salt beef might be anything), salt or dried fish, peas and beans, a live hog or two, fish from the sea, fresh potatoes when they were to be had. Our shipchandler shareholder in London supplied us well, and there were plenty of honest suppliers in Australia if they were dealt with honestly. We bought not one or two hogs, as was the custom, but ten or twelve at a time, small ones, and fattened them aboard. We also had plenty of preserved meat of good quality. It cost a little more but poor quality food was poor economy, too, and wholly stupid. Nor was food served out according to a strict allowance, as was the custom in most ships, particularly British, where the crew signed articles to receive their 'pound and pint' according to a minimum scale of provisions, which generally became the maximum. Our articles were for 'sufficient without waste', as in the Laeisz ships and most American sailing-ships. Bread was baked daily if it possibly could be, and there was always plenty of real coffee. The *Parma* was not overmanned with a crew of twenty-four all told and an average age before the mast of slightly under 18. We were aware that we had to nourish our boys.

This matter of food was very important at sea. Given good and sufficient food, decent quarters, and above all fair consideration and treatment by the officers and petty-officers, the crews were all right even though their pay was poor. Money as such meant little or nothing at sea, and the tradition was to squander it in port. To our boys, who almost invariably were in the ship because they must serve under square sail to obtain qualifying time in order to sit for officers' certificates, money was not such an important consideration. Moreover it must be remembered that the wages our able seamen were paid compared quite favourably with those ruling for similar artisans ashore in their own country, and this was the real yardstick. If the square-rigged ship, towards the end of her days, was surviving by a superlative practice of the art of spending nothing, this could be overdone. There were economies which were no economies at all, and yet many a fine ship went out of business through a master, or masters, who tried to please his owner by cutting down on the ship's maintenance and the welfare of the men. If the ship could not keep a reasonably contented crew, then she had better go under. There were many cases where the fruits of the false economies never reached the owner.

Under the British flag, in accordance with the Merchant Shipping Act, 1906, the master of every ship, except coasters of less than 80 tons net register, must provide, for each member of the crew who does not find his own food, rations in accordance with the following weekly scale:

3 lb of soft bread and 4 lb of biscuit
3 lb of salt beef
2 lb of salt pork
2¼ lb of preserved meat
¾ lb of fish
6 lb of potatoes
½ lb of dried or compressed vegetables

2   lb of flour
8   oz of oatmeal
1¾ oz of tea
4   oz of coffee
1¼ lb of sugar
⅓ lb of condensed milk
½ lb of butter
1   lb of marmalade or jam
½ lb of syrup or molasses
4   oz of suet.

Onions and condiments are also mentioned, and fresh meat and vegetables must be issued in port "when procurable at reasonable cost." Substitutes are allowed in certain circumstances, but it was illegal to supply margarine instead of butter.

These requirements were all very well, but the unfortunate thing about regulations is that there are always fools who think of ways to defeat them while pretending to comply with them. As far as the food was concerned, too, the standard of cooking could defeat the most generous allowance and, on the whole, the standard was poor in British ships. It was good in Scandinavian and American ships. Good cooking was essential when the where-withal to cook was as limited as it necessarily was in sailing-ships, which could carry only such foods as were preservable without refrigeration. The trouble in many British ships was that the masters would not have known, or appreciated, proper cooking if they had the chance to enjoy it. A man once inured to a diet of salt horse and pea soup had his palate spoiled for life. I speak from experience. I can recall now my horror as a boy, introduced first to this sort of thing, imagining that it ever could be regarded as food at all; yet after ten years I actually liked the stuff, though never well enough to go looking for it. Many old sailors used to come aboard in pleasurable anticipation of eating a meal of real pea soup—they asked for it to be made so thick it stood up of its own accord and required no plate, and they were not joking. They would complete the meal with a plate or two of salt horse. In ports, of course, there was the luxury of fresh vegetables to go with such things.

I have spent a little time discussing this matter of ship's food because it is important and was very closely allied with the much more important matter of morale. Without good morale, we could never have sailed the *Parma* or any other big four-masted barque with twenty-four hands. Indeed, we could not have sailed the *Parma* at all.

Crew costs were only part of the ship's disbursements. A master had to watch everything and everybody. In European ports (and in most others, too) he had to engage an agent, and the ship could never be chartered without the aid of brokers. This meant paying agency charges and brokerage, which were not excessive and were usually well earned. The port of discharge was a very important matter, economically, because expensive cargo-handling or an expensive port could play havoc with the voyage accounts, and the ship was helpless in these major items. No matter what it cost, she had to get the cargo out and buy some ballast to replace it, and she had to tow to sea from up-river ports, or at least tow to a safe anchorage. In the last days, when the few surviving ships could hope only for the one cargo annually, it was customary for them to sail back to the Åland Islands after each voyage, for the reasons that it cost nothing to lie there, the crews belonged there and were the more cheaply discharged and re-engaged, and there were good tradesmen to get on with any maintenance that might be necessary, at low cost.

In order to maintain what was called their 'class'—which means really their guarantee of seaworthiness—all ships are required to pass regular surveys. Whether they are insured or not makes no difference, for the cargoes must be insured or shippers cannot ship by them. Reclassing an old sailing-ship could be a very expensive business: the rule was that whenever the expense of retaining her classification was a sum greater than the ship could reasonably be expected to earn in the years that were left to her, she was scrapped, sold to ship-breakers who tore her apart for the sake of the metal in her. It was therefore no sense for an owner just to collect old ships. He had to buy *good* ships, preferably with several years of class still to run before they were due for survey.

This was one of the points we were well aware of when we bought the *Parma*. Another was employment for her, for cheap properties are worthless if they cannot be used. The weekend we bought the ship we had her fixed on the Baltic Exchange, through Clarkson's in London, to load a full cargo of wheat in Spencer Gulf for 31 shillings and sixpence a ton. This was a good freight and, as soon as the ship was fixed, we could draw a third of it for disbursements. This freight grossed approximately £8,250, out of which we had to finance the ship for the year, sail her round the world, and pay for loading and unloading the cargo. The whole voyage, including time fitting out at Hamburg and waiting in Spencer's Gulf to load and in Falmouth for orders, and sailing back afterwards to Mariehamn to lay up, took about nine months. So the costs worked out something like this:

Crew costs, at £100 a month	£ 900
Victualling costs, at 30/- a day for 270 days. Approx.	405
Stores, pilotage, drydocking, dues, brokerage, agent's fees, etc., including insurance	1,250
Loading costs in Australia, and all disbursements in that country	1,535
Discharging costs in Europe, and all disbursements including purchase of ballast for next outward passage	2,650
TOTAL	£6,740

The actual tonnage of wheat discharged was 5310 tons, not including the weight of the sacks (which was not paid for). The freight received was therefore about £8,365. On the credit side there was also the item of cadets' premiums, which had come to some £600. So on the first year's operations the *Parma* had grossed about £9,000 and spent considerably less than £7,000, and so she actually earned back her purchase price on that first round voyage. We were well aware, of course, that in the 1930's this was not shipowning, though some of the great American clippers had done it in the California gold-rush days. It was a piece of extremely good fortune. Moreover, in the rough balance-sheet which is presented here there was no allowance for the master's emoluments. The good result achieved was possible only by looking after *every* expense ourselves (especially with the aid

of the shipchandler shareholder and an excellent old Scot with
Clarkson's in London), by the goodwill which de Cloux had built
up over many years in the South Australian wheat trade in sailing-
ships, and by having no accidents at all.

That Scots broker's wife, incidentally, had had shares in a
good many sailing-ships which had been similarly run under the
Norwegian flag, and wanted to invest money with us if we could
find another ship to buy. We did, but unfortunately someone else
bought her. This was the *Pamir* which Gustaf Erikson bought
from Mr. Laeisz while we were away. The *Peking* was also for
sale and was an excellent ship, but she was bought by the Shaftesbury Homes as a stationary schoolship for boys.

The old Scots broker told me that it was a bad year if the
Erikson sailing-ships did not clear £1,000 each, at least, for the
owner, excepting any which were due for reclassing or which
might have had accidents. Erikson then owned some twelve large
Cape Horners and was buying more wherever he could find such
ships worth buying, such as the four-masted barque *Moshulu* at
Seattle. He did not insure his ships, and he had very little overheads. He paid his masters £14 or £15 a month, and in 1933
was offering sailors 50 Finmarks a month—less than ten shillings.
This did not cover their slopchest purchases. After a long voyage,
they owed the ship money for working in her, and there were
plenty of apprentices who paid to go. There were also passengers
who paid 10/- a day for the run to Australia and back, and
worked as well. There were never many passengers, never really
enough to cater for them, though Erikson certainly thought of it.

The Laeisz Line had many expenses which 'owners' like ourselves were spared. The Laeisz Line was a real shipowning
business—very much so—and had to cover such items as depreciation and replacement costs, and so on. The Laeisz ships could
not be made to pay on the one Australian voyage a year. Indeed,
it was difficult for us, at times, for freights went down to 24
shillings a ton and less than that, and an accident such as the
loss of two expensive anchors in a blow in the Bristol Channel
and some damage to the windlass proved rather costly. There
were almost no other freights we could hope to earn, though on

one occasion instead of going to Mariehamn to lay up we went
to the White Sea and loaded for London a very large cargo of
poor quality sawn boards, mill-ends and the like. This was called
'firewood', but in fact it was used mostly in the furniture trade
in England. This cargo took a long time to load and a long time
to discharge, for every piece had to be handled in and out. Though
it used the lay-up period quite well and kept the ship in commission (which was good for her), in fact it left almost no profit
margin.

Cargoes of Baltic boards for South or East Africa helped to
defray outward expenses, and there were a few of these on offer
occasionally. Another possible freight was guano from the Seychelles Islands for New Zealand, but this paid poorly. We were
offered a freight of chemicals once from Hamburg to Newark,
New Jersey, but this we refused for two reasons. The first was
that we did not know the trade and therefore could not accurately forecast the probable costs of handling the cargo, and the
second was that there was too much crew trouble and desertion
in American ports, and the ship would be put to a lot of expense
on that account. It was better to go empty to Australia, for if we
made a serious mistake we would be paying to handle those chemicals, instead of the shipper paying us. We could compute our
costs fairly accurately in the Australian trade, and so we knew
where we were.

Steamships would have taken all the grain, if they could, but
what gave us our chance (in addition to our very low capital
investment and costs) was the fact that we could load at outports,
and so saved shippers the expense of sending their grain to the
larger ports. Steamers had to have a delivery alongside of 500
tons a day in order to load with reasonable despatch and, if this
was not done, then they had to be paid demurrage. I think we
allowed a month to load, but of course we had a demurrage clause
in the charter party. Otherwise deliveries might have been too
slow altogether. Steamers took all the wheat from the big ports.
Insurance of wheat sent by sailing-ship cost the charterers about
2/6 a ton more than that sent in steamers. In 1932, for instance,
the steamer premium was 10/- percent and ours was 55/-. This

meant that sailing-ships had to accept a lower freight rate than the steamer, or the shipper would be paying considerably more to send his cargo under sail. When we had 31/6, steamers were being chartered at 34/–.

The following year freights were down and steamers were taking 25/–. I heard from one steamer owner (who was very interested in how we managed) that one of his ships—a big fellow carrying 9400 tons, which was about three times her net register—had made much the same voyage, going out on two boilers empty to Sydney and home on three boilers with the grain in bulk. She was 55 days steaming out from the Tyne, round Good Hope, and 53 days to Cork on the homeward passage. Her average out and back was about 9 knots, and she had every expense down to the minimum. Even so, her margin of profit was very small. The advantage she had was that she could do the same thing three times a year, and she could be sent anywhere a cargo might be offering. Though we took only about a month or so longer than she did, each way, it was out of the question for us to handle two charters a year. We lifted new season's wheat and that was all.

Of course, voyages of that sort were over-simplified compared with those big sailing-ships were making before the first World War. Then a considerable degree of skill was necessary to convert a probable loss into a tolerable profit, and an owner had to know *all* the possible trades his ship might be called upon to work, not just one of them. He had to have more than an approximate idea, for example, of the costs of loading case oil in Philadelphia or Bayonne, New Jersey, and of discharging the same cargo in at least three ports in Japan. He had to be in touch with costs on the coast of Chile, in the guano islands, in Newcastle N.S.W. and in the small and large ports on Puget Sound, at Delagoa Bay, and in Rangoon. He had to know stevedoring charges and practices in places as far apart as Honolulu and Campbelltown, New Brunswick. And he had to plan out his ships' voyages—if he could— so that, instead of keeping them idle in an expensive port waiting for some possible cargo to ripen and be harvested, their waiting periods and their ballast voyages were at a minimum and they spent the maximum possible time carrying inexpensively loaded cargoes to cheap discharging ports, at a high rate of freight. Above all, he had to see that his ships had the chance to earn more than he was called upon to spend on them, and the greater the margin the better. He could afford some long ballast passages for indeed these were unavoidable, but he could not afford to lose money by handling cargoes at a loss.

His greatest asset was not so much good ships as good masters, for the master was the real business agent once the ship sailed from her home port. The owner fixed the ships, but the master handled the ship's disbursements and collected some of her freights, in order to have the ready money to pay the ship's bills. A sailing-ship could not be controlled by cablegrams. The master was the man on the spot, and he could make or break her. For that reason, many owners paid good masters substantial bonuses, though there were some who were too stupid and too mean to do this. Very often, a master had some owning interest in the ship, and this was especially the case in Norway.

Sailing-ships, too, were liable to more accidents and mishaps than could be covered by insurance that was not prohibitive, even at Lloyd's. And so it was customary for owners to bind themselves into mutual societies, usually called clubs in England. Each owner paid in according to the number of ships he owned, and club-members were entitled to draw from the common funds to meet costs of accidents not covered in the ordinary marine policy. These clubs were very useful and survived, in Britain at any rate, until the end of the sailing-ship.

The whole sailing-ship economy, in the last analysis, rested upon men. Men had to accept what would now be regarded as primitive living conditions. They lived hard in communal quarters, and it was usual for them to supply all their own wants. Just as masters had to find even such things as their own charts and chronometers, sailors had to provide bedding, eating utensils, and everything else. The owner, under the British flag, provided the employment, the ship to work in. A foremast hand had a bunk in the forecastle (which was either a house on deck abaft the foremast, the space below the forecastle-head right forward, or part of the midships superstructure if she were a 'three-island' ship), a seat at a bench for his meals, and space for his sea chest if any. In good ships, he had also a place to hang his oilskins. But he bathed on deck in a tin or a wooden bucket of rain water, and he washed his clothes the best way he could. (He did wash them, and beautifully.) An officer had a cabin to himself, if he were a senior: if junior, he shared a cabin. There was a small mess-room to eat in. Petty officers shared small hutch-like places usually in the wettest part of the ship, and generally ate their meals on a bench in the galley. This was regarded as a privilege. Masters lived in their saloons.

The whole costing of the ship was based on this sort of life and there was nothing wrong with that. But the mechanical life in steam vessels, giving the men more leisure and less satisfaction, led in time to ever-growing demands for improvements—better food, better quarters, ever more leisure. Each generation of seafarers in consequence became unemployable in the ships of its fathers. Good conditions did not always achieve their object. The sailing-ship, of course, could not compete with the steamer in supplying such things as single-berth cabins with reading lights for deckboys, nor would she want to provide such things. The steamer could only afford them while she was able to ride upon a wave of prosperity which was at its base completely false. After all, unnecessary luxuries are a charge upon the community in some form or other, and especially a charge upon the general business community which it could only afford to pay with prosperity abounding—*worldwide* prosperity, which is not with us, nor likely to be. All deepsea shipping must survive in the face of fierce international competition. A more virile nation with mariners not accustomed to expensively too-good conditions can always arise and run the softer ships off the face of the sea.

The sailing-ship had to survive on a common-sense basis, a

fully factual economy, or not at all. What defeated her in the
end was not the lack of work for her to do but that she could
not afford to do it. Under the British and American flags, bureaucracy had made it impossible for her to keep even the nucleus of
trained crew without which it would be foolish to go to sea, and
a good many other flags were little if any better. The quoted cost
of building a full-rigged ship of about a thousand tons in 1953
was £125,000, plus whatever increases might be necessary because of the ever-rising costs of steel and everything else she would
need. The cost of providing the standard of accommodation
which had been agreed between the owners and the officers and
men's organizations, and of paying the crew, providing them with
agreed leave, insurance, and so forth, was quite impossible, even
if a crew could be found. Unless such a ship could get dispensa-
tions from the almost infinite requirements which bureaucracy
has inflicted upon all shipping, or a very large subsidy, it would
be ruinous to contemplate building her at all. If she were built for
any purpose other than training, she would be a freak. As a training-ship such a vessel would undoubtedly be magnificent, with the
right type of officers to run her. But as a commercial proposition,
having to comply with the same standards as the powered vessels,
she would be hopelessly handicapped against them and would
have no chance at all.

A six-masted barque carrying 9000 tons (with a Hilgendorf,
a Learmont, or a Jarvis to drive her) might stand a better chance,
but to build such a ship—if there were a builder and a rigger to
take on such a job—might cost half a million, and there are no
Hilgendorfs today. Such a ship would be a perfectly feasible ship-
building, rigging, and sailing proposition (the limit of size is
governed by the dimensions of the yards, which must not be so huge
that the men are unable to use the footropes properly and to work
on them: the *Potosi's* yards were no larger than the *Peking's*,
which are still to be seen where she lies at anchor in the Medway).
She should be able to sail at 18 knots or perhaps a little better.
But she could not be handled by a crew which consisted only of
boys. A proper nucleus of officers, petty officers, and first-class

seamen she must have, and at least the majority of them should be under 50—under 40, preferably. We may as well accept the fact that they are gone. So also—under our flag—is the whole tradition which they served so splendidly.

If it is to be restored it must first be built up in little ships, and that may take some time, preceded by a very painful re-awakening—not only in the field of economics.

Chapter ten

STANDARDS OF CONDUCT

THE sailing-ship sailor was a rugged individual. He had need to be. No sailing-ships but those which carried passengers or emigrants had a medical man aboard. The crew's health was another responsibility of the master's. I have heard of many masters who had curious fads and unusual activities, but I have never heard of one who was a health maniac. The life itself was healthy, and they left it at that. The fit survived and were still with them: the unfit had gone elsewhere, with or without a piece of canvas sewn about them. Many ships and many voyages were a demonstration of the ability of man—and boy—to triumph over the most appalling dietary conditions. That worried nobody but the apprentices, who dreamed of steak and eggs. Scurvy was rare, and it is unlikely that the compulsory issue of synthetic lime-juice after the twelfth day at sea (which was the rule in British ships: hence 'Limejuicers') had anything to do with that, for the men mixed the stuff with a little water and washed in it, or cleaned their teeth. The mere fact that it was intended for their good— allegedly—was enough to set them against it. Even on such passages as the *Lawhill's* 176 days between Hongkong and New York, there was no scurvy.

I have not been at sea that long but I have been over 160 days between the anchorage off Melbourne and St. Nazaire, and there was no sign of scurvy then. It was probably the splendid physique of the mariners which guarded them against this ancient enemy. It was certainly not their diet, either afloat or ashore, for as soon as they came ashore they tried to pickle themselves in

237

alcohol. There was scurvy in some ships but, oddly enough, the cases I know of occurred in ships which had departed from the usual deplorable diet, such as the four-masted barque *Olivebank* which embarked a number of turtles when she was loading guano in the Seychelles once, under the impression that they would provide fresh food for the passage to New Zealand. Scurvy struck her crew so badly that she had to put into Melbourne in distress, and some of her boys died there. This was in the 1930's.

In British ships, masters were required to have a medicine chest aboard, but this contained only the simplest remedies. In later days there was a book which went with it, called the "Ship Master's Medical Guide". The use of simple dressings and opening medicines was about the extent of most masters' medical knowledge. Many went on the assumption that man should not be ill and, if he were, he was probably malingering. In any event, some opening medicine would do no harm. The death-rate was certainly not high except from fevers caught ashore. Captain Irving, who served most of his apprenticeship with Captain Woodget in the clipper-ship *Cutty Sark,* told me how Woodget — a famous character—treated illnesses. Irving was 12 years old when he went to sea in *The Tweed* and thirteen when he transferred to the *Cutty Sark*. One day, feeling somewhat lethargic, he reported sick, against the advice of his fellow apprentices, aged 14.

"What ails you, lad?" said old Woodget, not unkindly, looking up from grooming a collie dog.

"I'm sick, Sir."

"Sick? How sick?"

"Just sick, Sir. Just sort of sick all over. There's no particular pain anywhere."

Woodget looked the boy over with his mild blue eyes, his kindly old whiskers bristling. Sailing-ship masters were good judges of human nature in man or boy. The collie dog joined in the examination, and so did its litter of pups.

"What you need, my boy, is a good cleaning out," said the captain at last. "We'll fix that. Run along to the galley and tell the doctor * to hot up some water. Then come back here."

* "Doctor" was a sailing-ship's name for the cook. Reasons unknown.

When young Irving returned it was to find the captain busily 'marrying' the end of a piece of codline to a long, thin, implement, which he knew was used as a bottle-washer. He was securing one piece of codline to the eye of this wire brush, and another at the other end of it. In came the cook with a basin of hot water which he solemnly put down. Irving watched these preparations with some sense of alarm.

At last he could suppress his curiosity no longer.

"What—what are you going to do with me, Sir?" he asked.

"We'll clean you out fore-and-aft with this," said the captain, brandishing the bottle-washer. "I'll reeve the fore-part down your throat and the doctor will haul the after-part out through your stern. Come here, now. It's going to do you the world of good!"

But young Irving was out of the saloon like a shot and away up to the foremasthead, nor did he come down until the evening. He was never "sick" again. "I didn't dare to be!" he said.

If masters and seafarers alike were apt to look on illness as a luxury best left ashore, they could cope with the serious accidents which were an ever-present risk of their calling. Broken arms, broken heads, broken legs were commonplace. Men were pitched about the decks in bad weather with the ships rolling violently and the sea sweeping unchecked aboard, and their heads or limbs would be banged against the belaying-pins or the stanchions, or the spare spars. Most masters were adept at such surgery as they were called upon to perform. They were, as a rule, handy men, whose hands did what they wanted them to do, which after all is the first and principal requirement in most surgery. They looked upon splicing bones together or mending broken heads as exercises in seamanship, or the shipwright's trade, and they generally did such things splendidly. Their methods might be primitive and their instruments were in fact a carpenter's, not a surgeon's. But when they had to, they could get results.

I remember on one occasion a big full-rigged ship came into Melbourne, 100 days or so out from Norway with a cargo of tongued-and-grooved boards for the building trade. A block had fallen from aloft on a man's head and a piece of his skull had been pushed in until it touched his brain, according to the medical reports. The master of the ship—she was Norwegian, I think—did not know what had happened, medically, but he could see that the bone of the skull had to be hauled back into position or at least to something like its former place. How could this be done? There was nothing in the "Ship Master's Medical Guide" about it (if he had a copy). That master was a former ship's carpenter, and he made the injured man a wooden skull-piece which fitted most ingeniously over the injured part, and had attachments skilfully contrived from a couple of sail-needles which lifted the bone away from the brain. It was a great success and the man reached port quite well. That master possibly did not know that he was deciding the life or death of this particular seaman. He took the job in his stride, saw a remedy, and applied it. In the same way he had delivered his wife of a child during the passage, but he was an old hand at midwifery.

So were a good many sailing-ship masters. They had to be. I have heard of younger masters who made such study of this art as they could, knowing that their wives must go through childbirth at sea. They went to hospitals and took a few lessons. They did not read the subject up in books. The books were much too alarming. A good many masters had their wives with them at sea in American, British, and Scandinavian ships, but in British ships at any rate, it was most unusual for any other female to be aboard. Though women went to sea freely in the short-trade Baltic sailing vessels, I have never heard of women working in deepsea sailers, in any capacity, until some of the last of the Finnish ships signed a few women on as 'cadets' or stewardesses.

Some of these captains' wives distinguished themselves by feats of heroism. At least two of them, one British and one American, brought their husband's commands safely into port from long voyages. The British woman was Mrs. Wilson, wife of Captain Joseph Wilson of the four-masted barque *Primrose Hill*. The *Primrose Hill* was bound round the Horn from Rio towards Tacoma, in the state of Washington, to load grain for Europe. Smallpox struck the crew. Captain Wilson, his officers, and most of the crew were down with it, but Mrs. Wilson was not ill. There were barely enough men left fit to work the ship. In this extremity Mrs. Wilson took command. The men murmured. A deputation of two came aft and asked that she put at once into whatever port she could find.

"Not while my husband is alive!" said Mrs. Wilson. "You men go back for'ard."

They went. Mrs. Wilson sailed the ship to Tacoma. She nursed her husband and the mates, and looked after the men. She had a small baby which also took the smallpox, and she nursed that, and saved its life. The *Primrose Hill* had a good charter to load at Tacoma but, to keep this, she had to be driven. If she arrived late the charter would be cancelled. Mrs. Wilson kept the charter. This was in 1891.*

The American was Mrs. Patten, wife of the captain of a clipper named the *Neptune's Car*. Her husband was taken ill off the pitch of the Horn with a brain fever. The mate was in his cabin—in irons, I believe—for alleged insubordination (which may have had some connection with the captain's breakdown). The American clippers often had curious crews few of whom were American, and the second mate of the *Neptune's Car* was unable to navigate. So Mrs. Patten took command. She was a girl of nineteen. She had studied navigation on a previous voyage, for she had been married to the captain at sixteen and had been three years at sea. She took the ship to San Francisco, and made a good passage of it.†

* The London shipping journal, *Fairplay,* reported in its issue of February, 1891: "The four-masted ship *Primrose Hill* sailed last summer from Dundee for Rio with coal, Captain Wilson being in command. The ship left Rio in ballast for Tacoma, and as she arrived at the latter place two days before the end of last month, her owners obtained 1s. 3d. more for freight than they would have done at the commencement of the year, rates having fallen to that extent. The owners were also saved about £350 through the heroism of the captain's wife, who refused to take the vessel out of her course to the nearest port, Valparaiso. It is the intention of the owners suitably to reward such gallant conduct, and no doubt the underwriters will do likewise. Nearly all the hands, and Captain Wilson, being struck down with the smallpox, Mrs. Wilson took command and navigated the ship to her destination. Her conduct was that of a true heroine."

† This story is vouched for by Professor Samuel Eliot Morison in his *Maritime History of Massachusetts.*

Navigation as practised even by the clipper masters was often a somewhat haphazard science. The aim of most sailing-ship captains was to keep away from the land. In the tea trade, this was impossible, and sailing through the South China Sea and the chain of islands in the East called for precise knowledge of the ship's position, at all times. The tea clipper masters, however, were an elite, as the East India Company's commanders had been before them. The general standard of accomplishment among most other masters was remarkably poor. Perhaps because they lacked confidence in the results plotted upon their charts, perhaps because it was simply the tradition, it was the practice in most British sailing-ships for the master to lock his chart away immediately he had pencilled his guess at the ship's position on it. After all, he had bought the chart. Nobody else had one. Neither mate usually navigated at all in far too many ships. Captain Learmont speaks of his horror at observing a master in a ship he was in, who thought nothing of snatching a hasty shot of the sun through a charthouse window, and that with an ancient and unreliable sextant. Under such conditions, it was impossible to navigate accurately. For most masters, the sun gave them the data they needed to solve their simple daily problems, and if the sun was not to be seen there was no navigation. Instead, they used what they called D.R.—dead reckoning—and 'dead' was the proper adjective to apply to much of it. In fact the term was properly 'deduced reckoning', but perhaps they did not know that. It was kept on a slate, and entered into the log by the mate at night.

The deepsea sailing-ship's normal navigational equipment consisted of one or two steering compasses (two for the very big ships which required tremendous hand-steering wheels, and so placed a compass in a binnacle in front of each side of the wheel) and a standard compass, whose accuracy was generally left to the professional compass adjustor. They had one chronometer or possibly two—three, in some well-found ships—such sextants (or even quadrants) as the officers might possess and brought aboard, the minimum books of tables (usually one volume only with logarithms and everything else necessary), one Nautical Almanac, one pair of parallel rules and one pair of dividers. The custom was to work up a time sight for longitude and to get a noon sight for latitude. This sufficed, if the chronometer was in order. The usual thing was to have chronometers rated ashore and to rely upon one or other of them keeping their rate. There was no alternative before the days of radio and checks by time-signals.

There were masters who were expert and most thorough navigators who made a hobby of the science and were glad, too, to pass on their knowledge to their cadets. But I am afraid these were the minority. Most were extremely anxious about their landfalls, and had good reason for the anxiety. Learmont speaks of other dangerous navigators with whom he served. "It was far too common for observations to be worked out in a slipshod manner," he says. Ships were lost sometimes because of the failure to use stellar observations. Learmont instances the case of the Liverpool four-masted barque *Bidstonhill* which piled herself up on Staten Island. At the subsequent inquiry, the master's explanation was that he had been running on D.R. for many days because there had been no sun. It so happened that Learmont had been working his own ship at the same time in the same place, and reference to his workbook showed that while there had in truth been no sun, he had been able to get good fixes night and morning by stellar observations. It was more trouble to work up star sights and many masters, having perhaps qualified with difficulty or afterwards becoming lazy, did not try. The loss of the *Bidstonhill* was unfortunately by no means a rare case.

As for Sailing Directions, most ships carried the standard Findlay's * covering the oceans of the world, and that was all. Findlay's works were interesting and voluminous, but in some respects they were not much ahead of a sixteenth century Mariner's Guide which I saw recently at the National Maritime Museum down at Greenwich. Giving directions for the passage from Taprobane towards Cathay—Ceylon to China—this counselled

* Alexander George Findlay, F.R.G.S., compiled Directories in the 1860's for the Indian, Atlantic, and Pacific oceans, and for the Eastern Seas. They were published in London by Laurie, at the Minories. When we bought the *Parma* she still had a full set aboard, supplied to her when she was the Anglo-American Oil Company's *Arrow*.

master-mariners to leave the Malay peninsular on the left and the
Philippines, etc., on the right, adding that the distance was about
2000 leagues.

All navigation was a closed book, normally, to the foremast
hands. They were neither told the ship's position nor had the
slightest interest in it, though they took a pride in good day's
runs and in fast passages. In the majority of ships the apprentices
were no better off, except that they did take some interest. They
were often able to learn the ship's position through the steward
though generally it was through some go-between, for stewards
and apprentices were not normally friends. The apprentices were
far too expert at thieving from the steward's stores.

Shortsea masters were even worse than their deepsea brethren. There is a story of an old Geordie collier master who, blown
away from the coast in thick weather somewhere into the Norwegian Sea, appealed to his mate to know whether he had seen
the ship's chart anywhere, remarking that he had a feeling she
had one. In due course, the two old-timers found the chart carefully rolled up and stowed beneath the dust of ages. The master
unrolled it, took a careful look, and jammed his right thumb
down upon it.

"We be about there," he said.

"Gawd, mon," said the mate, "let's have a look!"

The old man lifted his thumb and, with the mate, stared at
the chart horror-struck, for there was a black mark upon it just
where his thumb had been.

"If yon's fly-muck," said the old man at last, "we're all right.
But if it isn't! . . . Stand by to wear ship!"

The standard in the deepwatermen was perhaps not quite as
bad as that. There was a lot less fly-muck about.

One quality the shortsea masters had which was denied far
too many deepwatermen. They were magnificent at pilotage.
Navigation is the science of conducting a ship across the face of
the sea out of sight of land, by observing her position, correcting
the compass, and conducting her in safety to her destination. By
pilotage is meant the safe conduct of vessels within sight of the
land, and it is a very different matter. Most deepwatermen were

happy to pass control of their ships over to pilots at the first opportunity. What they were accustomed to was the safe conduct of ships with the whole ocean about them, to *sail* first and navigate afterwards, and the bee-line navigation of modern vessels would be quite beyond them. The young officer of today, whatever else he may or may not be, has no excuse for not being a highly proficient navigator and that indeed he is. After all, in most cases that is the main reason for his employment.

Apprentices were supposed to be taught navigation and instructed in the arts of seamanship, but in fact they were usually exploited as cheap labour. Almost every big British sailing-ship carried a contingent of them, usually anything from four to twelve. They lived in their own quarters which were known as the half-deck quite regardless of its actual location. Generally it was a house in the waist of the ship where the heaviest seas broke over the maindeck, though sometimes the 'half-deck' was a sort of hutch in the forepart of the poop. The apprentices were any boys whose parents or relatives had paid a premium to send them to sea, and they had to sign indentures with the owner to serve him for four years. Some—many of the best—came from the training establishments, the moored ships *Conway* and *Worcester,* where they began pre-sea training at 12 or so, and then were required only to serve three years at sea.

The training-ship boys, coming usually from families which knew something of the ways of the sea, were only in the better ships, as a rule. But they were exploited too. In the very great majority of ships, anything they learned was entirely their own business. They lived and worked as crew-members and ate the same sort of food, though they kept themselves apart from the forecastle crowd. In cases of mutiny or other crew trouble (which happened only in bad and badly-run ships) they were expected to take the ship's side regardless of the merits of the case, and this they did. On the whole they were a loyal, competent, cheerful, undernourished, reckless group of young fellows who lived life to the full afloat and ashore. In the heyday of sail there were thousands of them.

They wore double-breasted brass-buttoned suits with small peaked caps carrying a badge with the owner's house-flag emblazoned upon it and, apart from the officers, they were often the only members of the ship's company who possessed a suit. The men did not wear suits. They carried their gear usually in a seabag and not a chest, because chests were too cumbersome and never survived a stay—however brief—in a crimp's boarding-house. Suits could not be carried in a seabag. Besides, they were considered unnecessary. A decent pair of trousers and some sort of coat, with a jersey or a guernsey and anything at all for headgear from a cloth cap to a bowler, was the shoregoing rig. Shipboard rig was anything, usually dungarees for warmer weather and heavy stuff in bad weather. Sea boots and oilskins—oilskin *suits,* never oilskin coats: these were for officers who did not go aloft—with a guernsey, a sheath-knife, a belt, and a few working-shirts, completed the outfit.

Many apprentices went to sea in sailing-ships through a sense of adventure, and this was sometimes mistaken. The sailing-ship quickly weeded out those who had misjudged their calling, but many lads of character and spirit also deserted. California and parts of Australia still know many of these as respected and frequently wealthy citizens. The only redress an apprentice had, in a really bad ship, was to desert, and to do that took character. It took character, too, to stay the course. Out of the thousands who served their apprenticeship under sail, there emerged a very high proportion of excellent officers. The experience was fundamental, and it was ideal character-training. Until this year, none of the great Atlantic greyhounds—the really important liners—had ever been commanded by a seaman not trained in sail.

One thing among many others the sailing-ship apprentice learned, and that was how to live a man's life among men. The sailing-ship man, whether apprentice or seaman, knew how to live. It may seem strange, but he had also natural good manners. Living together for years on end at such close quarters, of course

ABOVE   At the pumps—the most dreaded job of all

BELOW   The food was plain and often bad in too many ships. Usually it was good in American, German, Scandinavian, and Latin Cape Horners.   →

↑ On her beam ends—the crew are below re-stowing ballast. This was aboard the *Herzogin Cecilie*. Note the rail washed away.

The sailor had to be able to work anywhere. →

A whole watch was lost from the ship *Pampa* under conditions such as these. →

A little square-rigger sailing by-the-wind. This is the *Joseph Conrad*, off Sydney Heads under all sail.

the rough edges had to be smoothed off. Such things as personal habits, table manners, cleanliness, and so on had to be at an acceptable standard if there were not to be intolerable friction and even murder. There was friction at times, especially when some crimp unloaded a group of landsmen and derelicts on an unfortunate ship. But by and large, forecastle and half-deck groups lived each in their own ways but both quite pleasantly— at sea, of course. There was often a sad deterioration in big ports, among the forecastle men.

I remember poor Charlie Müller's dismay when, at the age of 73, he had at last to enter an Old Persons' Home. The quarters were fair and the food was good, but Charlie lost about twenty pounds in the first month. He just couldn't stand the awful pig table manners of too many of his landsmen comrades. Charlie was a man who had knocked about the world since early child-hood; he had survived two wars, and escaped from the Russians after the second one. Yet until 1953 he had been able to look after himself, to choose his company. He had always worked very hard but he had also always lived decently.

I was astonished, in the British navy during the war, to notice how many young fellows from great public schools had not mas-tered the simple rudiments of communal life. Their ideas of per-sonal cleanliness (once removed from the facilities they had always known) were deplorable. It seemed to me they had been trained to conform to a standard but not developed as individuals, and that standard slipped under the stress of war.

It is true to say that the sailing-ship man's standard, once established, did not slip away from him. It was his for life, and he was a wholly developed individual too.

I have recently come across an interesting document which, I think, throws a deal of light on the attitude of the old-time sailor towards his employment and towards life. There was a master-mariner who, in his time, had commanded several fine full-riggers and at least one big four-masted barque. He had a number of sons who went to sea. As he rarely had an opportunity

← The sailing-ship sailor was a rugged type.

to counsel them in person before they went, it was his habit to
give each a long letter of advice, very thoroughly prepared.
Through the kindness of a grandson now serving in a motorship,
I have a copy of one of these letters which was written in the
1890's. It well repays reading, though there are over 40,000
words of it, giving excellent advice under sixty-three main heads
ranging from "A Few Words on Sea Boots" to "Drinking",
"When in Boats", "Furling a Royal", "Liberty Day", "Your
Health", and "Mother's Bible". The very first note is on contentment, the keystone of success.

"Make yourself happy where you are, and not where you wish
to be," writes the old master-mariner.

"If you wish for this and that and the other, it only unhinges your mind
and leads it away from your daily important duties, and in the end makes
you dissatisfied with your present state.

"I remember well once long ago, when I was chief mate of a fine
barque in the Australian trade. The Master was a terrible hard man, and
the crew were simply a lot of cut-throats, who had been beachcoaming *
in India for years. The 2nd Mate was a horrid old growling dissatisfied
man, so between the three (I was then only 20 years of age) I had a
pretty rough time. I had one day been brooding over my troubles a bit
in the cabin in the early morning, thinking I had not a true friend in the
ship, and the world looked to be very shady, when our little canary that
hung in our skylight began to warble and sing his merry song. Ah,
thought I, you are one living friend I have, my canny little bird, any-
how—and how happy you seem to be although you are in prison! No
chum on board to even look at, not a blade of green grass or a tree within
a thousand miles of you, and yet in your little prison, on seed and pure
water, you roll your pretty song out from dawn to sunset. If you are
so eternally happy with so little, I must be a vile fellow if I am unhappy.

"This cheered me up at once and I determined, come what will, I will
try my best to be joyful and happy from this day. So I sang like my bird
when alone on the poop. I drove unhappy thoughts away, when they
came, and was cheerful to all, the next day after I began this treatment
of my mind, I felt half my sorrow was gone. I went on gradually improving till we got to Adelaide, and at that port, I was called *Happy
Jack* the mate of the *Rowena*. My joviality and merriness actually drove
the old second mate out of the ship. One morn he cleared out bag and
baggage, and we got a splendid young fellow for second mate, and what

* Beach-combing—men 'on the beach', without a ship.

with our singings and dancings and sky-larkings, we made the old man quite young again and before the voyage was ended I was as happy as the day was long, and finished the round trip of 14 months in her. Half a person's trouble is often brought about by brooding over evils that really have no existence except in the brain. So make yourself happy where you are—and not where you wish to be."

On duty, the old seaman has this to say:

"At all times when addressed by your officers never forget to add Sir to your responses. It shows good breeding, and besides being your duty to do so, it causes your officers to have a kindly feeling towards you. I never lost anything at sea by being courteous. The best seamen are invariably the most courteous men in the ship, and the same rule applies to the officers abaft the mast. When an officer calls out to you aloft, answer him quickly. Nothing riles an officer so much as when he calls out to a man aloft, and cannot get an answer from him. (*Mind this.*) When the Royals or light sails are to be taken in, try to be *first man aloft*, this alone will cause all hands to respect you. Smartness and cleanliness is next to Godliness as all sailors were wont to say. Smartness alone covers a multitude of sins on board of every ship afloat.

"When the watch is called turn out *at once*. Do not lie for a minute or you will fall off to sleep again. Directly you hear the call—*Jump out*—learn yourself to do this, and in course of a little time it will become natural of you to do so. A smart relief is a sailor's blessing, a long relief a sailor's curse. When you hear the call 'All hands shorten sail', try to be first on deck. Dress as smart as you possibly can, for the safety of the ship may depend on the crew coming on deck very quickly. A good officer or seaman is sure to be first man on deck when called. No sluggard *can possibly* be a good seaman so mind be smart on deck when called."

The old seamen had a sure belief in God, which was not always apparent while they were in ports. The old man goes on:

"One of the boldest and best captains I ever sailed the seas with in the Blackwall liners, was Captain W. Deacon, as fine a seaman as ever trod a plank, and as brave a man in emergency as you could find. Yet he never forgot when the weather would permit of it to read a short prayer to all hands on the head of the main deck capstan every night at 6 pm. He was a most successful sea captain, a strict disciplinarian yet a very kind true-hearted man who feared no danger. People who mock and scoff at true religion are cads, and never worth much. When danger comes upon them, they invariably show the white feather. So my advice is:— do not forget God and he'll not forget you.

"All old sailors of my time considered it very unlucky indeed to go to sea without a Bible. I am not superstitious by any means, yet I firmly believe without God's book with you on the ocean you will assuredly not prosper that voyage."

He has a lot to say about ordinary shipboard duties. "On the Lookout," he counsels,

"do not sit down on a bitt or capstan and rest your head against anything, or you are bound to fall asleep. Sleep is an overpowering thing, and it is only by great energy it can be overcome at times. Many a fine ship has been dismasted through a sleepy-headed officer, and mind directly you observe anything unusual on the water, report it to the Officer of the watch in a respectful tone of voice. A smart fellow on the look-out is a treasure to the Officer of the watch. Whenever you relieve the look-out, see the lamps (side-lights) are burning brightly and if they are not as bright as they should be, report the matter to the Officer of the watch in a respectful manner at once, as the safety of the ship and all the lives of those on board may depend on the side-lights on a dark and dirty night.

"When it is your look-out, relieve the man on look-out as smartly as you possibly can. When relieved, report to your relief the lights burning properly, and any vessel that may be near or the land and so on, so that he is in a position to grasp the vessel's surroundings, and mind never go off the look-out till you are properly relieved. Also when you call the Watch do so in a proper manner. Don't be frightened of shouting too hard; sing out 'Starboard or Port watch ahoy—eight bells there; do you hear the news'—and repeat it again in a minute or so if you are led to suppose none of the watch are astir. See they turn out."

Here is some of his voluminous advice on working aloft.

"In knocking about aloft on the Royal yards, mind *don't let go one rope* till you have hold of another, and if you keep in mind this good advice you will never fall from aloft. This is a golden rule rigidly kept up by old sailors, and no one need be ashamed of acting on this advice. The want of it in practice has cost more lives in young boys falling from aloft, than any other cause that I know of. Never go aloft up the lee rigging: 'tis unseamanlike and lubberly in the extreme. Always shin aloft to windward in all cases, and cross over to leeward when you get up as high as you require to go."

Temperance is strictly enjoined.

"Two things have created all the disturbances I have ever seen at sea, and I have been 37 years to sea, 25 years of which I have been in command. I served 5 years as apprentice, 7 years as 1st and 2nd Mate, and the rest as skipper. I have been all over the world, and in all classes of ships from 4 thousand tons down to 50 tons—and in all this long experience nine-tenths of all unpleasantness at sea only arose from these two things: —*Drink* and *bad food.* Bad food you cannot avoid if you are unlucky enough to get in a poorly found vessel. But drink you can and must avoid."

In the course of his thorough and comprehensive advice, the old sea captain has a few words to say about accidents, especially falling overboard. The thing to do, he says, is to keep cool, to turn from the wind and sea and paddle quietly, raising a hand from time to time in order to direct the boat which is seeking you, but not shouting, and not trying to swim back to the ship. By following this advice he reckoned that a man overboard could keep himself going, even in a strong wind and sea, for half-an-hour, by which time a boat should be able to pick him up.

A good many sailing-ship men went overboard and a surprising number came back again. Every ship had at least its yarn about the man who was swept out by one sea and rolled back in again by another, or perhaps swept out and in again by the same sea. It *could* happen quite simply when a deeply laden ship was rolling heavily without making appreciable way, as when she was hove-to. Men who went overboard in bad weather, however, were almost invariably lost though the loss of life from this cause, on the average, was not great. I was looking at the records in the Laeisz office in Hamburg, for example. Those 'P' ships were hard-driven and deeply-laden, yet for the year 1903–04 I found that the loss of life from all causes in the whole fleet of twenty-two big square-rigged ships was eight men—two from the *Persimmon,* and one each from the *Pamelia, Posen, Plus, Petschili, Pangani,* and *Pisagua.* That is, eight men from a total of about 600. Sometimes a whole watch might be lost over the side, as happened once

in the ship *Pampa*. This was when she was under the Finn flag,
not the German.

In an ill-found ship, it would take more than half-an-hour to
get a boat back to a swimming man. There was little pretence
at lifeboat drill, despite the strict Board of Trade regulations.
Lifeboats in many ships were lashed down on the skids and that
was that. Perhaps there was a certain fatalism about it, for the
mariners were aware that conditions which overwhelmed their
ship would give little chance to the old-fashioned ship's lifeboat.
There is little doubt that the great majority of the square-rigged
ships which went missing foundered, and did so quickly, either
because the sea stove in their hatches, ice stove in their sides, or
they were flung upon their beam ends through the cargo shifting
and sank almost at once because the sea washed the hatches open,
and poured in. It took a Hilgendorf to get men safely away in
boats from a ship lost through causes such as these, for this sort
of accident overtook ships in the bad weather zones of the world
as they fled before, or fought against, the wild west winds.

Men who fell from aloft had little chance, whether they fell
on deck or into the sea. The only chance for them was if they
struck lines on the way down to break the fall, and then fell not
more than thirty or forty feet at last, into the sea. Captain Jarvis
told me of an occasion when he picked up a man who was knocked
out of the jigger-top in the *Lawhill* by a blown-out gaff tops'l,
but the man rolled down the weather rigging and fell from the
rail into the sea. Jarvis had a boat away quickly and the man
was no more than slightly injured. On another occasion when
he was serving his time, Jarvis was not so fortunate. It was his
watch below and he rushed out at the cry of 'Man overboard!'
The ship was already being hove-to by letting the mainyards go
forward. Without a thought, he jumped into the boat which was
being lowered. They got away from the ship safely—that can be
dangerous—and pulled about for a long time. But they found
nothing. Jarvis wondered why the men in the boat were so silent.
After a couple of hours, darkness coming down, they were recalled.

"Who was it?" said Jarvis.

The men looked at him, astonished.

"Your brother," said the second mate.

Jarvis himself had survived a fall from aloft. The lower top-sail, being clewed up to change it in the trade winds, knocked him from the yard, but he fell into the belly of the course below it and was able to swing down to the deck on a buntline. That was in a very small ship, and it was in the days when sails clewed into the bunts of the yards, and the tops'l had been badly clewed up.

Sailors took this sort of thing for granted. The rule was one hand for yourself and one for the ship, but it was often neglected. It took two strong hands and a good many pairs of them to do any real job of work aloft in a big sailing-ship. Though there were beckets stropped along the jackstays here and there for the men to thrust an arm through, they rarely used them. It was not that they were careless. It just did not occur to them that their work was dangerous, and it was as well that it did not. When it *was* really dangerous, it was usually bad gear that made it so.

The sailing-ship man generally stayed in sailing-ships, long after he could easily have gone in powered vessels if he wanted to. I am speaking of the genuine working seaman who stayed at sea. His preference for sail was real. He liked the kind of ship-mates he met there. He liked the life. He liked the feeling that *he* was making a real contribution to the ship's voyage, and he loved to do the work he called 'sailorising'—the skilled rigging work with his hands. He liked the cleanliness and the peace of the life, and he appreciated the wholesome goodness of the trade wind days, and the comradeship of his fellows. At the wheel he liked to feel the response of the ship to his own hands upon the spokes, and this was spoiled by any intervening mechanism.

There were other and perhaps more practical reasons for preferring the sailing-ship. The food was no better in the average tramp steamer, and the conditions of employment were if any-thing worse. Both ships, steam and sail, worked internationally on the watch-and-watch system—two watches working four hours on, four hours off, or some variant of that basic system. But in the

sailing-ship there had to be a watch big enough to work the ship
and so, even in the very good weather when there was normally
little work with the sails, there were more men on deck than were
necessary to keep the routine turns at the wheel and look-out.
The custom in most ships, under such conditions, was that men
not actually on turn could stretch out somewhere on deck, and
take their ease, in the trade wind nights, so long as they were
ready for an immediate call. The watch appointed one of its
number, by turns, to remain alert and act as 'policeman', and the
officer of the watch summoned the men by blasts on his whistle—
one for one man, two for the watch, and three for all hands. The
policeman roused them and they were ready. So, although the
Cape Horn ship could be relied upon to try her hands to the
utmost limits of their endurance, she also gave them their good
times.

This the steamer never did. Her crew was at the irreducible
minimum. The watch on deck was often just two men, one at the
wheel and one on look-out, spelling each other. This was mo-
notonous, especially as the older tramps spent a good deal of their
time at sea and very little in port. When the usual Cape Horner
came in from sea she took her leisure. Even a *Preussen* took a
week or two to turn-round. But a tramp could have bulk cargoes
poured into her in a few days, and be off again. She could use
water ballast, and so required no appreciable time to get rid of
that. She might quite easily spend fifty or so days at sea, then
three days in port, and then another fifty days at sea, and then
go and do the same thing the next voyage.

The sailing-ship offered far more chance of variety and an
altogether more satisfying sort of life. The old sailor used to look
forward to his 'pay-day', though he so rarely profited by it.
Steamers on short trades gave him no pay-day, and that was
another reason why he did not like them. He was a man accustomed to being exploited and he was inured to having to work
off an advance—which he himself had very likely never seen—
for at least the first month of his voyage, and possibly for three.
One other advantage the sailer had or appeared to have, and
that was a greater security of employment. Ships paid off—dis-

charged the crew—after every round voyage, but a voyage in a
deepsea sailing-ship might go on for years. Tramp steamers paid
off far too frequently, and a man was far too often what he called
'on the beach'—without a ship. When he had no ship he had
to live the best way he could.

The work the steamer offered was distasteful to true sailors
and it was not mere scorn that made them speak of 'leaving the
sea and going into steam'. They abominated the endless round
of chipping, scraping, and paint-washing which the steamer demanded. All ships had plenty of this kind of work, of course, but
again, the long-voyage sailing-ship offered a much wider variety
of jobs. Though he might be regarded as a sort of international
vagrant by most officials ashore, the sailing-ship sailor, in his own
way, knew what he was doing and had his eyes well open. He
was deliberately leading the kind of life that he preferred.
Apprentices went on to steamships as they had to do so, but the
sailors did not.

Such men were poor material for the labour organisers. To
the end of the sailing-ship era crews were not unionised, even
in Australia. Union organisers left the sailing-ships alone. Though
there was plenty of scope for an intelligent organiser among men
who were frequently so shamelessly exploited and whose hope of
redress was practically non-existent, the sailing-ship man had an
abiding distrust of all persons he regarded as sea-lawyers. Unless
he was goaded beyond endurance, the improvement of his lot—
or anyone else's—did not bother him at all. He was essentially
an individualist, and his team-spirit was confined to the ship in
which he served. He let the future take care of itself. If the end
of his days found him forced into some old people's home he
hoped it would be strictly for sailors only, for there he would be
among his kind and be happy.

But normally his chances of becoming an inmate of an old
sailors' home were not great.

Part V

STUDY OF A CLIPPER

Chapter eleven

THE CUTTY SARK: A BIOGRAPHY—I

I HAVE selected the *Cutty Sark,* because hers is a good story and because she is still afloat. The *Cutty Sark,* a full-rigged ship of 963 tons gross, was built at Dumbarton in Scotland to the order of a well-known London sailing-ship owner, Captain John Willis. Captain Willis was one of those old-fashioned shipowners who had themselves been masters in sail. His father had been an owner before him, and he sent his son to sea in order to learn his trade. He was a shipowner of a type now practically extinct, a *personal* shipowner. It was not so much that he owned his ships outright, himself, and did not just head some public company which really owned them. He was more than that. He looked after his ships in much the same manner that a racing man would look after his best horses. Yet he was more than that, too, for his ships lasted longer than horses did, and they could involve him in losses even heavier than race-horses could, if he allowed them to do so. John Willis owned many clipper-ships, among them such famous vessels as the *Lammermuir* and *The Tweed.* He had been brought up in the China tea trade, and he was far from alone in his opinion that the clippers would hold their own there for a good many years to come, despite the Suez Canal and despite the increasing fleets of steamers. Steamships then were more often auxiliary sailing vessels. Willis liked his ships real, without noisy engines in them and hordes of ship's firemen, and a great propeller floundering away to spoil their sailing qualities.

Steam coal was expensive then, and steamships used prodigious quantities of it. An auxiliary steamer would take almost as

259

long on the long voyage to Australia as a sailing-ship would, and
it seemed then that the day when the steamer could possibly
carry bunkers enough to steam the whole way and somehow contrive to fit a paying cargo in her hull as well, was in the unforesee-
able future. As for Suez, it was enough for the old die-hards that
the ditch, as they called it, was French. It would probably cave
in, or silt up; or, if it succeeded, be taken over by Egypt sooner
or later, and made impossible to use. There was a real case for
continuing to develop sailing-ships. After all, it must be remembered that sailing-ships had been doing the world's work then—
all of its sea-borne trade—for a good many centuries. The ocean
winds were reliable. There was an abundance of good sailing-
ship sailors, and plenty of experienced masters. Sailing-ships were
still comparatively small and were not costly. Voyage costs were
predictable. Owning principles were well established, and thoroughly understood. Defects in ships became immediately apparent, and could be dealt with. The trade in Eastern products had
been, like every other trade, developed entirely by sailing-ships.
It was the use of power in ships that seemed the anomaly then.
'Bought wind', the old-timers called it, and asked with good
reason, why buy ocean winds? To use them better was the real
answer.

It was to demonstrate, for her owner's profit and the good
of the sailing-ship generally, just how best to make use of the
ocean winds for the benefit of sea-borne trade, that old John
Willis ordered the *Cutty Sark.* He was far from being alone in
his optimism. The year she was built—1869, the year that the
Suez Canal was completed—a dozen other lovely clippers were
launched, on both sides of the North Atlantic. Donald Mackay
launched that lovely ship, the *Glory of the Seas,* and the famous
Great Admiral also began her career that year. In the United
Kingdom the *Caliph,* the *Normancourt, Ambassador, Duke of
Abercorn, Oberon, Blackadder, Doune Castle,* and *City of Han-
kow* were among the clippers to begin their careers that year.
The Australian emigrant trade was doing very well, and this was
carried on almost exclusively under sail. The famous Scottish
Loch line was ordering its quartette of beauties, the *Lochs Ness,*

Tay, Katrine, and *Earn.* A good deal of the transatlantic passenger trade was still in the hands of sailing-ships, which had built it up to a state of remarkable efficiency despite the opposition of Samuel Cunard, and others. The Aberdeen White Star Line was building its first iron clipper, the *Patriarch.* The famed *Thermopylae* was a year old and had just made her wonderful maiden passage to Melbourne in sixty days. Sixty days to sail almost 15,000 miles! No steamship could hope to make a long passage like that. Neither could any other sailing-ship, and none ever did again. But old John Willis cherished secret hopes that his *Cutty Sark* would sail the sticks out of the *Thermopylae.* London to Melbourne in 60 days! Why not 55?

This was in the days before model experiments in tanks, or cold mathematical calculations, could compute the maximum speed a ship could do before she was ever built. An owner backed his own fancy, and an owner who had been a clipper master himself and owned such ships as *The Tweed* with conspicuous success, felt competent to dictate his ideas to designers and builders. When John Willis ordered the *Cutty Sark,* it was deliberately to lower the records held by the cock-sure *Thermopylae*—she already wore a gilded cock at her main truck—and to make such passages from China and from Australia as never had been made before.

In perfecting his ideas for the ship to beat all ships, John Willis drew heavily on the hull-shape of *The Tweed.* This was a most unusual ship. She was one of the early vessels which had been built as a steamer—with paddles, not the hull-spoiling screw—and then, after a useful life, had the engines taken out of her and was made into a sailing-ship. She was built as a paddle-frigate for the Hon. East India Company, as the *Punjaub.* Ship-owner Willis bought her and her sister-ship for £40,000, then promptly sold the sister for £42,000 and the engines and other junk out of the *Punjaub* for another £10,000. That is the sort of ship that owners liked. Before she ever sailed to begin earning for him, the only capital he had in her was the sum he had spent on lengthening her and converting her into a cargo-carrier.

With such a beginning *The Tweed* could not go wrong. She

was a powerful ship with a heavy stern and a look of massiveness and solidity. She looked more like a well-kept carthorse than a racehorse to the connoisseurs, who liked their clippers graceful almost to the point of fragility. But the connoisseurs were wrong, for *The Tweed* proved herself a handsome racer. More than that, she was a money-maker. Like the four-masted full-rigger *Lancing* of later days—which also began life as a steamship, and did not look a particularly fast sailing-ship—*The Tweed* was in the class of the record-breakers. Above all, she paid handsome dividends.

Tradition has it that, before Hercules Linton was entrusted with the task of designing the new ship, John Willis took him to have a thorough look at *The Tweed*. Doubtless old "White Hat" (as he was called because of the immaculate white topper he always wore) expounded at length on the merits of his favourite, and doubtless, too, the young designer didn't really get a great deal out of the visit. *The Tweed*'s was a wonderful sailing hull, without a doubt, but just *why* it had proved so easy to move through the sea, no man could say. She was something of a fluke, owing a little to the lines of an old French Indian Ocean privateer and a little more to the Asians who built her, and more again to some happy circumstance in her lengthening. But how to reproduce these things? That was the problem. Even sister-ships could vary greatly in performance. Hercules Linton was a first-class designer; with or without *The Tweed* to help him, he was going to produce a lovely ship.

One thing he did get from old White Hat's discourse and maybe that visit to *The Tweed* was the idea of giving the *Cutty Sark* a more powerful stern than most other British clippers had. Though the first requisite of a clipper-ship was speed, her hull was not meant just to race through the water. It had to survive in it, too. Many clippers were unduly fine. They flung their sharp cut-waters into the seas and their fine hulls followed through without, sometimes, bothering to rise at all, so that life aboard in bad weather was like living on a half-tide rock. This could be dangerous, especially in a heavy following sea. If the great walls of water rushing at the running ship found nothing aft to lift, then they were prone to break right over her. It was dangerous for a sailing-ship to take seas over her stern. Her controls were there. Her controls were simple, for they consisted only of a hand-steering-wheel, a binnacle to house the compass, and an officer of the watch. But they had to be safe. Watch officers were not to be washed overboard. Neither were helmsmen nor compasses. They could not be spared. In many clippers the helmsman was lashed to the wheel in bad weather, and the idea of that was two-fold. He had a better chance, probably, if a pooping sea broke over him; and he could not lose his nerve and run away if a glance aft frightened him. As well it might!

But the *Cutty Sark*'s helmsman had to be lashed to the wheel often, too.

Hercules Linton was a partner in the young shipbuilding firm of Scott and Linton, and this was the firm old White Hat trusted to build his super-ship. Anxious for the business of so important a shipowner, they cut things very fine. The contract price for the *Cutty Sark* was £21 a ton, and the specification was ruinous. Nothing but the best was to go in her—iron for her frames and the very best of timbers for her planking, and perfect teak for her decks. Every piece of timber, every fastening that went into her had to be perfect. Perfect timbers cost a deal of money and a ship built of them cost more than £21 a ton, even in 1869.

The firm of Scott and Linton went out of business over the *Cutty Sark,* but not before Hercules Linton and his partner had produced the hull of a perfect ship. She was no copy of *The Tweed,* nor of any other ship. She was perfection in her own right. Others finished her when the young perfectionists could no longer pay their men. But she is their memorial. Her perfectly balanced lines and the magnificent Scots craftsmanship that went into her building made it certain that the *Cutty Sark* was no ordinary ship, even among the clippers.

It was with high hopes that the new ship was brought round to the London river, towards the end of January, 1870, to load general cargo for Shanghai. Her master was Captain George Moodie, who had come to old Willis's favourable attention some years earlier as mate of *The Tweed.* Moodie had commanded two tea clippers, the *Laurel* and the *Lauderdale*. He was appointed to command the *Cutty Sark* shortly after the keel was laid, and it was the experienced eye of Captain Moodie that watched every piece of wood that went into the ship. He was a Scot, brought up as a fisherman and trained in the coastal and North Sea trades. He was forty years old—a little old, perhaps, for a clipper master. Driving clippers was an exacting life which threw an immense strain on body and mind. There were always more clippers than good clipper captains, but Moodie was a first-class man. He was a good reliable Scots shipmaster, a good sailor and a good handler of men. He was a good business man too, and that was an important part of his qualifications, for the business success of a voyage was very much in the hands of the captain.

But Moodie had no luck with the *Cutty Sark*. Light winds and annoying petty accidents aloft dogged the little clipper almost the whole way to China. It was a running-in voyage, of course. In those days the making of ironwork to fit properly into the rigging of a deepsea sailing-ship was not thoroughly understood. A clipper's masts had to be stayed perfectly to do their work. Her standing rigging had to be set up with the fineness of the strings of an expensive violin, and it was by no means easy to achieve this perfection or, once achieved, to maintain it. Yet it had to be maintained for months on end, under all sorts of climatic conditions, and through great gales and long calms. New rigging was the devil, and it took time for all its parts properly to function. Moodie was a master of the art of rigging, but it took him most of the run from London to Shanghai to get the *Sark* right. Meanwhile, her passage was spoiled. She did well, but she broke no records.

It was not the outward passage that mattered so much, though the masters did their best to achieve as good a run as possible. There were no premiums to be gained by bringing general cargoes to Shanghai more rapidly than other ships could sail there. It was new season's tea on the London market that made real racing worthwhile. The *Thermopylae* had gone to Melbourne with a full hold of general cargo, and went on from

Australia to Shanghai. The *Cutty Sark's* time from London was 104 days, and the old-timers *Sir Lancelot* and *Taeping* had little difficulty in bettering her passage. The *Lahloo* ran out in 98 days. The *Thermopylae,* on that run to Melbourne, was off the Cape only five weeks after leaving the English Channel. The *Cutty Sark* would obviously have to work hard to beat that handsome vessel—if she could do that at all.

The *Cutty Sark* was fortunate in getting a charter to load tea for the London market at a freight of £3–10 for 50 cubic feet. Steamers had shown already that they could make the run to London in 60 days, despite the sailing-ship men's forecast that their stokers would all drop dead in the Red Sea. Liverpool owners and Liverpool firemen made the steamers a success, as much as anyone did. That remarkable specimen of humanity, the Liverpool Irishman, soon showed that he could stand up to the really devilish work of firing a coal-burner in the Red Sea, with a following wind, as easily as his mates stood the icy blizzards of Cape Horn. Liverpool Irish were strong, too, in the forecastles of square-rigged ships, and there were plenty of them in the *Cutty Sark*.

The Suez Canal showed no signs of silting up or caving in, and coal bunkering firms were doing very nicely at Aden and Colombo, and Singapore. Steamship competition was more than a menace. It was soon going to be fatal.

The new clipper loaded her first cargo of tea, and off she raced. She had no hope of being first on the market, unless all the steamers blew up on the way home. But at least she could hope to be the first sailing-ship, and there were many in the trade who still believed that tea was contaminated by iron hulls and the fumes from stoke-holds. Back in London, old White Hat was doing his best to foster this belief, which died hard.

The *Cutty Sark* was 110 days from Shanghai to London that first voyage. It was a good run and better than most that season. But the *Thermopylae* was only 105 days from Foochow, and old Willis must have cursed. Owners and masters alike took a fierce personal interest in their ships and their passages, in those days. Captain Kemball of the *Thermopylae* was not as popular a figure in shipping circles as was Moodie. His wife, who sailed with him, was not very popular either. In fact there was no real comparison between the two passages. The *Thermopylae* sailed a month after the *Cutty Sark*. It was only when two ships could sail from the same port on the same tide that there could be a real match between them. White Hat bided his time, and went through the logs with a large magnifying glass. He could find no fault in the seamanship recorded there, nor did he expect to find any. Moodie had had to beat the whole long and reef-strewn way down the China Sea from Shanghai to Anjer. The new clipper had more than her share of calms later, where the trade winds should have been fresh. This was especially the case in the Indian Ocean. Moodie complained that he had no luck. Nonetheless he made the best passage of the group of clippers which sailed about the same time, and White Hat, though not elated, was still hopeful. The *Cutty Sark* came storming up the channel in a south-west gale and arrived in the Thames with many of her yards fished where they had been overstrained by Moodie's driving.

She had time enough to lick her wounds before setting out on her second China voyage. This was in the spring of 1871. Once again, the little full-rigger took general cargo to China while the *Thermopylae* went to Melbourne. Tea clippers which took cargoes to Australian ports then went on to China through the Pacific, sometimes with general cargo or coal and sometimes in ballast. Since they needed some ballast to go with the tea, this was not necessarily a less profitable way of reaching China than by going there direct. The *Cutty Sark*, however, was in time to earn some money for her owner by making a short run in the South China Sea—down to Bangkok for rice which she delivered to Hongkong. She made this run while the new season's tea was being prepared for the market. When the tea was ready, however, the steamers took most of it. The previous year the steamers *Diomed, Agamemnon,* and *Erl King* had taken tea to the London market in sixty days, via Suez, and though many old-timers sniffed at the stuff and swore that it smelled of anthracite and bilge water or that it had obviously been roasted in the Red Sea, neither the trade nor the increasing number of tea-drinkers could detect anything really wrong with it. So there was a regular rush to build steamers. The clippers were offered only a miserable £3 for each 50 cubic feet of tea they loaded.

This would not do for the *Cutty Sark*. Though she was actually on the loading berth—and the *Thermopylae* was there with her, promising a great race—she was pulled off again by her agents, and sent down to Foochow. It was a foolish move. She couldn't even get an offer of £3 at Foochow and had to come sadly back to Shanghai again. This time she was lucky to get a cargo at all. Seven of the clippers loaded for New York, where the new competition of the powered vessels was much weaker— they hadn't the bunkers to get across the Atlantic easily—but the *Cutty* had to eat humble pie, and accept £3. She raced homewards with the famous *Ariel* and beat her by a week. It is fair to add that the *Ariel* was handled that voyage by a new commander who possibly did not get the best out of her. The *Thermopylae* had a better run than both of them, but once again the result was inconclusive. The *Thermopylae* had sensibly accepted what was offered and spared herself the waste of time in going to Foochow. Old Willis consoled himself with the reflection that it was not the hated rival which had the best passage. The little *Titania* brought her tea into the London docks 93 days after clearing from Foochow.

That freight of £3 for 50 cubic feet bothered Shipowner Willis, but it did not deter him in his resolve to stick to sail in general and, in particular, to the *Cutty Sark*. This freight was less than half of what the clippers had been getting before the Canal was opened. It cost a lot of money to keep a clipper in good trim, and she could only pay her way if she received good freights. She was essentially an express and she had to be paid express rates. The most serious thing was that the steamers could pay dividends on lower freights than the fine-lined clippers could, for they loaded much larger parcels. It was all very well for the clippers to pick up a little money by coasting voyages, but there was not really much profit in these, and the steamers were not handicapped by the sailer's ability to make only one China voyage in a year. The steamers could make two quite easily, and soon they could make three, and even four. So they began to take out all the general cargo, too. They had another great advantage. They were *regular*. Shippers soon learned to appreciate that. After all, it was a great help all round, in the business world, if everyone concerned knew when expected cargoes were going to arrive. The clippers could still race one another, but it became painfully obvious to far-sighted merchants, owners, and masters alike that it was a dying gesture and, really, a useless one.

But it took a long time for the die-hards like Willis to admit defeat. He managed to get a general cargo for the *Cutty Sark* outwards again to Shanghai in '72, and deliver it in 108 days. He still had many friends among the shippers. The *Thermopylae* again went to Melbourne and in sticking to that trade, her owners showed good business sense. It was much more difficult for powered vessels to compete with square-rigged ships when the sailers had the advantage of the almost ideal wind conditions of the Australian voyage. To get to China a square-rigger had to work through the whole dangerous area of the South China Sea and, once she passed the barrier of the chain of Indonesian islands, the rest of the passage could be a nightmare. In that area the wind blew either from the south-west or the north-east, in alternating seasons called monsoons. If a shipmaster naturally preferred to wait for the monsoon which favoured him, the shippers did not. A monsoon in the face of an efficient steamer—and they were steadily becoming more efficient—did not bother her much, but it added weeks to a sailing voyage. On the Australian run, the sailer knew that she could 'run her easting down'—storm along south of Forty S. from Tristan da Cunha to landfall off her Australian port—with an almost unbroken succession of westerly gales behind her. There were no bunker ports serving those wild waters. A steamer would have to stagger from Durban across to Fremantle, or from the Cape, which was further. If she sailed (as many did) then she stood to lose her advantage of predictable arrival date. If she steamed, her boilers needed so much coal that she couldn't carry a paying cargo.

So there was still a future for square-rigged ships in that trade, and the *Thermopylae*'s owners knew what they were doing. There were freights offering homewards from Australia in increasing quantities, too, and the square-rigged ship—for the time being—had an advantage over steam with these, also. The shortening of the route to Australia by using Suez Canal was more theoretical than real until steamers were more efficient.

In 1872 the *Thermopylae* ran out to Melbourne in 67 days, which was a week longer than that beautiful ship had taken on her maiden voyage. It was an excellent run, and when at last she was on the loading berth together with the *Cutty Sark* in Shanghai later that year, a good many knowledgeable shipmasters put their money on her to win. At last there was to be a real race. The ships were well matched. The *Thermopylae* was a little the larger and had the better record. Her record was comparatively free of the minor accidents which had marred the *Cutty Sark's*. She had been luckier with her winds, too—and that was an important matter to a deepsea sailing-ship. Her master, Captain Kemball, was well-known as a competent and fearless navigator as well as a master driver of clippers. He knew his ship well, and he knew, too—better perhaps than Moodie did—how to make the best use of all the divers channels and the changing conditions down the long and trying South China Sea. He had first-class officers and a good crew, well accustomed to the ship.

The *Cutty Sark* was well-manned, too, and everybody aboard her was equally determined and confident. They had easily defeated the famous *Sir Lancelot* on the outwards passage. They swore, indeed, that they had never seen the ship they could not sail past. That was an old sailor's boast which was heard more often than it was substantiated, but in the *Cutty Sark's* case there was a good deal of truth in it.

The two ships dropped out of the Chinese port on the same tide and were promptly held up for three days in heavy fog. This was a poor way to begin a race which should have been so stirring. It was to have a poorer end. After a first-class sailing match all down the China Sea with now the one ship leading, now the other, the *Cutty Sark* had the misfortune to lose her rudder in a gale in the Indian Ocean. She might as well have been dismasted. The *Thermopylae* suffered no such accident and raced onwards to come in an easy first. But Captain Moodie and his men, far from being deterred by so serious an accident—for the ship was quite helpless without her rudder—set to at once and made her a new rudder, fitted it at sea, and sailed on. Again the makeshift rudder carried away and again they fitted another, and they put up such a splendid performance bringing the deeply-laden clipper over 8,000 miles in her semi-crippled and hope-lessly handicapped condition that the whole shipping world awarded the *Cutty Sark* the moral victory.

Moodie's seamanship indeed had been magnificent. Think of it! There was the ship, less than a thousand tons, jumping and leaping in the confused and dangerous sea left by three days of continuous gale. Always a wet ship, now she was almost as much under water as above it. The gale had been a very heavy one even for those down-south latitudes, and had blown out some sails which were sewn to stand up to hurricanes. However, she was holding her own and indeed doing quite well, until a tre-mendous sea broke under her counter and wrenched the wooden rudder from its pintles. The ship which had been rolling and plunging enough before, now began to roll as if she was falling right over. She fell into the trough of the sea, and the great combers creamed aboard her and smashed along her maindeck. It was just as well that she was not opposing them or they would have smashed her. It was all very well to lie hove-to under a few rags of storm canvas, but somehow the ship had to be brought under control again, and that as quickly as possible.

There were not even any planks stout enough to make a tem-porary rudder. Captain Moodie at first tried steering with a spare spar out astern like a big sweep, but this was no use to the thoroughbred. He had to make her a real rudder, somehow. Undeterred by his wretched ill-luck, the gale or the obvious handicaps of trying to carry out a major dry-docking job in the open sea with a deeply-laden ship which was trying to roll under, Moodie had all hands turned to. First they made heavy planks by sawing them bodily out of some spare spars—all clippers

ABOVE RIGHT   Captain Richard Woodget

ABOVE LEFT   The clipper *Cutty Sark* is the last surviving real clipper anywhere.

BELOW   This is Captain Woodget's own picture of the *Cutty Sark*.   →

A great Tea Clipper race—neck and neck up the Channel after over three months at sea

The American-built Australian clipper *James Baines*, of the famous Black Ball Line

carried plenty of spare spars, for they knew that they might need them—and, at the same time, contrived the necessary ironwork to replace the lost pintles. The little ship had one good break. She had two stowaways aboard who turned out to be excellent craftsmen, one a shipwright and the other a blacksmith. These two worked splendidly, and this must be one of those extremely rare instances when stowaways turned out to be of use to the vessel they were stealing passage in.

There was another person aboard who was no help at all. This was old White Hat's brother, Robert Willis, who was making the voyage for the good of his health. (He must have been a very healthy man to embark upon it.) When the rudder was carried away, Robert Willis cursed and raved about the poop like a madman, clamouring at poor Moodie to make for the nearest port. This must have been a trial, and Moodie promptly swore back at him and told him to go to hell. Robert Willis remained a sullen and useless critic throughout the proceedings and the rest of the passage, and the incident so rankled on Captain Moodie that he resigned his command as soon as he got home.

Despite the useless protests of the loud-mouthed passenger and all the other disabilities, a temporary rudder was made and properly secured, and the *Cutty Sark* was brought under control again. Still the gales continued to howl at her. The new rudder was manhandled by a system of wires and chains leading to a spar across the poop and thence to the wheel, and she steered quite well. But the fresh onset of a row of gales on end put too great a strain on the jury rudder, and it had to be hauled inboard again for repairs. A second time it was shipped, successfully.

Fitting a jury rudder to the inaccessible stern-post while the ship was under way and leaping all over the place like a frisky two-year-old at a reluctant barrier, was a prodigious job. Seas washing aboard continually upset the blacksmith's forge, which was a primitive arrangement at the best. One sea knocked down not only the forge but also the blacksmith and the apprentice— Moodie's son—who was helping him. The forge full of hot coals fell on young Moodie's chest and the blacksmith was swept about

the decks in the huge sea, still clinging to the bar of redhot iron
he had been working on. He did not let it go. Young Moodie,
sworn at for wasting the fire, carried the scars of those burns
all his life and the blacksmith had his beard singed by the bar
of iron. But they got on with the job again as soon as they could.
The rudder was shipped, though, on the second occasion, this
was only possible by slipping it over the stern and then *backing*
the ship on to it with sternway, and reeving the rudder-post up
through the place for it. This was superb seamanship.

Men who took this sort of thing in their stride deserved to
win. But the *Thermopylae* had stormed along hundreds of miles
ahead, and when she arrived an easy first in the Channel, Kemball was cocky about it. Of course, he did not know of his rival's
accident. He knew only that he had last seen her a few miles away
off Anjer and had heard nothing of her since. When a few days
later the *Cutty Sark* came limping gamely up the Channel, racing
under a cloud of sail right to the last, even Kemball stared when
he heard she had come from the wrong side of Good Hope with
no proper steering-gear.

But he still declared that he had won. Argument was hot, for
the *Cutty Sark* was a London ship and Kemball's a pure Scot,
and the excellent show she had put up—it is doubtful if a
handicapped sailing-ship ever sailed from Good Hope to the
Channel faster, and indeed not a great many in perfect shape
could show a better passage—made the *Sark* many friends. The
English love of the game loser made a real heroine out of her and,
before long, it was Kemball who was being commiserated. He
refused point-blank to produce the *Thermopylae's* log in order
that it could be proved which ship was ahead up to the time the
Sark lost her rudder—there is little doubt that the Londoner *was*
ahead then—and that piece of poor sportsmanship lost him many
supporters.

But Captain Moodie had had enough. He left the *Cutty Sark,*
and sailing-ships, and went into steam. He had saved a little
money and he put it into a steamship company in Glasgow, with
which he took a command. And there, poor man, he lost everything. But the *Cutty Sark* sailed on.

Chapter twelve

BIOGRAPHY OF A CLIPPER—II

CAPTAIN MOODIE'S decision bothered old White Hat. Good masters were becoming ever harder to find. Even at their best, some of the crack clippers were poorly commanded. The ideal combination of qualities necessary to get the best out of a racing square-rigged ship, week after week and month after month, and to make a commercial success out of her voyage as well, was not often found in the person of one man. Yet one man was master, and had to be. No committees could run a sailing-ship. Consummate seamanship, magnificent leadership, iron nerves, an equable temperament and the ability to go without sleep for days on end and with insufficient rest for months, perfect judgment of wind and gear and weather and sea, mastery of a huge mass of sailing-lore painfully acquired (often its very acquisition would break down many men), the ability to withstand temptation of all sorts, especially of the bottle—these were only a few of the necessary qualities. A great clipper-captain had to have the feeling of a magnificent conductor, the brain of a tank general, infinite practical ability, unquestioned power of command, and the body of an ox. He was a master-sailmaker, master-shipwright, master-stevedore. He was his ship's brains, eyes, thoughts, and controlling hands. He had complete charge of a great seafaring entity—great though so small—in such a manner as is not now known, and little appreciated. No wonder that good clipper-captains were hard to find!

Captain Moodie was succeeded in command of the *Cutty Sark* by Captain F. W. Moore, who was the Willis marine superintendent at the time. Moore was a great captain and had a splendid reputation, but he was past real driving when he took over the new command. As a marine superintendent, he hated to see ships damaged in any way, and he was most reluctant to place too great a strain on wooden masts and yards, and hempen running rigging. So the *Cutty Sark* rarely did her best for him. She needed driving. The spirit of the wanton witch implied in her curious name could cope with gales and heavy winds, and did not like lying down to them. She did not care for the sedate hand of Captain Moore. He had her only for one voyage. First, she sailed to Melbourne with general cargo. She left London, very deeply laden, on November 26, 1872, and was anchored in Port Philip Bay on February 11, 1873. But the *Thomas Stephens* sailed a week after her and reached Melbourne on the same day. The *Stephens* was lucky enough to miss a gale that the *Cutty Sark* met in the Channel. The two ships took their departures * on the same day, the *Sark* from the Lizard and the *Stephens* from Start Point. From Melbourne the clippers shifted round the coast to lift New South Wales coal for Shanghai. The *Cutty Sark* ran up through the SW Pacific—up through the Coral Sea and then outside the Philippines and through the chain of the Ryukyu Islands—in 41 days, which was two days better than the *Thermopylae* did that year. But the *Hallowe'en* and the *Doune Castle* made the same run in five weeks. Coal was a heavy cargo for the clippers, and the *Cutty Sark*'s powerful stern dragged a bit in light winds when she was deeply loaded. She had to weather a typhoon near the Ladrones. Captain Moore had her in beautiful shape alow and aloft, and even the hurricane winds failed to shift a spar, though the *Blackadder* was badly dismasted in the same blow.

This year the famous ships *Sir Lancelot, Titania, Thermopylae,* and *Cutty Sark* loaded tea together in Shanghai and a wonderful race was promised, despite the steamers. These ships had to beat down the China Sea at the time of the unfavourable

---

* "Took their departures" means, to sailors, to set out on the actual ocean passage, from the last of the land. The position of the ship, plotted from the last bearings as accurately as possible, was placed on the chart. This was her "point of departure".

monsoon, and that year the weather was particularly violent. It was not just the ability to sail fast when she had a good wind that made the China tea clipper's reputation. It was her general sailing ability—her capacity to ghost along with next to no wind at all, and above all her weatherliness, by which is chiefly meant her dexterity in biting her way to windward against wind and sea. It was her sailing qualities in *adverse* conditions that gave her a lead over her peers. It was of no use merely to go outside, pick up a fair wind, and then hang studding-sails all round the ship like the Monday washing. Studding-sails, so beloved by artists, were essentially fine-weather kites, morale builders in light winds more than really useful canvas. They looked well though they were an infernal nuisance to set, and a worse nuisance to trim.

There was no use for such sails when the clippers were engaged in the dour beat right down the China Sea. Here everything was against them. There was no hope of a fair wind in the wrong season. Worse than the constant head wind was the fact that it also brought up a strong adverse current and, though the ships might avoid the worst of this by getting over on the western side, the waters were badly charted—they still are—and full of reefs and sets, and shallows and all sorts of traps for the deep hulls of sailing-ships. There were many narrow straits to beat through, and nothing but dour slogging to wind'ard could get a ship past such places. There was no other way she could go. So day and night, day after day and week after week, the little ships would beat and fight their way along against rising wind and short steep sea, and rain and poor visibility, with the chance of a stray typhoon as well, until they got well down. It was often more than a chance. The *Cutty Sark* had to fight another typhoon that passage, near Formosa. She came through all right but it set her back, and she was twelve days astern of the *Thermopylae* by the time she reached Anjer. Kemball of the *Thermopylae* was always noted for the splendid passages he made down the China Sea, no matter what the season. He must have been a magnificent ship-master.

Moore brought the *Cutty Sark* home that year in 117 days.

It might have been worse. But the *Thermopylae* beat him by more than a fortnight, and the *Hallowe'en* was only 90 days. It is fair to add that the *Hallowe'en* sailed over four months after the others and had a favourable monsoon down the China Sea—a very different story, indeed. The old-timers never spoke of a tea clipper's passage without mentioning the time of year she passed through the China Sea, for it was obviously unjust to compare the passage of a ship which romped along before a soldier's wind with others which had to beat the first 2,000 miles—and *knew* they would have to, when they sailed. The difficulties of that beat were well known and indeed, Lloyd's underwriters generally charged higher premiums on ships which chanced it. This was offset by the ship's better freights. The *Cutty Sark,* for instance, had tea at £4 for each 50 cubic feet, and the *Hallowe'en's* freight was only £2–10. So it made business sense to buck the wrong monsoon. What was business sense had to be maritime sense too.

Captain Moore was followed by Captain W. E. Tiptaft, who seems to have been a modest and competent seaman but without the verve of the true racing master. He had not commanded a real clipper before, and he appears to have taken things a bit easy in the *Cutty Sark*. He took her to Sydney first—Sydney was a handier port than Melbourne for a coal charter on to China— and his log indicates that he was reluctant to go much south of Forty South in his quest of west winds. The *Thermopylae* went down to Forty-five and Forty-seven and raced to Melbourne in 72 days, which was a week better than Tiptaft's time to Sydney. Most of the tea clippers went down to Australia that year, for the steamers by then were taking almost all the general cargo to China. There was plenty of business for the sailers on the loading berths to Melbourne and Sydney, and the coal business to Chinese ports was also doing well. The increasing number of steamers made considerable, and growing, demands for bunker coal, and the sailing-ships brought it for them—not willingly. They hated coal cargoes almost as much as they hated steamers. But it was business. It was obviously cheaper to stock Pacific bunker ports with coal from New South Wales than to ship the stuff from the

United Kingdom. So the sailing-ships would arrive at Shanghai having already earned two freights, and there was still a profit to be made from them.

There was no tea at Shanghai for the *Cutty Sark,* and for a while it was thought she might have to go back to Australia, empty, to bring more coal. However her China coast agents— Jardine, Matheson—were enterprising fellows, not so greatly carried away by the obviously increasing steamship business that they threw the clippers on the discard. Perhaps they were not yet quite convinced about the Suez Canal, either. So they sent the little ship 600 miles up the Yangtze-kiang to load new season's tea at Hankow. Their London correspondents were still writing them that the London market would pay well enough for a few clipper cargoes brought round the Cape, even though the tea was at least a month longer at sea than in any steamer. The old myth that it was better carried in sail was still much alive, and the *Cutty Sark* was able to get her Hankow cargo without much difficulty. Hankow was a dangerous place to load, with swift currents, and mudbanks, and plenty of jagged rocks—and a 600-mile tow to pay for, too, both ways.

Tiptaft, by loading at Hankow, was able to bring the first sail-carried new season's tea to the London market. But he did not hurry over it. There were several ways down the China Sea and the more dangerous were the faster. He took the easiest way and was 118 days to London. Again, the *Thermopylae* beat him by a fortnight. The redoubtable Kemball was still in command of the Aberdeen ship, but it was his last voyage in her. He left when she arrived home to take over the iron clipper *Aristides,* a green beauty of a ship which also was to achieve fame in the Australian trade, though she was not the equal of the lovely *Thermopylae.*

The *Cutty Sark,* though she was beaten so roundly by her old rival, made a better passage than most of the other racers. Again, when the tea cargo was out, she sailed to Australia and made the best passage of 1874–75 to Sydney. This was 73 days: but the *Thermopylae* was only 64 days to Melbourne. Again, it was the chance of a fair wind down-channel, where the *Cutty Sark* had had to slog against a south-west gale and lost a man washed overboard, that gave the other ship the edge. If one ship sailed a week ahead of another and then had to spend that week beating against an appalling head wind, which had blown itself out and been replaced by a favouring wind by the time the second ship sailed, then of course the later-sailing ship had a very great advantage. Though her hull might never move through the water any faster than her rival's, though her master, officers and crew were of equal abilities and she had nothing whatever else in her favour, she might well make the better passage through luck and not merit, and win the 'race'.

It was for this reason that the old-timers paid heed only when ships left the same port, in the same trim, on the same tide. It was just because the *Cutty Sark* continued, voyage after voyage, to miss slight initial advantages which the *Thermopylae* had the luck to gain, that the rivalry between the two ships remained at a high pitch and old Willis continued doggedly to believe that he had, after all, the better ship. Had he? The point is still arguable. At any rate, it is certain that he had no Kemball for his clipper until it was almost too late. Tiptaft did well, but not well enough. He picked up new season's tea again at Hankow, but was over four months delivering it to London. Once again, the *Thermopylae* beat her—this time by almost a week. But the ships did not sail from the same port nor at the same time. The *Hallowe'en* was only 92 days.

The *Cutty Sark* was back at London on October 21, 1875. A month later to the day, she sailed for Sydney. On this passage she ran 2,163 miles in six consecutive days, in the Roaring Forties; but at the same time the *Thermopylae*, which had sailed almost a week after her, was romping along at an average 270 miles a day. Again the rival had the better passage, this time by a week. The *Thermopylae* went to Melbourne, as usual, and the *Cutty Sark*'s Sydney supporters pointed out that it was further to their port, and—according to them, at any rate—if she had been bound to Melbourne, the *Cutty Sark* would have arrived there only 64 days out. Perhaps she would, for she was certainly in Bass Straits at that time and *could* have made Melbourne Heads when the wind forced her to turn south of Tasmania.

The log line—a contrivance to measure speed, made of high quality light hemp, marked with knots up to 15½, which used to be paid out from a reel held in the hands of two large apprentices—often ran out of its full length before the sand was all out of the glass, during that run. The clipper's speed was computed at 17 knots or possibly a shade better, and that was a wonderful speed for a deeply-laden ship with a waterline of little more than 200 feet. Neither she nor the *Thermopylae,* nor any other of the British tea clippers, had the great advantage of the big passenger ships in the Australian run, like the wonderful *Lightning* and the *James Baines,* the *Sobraon* and the rest. These kept their tweendecks empty of cargo to give the passengers room to sleep, and so they were always comparatively lightly loaded. This meant both that there was less of their hulls immersed to be driven through the water, and their decks were up out of the sea and drier and safer. They could be pressed even more than the tea clippers were.

After all, it made no sense to sail a clipper under. If too great a weight of water ever descended at once on her decks from the great snarling seas in which she raced, she most certainly would go under. Some did. Many had narrow escapes. They were very much *in* the sea, and when they were deep-loaded they had no great reserve of buoyancy. Neither the name of the *Cutty Sark* nor of the *Thermopylae* appears in the list, published in Lloyd's Calendar, of sailing-ships which claimed the greatest day's runs. Yet it is curious that it is the *Thermopylae* which holds the record for the London-to-Melbourne run, and the *Cutty Sark* is little behind her. It is the *Thermopylae,* again, which holds the record —28 days—from Newcastle to Shanghai. The *Cutty Sark's* 67-day run from Sydney to the Channel in 1885 is very little behind the *Lightning's* record 63 days from Melbourne to Liverpool, though the big, flat-floored *Lightning* was over twice her tonnage.

The difficulty with a deep-loaded little ship, trying to race before a gale, was that continuous gales brought up seas that she could not survive in, for, if she were driven too hard, the seas would race over her. A big ship with more freeboard could run much longer. If a sailing-ship once began to take seas badly over her stern or roll them in over both quarters, the Lutine Bell * would toll for her at Lloyd's in London.

Under Captain Tiptaft, there was little chance that the *Cutty Sark* would sail under. She went from Australia up to China again with coal, and after that was discharged, loaded tea again at Hankow. Tiptaft made a splendid passage home and beat the *Thermopylae* by a week. She had the better freight, too—£4–5 as against the other's £3. Altogether, it was an excellent round voyage, and old White Hat was pleased.

But the Glen Line's steamer *Glenartney* had her tea home in six weeks, and so did the *Glenearn* and a dozen other steamers. Though there was still thought to be room for a sailing-ship parcel or two brought round the Cape, it was becoming increasingly difficult to maintain the idea or to get a decent rate of freight for bringing the tea. Others of the surviving clippers had begun to take silk and anything else they could load, as well as tea. Altogether, only eight of them loaded in China in '76, full or part cargoes. The *Titania* went to New York from Shanghai and the lovely *Sir Lancelot* ran out to Otago and thence to Yokohama to load for France. Tea was all but finished as a cargo for clippers, or for any other kind of sailing-ship. Loading costs were high, and the clippers had always been accustomed to wait for a cargo. A cargo worth waiting for had to pay a good freight and, since the steamers could time their voyages to arrive when the cargo was ready, they could afford to undercut. Tea was, moreover, only one of their cargoes. They were well stowed with other goods. Nor did they have to buy sailing ballast, or waste good paying space on its stowage. A clipper had to be in perfect trim to do her best; a steamer could hog along with a hog's load, and make a good enough passage of it.

Old Willis did not speak of 'bought winds' any longer, though he continued to hope that the Suez Canal would cave in. The Canal Company, however, was doing very well, and the canal was splendidly maintained. The clipper's hopes now lay almost en-

* The Lutine Bell is sounded on the floor at Lloyd's to announce important news, such as tidings concerning missing ships.

tirely in the maintenance of the fiction that tea carried round
Good Hope in their hulls reached the market in better condition
than tea carried in the steamers. Tea, however, was steadily
becoming more and more a popular beverage, and the number
of consumers who could distinguish between sail-carried and
steam-carried tea—or who imagined they could—was diminish-
ing. Tea was available at lower prices, too. A great many new
consumers didn't know the taste of sail-carried tea—if it had any
special taste. There was no hope that clipper freights would ever
rise again, even if the sailers could get a cargo.

The *Cutty Sark* had her last China tea cargo in '77. She
cleared from Woosung—after loading up-river at Hankow—on
June 6 that year, but it was not until 127 days later that she
arrived in the Thames. The *Thermopylae* sailed a month later
but was alongside in London only a week after her. The *Cutty
Sark's* freight had to cover her river towage costs over 1500 miles
and the cost of two good anchors left in the deep mud of the
Yangtze. Some of the clippers had had to take £2. There were
poor dividends that year, and there was plenty of pessimism. But
those personal shipowners were courageous old bull-dogs who did
not know when they were beaten. Willis refused to accept the
obvious. He put his best clipper on the loading berth for Sydney
again and, once more, she raced out in less than two and a half
months.

But first she was very nearly wrecked on the Goodwins the day
after she left London. She was caught in an exceptionally violent
November gale which flung squalls of hurricane force at her.
Compelled to shelter in the Downs, she was one of scores of ships
which could not keep their ground tackle in the furious storm.
In the days of sail, casualties were much more commonplace than
they are today. Ships were exposed to much greater risks near the
land. Unable to beat against the terrific wind and unable to
shelter or keep her anchors in the turbulent seas in the Downs,
she drove about helplessly. It was a black night, and the Downs
was full of driving ships, crashing into one another, driving on
the sands, sinking, capsizing, sending up distress flares. Every lifeboat on the east coast of England went out that night, and the

surf breaking on the Kent beaches in the morning rolled the bodies of hundreds of drowned seamen on the sand. Once, twice, the *Cutty Sark,* driving helpless, collided with unknown ships, crunching and grinding together, smashing each other's yards and long jib-booms. Tiptaft tried to get sail on the clipper, but her canvas soon lashed to ribbons. Her bulwarks were stove in and much of her running rigging was cut away by the collisions. It was in the nick of time that the tug *McGregor* got hold of her in the morning and, even then, could barely hold her off the sands. A second tug had to help before the crippled ship could at last be brought safely back into the Thames.

This was salvage. The two tugs claimed £8,000. The value of the ship and cargo was put at £85,000. With an award of £3,000 the tugs were not overpaid. But it was a costly night. Other ships which had been damaged sued the *Cutty Sark* as the ship—they said—which had collided with them. But they couldn't prove it. One at least of them might have been able to, for her name-board fell into the clipper's scuppers while the ships were locked together. The carpenter, an old man who had been in the ship since she was launched, saw the name-board lying there in the morning and quietly threw it overboard, without a word to any-one. He wasn't going to have his beloved ship paying out money to any strange vessel, especially to one which had damaged her.

When she finally reached Sydney, the *Cutty Sark* discharged her general cargo and at once took in coal for Shanghai. While she had been storming out to Sydney, her great rival had run magnificently from the Lizard to the Line in seventeen days, though she was 74 days London to Melbourne compared with the *Cutty Sark's* 72 to Sydney. When the small group of surviving clippers reached Shanghai, it was to find that what little tea was left for them could pay a freight of only 25 or 35 shillings. This was ruinous. The *Cutty Sark* managed to get half a cargo at Hankow and then shifted to Shanghai, hoping to complete. This she could not do, for there was no more tea there. So the Hankow parcel was discharged, and she went tramping with coal cargoes across to Japan. Back again in Shanghai, still no tea was offering. The season was a bad one and there was nothing like the usual quantity of tea on the market and, in any event, the steamers had taken almost all of it. The *Thermopylae* took a cargo at 35/– for the standard 50 cubic feet and was home in 110 days.

While the *Cutty Sark* was waiting, Captain Tiptaft died. He was succeeded in command by his mate, Captain Wallace. This was towards the end of '78. Tiptaft had done well in bad times. He had shown what the little ship could do, especially in the Australian trade. He had nursed her and looked after her well and made quite tolerable passages. But Wallace was a real driver.

Wallace might have been a driver but there was no tea to be driven, and after hanging about Shanghai for months, the *Cutty Sark* had to sail back to Sydney in ballast. This costly and time-wasting sort of thing was only a taste of the fate awaiting sailing-ships, although they were to be built in the United Kingdom for another quarter of a century, and, in Germany, for almost half a century. The new sailing-ships were not small, however, and none were built as racers. One thing they all had in common which such vessels as the tea clippers lacked. They could carry a lot, and earn good money when freights were offering. The day of the luxury cargo-carrier and racing passenger-sailing-ship was over. The crews which handled such vessels as the *Cutty Sark* were large enough to handle vessels three times her size. The clipper's complement was 28 men, all of them—at first—skilled and fearless seamen. When, in later days, Willis cut her crew to 23 and 24, and even to 19, that was the same number which handled big four-masted barques carrying anything up to 5000 tons of cargo. If sailing-ships were forced out of the better-paying luxury trades, they had to carry what offered—bulk cargoes like wheat and lumber, and rice, and nitrates.

At any rate, Wallace made a good passage down to Sydney. Sailing *from* Sydney to Shanghai was a comparatively easy romp up before the trade winds, up through the Coral Sea and the Western Pacific—a flying-fish passage. But going *to* Sydney was

a different affair altogether, for the square-rigged ship had
first to work her way down the South China Sea (just as if she
were bound to Europe), then through the breadth of the Indian
Ocean, and then run her easting down across the stormy seas
south of Australia and sail up the east coast, coming into Sydney
from the south. Wallace had the little ship off Anjer just over
a fortnight after leaving Shanghai and passed south of Tasmania
when he had been six weeks at sea. He was seven weeks to
Sydney.

Still sticking to that optimistic and ill-founded belief that
his thoroughbred could find tea to carry, old Willis ordered the
clipper to take coal back to Shanghai. This she did, with a good
passage of a little over six weeks. Again it was futile. The *Thermopylae* did not even try the market but contented herself with a
cargo of Australian wool which she took homewards round the
Horn. As no tea was offering, Wallace took the clipper to Manila
to load jute and sugar for New York, which she reached after
a passage of 111 days. Then she ran back to the Thames in 19
days. According to her crew it was only ten days from off Sandy
Hook, but the log does not uphold this. Maybe the crew's idea
of 'off Sandy Hook' was a few hundred miles off, out in the Atlantic. Clipper crews never belittled their ships or their performance. Even as late as 1952 there was a *Cutty Sark* survivor
who declared that she had sailed from the Channel to Cape
Otway in 54 days, and from the Lizard to the Line in 16, though
such records were never claimed by her masters or by Willis. Nor
are they in her logs. According to the same informant, the ship
was "never passed by anything, not even an albatross"—or by a
four-jet airliner. If by strange chance such an apparition *had*
caught up with her, no one aboard would have looked.

At this stage in their affairs the surviving clippers were dispersed. A few went to the Indian coastal trade, some to the
trans-Pacific. Even old White Hat had become a pessimist. No
longer did he spend money freely to maintain the pride of his
fleet. He reduced her rig, cutting down her heavy spars on the
plea that her racing days were over. This was one of the

best things he ever did, though his reason was proved gloriously wrong. Most clippers were unnecessarily over-sparred. They could afford to be reduced a bit and to have such airy kites as skysails taken from them. Even studding-sails were usually more nuisance than they were worth, and the designers who incorporated sufficient of their area into broad, double topsails and topgallants did seafarers a good turn. Of course, the old-timers kicked at every innovation. They scorned even double tops'ls for a quarter of a century, and used to leave the upper yard mastheaded because they held that the two yards together spoiled the look of their ships. (Even in 1952, one full-rigged schoolship was still rigged like that, because her predecessor had been a single tops'l frigate, and her master liked things the way they were.)

So there were plenty of kicks when the *Cutty Sark's* rig was cut down a little, even from those whose work was much lightened by that change for the better. Shortly after her rig had been reduced the ship was chartered to load best steam coal in the Bristol Channel, for the American Navy in Chinese waters. Naval ships were finely-strung then, as now, and nothing but the best steam coal was good enough for them. So off went the little ship round to Penarth to lift her first coal cargo from a British port. Her reduced rig and circumstances were, unfortunately, reflected in her crew. The days were gone when clippers could command loyalty from the best class of mariners. These went in the steamships, and the clippers, like other sailing-ships, had to take what they could get. There was, moreover, a great demand for good steady officers in the steamships, which by that time were doing very well in all the passenger trades—across the North Atlantic, to South Africa, to Australia—as well as in the cargo business. New great steamship lines were being formed, and they all required both mariners and officers.

So it happened that the crew the *Cutty Sark* was furnished for that voyage was a poor one. Worse than that, the officers were a poor lot too. The mate was something of a 'bucko'—which is another name for bully—and the second mate was a weak type. He had poor eyesight, too, and could scarcely see clearly from the poop to the fore royal yard. Captain Wallace was a good man and an excellent sailor, but he had one fatal weakness. He was too easy-going. He lacked the essential qualities of leadership. He did not put his bucko in his place, as he should have done. Instead, he suffered him. The crew, shipped at Penarth, perhaps was the better for a little bullying the first week out. But it went on for months.

Wallace did another foolish thing. He sailed on a Friday. This may seem a small thing, but in 1880 and for many years afterwards, it was flying in the face of all maritime tradition. Sailors before the mast were superstitious, and they were appalled at the idea of sailing on a Friday. It was *tabu*. It was just not done. They held the belief, firmly and against all possible argument, that to begin a voyage—any voyage—on a Friday was to fly in the face of Providence. They lived by the grace of Providence, and they were well aware of that. A man took his life in his own strong hands when he shipped away in a long voyage clipper or any other kind of deepsea sailing-ship. To begin the voyage by deliberately flouting such an ancient superstition was to ask for disloyalty. Wallace asked for it, and he got it.

Included in the crew were eight apprentices, good stout lads who, after a year or two in the ship, were as competent as most able seamen. Their parents had paid premiums for them to be taught the business of seafaring, and it was incidental that the lads also provided a solid core of cheap, efficient, and loyal labour. It was a good thing they were there. The foremast hands were a ragged lot, including several who had not been in that class of ship previously, and a notorious old croaker who went by the name of Vanderdecken. Sailing on a Friday horrified this man, and he forecast every imaginable kind of accident. He kept on forecasting accidents throughout the whole of his stay in the ship and, unfortunately, too many of his forecasts were accurate.

But at first the *Cutty Sark* raced along very well, after an initial setback from a south-west gale, and she was well on the way to making a splendid passage when she reached the south-

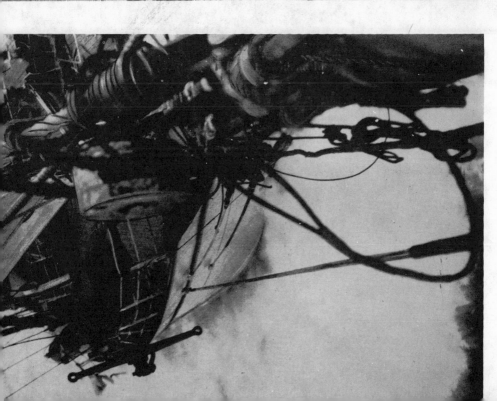

Studding-sails were more nuisance than they were worth.

Snoring along! A lee bow view

east trades of the Indian Ocean. The bucko mate had the crew working well, though one steamer hand named Francis, a coloured man, remained completely recalcitrant and useless. When the hard-driven clipper, already short-handed, shipped men who were no use aloft, a great strain was thrown on all the others. Francis was not popular either in the forecastle or abaft the mast, and the bucko mate went out of his way to haze him.

This was in accordance with the traditions of the sea of those days. Vanderdecken had no fault to find with this. But he continued to expect the ship to be dismasted, to run into icebergs in the Roaring Forties or to collide with the island of St. Paul, to lose a watch overboard, to spring a serious leak—in short, to be overtaken by severe calamity sooner or later. He never ceased expounding these views and, after a time, they began to get on the men's nerves. Vanderdecken was one of that strange class of seafarer, now extinct, who were excellent working seamen, born helmsmen and wizards in the rigging, and yet were unable to sleep or to mix properly with their shipmates at all. In six square-rigged ships in my youth, I knew only one such man and he was a severe trial. He paced the deck when he should have been asleep, waiting for the calamity he was sure would happen and determined that he, at least, would be ready for it. And ready he was, at all hours of the day and night. The little iron barque we sailed in *had* sprung a serious leak and all but foundered. It was common knowledge aboard that the old man had once been in a lifeboat for weeks and weeks where cannibalism had been practised, and it was pretty certain that he was one of the cannibals. This might have explained his difficulty in living with himself.

What dreadful background old Vanderdecken in the *Cutty Sark* may have had no one can now say, for no records remain of any other voyages the man made. But his croaking and the mate's bullying had an unnerving effect on the crew. It was a pity. Captain Wallace was respected, and the second mate's watch was a happy one. If either the bucko or Vanderdecken had been absent, the ship would have kept out of trouble.

In the better weather of the Indian Ocean the coloured man, Francis, became impossible. He had already had one battle with the mate, earlier in the voyage. One morning when a course alteration made it necessary to square the yards, Francis was on lookout. The lookout's duties included tending the gear on the forecastle-head, as might be necessary during bracing, and so forth. When the yards of a sailing-ship were trimmed there was a great deal of work to be done, for the set of all the square sails was altered. The lookout had to see to the fore-tack, which was usually taken to the capstan on the forecastle-head. When the yards were being squared in, the tack had to be eased. It was a simple job, calling neither for skill nor much muscular effort.

The crojack and the mainyards were squared in without trouble. The watch hurried along to the fore braces.

"On the lookout there! Slack away the tack!" the mate shouted.

No answer came. Nothing was done.

"Lookout there! Ease away the tack!"

No answer. No action.

Now no mate or second mate, or third mate or bos'n or any other person entrusted with the working of a sailing-ship, bucko or otherwise, could tolerate this sort of thing. It was not only insubordination. It was incipient mutiny. Failure to carry out any order promptly and efficiently could jeopardise a full-rigged ship and all aboard. One tradition could not be flouted, and that was the tradition requiring the immediate obedience of *any* orders.

The mate, breathing fire, made a rush for the forecastle-head. Whoever was there was in for trouble.

It was Francis, though the mate hadn't known that until he saw the wretched man. Just what happened in the next few seconds will never be known. The story is that Francis was lying in wait with a capstan-bar and some crazy idea of braining the mate. But the mate seized the bar from him, and promptly brained him. At any rate, very soon Francis was dead.

The ship then was in an uproar. Francis dead was more

trouble than Francis alive, and Vanderdecken stirred the hands to a state of undeclared mutiny. The mate locked himself in his cabin, and Captain Wallace took his watch. The clipper raced uneasily on with her good steam coal and, shortly afterwards, raised the coast of Java. Unfortunately the ship had to wait at anchor off Anjer for orders as to which port to deliver the coal, and Wallace foolishly allowed the mate to get away. If the mate had stayed to face his trial, there would have been a good chance that his act of manslaughter would have been condoned as necessary for the safety of the ship. There were precedents for that. Running away did no one good. As soon as the crew discovered it, they refused to do a hand's turn aboard the ship. Wallace tried to sail the ship with the apprentices and petty officers. But as soon as she entered the Java Sea she ran into a state of absolute calm which continued for three days. Calm is the great curse of sailing-ships. Poor Wallace showed the strain dreadfully. He never left the deck. The calm got on his nerves. All day long the ship lay silent upon the image of herself reflected in the sullen sea: by night the garbage that had been flung overboard at dusk stayed with her, not moving. Not a sail flapped. The ship lay lifeless where she should have been speeding before a favouring wind. Vanderdecken croaked about in whispers, and his bare feet padded upon the teak decks night after night—all night. He reduced many of the crew almost to a state of terror.

"You see; you see!" he croaked. "She can't go now. She *can't* go! There's a curse on her, that's what I say!"

The fact that he'd been saying the same thing for years, aboard every ship he'd been in, was irrelevant. The calm was eerie, oppressive, and foreboding.

At four o'clock in the morning of the fourth day of calm Captain Wallace walked over the side. They put out a boat at once, but nothing was seen of him again. Almost at once, a faint breath of air got up and began to grow. The *Cutty Sark* was sailing again. But where to go? The second mate was in charge as the only officer left aboard. All he had to do was to coax the ship along on the fine-weather run to Yokohama. What a chance for

a young man! But the second mate lacked both the competence
and the nerve. His bad eyesight bothered him, and he had been
unnerved by the hazing on the ship and above all, by Wallace's
sudden death. He had plenty of able lieutenants in the apprentices' quarters, if he had the nerve to use them and rely upon
them. More than one very junior officer, and some apprentices,
distinguished themselves in similar circumstances in the days
of sail by taking over command and bringing their ships safely
to the completion of their voyages.

This second mate was not in that mould, unfortunately. He
took the ship back to Anjer which was very close. There he
anchored, and promptly began to bombard the owner in London
with long cables which made nothing clear except that the poor
ship was in a great deal of trouble and no one in authority aboard
was able to cope with it. Willis ordered the second mate to go on
to Yokohama (for the freight on that Navy coal was good, but it
had to be delivered to the Navy). He might as well have ordered
him to hell. It was a pity, indeed, that the second mate had not
run with the mate, or jumped over the side with his captain.
Then one of the senior apprentices could have taken the ship.
Several of them were quite competent. Wallace had taken an
interest in their welfare and professional abilities, and most of
them were quite satisfactory navigators.

The upshot was that a still mystified Willis had finally to
order the *Cutty Sark* to Singapore, in charge of a Dutch pilot.
On the way, dead calm again cursed the ship, and at one stage she
was swept in a tidal race so close by the rocky cliffs of Thwart-the-
Way Island that the yards had to be braced sharp up to avoid
scraping the rocks.

At Singapore, Vanderdecken promptly left, vowing that his
life's work would be to track down the bucko mate and bring
him to 'justice'. On the face of it, Vanderdecken's quest seemed
hopeless. There is little doubt that the bucko mate got away
in an American ship which was lying off Anjer with the *Cutty
Sark*. But sailing-ship sailors were nothing if not inveterate
globe-wanderers. It is certainly a fact that the bucko, whose name
was Smith, *was* recognised by a member of the *Cutty Sark's*

crew—said to be Vanderdecken—years afterwards, and he *was* brought to trial. Smith was tried, under the name of John Anderson, for the wilful murder of John Francis, at the Central Criminal Court in London. It was brought out in evidence that he had acted under great provocation, and the charge was reduced to manslaughter. On this he was found guilty and, despite the fact that several witnesses who had known him many years testified to his good character and generally humane disposition, he was sentenced to seven years' penal servitude.

Among the witnesses to character was John Willis, who did the best he could for his former mate. Smith, alias Anderson, or Anderson alias Smith, served his time helping to build the Dover breakwater. When he was released, he went back to sea at once. He had lost his certificates, of course, but Willis got him a berth as bosun and second mate of a square-rigger bound to Australia. Bucko or not, Smith showed he had plenty of courage. He worked his way again through the various certificates of competency, taking his second mate, mate, and master as soon as he could. He rose to command with the Anglo-American Oil Company, which retired him on a pension for his good service. He died of cancer in 1922, when he was nearly 75 years old.

What happened to Vanderdecken no man knows.

When the *Cutty Sark* reached Singapore on that tragic voyage her troubles were far from over. There she was in that hotbed of the East, without a competent officer aboard, or a crew. (The foremast hands had soon melted away.) Willis, not wishing to send a new master out in a despised steamship, cabled to the master of the *Hallowe'en* at Hongkong asking whether the mate of that ship could be recommended for command. It so happened that the master hated the mate and would have recommended him for anything to get rid of him. So off went the mate full speed to Singapore to take over his first command. A worse choice could hardly have been made. The new captain's name was Bruce, and he was the worst possible type of man to command a full-blooded clipper. The *Cutty Sark* scared him into a state of nervous prostration which he covered alternatively by drink and an air of tremendous rectitude. This air he kept for shore consumption; the ship and her people soon found him out.

Bruce was a small man with an unctuous countenance and large, protruding eyes. A slobbery mouth and a high-pitched tenor voice, a false cheerfulness ashore and a real capacity for villainy and petty bullying aboard combined to make him the laughing-stock of his own apprentices, and he knew it. He was a man who found himself extremely hard to live with, and he was forever trying to make up for his appalling shortcomings by acts of silly braggadocio or senseless swaggering which everyone saw through, including himself. He was happy only in drink or in psalm-singing ashore, and there was considerable doubt about the psalm-singing. He certainly was a most extraordinary man. In the various ports of call, shore people thought highly of him. He was asked to conduct church services, and once a collection was made and a gold watch presented to him, as a mark of esteem for his great 'piety'. Yet aboard the ship he was a petulant little tyrant, covering his fear of the ship by tremulous shouting at the crew, and petty fault-finding of his officers. One thing he feared even more than the ship and that was landfalls. Any landfalls. Any land, indeed, anywhere. The man was a splendid navigator and had less cause to fear his landfalls than most of his fellow shipmasters. But he seemed quite incapable of rousing any self-confidence. Whenever the ship was approaching land he became quite unnerved, and often hove her to, wasting time stupidly, rather than trust himself and let her stand on to pick up the land. He dreaded coming into port; perhaps he hated to put on his shore-going manners and to pretend to be high-minded.

Under the ignoble Bruce, the poor ship wandered about the seven seas, tramping for cargoes. Sometimes he was so drunk that she ran away with him like the wanton she was, and when he hove her to, near the land, she kicked and bucked like a recalcitrant mule. From Singapore she went to Calcutta where, after several months of waiting, she loaded Indian tea for Melbourne. It was ironic that the clipper, forced out of her rightful business of carrying China tea, now opened up the great Australian market to the Indian product and then had no further share in carrying that. This cargo of the *Cutty Sark*'s was the first Indian tea ever shipped to Australia, where it soon became a popular beverage. From Australia the *Cutty Sark* took coal to China again; thence to Cebu for jute to deliver in New York. Owing to Bruce's goings on, the ship was out of food long before she reached the American port, and the proud little clipper was forced to beg provisions from passing steamers. This was inexcusable. The only reason for the ship's shortage was the misuse of the funds provided by the owner for buying food, for Willis liked to see that his ships were properly stored.

In New York at last, Bruce found a port where a faked appearance of sanctity did him no good at all. Between the bottle and the bible-punching he broke down, and was removed from the ship. So was his useless mate.

It was just in time. Any more of Bruce and buckos, and the clipper might as well have gone up in flames.

Chapter thirteen

BIOGRAPHY OF A CLIPPER—III

WITH the *Cutty Sark* stuck without a crew and without officers in the expensive port of New York, Willis was in a dilemma. The ship was already loading a full cargo of case oil for Samarang, and a crew she must have. New York was a bad place for crews and a worse for officers. Willis solved his difficulties by robbing another of his ships, the clipper *Blackadder,* which happened to be in New York at the time. He took her master, mate, and crew, almost complete, across to the *Cutty Sark.*

The master of the *Blackadder* at the time was a Captain F. Moore. He was no relation to the other Moore who had the *Cutty Sark* earlier, and he was a thoroughly experienced and capable seaman, and a good disciplinarian as well. He found the old tea clipper in a disgraceful state. Bruce had not been content to rob his owner only on the provisions. He had skimped the ship in every possible way, and generally neglected her. Sails, running rigging, and even some of the standing rigging were alike in poor condition. She needed thousands spending on her, but there was little prospect of earning thousands with the freight of case oil—a rather desperate one for such a fine-lined ship—and Willis clamped down. His orders were that expenses must be kept down to the irreducible minimum. She paid her dues, paid to have her cargo stowed—that could not be avoided— paid for pilotage out, and that was about all.

Case oil was indeed a desperate cargo for the ship. In the first place, she was unfitted to carry it. Case oil—really it was *cased* oil—was the trade name for the old-fashioned square cans of kerosene which used to be stowed two to a wooden case. To handle it, ships should be built of metal and properly ventilated. The *Cutty Sark*, never having been intended to touch such stuff, was not properly ventilated. Case oil could be jammed by the score-thousand cases into the box-like holds of more modern ships. But her hold was more or less triangular both for'ard and aft and was not box-like at all. If times had been good, she would have run—if necessary in ballast—back to London to load general cargo for the Far East or for Australia. But times were far from good. There was no chance of a general cargo for her to China, and the steamers were taking most of the Australian cargoes as well.

So the little ship went off with her case oil cargo and raced down both Atlantics, round the Cape, and across the Roaring Forties, through the Indian Ocean and up to Samarang. She would have raced better had she been in better order. Captain Moore's log of that passage is a sad commentary on her condition. Sails blew out, gear carried away, avoidable grief of all kinds harassed her the whole long way. But she skipped along when she could, as if anxious to get the case oil delivered and the reek of paraffin out of herself for ever.

From Samarang, after the oil was out, she sailed in ballast to Madras and lifted a cargo of eastern goods such as jaggery, myrobalans, and buffaloes' horns, from the roadsteads at Bimlipatam and Coconada. At any rate there was no shortage of sweetening stuff that passage, for the jaggery never stopped oozing a treacly kind of molasses which had to be pumped out from the bilges. When the taint of paraffin was out of it, this stuff went quite well in the apprentices' home-made dishes. They used to pound up hard biscuits with a belaying pin, or a capstan-bar, and mix the mess with old fat and jaggery-juice, and then shove it in the cook's oven to get hot. Probably only a sailing-ship apprentice could appreciate the result, but aboard the *Cutty Sark* it was something of a delicacy that passage. It may also have been a necessity for growing boys, for the food was not served out lavishly. Pea soup, boiled salt horse, the occasional piece of salt pork, and preserved meat warmed up for Sunday dinner—this was the weekly round. Breakfast was burgoo—a watery porridge with a flavouring of weevils—and supper was whatever could be saved from the other two meals, if anything. It was for this meal that the jaggery juice and the smashed-up biscuits came in handy.

The *Cutty Sark* was a little over four months to the Channel from Coconada Roads. She did not hurry. Captain Moore was busy the whole voyage getting her properly seaworthy again and, by the time she docked in London in June 1883, the little ship was in good condition once again, on deck and aloft. Her wonderful hull had never given any trouble. But Moore had difficulty inducing his owner to put up enough money to give the ship all the canvas and cordage she needed for another voyage, and again she went to sea rather parish-rigged. Willis was becoming more and more a pessimist. So long as he believed his ship could capture the record in the China tea trade, he lavished money on her. But in 1883 he knew that this was out of the question. The ship was fourteen years old, and the big iron clippers in the Australian trade were almost as much a menace as the steamers had been in the Eastern run. Nor was there the slightest sign that the Suez Canal would silt up. Old White Hat did not boast very much about his *Cutty Sark*, did not expect much from her, and began to cut down her expenses as severely as he could. As an old shipmaster himself, he knew how to be a shade too severe in this direction.

Captain Moore took the *Cutty Sark* on two Australian round voyages, going out in 1883 with a general cargo to Newcastle and coming home again round the Horn. He did extremely well, so well that he made old Willis sit up. He sailed out from the Channel in 79 days, and was home again from Newcastle in 82, making not only the best passage of the ships which sailed about the same time but the best wool passage of the year. She beat most of the other ships by anything between a fortnight and a month. This was a highly creditable performance. No one had believed that the little tea clipper could sail as well as that on a run for which she had not been designed. Tea clippers were a bit fine-lined for the Cape Horn run, as a rule. The fact was that Willis' powerful stern and strong rigging were paying off at last. The clipper he'd hoped would beat all-comers in the tea trade years before was at last showing her real merits, in a trade for which she had not been intended. Her power and her grace, her strong Scots hull and her good sail-plan, combined to make her queen of the Cape Horn wool race. It was an odd quirk that made the ship a record-beater in her middle-age.

It might have been an odd quirk of fate, but she certainly was consistent. Nor was the best passage of the year a mere matter for congratulating the master and his crew. It meant money, for wool was auctioned only at certain times on the London market, and cargoes which did not arrive in time for the auctions had to meet expensive storage charges. A ship which could be relied upon to catch the sales was assured of her cargoes. More than that, she could earn a bonus by taking the berth for last chance at the sales. Wool coming down late from the up-country stations in New South Wales could easily miss the January sales, and soon the *Cutty Sark* was promoted to the small band of super-clippers which undertook to leave Sydney late and arrive in London early. There was good business in employing clippers in such a trade, and there still was real merit—and profit—in racing. No wonder the *Cutty Sark* came into her own, at last!

In this she was immensely aided by the appointment of an outstanding captain, Captain Richard Woodget. Moore took her the first two wool runs, and did very well. Woodget had her for the following ten Australian voyages, and did magnificently. Moore's total pay from Willis for handling the little clipper was only £200 a year. There was still a tradition in those days that a shipmaster could legitimately add to his earnings by his own ventures, not by robbing the ship and crew as a fool like Bruce did, but by using his business sense (and a little space in the ship) to his own profit. A sensible shipmaster, accustomed to a certain trade, would soon have his contacts at both ends, and would know the items he could dispose of with advantage. He knew the port authorities. Many captains carried business men as passengers and made profitable contacts in that way. A venture might be liquor, or millinery, or a particular breed of dog—anything

that would sell readily, with a good demand. Part of a captain's
emoluments had traditionally been the right to space in his ship
for his own ventures. At £200 a year it was necessary. There
were no pension schemes for shipmasters in those days but, apart
from the inherently indigent (who did not often rise to command)
and the hopelessly drunk (who never kept command if they got it)
not many shipmasters ended their days in the poorhouse. Most
of them were able to retire ashore with at least a competence,
and set up a flagstaff in the garden of some pleasant country
cottage.

A shipmaster who could earn something for himself was
usually the best man for his owner, too. Woodget had shown his
merit by making money handsomely for his owner in one of
Willis' worst ships, the ancient *Coldstream*, and by getting better
passages out of that old-timer than anyone else had been able to
do throughout the previous 35 years of her undistinguished existence. He was the obvious choice for the *Cutty Sark*. He was
that rarity, the right man in the right place at the right time.
Richard Woodget was a great shipmaster. He deserved the
Cutty Sark, and the *Cutty Sark* deserved him. I can think of no
finer compliment to either.

His achievements with the grand little ship were the more
meritorious since he had nothing in his favour. Willis had discovered long before that he could reduce the crew by a third,
and he had promptly done so. Now, half the crew were not competent grown seamen at all, but a group of boys. It was Willis' good
fortune and in no way his merit—though it was Woodget's merit
—that these boys generally showed themselves to be even better
than men. Some of them were only twelve or thirteen years of
age when they joined the clipper. Years afterwards, one of the
last of the sailing-ship owners was to keep a fleet going on the
strong backs of boys, and to charge them for working for him
into the bargain. Old Willis had shown the way.

Another disadvantage Woodget had to face, and that was
the fact that each year it was becoming more difficult for a
small ship to pay on one Australian round voyage, and yet there
was no other work the *Cutty Sark* could do. Her actual sailing

time during most of the ten years that Woodget had her was rarely more than five months a year—about 70 days out to Australia, and around 80 days back. (It was further to sail, coming back: Cape Horn is a long way south.) She could load all the general cargo she was likely to get in a couple of weeks in London, and screw a maximum capacity of wool bales into her tight hull in Sydney or Newcastle in considerably less than a month. This meant that the ship was fully employed for little more than half the year. Yet she had often to wait for her wool cargo in Australia for months. Moreover, she had to be kept in full commission during this wait and, because she was such a fine-lined ship, she would not stand up without a good deal of ballast. This ballast had to be bought and people paid to put it aboard, and then to take it out again and dispose of it. Nobody gave sailing-ships anything. Apprentices were cheap crew, but they had to be fed. There were generally also six or eight able seamen, and there was an afterguard to pay and feed as well.

There was no hope of earning anything by taking a cargo of coal up to China or across to Chile, while she waited for the wool. That way she might miss the wool, and she would get no return cargo from either country. To romp up to Shanghai with the trade winds was all very well, but it was a mighty long way back again. A clipper like the *Cutty Sark* might run from Newcastle to Valparaiso in four weeks or less, but then she would have to discharge her own coal, pay for lightering, and then buy ballast expensively and wander back before the light Pacific trades. That might well take even a clipper fifty days. Nor could she carry coal enough to pay. As ships increased in size, freights had a habit of dropping. More and more had to be crammed into big square holds to hope to pay at all. The *Cutty Sark* could carry 1200 tons of coal at the best. Ships carrying 3000 tons, with a crew no larger than hers, were having trouble to make ends meet.

After all, there was one criterion by which the sailing-ship, clipper or whatever she might be, must stand or fall. She had to earn more than it cost to run her and, on top of that, she had to earn the cost of a ship to replace her. She was—and still is— a dreadfully expensive property, as soon as she could no longer

earn enough to pay her way. It didn't matter in the least how
beautiful she was or how astonishing her voyages were, if they
did not pay reasonable dividends, as well as her own working
and replacement costs.

These problems were worrying old Willis, diehard that he
was, more and more. They also worried Captain Woodget. He
was a good owner's man, and he did his best to keep the ship's
expenses down and give her a chance to pay. Those long waits
in Sydney were pleasant, but they were expensive. Year by year,
the increasing horde of hungry steamers was creeping into all the
ports of the world in endless quest of cargoes. The Sydneysiders
cheered the little clipper for her wonderful runs, but the business-
men could only afford to ship by her so long as a better means
of getting their wool to England did not come along.

Meanwhile, voyage after voyage, Woodget drove the *Cutty
Sark,* undermanned (by older standards) and cut-down, as she
had never been driven before. He kept the ship in perfect trim
and he sailed her perfectly, too. He was a seaman of skill and
endless energy, and his nerve was as sound as his ship. A strict
disciplinarian, he was a just man, and his officers, cadets, and
able seamen respected and admired him. Gone were the days
of foolish crew troubles, which had never been the fault of the
ship. The men, treated justly, responded; and they stayed in the
ship year after year. Woodget drove the ship and he drove them,
but he over-drove neither. He was one of those extraordinary
men who were supremely good at whatever they undertook to do.
He was a great navigator, an artist at sailmaking, a master-
rigger. He bred collies, and his dogs were better than most other
collies. He took up photography—in those days an almost impossible art to practise afloat—and he did excellently at that.
He took a keen interest in his cadets, though many of his fellow
shipmasters felt under no obligation to do that, and he trained
them—indeed, reared is a better word, for many of them came
to him as children—so well that most of them made their mark
in after-life, and many were outstanding.

The ship, while he was at Sydney waiting for the wool-clip

to come down, was a happy abode of hardworking mariners in half-deck and forecastle. While the ship lay off in one of Sydney's lovely bays, with other clippers at anchor near her and the ferries passing by, the favourite dogwatch pastime was making music. The apprentices and the seamen would gather by the main hatch and sing their hearts out, some playing tunes—more or less correctly—with whatever came to hand, old whistle or comb with a bit of old paper on it, moistened in the mouth, or a jews' harp. The bursts of song coming over the lovely waters of the Sydney bays as clipper after clipper would take up the chorus, were a familiar feature of the sailing-ship life, as the crews, hard-worked and hard-muscled, slim and magnificently fit, rolled out their songs. Picnics in the ships' boats at weekends, entertainments arranged by the hospitable Australians—who always took a great interest in the ships that were their link with 'home'— evening concerts, and the day's hard work, made the time fly.

Again it is a tribute to Woodget that none of his boys ever deserted, though desertions were common from sailing-ships then. Pay and prospects alike were better in Australia than they ever could be for a Limejuice lad bound 'prentice to a wool clipper, or any other kind of sailing-ship. But the *Cutty Sark* boys knew what they were doing. Their ships were their public school, their indentures to life as well as to the sea profession. It was their inestimable privilege to serve their time in a ship which called to all the best in them, under a man who knew how to bring that best out, and did. No wonder the *Cutty Sark* lads under Woodget became commodores in great steamship lines! The pity is that there were not more of them; that Willis, far-sighted as he was, did not keep on the ship as a cadet-ship under Woodget, and man her with apprentices alone— twenty or thirty of them—with a stiffening of petty-officers.

The apprentices were not the only interesting characters under Woodget in the *Cutty Sark*. Such an unusual shipmaster gathered unusual men round him, and even the cook was outstanding. The cook was a Chinaman with the very English name of Tony Robson. Many years before, a China clipper homeward bound came upon a small boat, drifting alone in the China Sea.

In the boat was a baby, and nothing else. No food, no message, no anything. The baby was well nourished and had not been long adrift. Where did he come from? What could possibly be his story? No one knew. No one ever did know. The little Chinese baby was adopted by the clipper crew, named Tony Robson, and brought up to be a splendid sailor. When Woodget had the *Cutty Sark*, this Chinaman was an old man. He had graduated to the galley, which was considered a 'soft' job for a good old hand then. He was a first-class cook and a wonderful yarn-spinner and though officially the cook, he still took a great interest in the rigging and a fierce proprietary interest in the foremast, which was nearest to his galley.

Out to New South Wales in 75 days, home again in under 80—these were typical Woodget voyages. He did so well that old Willis, who never was a man to give up anything easily, had a last fling at breaking the China tea record. In 1886 he sent the *Cutty Sark* to Shanghai for a tea charter, for the last time. She had to take out a cargo of scrap-iron, for nothing else was offering. This was a heavy, dead cargo which gave her poor chance of sailing. It was as well she earned the freight, however, for though she waited for months, no tea charter could be arranged. Willis had presented the ship with a golden shirt to fly at the main-truck before she set out on that voyage, but she was not to lower the *Thermopylae's* golden cock. The wonderful maiden voyage which that Aberdeen ship made—60 days to Melbourne, 28 days N.S.W. to Shanghai, 91 days back with her tea—was to stand. Willis had to order Woodget to sail the *Cutty Sark*, golden shirt and all, down to Sydney in ballast to try to salvage something from the voyage, with a cargo of wool. In that trade she showed that she could defeat the wonderful *Thermopylae*, and she proceeded to do it.

At that time, the ship that could outsail the *Thermopylae* could rate herself the fastest sailer in the world. The *Cutty Sark* put up records which stand today at Lloyd's of London—67, 69, 70 days, Sydney or Newcastle to the Channel. She was the *United States* of the wool clipper race, and the *Thermopylae* was a splendid *Queen Mary*. Under Woodget, the *Cutty Sark* was indeed a queen of the sea.

But it was all in vain. Soon Willis knew it was in vain. So did Woodget. None of the fine boys who trained under him stayed in sailing-ships. One after the other they graduated into the despised steamers, to make their careers in powered vessels. The almost incredible amount of effort that went into the making of a clipper's Cape Horn voyage made magnificent seamen, too. But the clippers were reduced to training seamen for their implacable rivals. The men they made helped to destroy them.

By 1953, a few men still live who served in the *Cutty Sark* in her heyday in the Australian trade. One of these is Walter Naylor, who was second mate when the little ship beat the mail steamer into Sydney, to the delight of the Australians who were carrying on a campaign for faster mail-steamers at the time. They applauded the *Cutty Sark* vociferously but they knew that her feat—though common enough for Woodget and her—was a rare gesture and really a useless one, a sort of kick from a racehorse at an automobile. They continued to book passage to England in the automobile, and to send their fast freight by the same means. There was a hollow ring to the cheers, spontaneous as they were. The march of progress was not to be stayed by a beautiful ship. The day was almost over when men could afford to send their goods in an ocean-going yacht, or care to do so.

Another ancient mariner still on deck from these stirring days is Captain C. E. Irving, C.B., R.D., R.N.R. (Retired). Born in 1871, Captain Irving went to sea at the age of 12 as an apprentice to John Willis in the ship *The Tweed*. At the age of 13, he was transferred to the *Cutty Sark* and in her he sailed from 1885 to 1888, with Woodget—out to China on the scrap-iron voyage, and in the wool races round the Horn. Before he was seventeen, the youthful Irving had finished his indentures and presented himself for examination as second mate. But the regulations were that candidates must have turned seventeen, and he had to go back to sea again for a Western Ocean voyage.

When he had his certificates, he presented himself for selection as an officer before the nabobs of the P. and O. Company.

The P. and O. was, to some extent, the successor of the mighty
Honourable East India Company, and it still kept up a great
style. Officers might not be paid very much, but they were expected at all times to present an impeccable appearance and to
behave like gentlemen. Frock coats and the complete set of
formalities that go with that rig, were necessary even to pass
the front door. Irving must have looked very youthful in this
formal rig. The morning he presented himself there were dozens
of other qualified officers, senior to and older than himself, some
of them from the crack training-ships. The personnel director
looked him up and down.

"You're young, aren't you?"

"Yes, sir," said Irving, meekly.

"What experience have you had?"

"I served my time in the *Cutty Sark*, sir."

"What, under Woodget? And you're still alive?"

"Yes, sir. With Captain Woodget."

The director looked hard at him for a moment. Then he
told him the firm of tailors which the company used. Irving
was hired.

It required no greater skill or good fortune to survive in the
Cutty Sark than in most other clippers in the Cape Horn trade,
though she was known as a wet ship and Woodget was a hard
driver. Shipowners were well aware that three or four years under
such a man, in such a ship, was the best possible introduction
to the seafaring world that a youngster could have. Trained in
such a manner, a young man knew not only his business, but that
seafaring *was* his business, his life's work. There was no doubt
that seafaring would be his career. The P. and O. regarded
their officers as an investment: a young man from Woodget's
Cutty Sark was worth investing in.

They were right about Irving. He rose to command the
greatest ships in the line, to distinguish himself by outstanding
feats of seamanship again and again, to have a long and honourable career in the Merchant and Royal navies alike. At 81, Captain Irving (having ferried small craft across the North Atlantic
during the second World War because the Admiralty thought

him rather old for front-line service) is still an active business man in London, with many shipping interests.

I talked with Captain Irving in the rooms of his club in London. Though it was then well over sixty years since he had left her, the *Cutty Sark* came booming through those London club-rooms under a stately cloud of sail and the Cape Horn voice of the long-dead Woodget roared in a gale of wind while Captain Irving yarned. What a life it was! Irving was at the wheel once when Woodget did something rare for him. He drove the sticks out of her. The ship was partially dismasted.

Actually, she was not being over-driven. Any fool could over-drive a ship, and there were some notorious masters who retired to their cabins in a gale with a bottle or a case of bottles and, from the alcoholic 'safety' of the poop, breathed fire at any who wished to reduce sail. Woodget was not that kind of driver. Far from it! He neither drank nor smoked, and he was a past-master at the art of keeping just that amount of sail on a ship which, with the winds blowing and the sea running, would allow her to do her maximum speed. His expertness and his daring alike consisted in keeping up that maximum speed. To overdo it was to invite trouble. This night it was a shift of wind that took the ship and the mate by surprise, and whipped some of the lighter sticks out of her. It was a dreadful night, blowing and howling—normal Roaring Forties stuff. Rain-squall after rain-squall overtook the running ship, and the huge seas threatened to knock her over in her stride. Woodget had a press of sail on her. Other ships would have been reduced to lower tops'ls (in part to ensure their captain's sleep), but he knew that she could stand her full suit. With that powerful counter old Willis had built into her, she needed driving and she could stand it.

But a flick of the wind a few points of the compass momentarily took the sails aback. The whole wonderful engineering job of a clipper's rig was designed to take stresses from one side only, and that was from *abaft* the sails. If the wind jumped round the sails—took them aback as sailors say, blew upon them from ahead—then the stouter stays helped to pull the masts down and not to support them. In the twinkling of an eye, the fore topmast and the main topgallant had come down on deck, and the masts and yards and thrashing sails were jumping and banging and clattering and smashing into the little ship's wooden sides, as if their only aim was to break her open, to bring her down in her stride. Still she ran on, for skilful handling brought her before the wind again. The sea was higher, the wind screaming. The little ship leapt and jumped and flung her jib-boom now into the pressing dome of the rain-filled sky, now, as she slithered down the slope of an enormous sea, towards the very bowels of the earth. Seas crashed and thundered aboard her. The blown-out sails were making terrifying noises like the thunderclaps of doomsday.

The main topmast—a solid spar—and the topgallant-mast above it, and the fore topgallant and all the main tops'l and topgallant yards, and the fore topgallant and the fore royal, were continuing their attack upon the sides of the ship and along her rail where they had fallen, as if the attack was under the demoniac brain of a monster, and the ship shuddered from the blows. How long could wooden sides stand such hammering? All hands were on deck, of course, under the Herculean Woodget who was at his best in such conditions. They had to clear the mess, save what they could, prevent the ship being stove in by the smashing of her broken rigging. They had to work more in the sea than out of it, for at the wheel where he was, Irving could not distinguish where the sea ended, and the ship began. If he had not been lashed, he could not have stayed there. The sprays were picked up from the mighty combers and flung at him like frozen needle-points, and the wind tried to pick him up and blow him into the mizzen rigging. The long, long hours of the dreadful night dragged by, and still the tremendous task went on.

Yet by the sullen daybreak of a morning young Irving had expected not to see, the wreckage *had* been cut away. The ship *was* under full and competent control again. She raced on under the reduced sail area forced upon her by the accident, and Woodget began at once—*at once*—to re-rig her thoroughly, to get another main topmast aloft and cross new yards (the clippers carried plenty of spare spars), and drive along. For three days, four days, five days, the work went on, steadily, despite the fact that even the wonderful Chinese cook could not provide a warm meal, for the galley was awash. The half-deck was awash. The poop was awash. The forecastle was awash. There wasn't a dry place anywhere, except in the hold, and that was hermetically sealed.

When she was rigged again, the *Cutty Sark* ran on to Sydney, storming two thousand miles in a week, running often at seventeen knots and averaging fifteen for days on end. Day after day, night after night, Captain Woodget stood on his poop, clinging with one hand to the weather mizzen rigging, or stamped the brief space between the binnacle and the rail. Standing under the wretched shelter of a minute weather-cloth lashed in the mizzen shrouds, a corner of his moustache gripped in his mouth to prevent it trailing off in the wind, his grey old beard glistening with salt and with rain—fearless, splendidly competent, ready to react instantly to any emergency that might arise and to react with precise and immediate knowledge of the right thing to do— the brains of his ship! There stood Woodget, a magnificent representative of a great profession. There stood Woodget, voyage after voyage, year after year, getting the best out of his ship and all on board, driving for ever from her graceful decks the taint of the buckos and the few fools who once had blemished them.

Storming through the Roaring Forties, dodging the ice-islands and the floe-ice on the long and gale-ridden road towards Cape Horn, nursing her through doldrums calm and slogging her down-Channel into some wretched south-west gale, getting always the best out of that wonderful ship as no man had ever done before or would do again, Richard Woodget was indeed a Man amongst Men, a Sailor with few peers anywhere, and no superiors at his chosen trade. Great ships made way for the *Cutty Sark*, and dipped their colours before her onrush. At last the *Thermopylae* was well beaten. The glorious *Mermerus*, the racing *Cimba*, the powerful *Rodney* and *Derwent*, the big well-handled *Lochs*, the iron *Aristides*, *Salamis*, *Patriarch*, *Orontes*, *Thyatira* —a hundred lovely ships with a hundred lovely names, she raced and beat them all, year after year.

Yet it was not just a picture of a supreme deepwater sailor man I gathered from my friend Captain Irving. Woodget was an outstanding character in other ways. The *Cutty Sark* had— still has—splendid decked tween-decks. When she was in ballast these were empty, and it was Woodget's joy to go roller-skating round them, and teach his officers and cadets to do likewise. He used to roller-skate on the main-deck too, but that was full of houses, hatches, masts, fife-rails, and the like. In the tween-decks there was only the chance of pitching into the lower hold. On the main-deck, you could go overboard. As a change from roller-skating, Woodget took up cycling, on the ballast run to Sydney from China, and he taught himself to be an expert cyclist in those same tween-decks. That was dangerous, for the hatches were all open, and a pitch of the ship could easily send him help-lessly down. His dogwatch amusement in the good weather of that run was to teach the apprentices to cycle, too, and some of them did not take kindly to it. His cycle was one of the early two-wheelers, a bone-shaker by name and bone-shaker in fact. The pedals were on the high front wheel, and it lacked springs and all other refinements.

Woodget took up nothing he was not thorough with. The bane of young Irving's life was, when recovering from bone-shaker saddle-sores or a bump on the skull caused by roller-skating on a rolling deck, to be chosen as one of the crews of the two life-boats old Woodget used to put out, lashed together with a plank across to support the tripod for his ancient camera, while he egged them on and somehow achieved the apparently impossible feat of getting a 'shot' of the ship under sail while the camera was properly steady, a thousand miles and more from the nearest land.

What a man to sail with!

Yet by the mid-nineties it was impossible for the *Cutty Sark* to pay her way. The wool-clippers were bigger and bigger, and the wool-ship race was dying anyway. The steamers by then had the lions' share of the general cargoes and the wool in the Aus-tralian trade, and the little clipper could not hope to pay on less expensive cargoes. No one cared if she raced home in 60 days with 1200 tons of grain. Indeed the brokers might well be annoyed, for she would give their cargo too brief a warehousing. Big sailers soon were getting grain because they could be trusted to deliver it slowly, not quickly. The day of the sleek and lovely little clipper-yacht was over. Small cargoes carried expensively could never hope to pay again, and she had to go.

By 1895, such giant sailing-ships as the five-masters *France* and *Potosi,* carrying well over six times the cargo the *Cutty Sark* could, and with less than twice her crew, were already in the water. The *Thermopylae* had been sold to Canada for five years and was still smashing records in the transpacific trade. The two magnificent ships were still fighting hard.

They had played their glorious part in maintaining the greatness of the sailing merchant service. Their day was really done—had been well on the way out, indeed, when they were launched. It was their own magnificence that had kept them going for so long, for they were better ships even than their owners, their designers, and their builders had dreamed.

In the end, both were sold to those good judges of good ships, the Portuguese. The *Thermopylae* became the training-ship *Pedro Nunez* for the Portuguese Navy, and the *Cutty Sark* became the trader *Ferreira* belonging to some brothers of that name, in Lisbon. By careful voyages, good care and good handling, they were able to use her successfully for almost the next quarter of a century. She was a strong ship and her hull continued in splendid condition. So long as she had a rag to show to the wind, she could sail. Again she was battered by hurricanes and dreadful gales. Again she had her rudder torn away by the sea, and sailed hundreds of miles with a makeshift rigged by her Portuguese master. She took the ground in a West Indies hurricane and was given up as a total constructive loss by the pessimists ashore. But she came off as good as ever, and continued in her Atlantic round—Lisbon or Oporto, New Orleans, Rio, the Portuguese possessions of the West African coast, the Cape Verde Islands.

Seriously dismasted once, she was re-rigged as a barquentine. Still she sailed splendidly whenever she had a chance. Still that noble hull, which was so light and graceful it looked as if a child's hand would give it way with a push from alongside a dock wall, moved wonderfully through the water whenever the wind blew. She sailed unscathed under the Portuguese flag through the '14–'18 war, except for the damage that hurricanes did her. Now and again she showed herself briefly in big ports—Liverpool, Cardiff, London—though generally her life lay at open roadsteads where a sailing-ship not in a hurry, and run with a minimum of outgoings, might hope to pick up slow cargoes and somehow make ends meet. The Portuguese did their best to keep her employed, but it was difficult. I have spoken to some of them who were in the ship during these years, and their admiration for her is still profound—profound, and based on understanding.

By 1922 the *Cutty Sark* was no longer able to earn her living anywhere. Too small for long trades, too big and too deep for short, too finely lined to drift with a dullard's load of hides or guano along South America's west coast—that last home of many square-rigged ships—she was caught, too, in the post-war shipping depression. There was no hope for her. In these circumstances, a public-spirited British shipmaster came upon her, driven by stress of weather into Falmouth. He could scarcely believe his eyes. The *Cutty Sark* still afloat? That noble model of the sailing art, that triumph of the adze and the rigging loft! The strange name and the strange flag, the barquentine rig, the line of painted ports along her sides like the old East Indiamen, could not disguise her. Captain Dowman had once been passed at sea by the *Cutty Sark* in the great days when Woodget had her. Once seen, never forgotten! Now he found that he could buy the great old ship, and preserve her. First she had to complete her voyage, and then he had her towed back to Falmouth from the Portuguese coast.

It was a great gesture, worthy of the ship and of the best of shipmasters. Captain Dowman restored the clipper to her proper status and made use of her as best he could, as a training-ship for boys. It was his desire to give her a full suit of sails again and send her off to sea. But he died before this had been done. His widow presented the ship to the Thames Nautical Training

College and, in 1938, the *Cutty Sark* was towed round to the Thames. She was moored close to the training-ship *Worcester*. There she remained throughout the second World War, with the bombers flying over her and, far too often in the war's early years, high-explosive and fire bombs falling close. But she survived.

There she remained until the *Cutty Sark* Preservation Society was formed to take over, in 1952, with the purpose of placing her in a permanent berth by the side of the Thames, and preserving her as the national monument she is. By then she was in fact the last of a glorious era. The others had all gone. All the Americans had gone, long since, the last of them sunk, or burned for their metal. The *Thermopylae* and the *Thomas Stephens* were sunk outside the Tagus when their working lives were over, though their great rival had then twenty years of hard tramping still ahead of her, and two World Wars. The lovely old *Samuel Plimsoll* was a coal-hulk in Fremantle for many years, and finally went down there at her berth. Few other real clippers saw even the nineteenth century out, though an odd one dragged on a few years in the Indian Ocean. By the mid nineteen-fifties all the big cargo-carrying sailing-ships were gone too—*all* engineless commercial square-rigged ships, gone from the face of the sea. Here and there a ship has been saved and preserved as a museum-piece, to show future generations what such vessels looked like—the rebuilt frigate *Constitution* at the Boston Navy Yard, the frigate *Jylland* in Copenhagen, the ships *C. W. Morgan* and my own old *Joseph Conrad* at Mystic, in Connecticut; the ship *AF Chapman* which is serving as a Youth Hostel at Stockholm; the four-masted barque *Pommern* at Mariehamn and the *Viking* at Gothenburg; the little barque *Seute Deern* at Hamburg where, in 1953, she was used as a restaurant. In this way a few odd old-timers still showed a yard or two at odd corners of the globe, and there was still a considerable fleet of square-rigged school-ships carrying no cargoes and engaged entirely upon short voyages designed for training boys.

Of all these ships—of *all* ships—only the *Cutty Sark* survived intact as a relic of the wonderful clippers.

Part VI

SCHOOL-SHIPS,
AND SOME OTHERS

Chapter fourteen

TRAINING

THE STORY of training under sail—*real* training under sail—in the British Merchant Service is the story of Messrs. Devitt and Moore's. Beginning as shipbrokers and insurance agents in London in 1836, Messrs. Devitt and Moore became in turn owners of outstanding passenger and cargo-liners in the Australian trade, pioneers in the use of Cape Horn ships as school-ships for officer-aspirants, and the last British owners to operate cargo-carrying sail-training vessels. They made, I think, a real contribution to the story of the Cape Horn ship, and that is why I have selected their story as the basis of this chapter. Sound old-fashioned ownership principles, a flair for good labour relations and, above all, an unblemished reputation for integrity, built up the Devitt and Moore Line.

Thomas Henry Devitt and Joseph Moore, Ship and Insurance brokers, had the courage to launch out on their own in the London shipping world, as young men, and their business acumen, sound common-sense, and enterprise soon attracted the attention of leading shipowners. Among the important owners who entrusted them with the management of ships was the well-known Duncan Dunbar, who owned such famous vessels as the *Rodney*, the *Canterbury*, and the great *La Hogue*. Devitt and Moore managed the extensive Duncan Dunbar line for many years and did it splendidly, and when Duncan Dunbar died, they took over the ships. These vessels were primarily first-class passenger-carriers. In those days there were all sorts of ships carrying passengers to Australia—the convict transports (of which the least said the better), troop transports, emigrant carriers, and a superior class of vessel which was the sailing counterpart of the large liners of the mid-twentieth century. Devitt and Moore handled the liner business, exclusively, and in that they were wise. The liner business lasted when the others passed away, and the goodwill which those great sailing-ships created still does the Red Duster good service. Passengers were carried in Devitt and Moore ships to Australia for 20 years after famous lines such as the P. and O. and the Orient were running good passenger steamships in the business.

The passenger-carrying sailing-ship took an unconscionable time to die and, indeed, is not quite dead even in 1953, for there is still one small group of ships carrying passengers under sail across the North Atlantic, the Cape Verde packets, which operate a brigantine and a schooner * between the Cape Verde Islands and Providence, Rhode Island. These Cape Verde packets serve a specialised trade which is perhaps unattractive to large liners, but the Devitt and Moore ships continued to hold a considerable clientele among the regular travelling public for years after steamships—and good steamships—were offering faster and cheaper passages. There were many people who preferred the sailing-ship for its restful qualities. They disliked what they regarded as the "dirt and bustle" of the steamer—the noisy coaling days in port, the smuts from the low funnels, the different (and much more trying) motion in the sea, the appalling heat of their cabins in the tropic zones. The sailing-ship took longer for the passage, say, from London to Adelaide or Melbourne. But it was not so much longer. Over half a century's passages in more than a hundred ships show that 80 to 90 days was the time usually taken for the run out, and 90 to 100 days for the run home again. People had 90 days to spare for an ocean voyage in those days, and knew that they would benefit by it.

The old sailing-ships catered for them properly in every way they could. Gone were the days of the Hon. East India Company when a passenger bought a place—very expensively—at the cap-

* The *Madalan* and the *Effie M. Morissey*.

tain's table, furnished his own cabin at his own expense, and settled aboard for nine months or so. The Devitt and Moore ships provided the best of food and plenty of it. The food served in the first saloon was much better than it is at sea today, for it was fresh—completely fresh—and butchered aboard. The Devitt and Moore records show that real farms went to sea in their passenger ships. The full-rigged ship *Sobraon*—she was built in 1866, sailed for many years in the Australian passenger trade, later becoming the Royal Australian Navy's training-ship *Tingira* moored in Sydney Harbour and only recently broken-up—carried, for example, three bullocks, three cows (for milking), ninety sheep, fifty large hogs and a number of sucking pigs, and between 300 and 400 fowls, ducks, and geese. Looking after these was an expert business and it was expertly done by the ship's butcher, a highly important member of the ship's company who sometimes graduated to become chief steward. He generally had at least two assistants. Large quantities of fodder were taken along to keep the beasts in good trim. The *Sobraon* (like all the other passenger-carriers) had substantial pens and houses built permanently on her decks to accommodate her animals and poultry. The fodder included bales of hay, straw, sacks of parsnips and swedes, corn, grit, pollard, and bran, and so forth, and the boats were stowed full of these things. All the greenstuff that possibly could be jammed aboard was also taken, filling the tops of the very large deck-houses.

The ships usually took care to sail from London in summer, calling at Plymouth for their saloon passengers, and they arrived at and sailed from Australia in summer, too. Theirs was a very pleasant life, with no winter at all. They went out round Good Hope, and they sailed beautifully because they were beautiful ships, but they were not driven. It was their custom to come back round the Cape of Good Hope and not around Cape Horn, except sometimes from Sydney. Ships leaving Port Adelaide and Melbourne in the summer months usually found easterlies enough to get them safely past Cape Leeuwin and into the trade wind belt of the Indian Ocean, where the sailing conditions were

ideal. The west-setting Agulhas current helped them round Good
Hope, and they often called in at Cape Town. They touched at
St. Helena, too.

There was plenty of diversion aboard. The passengers were
accustomed to produce their own newspaper, the ship providing
the press and the paper. Concert parties, sing-songs, theatricals
of all sorts, and long sessions of gossip and earnest Victorian
conversations helped to pass the time, which never dragged.
Those passengers went aboard prepared to entertain themselves
for anything up to 120 days, if needs be, and there was no nervous
dread of being left to their own devices. People did not continually expect to have something done for them, in those days, nor
find life insupportable without their own particular version of
the day's alleged news thrust under the front door every morning. They were a contented lot, and they settled down in the
sailing passenger-ships extremely well.

As for accommodation, that also was surprisingly good. In the
first place, it was without vibration and it was also without noise.
Except in calms (when the animals' presence would be somewhat obvious) it was without smell, too. Consider, for example,
the lay-out aboard the Devitt and Moore passenger liner *Rodney,*
which was put in the Australian trade in 1874. The Australians
took a great interest in their ships as their link with Britain. The
beautiful harbours of Sydney and Hobart and the broad bay of
Port Phillip at Melbourne were lovely settings for the stately full-
riggers. A ship fresh arrived was there for all to see. Her great
masts and yards towered over the new cities, her shapely hull lay
upon the harbour waters untarnished by the flotsam and filth of
a later age. The connoisseurs, of whom there were thousands, discussed each new ship with expert knowledge and an informed
all-seeing eye for the slightest detail. Even the small two-page
newspapers could devote at least half a close-set column to
description of the new vessel. Regarding the *Rodney,* we read:

> "To render voyaging as easy and pleasant as possible has long engaged
> the attention of shipowners, but it is only of late years that it has become
> a special study to make the accommodation for overseas passengers not
> merely comfortable but absolutely luxurious.

"The change in this respect since the time when only a certain amount of cabin space was provided is something akin to a transformation. . . With very little need for previous provision or preparation, the intending passenger can nowadays step aboard ship and find his cabin carpeted and curtained and fitted up with almost all the accessories and appointments of a bedroom in a hotel.

"An inspection of the *Rodney* will convince the most fastidious. . . The *Rodney* is an iron clipper of beautiful model . . . constructed specially with a view to the conveyance of passengers, and there are few sailing-ships coming to the colony which have such a spacious saloon. It measures 80 feet in length and has berthing accommodation for 60 people. No cost has been spared. . .

"The cabins are 10 feet square, and a number of sleeping berths can be drawn out so as to accommodate two people. For each cabin there is a fixed lavatory, supplied with fresh water from a patent tap, and by the removal of a small plug in the centre of the basin, the water runs away right into the sea, so that all slopping is avoided. The lavatory is fixed on top of a cupboard, which answers all the purposes of a little chiffoniere. . . There is also a chest of drawers in each cabin—a very great convenience—in which may be kept clothes, books, and many 'unconsidered trifles' which generally go knocking about in ships' cabins at sea.

"The windows in the cabins are large, admitting plenty of light and air, and the passengers have easy control over them. The ventilation is all that could be desired. Good-sized looking glasses and handy little racks . . . also abound. . .

"The bathroom occupies the space of one of the largest cabins, and hot as well as cold baths are attainable.

"The saloon is lighted by two large skylights, one of them being 21 feet in length. They are emblazoned with very pretty views of Melbourne, Sydney, Adelaide, and Cape Town, these being the principal ports to which Messrs Devitt and Moore's vessels trade. There is also a piano in the saloon . . . and the tables are so constructed that they can easily be unshipped and the saloon cleared for dancing.

"For gentlemen there is a capital smoking-room. . . The accommodation in the tweendecks for second cabin and steerage passengers is all that could be desired. . . Cooking can be done in the galley for 500 people, and there is a steam condenser which can distil 500 gallons of water daily."

Such a ship today would probably do well on round-the-world cruises, but she would have to add television to her amenities. The last of these really magnificent sailing passenger-carriers was broken up in Sydney in March, 1953. She was the iron full-rigged ship *Melbourne,* of 1857 tons, built by R. and H. Green in 1875 from some surplus plates left on their hands after building an ironclad. She was lavishly decorated and fitted out regardless of expense. Her 69-foot poop retained a real stern cabin with the large stern windows of the old East Indiaman, and her passenger cabins were beautifully finished. She was 270 feet long and cost £42,000 to build and equip, which was a lot of money in 1875. Devitt and Moore bought her in 1887, renamed her *Mac-Quarie,* sailed her as a passenger-carrier until 1897, and then made her into a training-ship. She was the ideal cadet-ship, but she was rather fine-lined and could not stow the big cargoes necessary for a Cape Horner to pay her way when the passengers were lost to her. Though some older travellers remained faithful to sail even after the turn of the century, the younger travelling public did not: ships could not be made to pay by catering only for what had become a small company of die-hards. So the *MacQuarie* was sold to the Norwegians and was hulked at Sydney in 1909. She refused to wear out. Right to the end, her good iron plates were in excellent condition.

Men served such ships for years and found a great contentment in the service. There was a crew of 69 in the *Sobraon,* including sixteen stewards and two stewardesses and one man described in the articles as an 'engineer', who looked after the condenser and the plumbing. Many men remained in the same ship, under the Devitt and Moore house-flag, from her launch until she was sold foreign. The famous Captain J. A. Elmslie commanded the *Sobraon* from 1867 until 1891, and the same carpenter and steward were with him throughout. The carpenter had assisted in the building of the ship, as a foreman shipwright, and took such a liking to her that he went with her for the maiden voyage and stayed with her as long as she sailed. The steward began as assistant butcher, then became butcher, and slowly rose to head his department. Able seamen stayed with the ship a decade or more, and several of her apprentices rose to be officers of experience in her.

Nor was this sort of thing unusual in the Devitt and Moore

sailing liners. What a life it was! Never a winter, just time enough in the Roaring Forties to wash the farmyard dirt thoroughly away, never a serious accident aboard, and a kindly master such as Elmslie to serve under. All those passenger-ship masters were selected with the greatest care. Like Elmslie, many of them had served in the last of the great East Indiamen in their youth, and carried on the noble tradition of gentlemanly seafaring. Their names were household words in Sydney, Melbourne, Cape Town, and Adelaide. Travellers did not inquire so much as to when the *Sobraon* was due as when Captain Elmslie was next expected, for the *Sobraon* was Captain Elmslie. Where she flew the Red Duster, he could be relied upon to be there. He had ample leave during the ship's turn-round in London, and did not miss a voyage. The ships made one voyage a year. It was a good life, and very nicely organised.

With the comfortable *La Hogue,* the popular *Paramatta,* the big *Sobraon* (she was one of the largest composite sailers built, registering 2131 tons; she was 317 feet long with a beam of 40 feet and a depth of hold of 27 feet), and the *City of Adelaide, South Australian,* and *St. Vincent* prime favourites in the Adelaide trade, the firm of Devitt and Moore were the Cunard Line of the Australian trade. Year followed year, gale followed gale, and still their lovely sailing-ships wandered pleasantly upon their sunlit ways. The Suez Canal opened and remained open, and functioned for almost 30 years before the advantages it gave the steamships finally put Devitt and Moore's out of the passenger business. Long before that happened, they had launched out in a sphere of activity which was destined to be the last employment of the deepsea square-rigged ship, and that was training.

The supply of good officers and seamen to the British Merchant Navy was a matter of great importance, and the growing horde of tramps and steamships of all kinds did not lessen the importance of an assured and ample flow of good men. Though the life in them was so completely different, in some ways the steamship required an officer of greater competence even than the sailing-ship did—in the care of cargoes, for example, and in the practice of pilotage and of navigation. Where the sailing-ship made the best passage she could between two points, the steamship went directly and therefore called for precise navigation. Her economy depended to a great extent on her consumption of the minimum amounts of fuel, and this again meant precise navigation in order that no time would be wasted, and no fuel. She handled more cargoes, loaded and discharged at more ports. She was usually worth a great deal more money, was a much greater liability in case of accident, carried more passengers. Her compliance with the Rule of the Road must be instant and correct at all times, for two steamships running into one another were a far greater source of potential danger—and damage—than two sailing-ships might ordinarily be. Moreover, the regularity of the steamship made her control from an owner's office more real and much more effective. A sailing-ship master did his best, but a steamship master had to keep a schedule: his costs could be estimated rigidly, and he was required to keep within them.

The coming of the powered vessel by no means robbed the sea of its dangers nor lessened the need for the utmost competence and vigilance on the part of watchkeeping officers. In a square-rigged ship, the need for vigilance was at all times apparent. An officer took the deck and, with a quick sweep of his experienced eyes over the rigging and the horizon, knew what he was in charge of and how things were. Alertness was an ever-present requirement of his calling, and he knew that. Watch-keeping aboard a steamship could be extremely boring over long periods of a voyage and, though the need for alertness was disguised for much of the time, it was still there in just as great degree, if not greater. Far-sighted shipowners concerned themselves with maintaining a flow of good recruits and fostering the good qualities of alert and competent seamanship. More and more boys, by the 1890's, were beginning their careers in steam. Many others went as apprentices in Cape Horn ships where they were treated as cheap labour. Though the experience under sail almost always did them good in some way or other, it was a fallacy to regard the ordinary period of apprenticeship in the usual run of Limejuice ships as training. It was invaluable experience, even at the worst; but in a properly conducted training-ship it could be so much more than that.

The older masters and owners remembered the great days of the East Indiamen and their midshipmen system, which had assured an excellent flow of first-class officers for first-class ships. The Blackwall frigates had continued this, though the great rewards of the East Indiamen had gone, then. A midshipman in an East Indiaman had two great assets to reward him for accepting the life at sea as his career. He had social status and the chance of fortune. Tramp shipping wiped both off the face of the sea. British shipping consisted largely of tramps, by the 1890's, and life in by far the great majority of these was plain servitude. They were run on the watch-and-watch system with two officers, and two (or, at the most, three) men in a watch. A great cloud of meanness had descended upon too many of them. The food was poor and so was the accommodation. In addition to the sailing-ship's disadvantages the steamer provided also the dirt of coal, and the draughtiness of an open ugly bridge was a poor exchange for the airy poop of a Cape Horn ship. More than these things, the steamship robbed masters and watchkeepers alike of the sense of achievement the sailing-ship gave them in such abundance. By comparison, the tramp life was almost intolerably humdrum, and the rewards were humdrum too.

In such circumstances it was no cause for wonder that there was some increase in the drift of good men from the sea. There had always been a considerable wastage from the sea, for men are not fish and women have always wanted their menfolk ashore, where they were. But there were indications, particularly in periods of comparatively full employment ashore, that it might become difficult to man British ships with a sufficiency of the best type of recruit. One remedy for this was to introduce some form of training which would take the place of the old East Indiamen. When Clark Russell, the sea writer, went to sea in a Blackwall ship in 1858, there were twelve midshipmen in the vessel, more than half of them from the great English public schools. Several were from Eton, and others were from Harrow or from Winchester, and there was at that time regular recruitment from these great schools for the Merchant Service. Servitude in tramps had scant appeal for such recruits as these. Their parents paid large premiums for midshipmen's berths, and the sea life must offer the prospects of a really good career. A first voyage premium was £63, second voyage £52, and third voyage £42, with an extra ten guineas to cover messing during each voyage. The great sailing lines such as Green's, Money Wigram's, Duncan Dunbar's and the rest all carried such midshipmen, and there was never a shortage of them while there were good prospects of worthwhile commands.

The idea of reviving the old midshipmen idea, to a great extent, was Lord Brassey's. Lord Brassey knew the Devitt and Moore ships very well, both in London and in Melbourne. He was well acquainted with Sir Thomas Devitt. Sir Thomas was more than shipowner of great experience and remarkable reputation. He was a far-sighted and public-spirited citizen as well, and he took up the training scheme with enthusiasm. Many of the best shipowners promised their support. He had the ships, the men, the tradition: and he had the trade too. Devitt and Moore were by no means merely a die-hard firm determined to keep to the older style of ship and methods. The very first full-powered steamer ever to round the Cape of Good Hope and make an Australian voyage was their *Queen of the Thames*. True, probably well aware that the Devitt and Moore houseflag really did not belong to her, she flung herself on Cape Agulhas on her first homeward passage, and stayed there. After that Devitt and Moore restricted themselves to the big sailing-ships they knew so well how to run, but they were also interested in the Orient Line, which successfully changed from sail to steam and ran—and still runs—splendid liners in the Australian trade. Such lines as the Orient, the P. and O., the Union-Castle, the White Star and Cunard offered commands comparable with those of the crack sailing liners of the past, if not the same chance of fortune.

The first ships Devitt and Moore commissioned as training-ships were the beautiful *Hesperus* and *Harbinger,* two former

Orient Line passenger-carriers which the Orient Company had given up for steamships. The *Hesperus* and *Harbinger* were especially graceful full-rigged ships. Both were built by Steele of Greenock, who built splendid clippers. The *Hesperus* ended her days as the Russian sail training-ship *Grand Duchess Maria Nikolaevna*. I saw her lying alongside in Bordeaux in 1921 when she was almost half a century old, and had been unavoidably neglected after the downfall of Czarist Russia. Even then her gracious looks put the big steel 'windjammers' to shame. She was riding high out of the water, sails unbent, yards askew the way the riggers had left them, odds and ends of gear about. The water in the dock was dirty and the surroundings generally were not those to show a ship at anything like her best. But her grace of hull and her supreme seaworthiness shone in that dingy dock, and there was about her still an irrepressible air of readiness to do battle with the wild west winds, to sail magnificently wherever competent man might need to take her. Maybe the shades of a few hundred British apprentice lads still stayed with her, not haunting her but loth to go, though it was twenty years and more since her training-ship days. The *Harbinger* was a beauty from Steele's shipyard at Greenock, too, a lovely iron clipper built especially for passengers, to sail well, to behave well, and to provide all who sailed in her with a sense of comfort, of security, and supreme seakindliness. Frank Bullen sailed as second mate of the *Harbinger*. "I never saw anything she would not do that a ship should," he wrote of her. "She was so truly a child of the ocean that even a bungler could hardly mishandle her, for she would work in spite of him. . . For all her bulk she was as easy to handle as a 10-ton yacht. . . Her docility was amazing."

The idea behind what was called the Brassey Cadet Training Scheme—Lord Brassey took a financial interest in it—was that this pair of lovely ships should provide all-round experience for boys, recruited either from the stationary training-ships in the great ports or fresh from their homes, among their own kind, in working ships carrying cargoes, and under the care, instruction, and surveillance of officers who were interested in them. A special instructor was carried. The boys were the crew but there were enough of them, yet not so many that they got in one another's way and the ship had to be run by a system of drill. An excellent nucleus of experienced sailing-ship men was carried as well. The boys had their own quarters which were good and well-kept. They were required to be properly dressed at all times, and to conduct themselves as gentlemen in port and at sea.

The serious decline in recruitment for the sea is shown clearly in statistics. In 1870 there were some 18,000 boys under indentures in British ships, nearly all of them under sail. By the turn of the century there were about 5000. (In March 1953, the precise figure for apprentices and cadets in the 3021 British-registered ships is 4923, none of whom have the privilege of serving under sail.) In the days of the comparatively small sailing-ships there were of course more ships, and in consequence more officers, more commands, and more wastage of human life in losses at sea.

To provide first-class training costs money. There was no way round that. The Hon. East India Company could do it because, with its wealthy monopolies, both the company and its servants could make enormous fortunes. But the days of fortunes by merchant-venturing were past and could not be recalled. If the Devitt and Moore experiment was to be a success, adequate premiums had to be charged. The premiums charged the sons of gentlemen in the ocean training-ships of Devitt and Moore's Australian line amounted to £250 for five voyages, beginning at £70 for the first and ending with £30 for the fifth voyage, with boys from the established stationary training-ships paying £10 less a year and making not more than four voyages. The charge for laundry was £1–10, a voyage, and cadets supplied their own bedding and outfit. This included a 6' by 2' horsehair mattress and pillow, a superfine blue cloth uniform suit, two straw hats, a sea chest 34" by 20" by 20", and oilskins, sea boots, working clothes, and so on. The cost of the lot from a good outfitter was reckoned at £35.

The boys got good value for their parents' money, and the Brassey scheme was a great success. The mainstay of the ships' earnings, however, was cargo, and it was steadily becoming more difficult for a ship to pay on the one Australian round each year, even with assured general cargo to carry out, and wool home. Soon the *Hesperus* and the *Harbinger* were too small and they had to go. In 1899, after only eight years under the Devitt and Moore houseflag, the *Hesperus* was sold to Russia and replaced in the training-ship scheme by the larger *Illawarra*. The *Harbinger* went to the Russian Finns in '97, being sold then for £4,800. She was replaced by the beautiful *Melbourne,* renamed *Macquarie*. There could hardly have been a better ship for the purpose.

One thing all these ships had in common, which was of inestimable value for character-building in youth. They were inspiring ships to serve. Their grace, their good sailing qualities, their harmony of line and of towering sail-plan, their unfailing response to skilled control—these were endearing qualities, not easily to be duplicated in powered vessels. The square-rigger was a *whole* ship, so to speak. Her masts, her yards, her bowsprit and jibboom, her shapely hull were *all ship,* all part of her and all necessary to her: and so a sailer of 2000 tons looked, in a way, larger than a steamer five times her size, for the steamer was a hull with engines and fuel space, the minimum of accommodation, the minimum of cargo-handling gear, and a bridge erected 'thwartships atop the lot to give the watch-keepers a place to work.

But the *Macquarie* and the *Illawarra* were soon too small, too, and in their turn, they had to go. The last of the Devitt and Moore ocean training-ships were the four-masted barques *Port Jackson* and *Medway*.

In the meantime, Lord Brassey had become Governor of the state of Victoria, and the Australian steamship owners, much impressed by the Devitt and Moore training-ships and aware of the need of something similar for their own shipping, had tried to introduce something of the kind. One idea they had was to use a stationary training-ship along the lines of H.M.S. *Worcester* in the Thames, and to moor her in Port Phillip Bay. The Victorian Steamships Owners' Association entered into negotiations to buy the *Rodney* for this purpose, but had reluctantly to give the idea up as too costly for their resources. They then considered the running of a trading sailing-ship similar to the *Hesperus* and *Harbinger,* but one difficulty was the expense of maintaining a large crowd of boys while the ship lay in London. Devitt and Moore sailers (and most others) were accustomed to lie upon the loading berth in London for several months. Their boys went off to their own homes, on leave, for to keep a commissioned training-ship going in the London docks was not a good idea. The Australian boys would have no homes to go to, and so that idea was given up, too.

It was a pity. Lord Brassey was very keen to see something of the sort established, but the best that Melbourne could do was, some years later, to buy the Loch Line's barque *Loch Ryan* and make a reformatory ship out of her, anchored in Port Phillip Bay. One idea which was gone into carefully was to accommodate the Australian boys in the training-ship *Worcester* during the time their ship was in London, but this was not practical. The *Worcester* had no spare room, and, in any event, it was difficult to fit a group of seagoing cadets into her curriculum without upsetting things. So the Australian lads went individually into the Devitt and Moore ships, and there was never an Australian merchant service training-ship as such (New Zealand had the barque *Dartford* which did good service until the first World War).

The *Illawarra* was a big full-rigged ship registering not far short of 2000 tons, built in 1881 for Devitt and Moore. She was a cargo-passenger liner employed in the London-Sydney trade, and she was a training-ship only from 1899 to 1907, when she was sold to Norway and the *Port Jackson* bought in her place. The *Port Jackson* was an iron four-masted barque of 2132 net register tons, 286 feet long, 41 feet in beam, and 25.2 feet depth of hold. She was built by the famous builders Hall of Aberdeen in 1882, and she cost £29,000. She was a beautiful ship to look at and, like most of the Hall ships, she sailed splendidly. She was a worthy successor of the *Hesperus, Harbinger,* and the other full-riggers. She had a good turn of speed and was the first four-masted barque to run from London to Sydney in less than 80 days. Her maiden passage was 77 days from the Channel to Port Jackson, where she was acclaimed. Later she ran from San Francisco to Sydney once in five and a half weeks, which was only a day or two longer than the mail steamers' time for that passage then. She had been laid up for two years for lack of employment when Devitt and Moore bought her for £8,000. She was a good buy.

One reason for acquiring the *Port Jackson* was because Devitt and Moore, together with the Marine Society, had conceived the excellent idea of extending the kind of training available in their ships to boys who were going to be deck-hands, as well as for the officer-aspirants. The Marine Society had a stationary training-ship in the Thames, the *Warspite,* and boys went from this ship into the merchant service direct. It was thought that the advantage of a round voyage under sail to Australia would be of life-long benefit not only to the boys themselves but, by maintaining a flow of well prepared personnel, for the merchant service as a whole. So the Marine Society agreed with Devitt and Moore to send a hundred boys aged 14 to 17 in the *Port Jackson* for an experimental voyage, and to pay £25 each for their keep. The *Port Jackson* was given an additional steel deckhouse for'ard of the poop with space to sling a hundred hammocks, to accommodate the *Warspite* boys, and off she sailed for Sydney with 136 hands all told. Only boys of good character were allowed to go and there was no question of unloading undesirables (as had been done far too often in the annals of the sea, though never with Devitt and Moore).

The *Port Jackson* was in collision with a steamer in the Channel within a day or two of leaving and had to come back for repairs, but the Marine Society's boys behaved very well in the emergency. One regrets to note that the boys were not allowed aloft at night, which was surely an error. There were 33 of them in a watch, with three watches, and plenty of activities of all sorts. The voyage was an unqualified success, and on the arrival of the four-master back in London, it was reported that the whole hundred of them were "ready to go anywhere and do anything". Not a single lad had deserted in Sydney, though it had been expected that some might decide that a life in Australia was preferable to a life before the mast. The Marine Society had taken the precaution of putting the lads under indentures for two years, in order to prevent them from making the one voyage and then leaving the sea. But indentures had never prevented any mariner, young or old, from deserting in Sydney if he wanted to.

The following year, fifty more *Warspite* boys were taken, and again the experience proved invaluable. But unfortunately it was expensive. The £25 a year which the Marine Society paid by no means covered the cost of maintaining a boy in such a ship. The *Port Jackson* had a full crew in addition to the boys. (She carried a master, three mates, a chaplain, doctor, three instructors, three stewards, three cooks, four quartermasters, a boatswain, sailmaker, carpenter, and fourteen able seamen—36 all told, which was twice as many as would have been considered an adequate crew for her under the Finnish flag, say, twenty years later.) It was expensive to maintain a square-rigged ship in immaculate condition. The *Port Jackson* spent four or five months of the year in port, which was very costly, and, though she carried a full general cargo outwards and wool and tallow back again, it was difficult to make ends meet. The Marine Society, too, had the *Warspite* to maintain, and could not continue indefinitely financing the boys' round voyage under sail as well. The *Port Jackson-Warspite* scheme was acclaimed everywhere and shipowners snapped up the boys (Cunard took twenty of them), but when the Marine Society announced that it must appeal to the public for support to continue the scheme, no support was forthcoming. An appeal brought in a miserable £26 (as reported in *The Times* on October 21, 1907). The Marine Society did very well to send fifty boys for the *Port Jackson*'s second voyage. After that the scheme languished. It was a pity.

It is perhaps significant that almost at the same time as the poor response to the Marine Society's appeal was announced, the German Training-ship Society was meeting at Dresden, with the Grand Duke of Oldenburg in the chair and the King of Saxony among those present. Nor was there the slightest difficulty about support from either the German public or from shipowners. The German Training-ship Society ran a beautiful little full-rigged ship, the *Grossherzogin Elisabeth*, which in 1953 is still afloat. This ship carried no cargo but was purely a training-ship, making short voyages such as to the West Indies in the winters and round the Baltic and North Sea in the summer months. Several of the big German lines ran their own cargo-carrying schoolships, such as the two four-masted barques *Herzogin Cecilie* and *Herzogin Sophie Charlotte* for the Norddeutscher-Lloyd Company. These were comparatively new ships, built in the early years of the twentieth century; the *Herzogin Cecilie* was a magnificent big four-masted barque carrying well over 4000 tons of cargo, with her boys quartered in a raised continuous poop which extended for'ard of the mainmast. The *Herzogin Cecilie* and the *Port Jackson* were together in Sydney in 1911, and there was considerable friendly rivalry between the cadets.

Not only the Germans had taken up the Devitt and Moore idea. The Belgians were having the four-masted barque *L'Avenir* built in Germany as a seagoing school-ship for their merchant service, having sent twenty-four cadets in the German five-masted barque *R. C. Rickmers* in 1907 and being very pleased with the results. Denmark had built the four-masted barque *Viking*. The Japanese were introducing their sail-training scheme with the four-masted barque *Taisei Maru* (which also met the *Port Jackson* in Sydney once). The Scandinavian countries had long maintained small sailing school-ships for pre-entry training for boys going to sea in their merchant ships, but they did not use the British apprenticeship system or—except for the Danes—cargo-carrying deepsea training vessels. Many countries used sailing-ships to train boys for their navies. The Russians, for instance, had the *Hesperus,* the Portuguese the clippers *Thermopylae* and *Thomas Stephens*, and the Italians, the Greeks, the Spaniards, the Brazilians, the Argentines, the Chileans were among others using similar vessels.

In Britain, the Devitt and Moore scheme was doing fairly well, despite the failure of the Marine Society's idea for the boys. On the second voyage of the *Port Jackson* in 1907, she carried 22 cadets under the Brassey scheme in addition to the 50 *Warspite* boys. The premium for cadets had been raised then to £255

for four round voyages of nine months each, with an additional
£7–10 a month for any voyage longer than that. The cadets
looked after the mizzen and jigger masts and the *Warspite* lads
looked after the fore and main. The London County Council,
which has always taken a progressive and practical interest in
education (and has a considerable interest in the sea) did what
it could to help the *Warspite* scheme, for which it offered several
scholarships. But the scheme died. That year, the *Port Jackson*
was the only Devitt and Moore sail training-ship left, and it
began to be obvious that she, too, was too small to hope to pay
her way much longer. Devitt and Moore were not conducting a
philanthropy but were engaged in a straightforward and highly
desirable business of national importance, and it had to pay its
way or go under. There was no such thing as state help, nor was
any sought, for shipowners had good reason to fear the stifling,
clutching fingers of bureaucracy. The better shipping lines were
taking the Devitt and Moore boys and were glad to have them,
but there was no question of forming a society among the owners
to run sail training-ships as the Germans had done so successfully.

By 1908, the White Star Line had introduced a sail training-
ship of its own, the full-rigged ship *Mersey* of 1829 register tons,
which it had acquired for £7,000. The *Mersey* was a Liverpool
ship and the *Port Jackson* was a Londoner. The *Mersey* carried
premium cadets—the premium was £200 for four years—and
sailed in the Australian trade. She was a real school-ship just as
the *Port Jackson* was, and carried fully qualified instructors. She
sailed on her first voyage in 1908 with 39 cadets, who were guar-
anteed preference—subject to good conduct and obtaining their
qualifications—in the White Star Line, Leylands, the Dominion,
and the Atlantic Transport lines. Liverpool was always a considerable sailing-ship port and the *Mersey* scheme did well for
some years, but the ship was sold to the Norwegians before very
long.

Stimulated perhaps by the Liverpool rivalry, the *Port Jackson*'s cadet accommodation was increased in 1909 from 30 to 40
places, which was considered the maximum number of boys which
could usefully be carried and trained. The *Port Jackson* boys,

provided they qualified reasonably well and received good reports, were assured of employment in the best London steamship lines: but the British character is odd. Though these lads had a fine bearing, were well behaved, and had had the advantage of the best possible training and preparation which could be provided for them, they could only be selected by personal interview from those whose parents were prepared to pay the substantial premiums. In the view of many shipowners and masters, there was in truth no discernible advantage they possessed over other boys who, having perhaps enjoyed pre-sea training in the *Conway* or the *Worcester* or perhaps not, served their time in, say, the little Milne barques of Aberdeen or the Scottish Shires. The hard-run Limejuicers did the service of effectively screening all who were not really destined for the sea, and these had departed before reaching officer status. The survivors were generally boys of character, with the stuff of true leadership in them. Perhaps because they had not been regimented, many a braw Scots lad or a North-country boy had developed into an excellent embryo-officer by the time he was 19 or 20 and, at the expense of much midnight oil and a minimum of expensive tutoring, had qualified for his second mate's certificate. Most of the better steamship lines still insisted that officers employed by them should be qualified in sail, but many of them were not particular how their recruits had gained that qualification. Some boys, too, had the advantages of the Devitt and Moore ships wasted on them.

Nonetheless the *Port Jackson* was a considerable success, so much so that Devitt and Moore acquired a second four-masted barque in 1910 and formed a special company—Devitt and Moore's Ocean Training Ships, Limited—to run the two vessels. The second four-master was the 2516-ton *Ama Begonakoa*, of Montevideo. She carried 4000 tons and was built at Dumbarton in 1902, at a cost of £30,000. She was towed to the Thames from Bilbao, refitted as a cadet-ship, and renamed the *Medway*. The purchase price was £11,000, but, by the time her refit was completed, towage charges met, and so on, she had cost £13,744. Her equipment cost £1,712-15-4, and towage, runners, dry-docking, port charges and so forth ran up to another £908. But she cleared a profit of £286 on her first round voyage, and the same year the *Port Jackson* made £500. These are very small sums, made possible by the very low overheads, but they sufficed. Both ships were employed in the Australian trade but, by that time, the *Medway* was loading wheat, not wool. Steamships had taken all the wool. There were 64 cadets in the two ships, fifteen of these coming from the *Conway* or *Worcester*, or from the R.N. College, Osborne.

The annual report of the Managers for that year, as presented to the shareholders at the meeting on Tuesday, January 23, 1912, disclosed a healthy state of affairs. Both four-masters were then in Sydney, loading homewards. Shareholders were assured that "there is an increasing demand for properly trained officers, and there is no difficulty in placing all the best men with the most important Steamship companies which will only employ officers who hold certificates of competency showing that they have had experience in sailing-ships. It is unfortunate that so many owners are content to take officers who have only steam experience," the report continues, "but the scheme in which the company is interested will certainly do much to provide men of the best type for those who desire to employ officers of resource instead of mere navigators."

But the "mere navigators" were a growing horde and, before very long when the '14–'18 war began, shipowners had to take what they could get. Many of them had had no scruples, and the merchant service was thirty percent foreign-manned from the turn of the century. As for most North-countrymen, a good many Cardiff shipowners and the like, their main concern was to assure a flow of cheap labour on the bridge, on deck, and in the engine-rooms, and they had little care how they got it. However, the Ocean Training Ships scheme was not for them. It was meant to produce an elite of the merchant service, as there had always been, at any rate since the early days of the East India Company.

The annual reports tell the story. At the meeting held on January 15, 1913, shareholders learned that there was to be a dividend of six percent, which was pleasing news. The *Medway*'s good carrying capacity was paying off, and both ships continued

The *Joseph Conrad* was the last Cape Horn school-ship. Note the triangular mainsail, and the big single topsails.

The training-ship *Macquarie*, belonging to Devitt and Moore   →

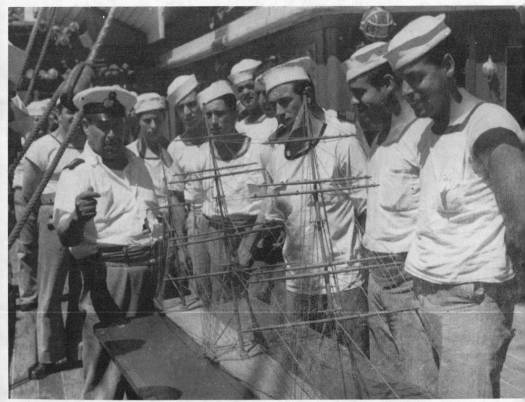

to handle cargoes outwards and homewards. (In this they were favoured: it was more than most other sailing-ships could do.) The *Medway* had cleared £2,305 but the *Port Jackson* had made only some £29. One reason for the older ship's poor earnings was that she had carried general cargo and had to pay to transship a good deal of it to continental ports, which she could not visit herself. The *Medway* did a lot better with her 4000 tons of wheat, and when she was required to discharge some at Lisbon, an extra freight was paid for that.

But there were problems. Parents of boys who were good officer-material could not always afford to pay the rather high fees which the Ocean Training Ships were forced to charge if they were to continue running, and it was not easy to get good officers for the ships themselves. Both ships were fortunate in their masters, who were excellent men throughout the ships' careers but, very naturally, most younger officers felt that they had to go in the steamship lines to assure their futures. The company told its shareholders that it was thinking of acquiring another large four-masted barque—there were plenty on the market then, going very cheaply—to use for training lads on less expensive terms, and the success of the *Medway* was encouragement that this could be done.

The following year both ships came home with Australian grain, though the *Medway* went across from Lisbon to New York to lift case oil for the outward passage to Australia. The two ships carried only 32 cadets between them, but one reason for the low number was that the Admiralty had taken eight of the cadets to train as Midshipmen, R.N.R. The two ships cleared £1,373–16–4 that year, but this went to depreciation and reserves. They then loaded coke outwards to Australia and brought wool back, for the Bradford buyers had become interested in bringing a few cargoes back under sail in order to save warehousing charges ashore in Yorkshire. The coke and wool voyages, however, did not pay. Some 600 tons of pig iron had to be put in the *Port Jackson*

ABOVE
Sail-handling made real sailors, and its character-building could not be duplicated in powered ships.

BELOW   A lesson in rigging
←

for stiffening, and this cost £1,702. She was caught discharging at Immingham by the outbreak of the war and was held up several months there before being allowed to sail. Twenty-four of her cadets went straight into the Royal Navy. The war upset all trades, and the *Port Jackson* went off with cement for Buenos Aires while the *Medway* loaded at Liverpool for Hobart, Tasmania, after taking out coke to Port Alma in Queensland and sailing home with grain, at a loss.

War spoiled the Devitt and Moore training-ship scheme, though the two ships continued to sail for a while. The *Port Jackson* was sold to British buyers in 1916, after clearing a profit of £6,892 on a two-year round voyage. "In view of this ship's age, which so greatly affects the cost of insurance both of ship and cargo, we deemed it advisable to close with an offer made to us at a price which in our opinion is never likely to be repeated," said the managers. But she would have brought a fantastic sum if they had kept her a year or so longer, provided she was not lost to submarines or mines in the interval. The two ships carried only 27 cadets between them, just before the *Port Jackson* was sold. There was a great upsurge of interest in the sea because of the war and there was no dearth of interested boys of the right kind. War, however, made it difficult to take long views, and the advantages of the rather costly training in the two Cape Horners were apt to be overlooked.

War took a heavy toll of merchant seamen. It also killed the idea of sail training in the British merchant service. One reason for this which no one could deny was that the steam-trained men had done very well. Another reason was that many steam-trained men showed an understandable antipathy to their sail-trained fellows, who had enjoyed something they had not. Nor did the merchant service as a whole take kindly to the idea of maintaining an elite among its officers. War was a great levelling-down process. The mass-produced had no interest in levelling *up,* and often resented the idea. Many younger officers, never having had the chance to serve under sail, resented, too, the airs of superiority which some of their seniors were accustomed to assume, for they knew quite well that all the sailing-ship experience some of those seniors had "enjoyed" was perhaps twelve months cleaning out the heads and striking the bells in some sluggard old barque, run on a miserable pittance. If *all* were not required to gain experience in deepsea sail, it was inevitable that in course of time, the sailing-ship would become unpopular.

The profit from the *Port Jackson*'s voyage helped to pay for the £2,300 which had to be found to get the *Medway* through her number three survey and to meet the loss on her 1915–1916 voyage. The *Port Jackson*'s profitable round had been London to Buenos Aires with cement, thence to New York with linseed; thence case oil to Adelaide (she was only 93 days delivering this), and wheat from South Australia back to England. The *Medway* took steel rails for the Tasmanian government to Hobart but had to move across the Pacific in ballast in order to lift wheat from Portland, Oregon, for the United Kingdom. The *Port Jackson* left the Thames with no cadets.

The best way of continuing to use the sail training-ships at that time was discovered when the *Medway,* with a full complement of cadets, was put on the trade between South America and South Africa. This kept her out of the war zones and at the same time gave her cadets the classic training of a number of Cape Horn roundings. But the bureaucrats stepped in. The ship was seized—requisitioned is the official word—by an official styled the Shipping Controller. She was rigged down and engined as a sort of oil-tanker. This was the more criminally stupid in that Devitt and Moore had already arranged, at the request of the Anglo-Saxon Petroleum Company, to dispose of the ship to them for use as a sailing tanker. She would have had an auxiliary engine but the cadets could have remained. She would not have been rigged down. At least the tradition would be maintained. But the bureaucrats sent the cadets packing, and the *Medway* was ruined.

That was the effective end of Devitt and Moore's Ocean Training Ships, but it was by no means the end of their interest in training an elite for the merchant service. The Managers had for some time been concerned with that old problem, wastage of good men from the sea. One of the best ways of avoiding at least some of such wastage was by trying the boys out before they went to sea, by means of some sort of thorough pre-sea training. A year or a couple of years spent at a training establishment—either in the form of an old man-o'-war moored in an estuary or buildings ashore—could do nothing but good, both in eliminating those who were unfitted for a career at sea, and making those who were suited to the life even more fit. So the Nautical College, Pangbourne, came into existence, to form the pre-sea side of Devitt and Moore's Ocean Training Ships activities. The first term was entered on September 1, 1917, and a retired captain of the Royal Navy was the captain superintendent. The establishment was modelled partly on the lines of the Royal Naval College, Osborne—according to some critics, perhaps too much so for its purpose—and the idea was that suitable boys should graduate from the shore establishment into one of the sailing-ships.

Having had the *Medway* taken from them, the managers acquired the barquentine *St. George,* in August 1919. It was a bad time to buy a ship. The *St. George* was a vessel of 871 tons, a former yacht. She cost £30,000 purchase price, plus another £2,500 to fit her out and equip her. She could earn nothing, and her running costs were ruinous. For a while, she sailed between the English Channel and the Atlantic islands—from Plymouth to Las Palmas chiefly—but she was altogether too great a drain on the college income and she had to go. It was a great pity she was ever bought, but the Pangbourne cadets had been promised experience under sail and, at the time, a more suitable vessel was not available. Within a twelve-month, however, magnificent vessels such as the Laeisz Line's almost new four-masted barque *Pola* and the school-ship *Herzogin Cecilie* were going begging, as reparations. The *Pola* went to the French, who renamed her *Richelieu* and used her for a school-ship until she blew up in Baltimore, and the *Herzogin Cecilie*—the best ship of them all from the Devitt and Moore point of view—was sold to the late Gustaf Erikson for £4,250.

Another vessel acquired by Devitt and Moore was no better than the *St. George* (which had gone off to the South Seas on a sort of paying guest voyage by 1923) and that was Lord Brassey's auxiliary steam yacht *Sunbeam*. Lord Brassey had willed this vessel to the organisation he had helped so much to found and to foster through the years, but she was not really suitable for a training-ship. Moreover she was in Indian waters, under requisition and, when she was released, it was a most expensive business to bring her back to the United Kingdom. Coal was a ruinous price at the time, and the group of officers entrusted to sail her back steamed her instead, and all the bills were given to Devitt and Moore's.

The Nautical College at Pangbourne thrived and has continued to do good work. But Pangbourne, by the banks of the Thames between Oxford and London, is a long way from the sea and, as the years pass, even further from the roar of the Cape Horn gales and the tradition of the sailing-ship. As an educational establishment it is magnificent and I understand there is a long waiting list. The boys sail a little in dinghies on the Thames nearby and, when they graduate, about a third of them do not go to sea at all. Devitt and Moore's Ocean Training Ships have become the Devitt and Moore Nautical College, which perhaps was inevitable. But I think it is a pity that the sailing tradition was not maintained by this firm which had done so well and which, before all others, was so well fitted to keep it going. But neither Devitt and Moore nor anyone else could persevere indefinitely with something which, excellent as it was, was not really wanted.

Chapter fifteen

BETWEEN THE WARS

AFTER THE first World War, the Cape Horn ship declined very rapidly in numbers. Within five years of the end of hostilities practically all British, all American, all French, and even most of the Norwegian, Danish, and Swedish Cape Horn sailing-ships had gone out of commission. They had been lost, hulked, or scrapped. The war, with its high freights, had given a false fillip to the surviving sailing-ships. The harm it did far outweighed the little good. Though the lure of profits caused some hulks to be rigged again and a considerable fleet of big wooden schooners and barquentines was built in the United States, the worst effect of the war as far as the sailing-ship was concerned was its spoiling of the men. Sailing-ship men who survived the war had become unemployable under sail in the process—a hard fact, but a fact nonetheless. High wages, conditions of employment which were beyond those which sailing-ships could hope to finance as soon as the freight market dropped, a constant drift of the younger men into powered vessels, the autocratic dispersal of the truly international sailing-ship sailors as they were paid off their ships after post-war voyages, a far slower rate of decrease in running costs as compared with the very steep drop in freights—these things combined to make the sailing-ship very difficult to operate.

There was a severe shipping slump quite soon after the first World War, and tramps and sailing-ships alike scoured the seas in vain for paying cargoes. Big Cape Horn four-masted barques, barques, and full-rigged ships were tied up two and three abreast in many ports in Europe. I saw them particularly in Nantes,

St. Nazaire, and Bordeaux, though almost every port of consequence had its quota. Not many of these ships went to sea again.
The presence on the market of a considerable fleet of German
sailing-ships, including all the surviving ships of Mr. Laeisz's
excellent line, further depressed the market. In ports as far apart
as San Francisco, Dunkirk, and Antofagasta, the German and the
former German Cape Horners lay, and most of them were
wasted.

For a year or two, a few British and fewer American Cape
Horn ships struggled to make ends meet. In Britain, the John
Stewart Line was the last, though a few old ships bought by
Sir William Garthwaite and registered—for some reason—in
Montreal (though sailing on English articles) sailed for a year
or two longer. The last British Cape Horn cargo-carrier was lost
when the *Garthpool* (which had begun life in 1892 as the
Lawhill's sister, *Juteopolis*) threw herself on the Cape Verde
Islands on a day of poor visibility in 1929. Over-capitalised, expensive to run, too greatly harassed by the infinite and useless
upsurge of bureaucracy which was one of the evil effects of the
war, and, in some cases at least, indifferently handled and sailed,
most of these last ships were poor shadows of their illustrious
predecessors. Old sailors almost breathed a sigh of relief when
they were gone.

The United States emerged from the war with an excellent
fleet of former German ships, under the Dollar and Hind Rolph
house-flags in San Francisco, but of all maritime nations the
Americans were the least able to sail such ships economically
in the face of the fierce post-war competition. The Stars and
Stripes had been made too costly for a Cape Horn ship to fly,
and most of these vessels made one voyage only, if that. One or
two sailed across the Pacific with lumber, to become bankrupt
at their arrival ports. More than one, financed briefly by some
fly-by-night who pocketed every advance he could lay his hands
on, was abandoned in Australian ports, and sold there for a few
dollars. Others sailed a last voyage to reach some break-up port
(usually in Japan) or place where there was a market for a big
coal-hulk. The increasing use of oil fuel and of diesel engines in

deepsea ships made even the market for hulks very uncertain.

The result of all this was that, within a year or two of the war's end, the only considerable fleet of square-rigged ships to fly the American flag was that of the Alaska Packers' Company, of San Francisco, and these were sea-going depot-ships and in no sense real Cape Horners. They made the one voyage annually, from San Francisco to the Alaska salmon-packing stations, carrying men and stores, and they came back again with the salmon pack. After a few years most of them were considered unusable even for this employment, and for years in the 1920's and as late as the early '30's, the masts and yards of the laid-up Packers' fleet towered above the creek at Alameda. Some were sold to Japan for scrap. One or two went to Hollywood for use in the film industry. Others were moored off Long Beach where they were useful as gambling houses, for they lay outside United States territorial waters. By 1939 one only was fit to go to sea, the barque *Kaiulani* which had been the *Star of Finland,* and she did not last long. The *Kaiulani* was the last Cape Horner to fly the American flag. She was a steel barque of 1699 tons, built by A. Sewall and Company at Bath, Maine, in 1899, under the name of *Kaiulani*.

From all the upset of the first World War, only two sailing-ship owners emerged who were capable of carrying on the tradition of the sailing-ship. One of these, since he used old ships exclusively and could remain in business only while there were old ships to use, was merely delaying the time when these ships must reach the inevitable scrap-heap. This was the late Gustaf Erikson, of Mariehamn, in the Åland Islands. Captain Erikson was a collector of old ships and he ran them well enough, but in this he was aided by several factors which are ordinarily denied to more orthodox shipowners. Since he built up his fleet *after* the post-war slump, he was able to buy ships at scrap values. He secured many magnificent four-masted barques at prices ranging from £4,000 to £6,000, and once got a trio of barques at £4,000 the lot. He was certainly not over-capitalised. He was not bothered by depreciation at all, for as long as they remained afloat, his ships could not become worth less than he paid for them. In such circumstances, he could afford not to insure his ships, nor did he do so. From the 1920's to the outbreak of the second World War, his usual fleet was some twenty ships of which at least twelve were Cape Horners, yet the capital invested in the lot probably never exceeded £100,000. Gustaf Erikson was a capable shipmaster before he was an owner, and he was always a shrewd and energetic business man who carried his own risks. He was virtually his own marine superintendent (and an excellent one, for there could have been none better), and he had the minimum overheads. He was well served by a firm of London brokers—Messrs Clarkson and Company, of Fenchurch Street and later of Bishopsgate—who well understood the sailing-ship business.

Though he loved Cape Horn ships with an understanding and abiding affection, he did not scruple to scrap any which became unprofitable to him, always putting the money from their sale to the purchase of more ships while there were any such ships to be had. When an old ship, unable to carry a big cargo—like the full-rigged ship *Grace Harwar*—was due for an expensive survey in order to carry her insurance classification (without which she could not be chartered to carry insurable cargoes and therefore would have been unusable), he sold her for breaking-up. Despite this, he was able not only to maintain his considerable fleet but to add to it, so long as there was a square-rigged ship left anywhere which was worth buying. Before long, there was an end of them. The three former Danish logwood barques from the depressed West Indies trade—the *Claudia, Suzanne,* and *Germaine*—and the four-masted barque *Moshulu* (which was the former German training-ship *Kurt*) which he found in Seattle, were about the last worth buying.

In 1935, the Erikson ships totalled fifteen Cape Horners, three former Cape Horners (the *Lingard, Kylemore,* and *Pestalozzi*) then in the North Sea trade, five small wooden barques and barquentines also in the North Sea trade, and half a dozen motor-schooners, with a towboat (which burned wood) and a slip at Nystad. His Cape Horners included four former school-ships, the

Norddeutscher Lloyd's *Herzogin Cecilie*, the Belgian *L'Avenir*, the Danish *Viking*, and the ex-German *Kurt*. In these and his other deepsea ships, Erikson carried a considerable number of cadets, though never more than sufficient to make up the crews for the ships. There were over a hundred cadets in the various ships, but no instructors. These cadets came from many countries, including the United States. The premiums were small—£50 usually—and the lads received a wage which, if it was minute, was the same as the deckboys and ordinary seamen received. An able seaman was paid about £2 a month, or perhaps £3. Carpenters and sailmakers were doing well to receive £5 or £6 a month. Cooks had between £4 and £6, stewards from £8–10 to £10 (depending on the size of the ship), second mates £7–10 to £8, mates £9–10 to £10–10, and masters from £15 to £22–10, with a bonus in some instances.

With such a low wage scale (it was no lower than that offered a British crew to ship in the four-masted barque *Bellands* out of St. Nazaire in 1921) the Erikson running costs were at a minimum. There was one other great advantage which these Åland ships had, and it was vital. They had at all times a good and sufficient pool of experienced sailing-ship masters, officers, and men to sail them—men who had been accustomed to sailing-ships from childhood and had, in most cases, never been in any other sort of ship. It was all very well being able to draw cadets from every country which still insisted on sail experience for its officers without providing the sailing-ships for lads to serve in; but cadets were not crew. They were useful and they could be excellent, but without a sufficient cadre of experienced men steeped in the unbroken sailing tradition, the Erikson ships could not have gone to sea. The background of the little Åland firewood schooners, trading across to Stockholm, and the Baltic barquentines and the North Sea barques, provided the men, and the economic stress associated with most unfertile islands sent them to sea. The Ålanders were first-class seamen, and they did very well. Among them were some outstanding masters, of whom the greatest, without a doubt, was the late Ruben de Cloux. It was de Cloux who sailed the *Lawhill* to fortune: it was de Cloux who bought the *Herzogin Cecilie* and later the *Viking* for the Erikson fleet; it was de Cloux who sailed the *Herzogin Cecilie,* with boy-crews who were never more than barely adequate to handle that heavy ship—she had been designed deliberately to make as much work as possible for as many boys as possible; but the Ålanders sailed her with the minimum—and he sailed her time and time again from Australia to the Channel at the head of the fleet. Moreover, he did this without expensive loss of sails and at the bare minimum of expense generally.

It was de Cloux, really, who largely made it possible for the fleet to be built up. As a young man he commanded the big-carrying *Lawhill* at the end of the first World War, when she still was handling highly profitable freights. Instead of those freights being dissipated in heavy overheads and general costs and wastage (as they were far too often in other ships), de Cloux saw that every penny was laid by. He was never misled by easy money, which does not last for long. One round voyage to Buenos Aires, for example, yielded a surplus of some £60,000. Immediately afterwards there was a slump. But the *Lawhill* had never been geared to the boom. In other words, she did not require boom conditions to sail profitably. She had more than earned her own costs and a considerable surplus to buy other ships as well, and sailing-ships were cheap as soon as the slump began. No one else wanted them. No one else thought they had a future (except one other man who was handicapped out of business, for his were among the ships being sold). The Erikson crews were not spoiled. Any who were no longer satisfied with the conditions offered could go, and they were not missed, for the *Lawhill* was manned each voyage by a fresh crowd of youngsters from the Åland Islands where the supply was cheap, sturdy, and apparently endless. The *Herzogin Cecilie* was manned in the same way: it was only later that such luxuries as cadets and passengers (who paid 10/- a day and had nothing to complain of) were offering. The Ålanders, hemmed in in their islands during the war and accustomed to a hard life on their small farms and in their wooden ships, had not known the decadence of war-time affluence, the fibre-rotting ease of unsound too-good conditions. For them, life was hard, as it had always been. They were still good sailors.

There were other excellent masters—Mattson, of the *Olive-bank*; Boman of the *Grace Harwar* and later the *Moshulu*; Broman of the *Pommern*; Carl Granith, who lost his life in the *Olivebank* when she was mined; Hägerstrand of the *Woodburn,* the *Hougomont,* the *Viking,* and the *Passat*; the Sjögrens. These were good sailors and they made good voyages. Though it had setbacks (particularly the loss of the *Herzogin Cecilie* in the English Channel late in '36, and a freight-slump now and again in the depression years which left even some of the Erikson ships sailing round the whole world in ballast, unable to find a paying cargo anywhere) the Erikson line thrived. But the second World War cost it dearly. The barques *Penang* and *Killoran,* and the four-master *Olivebank* were casualties, with considerable loss of life. The *Lawhill, Pamir,* and *Archibald Russell* were war prizes, and the last-named was rigged down in England never to sail again, while the others finished the war under other flags. The *Moshulu, Pommern,* and *Viking* were caught in the Baltic, and only the *Viking* made a postwar voyage. The *Winterhude*—a rather ugly big barque—was scrapped. The *L'Avenir* had been sold before the war to a famous German company—Hamburg-Amerika—as a school-ship but, under the name of *Admiral Karp-fanger,* had gone missing on her first voyage.

The Erikson Line emerged from the war with a handful of ships only. Three of these—the *Passat, Viking,* and the returned *Pamir*—sailed briefly, but they made losing voyages. The bureaucrats had fixed the freights but they could not fix world-wide costs, and by the time the freight market was freed the Erikson ships had gone. Gustaf Erikson died at Mariehamn in the Åland Islands in August, 1947, at the age of 74. He had been a ship-owner for 35 years during which he had owned, at one time or another, 70-odd ships, of which 40 had been sailing-ships. He had served at sea in sailing-ships in all capacities from boy-cook to master and, in the end, he had made a success of sailing almost the last handful of big Cape Horners left in the world, when no one else would touch them. To do this took courage, foresight,

The Pommern

HAROLD A. UNDERHILL

and considerable practical ability. Gustaf Erikson had all these in good measure. But at the time of his death his fleet was reduced to three ships, and these were doomed.

It was not the war which defeated them, though in the second world war Finland had taken a very active part, and its seafarers were as affected as any others by the long tide of high freights, full employment, and the nerve-rack of the endless and awful risks of modern war. What ruined all hope of reviving the Åland sailing-ships was the disappearance of the local sailing schooners and barquentines, for, long before the end of the war, all these were powered. That was fatal. There was an immediate drying-up of the reservoir of sail-trained young men, willing and able to serve in sailing-ships because that was the only life they knew. Most countries had been compelled, during the war, to give up the requirement that officers for merchant ships should have experience under sail, because sailing-ships—with a very few exceptions—had been unable to operate during the war. This dried up the source of cadets: but it was the loss of the pool of sailing seamen and boys which was really fatal. Ålanders had been able to sail with profit in Swedish ships, and not many masters and mates were prepared to go back in the Cape Horners.

In 1953, the *Pommern* lies alongside at Mariehamn but the costs of keeping her, even in idleness, are very high. A big steel Cape Horner is a large area to paint, and paint is expensive. Her masts and yards and standing and running rigging must be kept up, and that also is costly. There must be ship-keepers, and they cost money too. The latest news is that an approach is being made to Ålanders generally to contribute towards the cost of keeping the ship. Meanwhile the port of Gothenburg in Sweden was debating the merits of using the *Viking* as a temporary navigation school, instead of putting up an expensive building ashore, and the *Pamir* and *Passat,* having been sold to Belgium for breaking-up and resold by the knackers to an over-optimistic Hamburg firm which put engines in them, lay bankrupt, one in a Dutch, the other in a Danish port.

Gustaf Erikson never built a ship. The only owner who built Cape Horners after the first World War was Laeisz. The Vinnen

line built five curious auxiliary five-masters, but these were abor-
tions and not Cape Horners. The Danish East Asiatic Company
took delivery of the big five-masted barque *Kjøbenhavn* from
Ramage and Ferguson, of Leith, in 1921. She was auxiliary, too.
Laeisz completed the four-masted barque *Priwall* in 1921 and
built the *Padua* in 1926: to date, she remains the last Cape
Horner ever sent down the ways, anywhere. The *Priwall* and the
Padua were splendid ships, and they were sailed until 1939 in the
full tradition of the great Flying 'P' Line. More than once, they
showed that they were still handled in the Hilgendorf manner,
and they still were capable of breaking records. Both ships sailed
from the Elbe to Spencer Gulf, South Australia, in between 65
and 66 days, in 1933. That was clipper time, though they were
both big, heavy four-masted barques with cadets as crew. Nor
was that wonderful run their only outstanding passage between
the wars.

The end of the first World War saw the Laeisz Line dispersed
to the four winds. The *Peking* became Italian, for a while. The
Pommern was Greek, the *Parma* British, the *Potosi* Chilean, the
Pola French, the *Ponape* Norwegian. Laeisz got them back again
as soon as he could—all that were still in first-class order. Except for the *Pola,* which the French kept as a training-ship, the
other countries did not really want the sailing-ships. Within a
year or two, the Laeisz house-flag flew once more from the trucks
of a fleet of fine Cape Horners which included the four-masted
barques *Pamir, Passat, Peking,* and *Parma,* and the ship *Pinnas.*
All were twentieth century ships, the first three German-built to
Laeisz order, the *Pamir* by Blohm and Voss in 1905, the *Passat*
and *Peking* by the same builders in 1911, and the *Parma* as the
Anglo American Oil Company's *Arrow* in Scotland in 1902, and
bought first by Laeisz in 1911 for £15,000. The four-masted
barque *Priwall* had been laid down with the *Pola* at the Blohm
and Voss yard at Hamburg in 1916, but was not completed until
1919 and made her maiden voyage in 1920. She was a four-

ABOVE RIGHT   The late Gustaf Erikson

ABOVE LEFT
The former Laeisz ship *Pola* became the French *Richelieu*. She was
burned out at Baltimore.

BELOW   The *Herzogin Cecilie* was lost in the English Channel.   →

→ Former German prizes rotting in San Francisco Bay

They were broken up, most of them in Japan.

← The barque *Kaiulani* was the last American Cape Horner. She sailed during the second World War.

The Alaska Packers ↓ up in Alameda Creek

masted barque of 3105 gross register tons and 2849 nett, built
in the usual three-island style of the Laeisz ships. The *Padua*
was added to the fleet when she was completed by J. C. Tecklenborg at Geestemunde in 1926. She was a strong and shapely four-
masted barque registering 3064 tons gross, 2678 nett.

The *Pinnas* was dismasted off Cape Horn in 1929 and had to
be abandoned in a sinking condition, as her fallen masts and yards
had smashed her sides in. This left the six four-masted barques.
They were employed again in the Chilean trade, but it was more
and more difficult to keep them going. The ships were all right
and so were the masters, officers, and crews. As late as 1938, the
Priwall was still breaking clipper records, for in that year she
made the classic westwards rounding of the Horn in five days,
14 hours. That was from 50 South in the Atlantic to 50 South
in the Pacific, and to the best of my knowledge, it is the fastest
westward rounding of the Horn that was ever made under sail.
The master of the *Priwall* at the time was Captain Hauth, and
her crew included some forty German cadets.

Under the redoubtable Herman Piening, the *Padua* passed
the Lizard deep-loaded with heavy general cargo on April 13,
1928, and was anchored in Talcahuano Bay 71 days later. Homeward bound that voyage with a full cargo of nitrates from
Mejillones, she was in the Channel 69 days out and was alongside
at her port of discharge three days later, 72 days from anchorage
to anchorage. This was the best voyage made by any deep-loaded
sailing-ship at least since the end of the first world war, and the
Padua and *Priwall* shared another clipper passage. This was
their ballast run from the Elbe to South Australia, already mentioned. I have the report of Captain R. Claus on the *Priwall*'s
run before me now. (In 1953 Claus commands a small steamer
out of Hamburg.) The *Priwall* left the Blohm and Voss floating
dock at Hamburg on the morning of October 31, 1933, and, with
the *Padua* in close company, towed down the Elbe bound in ballast for Spencer Gulf for orders, to load South Australian wheat.
This was a departure from the usual Laeisz procedure, but the
Chilean nitrate trade was in a poor state, and already the *Peking,*
Passat, and *Parma* had had to be sold to sail under the Finnish
flag. The ships were losing money on each voyage they made, and

it was impossible to continue to run all six of them. So the *Priwall* and *Padua* were sent off to try the Australian grain trade.

Their voyage under sail began on the morning of November 2, and the two big four-masters raced down the Channel logging 49 nautical miles in a four-hour watch sometimes touching thirteen knots. (Thirteen and a half was about their top speed with cargo: perhaps fourteen knots in ballast. Laeisz ships made good passages by their consistency and not by odd bursts of unusual speeds.) Claus in the *Priwall* was leading down-channel, but the *Padua* (which was commanded by the veteran Captain Jurs) was very close astern. The two ships did not sight each other again until November 20. Three weeks out, they were across the Line and storming along with the southeast trade winds. The *Priwall* was fortunate in picking up good westerly winds on 27 South. On Christmas day she ran the excellent distance of 342 nautical miles in the 24 hours and, in the 18 days from December 14 to December 31, she covered 4884 miles. During the same period the *Padua* sailed 4810 miles. Here are the days' runs from the two ships' logs.

Padua	Miles	*Priwall*	Miles
	178. 14/12		242. 14/12
	266		276
Miles from	273	Miles from	288
14th to 31st	288	14th to 31st	289
December,	287	December,	312
1933.	305	1933.	311
	280		300
18 days.	312	18 days.	273
Average,	236	Average,	245
267 miles	202	271 miles	93
a day.	308	a day.	250
	283		342
	309		312
	250		280
	351		317
	257		277
	284		276
	141. 31/12		211. 31/12
	4810		4884

During this time the *Priwall* touched 15 knots in a squall, but she could not keep that speed up. On January 5, 1934, she picked up the South Neptune lighthouse at the entrance to Spencer Gulf. Her passage was 65.1 days, and the *Padua* was only a few hours astern. It was a splendid performance. The *Priwall* loaded at Port Victoria and the *Padua* at Port Broughton.

But the voyage did not pay and, before long, the *Priwall* and *Padua* were back in the Chilean trade. The *Padua*'s passage of 68 days from Bremen to Corral in 1938 was splendid, and so was her crossing of the Pacific from Valparaiso to Port Lincoln in 52½ days, at an average speed of over seven knots. These were magnificent ships and the Germans could still sail them. But the *Priwall* was in Valparaiso at the outbreak of the second World War and, in June, 1941, the third Reich made a present of her to the Chilean navy. She was fitted with a strong motor and renamed the *Lautaro,* but a year or two later she burned out with a cargo of nitrates, somewhere off the coast of Peru, and that was the end of her. Not long after that, Claus was helping to put up scaffolding at the Deutsche Werft to keep his family alive.

As for the *Padua,* she survived the war (which she spent principally as a training-ship for young merchant seamen, in the Baltic) and was handed over to Soviet Russia at Swinemunde in January, 1946. She was refitted as a training-ship at Rostock when it was reported that she was to accommodate 400 to 600 young men. In 1953, as far as I am aware, the *Padua*—now named the *Krusenberg*—is still operating as a school-ship for the Russian Navy somewhere in Baltic waters, but where I do not know. She has not been seen since 1939 in the open sea.

In 1953, a handful of other Laeisz ships survives, here and there—the *Pommern* in Mariehamn, the *Pamir* and *Passat* bankrupt and ruined with engines, the *Peking* as a stationary training-ship in the river Medway in England, where she is known as the *Arethusa* and is run by the Shaftesbury Homes. Almost all her yards have gone though her four high masts still stand. I went to Hamburg and asked Erich Laeisz what he thought of the total abandonment of the science of handling the deepsea sailing-ship,

which had been worrying me. It worried him, too; but what
could be done about it? Ships are too costly to build and to run
and, even in Hamburg, the men and the spirit are no longer
available to provide the essential nucleus. In the long run war
is wholly dispiriting, win or lose. Men forced to begin life afresh
and to find somehow the will and the ability to overcome the
most crushing and ruinous disadvantages can scarcely be expected
to become enthusiastic for an ideal. The House of Laeisz was still
very interested in sailing-ships, though its fleet had been dispersed
for the second time in the same generation. Said Mr. Laeisz (this
was in 1949) :

"I personally, of course, would gladly grasp any opportunity of setting going again one or more of the most modern sailing-ships, but
besides all present restrictions as to size and the line Brest-Scillies there
is still the absolute lack of funds.

"After losing *all* my ships and after the so-called currency-reform, I
have practically nothing at all left to build anything. Even before this deplorable war my steamers and motorships had to make good part of the
losses incurred by the sailing-ships, with freights down to 10/6 from
Iquique to Delfzyl or 25/– from South Australia to Glasgow. If I were
to build anything reasonable it needs must be a paying proposition.

"In Germany there was a plan before the war, and elaborated upon
during the first years of the war, that all German shipping companies
and owners either should run one or two school-ships at their own
expense according to the tonnage owned or, if too little, participate with
others equally placed in one ship. These ships were intended to go into
regular trades for those shipments of grain and other commodities made
by organisations of the Reich—for instance the Reichsgetreidestelle. This
way the ships could pay their way without disquieting the open market
at times when otherwise they would have been compelled to accept insufficient rates. Thus a direct fixed subvention could be dispensed with.

"Having been in the regular nitrate trade with a line of well-found
ships gave our firm an opportunity to keep going, even after the slump
of the nitrate freights in the middle of the first decade of this century.
We did this by carrying real general cargo out, instead of being forced
to run out in ballast or with poorly paying bulk cargo as so many others
had to do. After the first world war the scope of the general cargo was
reduced to iron, coke and cement which did, of course, pay not so well.
After Chile started subsidizing her own cement industry even this cargo
fell off more and more. The European market for Chilean nitrate had by

this time deteriorated more and more, and what little quantities went to Europe were shipped in lots by regular liners.

"Being placed in quite another position from that of the Finns, and saddled with far higher expenses than they, it did not pay to keep our ships going on one cargo of wheat per annum.

"To sum up, I doubt very much that a sailing-ship can ever again pay her way, barring wartimes. So the only way left would be to do it internationally, i.e., to run cargo-carrying school-ships and train all-comers from western Europe to the U.S.A. It would surely be a grand thing on the road to international understanding. But can such an idea grow roots strong enough to sprout branches that carry the necessary funds?"

A few years after that, the Laeisz Line was building small fast fruit ships, a type it had launched between the wars with considerable success. Its last two four-masters, the *Pamir* and *Passat,* were bought back expensively from a firm of Belgian ship-breakers by a Hamburg shipowner named Schliewin, and the idea behind this was the excellent one put forward by Erich Laeisz in 1949—to make the ships into international school-ships for the good of youth generally and the retention of the Cape Horn tradition. But vast sums had to be spent on both ships and, in the end, they were impossible economically and they were not sailing school-ships either. They were given big diesels which robbed them of good cargo space, filled them with unnecessary and expensive people, and spoiled their sailing qualities.

It was difficult to get crew. There were plenty of powered ships. There was one other reason for the reluctance of seafarers to serve again in long-voyage sailing-ships, or to accept anything like the conditions which used to be considered necessary in such vessels. The older seafarers were never troubled by wives. Few of them were married. They were very young, very old, or confirmed bachelors. In recent years there has been a remarkable change. Nowadays many married men follow the sea, or try to, and wives are reluctant to agree to their husbands being away for what they consider too long. When the *Pamir* and *Passat* were recommissioned, not only was there a stipulation that voyages must be short—to the east coast of South America only—but the regular seafarers demanded steamer rates of pay, plus a sailing allowance. The old Cape Horn sailor was content to cut himself off from home life. He literally was a *sea* man. But his modern counterpart believes in keeping at least one foot ashore, and the wife of his bosom is intent upon getting both his feet there, at the first possible moment. No matriarchy is interested in providing menfolk for the sea.

Both propellers obligingly dropped off on the *Pamir* and *Passat*'s first South American voyages, and the vessels had to be sailed. But new propellers were *flown* out to them in Brazilian ports. (How can a sailing-ship pay which has engine parts flown thousands of miles? What sort of Cape Horn ship is that?) It was all very well while the Korean War kept freight markets temporarily very high, and the two four-masters might have cleared expenses. But Korean War or no Korean War, freights dropped soon after the ships were recommissioned, and they kept dropping: within a few months the two fine four-masters were held for bankruptcy.

It was a pity, but it was inevitable. Money had to be poured into them to make those two ships into full-powered auxiliaries and to fit them as school-ships, according to modern ideas. Nor did the international young men to go in them prove easy to find. Even in Germany, the requirement that officer-aspirants must serve twenty months in sailing-ships had to be dropped as no longer reasonable. Finland and Sweden had also had to abandon sail-training. A handful of British boys, sent by a few enterprising shipowners, joined the ships, but they took unkindly to the Schliewin idea of 'training' for first-voyage cadets. Except when the propellers fell off, the ships made most of their voyages under power. (To give a master engines which will enable his ship to average nine knots was a temptation few could be expected to withstand, for the ships could never average anything like that speed under sail.) In at least one of the ships, the principal idea behind the 'training' seemed to be to impress the newcomer with his complete uselessness and in no circumstances to permit him to benefit from the real advantages of service under sail. No, the scheme was ill-conceived and poorly executed, splendid as the principle was.

When I first heard that the *Pamir* and *Passat* had been bought back from the breakers I was astonished. If those ships were worth sailing, then the House of Laeisz would sail them: if Laeisz were not interested, then I was very dubious about the whole thing. I was the more dubious because I had been thoroughly over the *Pamir* when she was in London a year or two earlier, under the New Zealand flag. (The New Zealanders were able to man her because the Union Steamships Company still had a few real sailing-ship officers from the barques *Gladbrook* and *Dartford,* and the sailing tradition had persisted a long time in the Tasman Sea and round the coast of New Zealand. They handled the ship very well, though expensively—so expensively, indeed, that the New Zealand government, tiring of meeting the deficits, gave the *Pamir* back to Gustaf Erikson.) A group of us had the idea of acquiring her and converting her into a school-ship, though not with engines. She had had over a thousand tons of wet sand in her for years and there was no telling what condition some of her plates might be in. After all, she was an oldish ship in 1950. We estimated that it would cost at least £100,000 to do anything with her as a satisfactory school-ship: it was better to build a new ship. Just then, the Korean War caused such a flood of shipbuilding orders that there was not a yard left in all Britain where such a ship could be laid down before 1955.

So we had watched the *Pamir/Passat* experiment with interest. If the engines were flung out of the ships they would be good Cape Horners again, even now. But who would sail them then? It is futile to find one man who will handle such a ship. There has to be a living tradition, a free and willing acceptance of service under sail without benefit of engines, a sufficient reservoir of competent seamen able and eager to serve and to go on serving. Those things have gone.

Chapter sixteen

THE SCHOOL-SHIPS

THERE remain the sailing school-ships. These were of three types —the cargo-carrying Cape Horner which was manned largely by cadets, like the Devitt and Moore ships and the Swedish four-masters *Beatrice, C. B. Pedersen,* and *Abraham Rydberg* (which were the best and are now all gone); the non-cargo-carrying small full-rigged ship for *ab initio* training and indoctrination of boys intended for the merchant service; and the naval school-ship, such as the United States Coast Guard's barque *Eagle,* the Portuguese barque *Sagres,* and the Italian *Amerigo Vespucci.* They are all comparatively recent inventions in the history of shipping, as far as I am aware. Most navies and all merchant shipping managed without much organised training, until comparatively recent years. When children went to sea their indoctrination did not have to be arranged.

The first merchant service school-ship, to the best of my knowledge, was the Swedish brig *Carl Johan,* which was in commission from 1848 to 1878. She was followed by the first *Abraham Rydberg*—a ship—in 1879. From 1879 until 1942 there was always an *Abraham Rydberg*—first the wooden ship, then a steel ship from 1912 to 1928, and then the four-masted barque (which is still afloat in 1953, now as a Portuguese motorship). The Danes had built their first *Georg Stage* (another full-rigged ship) by 1882 and have preserved that tradition ever since. These Scandinavian ships were—and most still are—financed by successful shipowners and other philanthropists, and their idea was to pro-

359

vide a better source of recruitment for their ships, to give boys
their initiation to the sea in the best possible manner among their
own kind and in the care of interested officers, whose whole purpose was to look after them and provide them with the most satisfactory form of training.

There were several such ships also in Norway, which in 1953
still maintains at least three of them, the lovely little Kristiansand
full-rigger *Sørlandet*, the Oslo ship *Christian Radich*, and the
barque *Staatsraad Lehmkuhl*. The *Christian Radich* was built
at Sandefjord in 1937 and cost about £30,000. This was also the
approximate cost of the Danish full-rigged ship *Georg Stage,*
which was built in 1934/35 to replace the ship which I had
renamed the *Joseph Conrad*. The *Christian Radich* is 200 feet
long by 31 feet in beam, and accommodates some hundred boys.
Up to the end of the second World War at any rate, she had never
received a pennypiece in payment from the government of Norway or from the city of Oslo. Shipowners and merchants paid for
her (the late Christian Radich giving the original donation which
made the construction of the ship possible), and they found that
it was sense. These sailing school-ships gave lads a splendid indoctrination to the sea, and still do so. At the end of the war, in
1945, all the Norwegian school-ships had been damaged in greater
or less degree. It was an expensive matter to get them in commission again, but it was one of the first things the Norwegian
shipowners did.

The vessels usually sail in the spring, summer, and early autumn
only, sailing in their home waters, in the North Sea, and with a
transatlantic voyage now and then. They are costly to maintain,
but the Scandinavians consider them well worthwhile. The little
Sørlandet was financed by a gift outright from Shipowner O. A.
T. Skjelbred, of Kristiansand. Education authorities also help
to finance this vessel, as well they might. The *Sørlandet* registers
557 tons, was built in 1927, and can accommodate 95 boys. She
has the distinction of being the only one among the school-ships
which does not use auxiliary power and, indeed, she is the last
pure full-rigged ship left sailing anywhere, for the German
Schulschiff Deutschland does not now go to sea. The Danish

Georg Stage makes little use of her motor: but she is an auxiliary, and so are all the others—ships, barques, barquentines, and top-sail-schooners.

There is a surprisingly large fleet of such vessels, even today. If they could all be assembled together in a harbour which would accommodate them, they would be an astonishing sight—two four-masted barques (both Soviet Russian and former Germans, the ex-*Padua* and the auxiliary ex-*Kommodore Johnsen*): ten full-rigged ships (Danes, Norwegians, Poles, Italians, Finns, Germans): eight or nine barques (American, Portuguese, German, Brazilian, Spanish, Norwegian, Russian): a dozen or more barquentines and topsail schooners (Belgian, Spanish, Danish, Jugoslav, Indonesian), to say nothing of ten or more large ketches and two-masted schooners, all engaged in training youth for the sea. The Germans, until the second war, maintained the largest fleet, of two ships and four barques. A number of the other training ships (among them the *Staatsraad Lehmkuhl* and the Polish *Dar Pomorza*) began their careers as German. The Indonesian barquentine *Dewarutji* was launched from the shipyard of Stülcken Sohn's in Hamburg at the end of 1952, and the Danish topsail-schooner *Lilla Dan* was commissioned only in 1950. The U. S. Coast Guard barque *Eagle* (the former German naval school-ship *Horst Wessel*), the Russian barque *Tovarisch* (the former German *Georg Foch*) and a Brazilian barque which was the former German *Albert Leo Schlageter,* have all been commissioned in recent years.

The British contribution to this considerable fleet is a very small one. There never has been a non-cargo-carrying school-ship for the British merchant service, if one excepts a small brigantine tender or two. The present British contribution consists of a ketch, an ex-German pilot schooner, and an ancient yacht named *Moyana* which is run by the Southampton School of Navigation. The ketch is the *Warspite,* belonging to the Marine Society and chartered for 1s a year to the Outward Bound Sea School at Aberdovey in Wales, and the schooner is the *Prince Louis* which takes boys to sea from Kurt Hahn's school at Gordonstoun and from the Outward Bound Sea School at Burghead, in Scotland.

No sea-going British school-ship of any sort crosses yards: none has done so since I had to sell the *Joseph Conrad* in America at the end of 1936, and she was in no sense an official vessel nor sailing with any sort of official blessing. She was my venture because I believed in the value of such experience for all boys, whether destined for the sea or not, and she was the only truly international ship of the lot. My officers were Scandinavians and Australians; my seamen Americans, Australians, Danes, Germans; my steward a Finn and my cook from Suffolk, and my cadets came from the ends of the earth. The ship had to be truly international in order to be manned by active, real sailing-ship sailors. All other school-ships are strictly national, since they are either financed by philanthropists for the good of their own merchant service, or run by the state for its own navy.

I have sailed also in two of the other sailing school-ships, the Danish *Georg Stage* and the Portuguese *Sagres*, the one a merchant service and the other a naval school-ship. Both do excellent work. The *Georg Stage* is a fine little steel full-rigged ship of about 250 tons nett, rigged in the classic manner with double topsails and single topgallants and royals on all three masts, and she is about as small as a ship can be and carry such a rig. (Her predecessor was rigged with single topsails.) Her 80 boys live in the tween-decks, slinging 40 hammocks in each of two large tween-deck compartments, and these hammocks are stowed by day in hammock nettings along both sides of the upper bulwarks, above the pinrails. Each boy has a locker for his clothes, another for his boots and shoes, a hammock, a seat at a mess-table with nine of his comrades, and a number by which he is known throughout the five-and-a-half month cruise. The lads are carefully selected each winter from among physically fit and able lads aged 14 to 15½, who wish to follow a seafaring career, though they do not bind themselves to serve merchant shipping. No boy selected as a *Georg Stage* cadet may have been to sea professionally before, for the success of the system depends upon all starting off together in the same degree of ignorance. Boys come from all walks of life and all parts of Denmark;

whether a boy is destined to become master of one of the Danish
East Asiatic Company's great liners or able seaman in an Aarhus
galeass, all begin in the same manner.

This, too, is the idea behind giving the lads numbers. Shore
clothing, money, possessions of all kinds have to be given up when
joining ship at the Navy yard in Copenhagen each March 31.
Each lad is issued with his uniform (he pays £15 or so towards
its cost, but there is a grant for any who might be unable to do
this), and goes aboard. He has a few days to settle down and to
learn the rigging, which rarely bothers a boy. He learns to go
aloft, to find his way about the rigging by day and night, to
haul on the right line or tackle as and when required. His instructors are the ship's officers and four under-officers, who
are carefully selected from young men who have previously bene-
fited by the *Georg Stage* training and have been three or four
years at sea, where they must have enjoyed exceptional records.
These under-officers are really the backbone of the ship, and they
are very carefully chosen. They are changed each season, for experience has shown that this works best. They are generally
excellent young fellows who are just ready to go to mates' school
after serving their necessary qualifying time at sea, and they know
full well the lifelong benefit of the *Georg Stage* experience and
the value of a good report from the master, after a season's in-
structional work. A young man with such a report finds it the
best possible asset in his future career, and these under-officers
are indeed exceptional fellows. (I speak from experience. I took
two of them in the old *Georg Stage*, the *Joseph Conrad*. They
were magnificent. One has since become master of the Greenland
trader *Kista Dan* in the Lauritzen Line; the other, after a distinguished war career, became an officer in the State's Greenland
service.)

Such young men take a real and practical interest in the lads
entrusted to them, having been such lads themselves recently
enough to remember well the difficulties and the problems. There
is a nice democracy about the *Georg Stage*, as there is in almost all
Scandinavian ships. There are no class distinctions. The master
takes his meals in a messroom along with the mates and the

under-officers, and a ubiquitous genius who looks after the accounts, the engine-room, the health, and the wireless telegraphy. The boys are known simply as 'youngsters' and the afterguard are the 'grown-ups', and that is as far as the distinction goes. All eat the same food, share the same life. Yet there is perfect discipline, and—most remarkable, yet again not at all uncommon in Scandinavia—a discipline without threats and almost completely without punishment. There is never any physical chastisement.

In so small a ship, things have to be kept in their proper place. *Everything* has to be shipshape and *Georg Stage* fashion, even the wildest little boy. If he is too wild, he is packed off home and that is the end of him as far as the sea in concerned. But if he keeps himself spotlessly clean, attends to his business and learns his seamanship in a respectful and proper manner, he will come to look back upon his cruise in the little full-rigger as the highlight of his youthful life, and he cannot help but benefit from it. In Copenhagen today there is a society of old Georg Stagers which includes men from all over the world and every conceivable walk of life, and they are one and all the greatest of comrades. More than that, they are a considerable asset—and have been of lifelong value—to the state, whether they have served long in its ships or not. Most of them do serve in Danish ships.

In Scandinavian ships there is only one standard of cleanliness, and that is perfection. Though each lad has a stainless steel plate, mug, and cutlery, he really does not need these for the bare boards of the deck are clean enough to eat from. Everything is clean, including each of the 80 boys. (It is not at all to be wondered at that Danish ships—and indeed Scandinavians generally—have a clean look about them which few others seem to keep for long. Look round in any port with an unbiased eye.)

When the new boys have had a chance to settle down, the *Georg Stage* sails off to spend the first month in Danish waters. The lads are allocated their places on deck and in the rigging (for that is the only way to run things in a ship with so many boys), but they are changed frequently, in order to prevent any possibility of learning merely to do the drill and not to understand its purpose. In the short space of one month, a remarkable transformation has taken place among the 80 boys. They come aboard a typical group of landsmen—enthusiastic, often, but with the enthusiasm unchannelled and undisciplined; often with little or no idea of real team spirit; unaccustomed to living together and serving together something greater than themselves; educated to a certain standard, but perhaps not taught really to think through things at all. The little ship and the background of sails and the sea bring about a transformation which is strengthened by the endless demands of the sailing life. The lads acquire a stern sense of duty, a remarkable sense of brotherhood (as shown so clearly afterwards by the Old Boys' Association), a fine feeling of adventure satisfied and of living men's lives. These things are absorbed painlessly and to each lad's infinite benefit.

This whole matter of the worth of training under sail is still controversial, though the requirement itself has long been abandoned both by Britain and America. But there is no question that the character-building qualities of the small sailing-ship are unrivalled and cannot well be duplicated in power-driven vessels. Hard-headed business men support the *Georg Stage*, the *Christian Radich*, the *Sørlandet*, and the rest. They see their returns. (Again look round with seeing eyes in any great port.) There is a remarkable amount in common between the primary training aboard the *Georg Stage* and the aims of such an enlightened body as the Outward Bound Trust, in Britain, which controls the Outward Bound Sea and Mountain Schools. The aim of the Outward Bounders is to undo the harm done by the 'taming' effect of so much of what passes for education in the great democracies in the mid-twentieth century, where the emphasis so often is on finding somehow the equipment to furnish youth with a 'safe' job, regardless of the pallid stamp of mediocrity and the tame uniformity which are imparted in the process. Those Danish boys are no mediocrities. The little ship builds up upon themselves, and brings them on. Sooner or later, a nation which has the good sense to retain and to develop the real quality of its youth will profit from its foresight and intelligence.

For years now, Denmark has been in the front line of the so-called 'cold' war. If the cold war ever heated up, it is logical to rate her chances as somewhat slim. Yet one hears of no rising suicide rate or alarming extension of chronic alcoholism in that country. A country is as good as its citizens are trained to be, and education does not consist only of competing for scholastic 'distinction'.

At the end of their cruise, forty of the boys join the state school-ship *Danmark,* another full-rigger. The *Danmark* is a ship of about 700 tons, an auxiliary of the same rig as the *Georg Stage,* but her function is to provide vocational training. She is the secondary school of the Danish merchant marine and, in that way, the Danish merchant service is unique. The *Danmark* sails in the early autumn soon after the *Georg Stage* has laid up—rigged down by her own boys who are always her real crew—and is away eight or nine months, sometimes longer. She generally beats down the Channel and makes an Atlantic round—Madeira, the Cape Verde Islands, the West Indies, some port or ports in the Gulf of Mexico, and so home again—but sometimes she goes further. She is well known in the United States where she spent the war years doing splendid work, for there are countless thousands of young American and British boys who would benefit by such sailing experience if they had the chance of it. Unlike the *Gearg Stage* (which is financed privately) the *Danmark* is a state concern.

These two small ships, the *Danmark* and the *Georg Stage,* are doing a splendid job. But each year it is becoming more and more expensive and, even in Denmark, it is not always easy, nowadays, to get the right type of under-officer and officer to sail in them. The blandishments of the ordinary vessels, in a time of full employment—unsound as any experienced seaman may know all that to be—are very great; it is easier for a youth to go straight to navigation school and then join one of the big steamship lines. There are plenty of jobs, for the time being. But it is to be hoped the *Georg Stage* and her consort will thrive for many years, and the other sailing school-ships with them.

The Portuguese naval school-ship *Sagres* is in a different category. She is a former Cape Horn cargo-carrier, built of steel in 1896 as the German ship *Rickmer Rickmers* for the Rickmers Line of Bremen, and she sailed as an ordinary cargo-carrier under the German flag until 1914, first under her original name and later for other owners as the barque *Max*. She had been rigged down from a full-rigged ship to a barque, after a partial dismasting, at Cape Town in 1904, and she had been employed tramping about the world. She had made a number of voyages between Europe and the Far East, usually taking out coals from Cardiff to Hongkong, and bringing back rice from Burma. She had also made a number of case oil voyages principally between Philadephia and Japan, and in 1910 she took patent fuel from Cardiff to Iquique and then crossed the Pacific to Australia for more coal, and finally loaded nitrates at Pisagua for discharge at Delfzyl. She was homeward bound with another nitrate cargo when the '14–'18 war broke out, and she went into Horta in the Azores to wait. There, in 1916, she was seized as a prize, and has flown the Portuguese flag ever since, at first as an ordinary merchantman under the name of *Flora* and, from 1924, as the official naval school-ship, under the name of *Sagres*. In 1931, she was given two Krupp diesels of 350 h.p. each, with variable-pitch propellers, which could give her a maximum speed under power of seven knots, in a dead calm. She was also given four small Hotchkiss guns.

The *Sagres* has a register tonnage of 2008 tons and is a massively-rigged Cape Horner of more or less the standard German type. Her netted bowsprit, her whaleback forecastle-head and poop, her powerful steel masts and yards, are the same now as they were almost sixty years ago, but internally she has undergone a great transformation. She is practically all accommodation or stores space. She can accommodate 400 men without being overcrowded, the sailors slinging hammocks in the spacious tween-decks, which are well lighted and well ventilated. The officers' quarters are in the poop and the after tween-decks, and the captain's quarters are in a large deckhouse built under the boatskids on the main-deck. A schoolroom, an electric bakery, and a large galley (which is equipped to prepare 500 meals at a time) occupy the former forecastle, where the 18 sailors used to live when the ship was German. The petty officers live in cabins and dormitories and have their own mess, but leading seamen and all others sling their hammocks. The lower hold is given up to store-rooms. Below these is the sailing ballast.

The ship is fitted with electric light throughout, with radio, echo-sounding, patent logs of several types (including the Cherni-keef), a gyro-compass, a very large refrigerated chamber, flood-lights for night work on deck, a 14-bed hospital and a surgery equipped with X-rays, several large motorboats, eight large rafts, and two 40-foot schooners which are used for sailing in places such as the Cape Verdes and the Azores. She carries her own band. She has a barbers' shop, a tailor, a cobbler, and a shop where the mariners can spend their spare escudos to advantage. In the centre of the poop, lit by two large skylights, is the officers' mess with a sixteen-place table, and a bronze of the Prince of Sagres at the bole of the mizzenmast which passes through the for'ard end. (Another bronze of the great Infante is the barque's figurehead.) Tasteful lamps shaped like ancient iron lanthorns disguise the electric lights, and the blowers for the forced air ventilation are hidden in a decorative frieze. Off this saloon, across an encircling alleyway, are the cabins and some offices, with ports on the ship's side. Here lived the mate and second mate, steward and cook, in the Cape Horning days, and the whole afterpart of the poop was then the master's. The *Sagres* now carries an afterguard of eleven officers—the captain, first lieutenant, three senior and three junior lieutenants, a paymaster, engineer, and a doctor. There are also four mid-shipmen, three of them watchkeeping engineer-officers under training, and the fourth an assistant to the paymaster.

When I joined the ship at anchor off Cascais by the mouth of the Tagus, on an early June day of 1952, there were 372 ratings aboard, headed by a sailing master who was the first of that ancient calling I had come across. (Masters used to be carried aboard fighting ships to sail the ship and look after all the appurtenances of sailing, as separate and distinct from the gunnery and fighting. James Cook was one, Bligh another.) Under the master (who had general charge of the deck and masts and sails, directed by the first lieutenant) were a boatswain and four boatswains' mates, four captains of the tops (one being for the bowsprit), and large numbers of petty officers, leading seamen, seamen, and boys. The crew included a bandmaster, a shopkeeper, a shipwright, six stewards, five cooks, gunners, signalmen, electricians, sickbay attendants, wireless operators, instructors, and buglers. The ship's complement was 186 officers and men. All others were under training.

In addition to the boys and ordinary seamen, the entire class of young officers from the Naval Academy was sailing in the ship, for the usual procedure is to give these their indocrination under sail. There were twenty-six of these young men. The master, one José Tiago from Lagos, had been 32 years in the navy and eight years in the *Sagres*. Like most of the senior petty officers and captains of the tops, he had been in the ship when she had no engines.

The *Sagres* occupies a unique position in that she is the seamanship school of the Portuguese Navy, as well as the sailing school-ship. One result of this is that at any time, all sorts of ratings are to be found aboard qualifying in seamanship for whatever advancement they are competent to seek. Alongside the youngsters undergoing their *ab initio* training may be grey-headed old petty officers grown grizzled by long service; a group of cadets leaves the classroom to make way for a section of signalmen; a group of gunners' mates keep their hand in with the small arms while a crowd of boys swarms along the yards high above them. The *Sagres* is a busy ship—day in, day out, year in and year out, whether she is sailing or not. She spends much of her time in recent years at anchor in the Tagus close by Lisbon, sailing usually for three or four months on a round of the Atlantic islands—Madeira, the Cape Verdes, the Azores—though she sometimes goes as far as Rio de Janeiro and Buenos Aires, or across to New York and New Bedford. The purpose of the *Sagres* is two-fold, and her work as the navy's seamanship school goes on without interruption whether she is on her annual voyage, or at anchor in the Tagus. The indoctrination of the recruits, both officers and ratings, does not disturb this. Indeed it is the more efficient, with an excellent cross-section of the navy all round them.

The system works very well. The maritime traditions of Portugal are great and they are still vital: indoctrination does not take long, though the boys may come from the mountains by the borders of Spain or the sunny uplands of the lovely Algarve, and some of the cadets might have been better horsemen than yachtsmen a few months earlier. The Portuguese has a natural feeling for the sea. The great crowd aboard very quickly shakes down and, though at first it seems somewhat strange to hear orders given over an efficient loudspeaker system aboard an old Cape Horner and the array of electrical equipment is diverse and astonishing, after a day or two these things fit in. The electrical equipment is necessary, for the modern seamen must understand its use, too: and giving orders to two or three hundred simultaneously is a little different from working a merchantman's watch of able seamen. The loudspeaker system is useful.

I sailed from Cascais Bay on June 3, 1952. The *Sagres,* under the command of Captain Luciano Sena Dentinho, had come down the Tagus the previous day. Captain Dentinho, who had been in the small sailing-ships of the Algarve in his youth and in the navy since the first World War, had taken over command only recently from a captain who had been in the ship several years, and there had been many changes of key personnel. Almost all the officers and almost the whole crew were not only new to the *Sagres* but quite inexperienced in any big square-rigged ship, though a sufficient nucleus had been retained and the ship soon settled down. In the Portuguese navy, any officer or rating may be drafted to the *Sagres.* She got under way under sail, setting off before the fine north wind in good weather towards Madeira. The sail to Madeira was purely a shake-down cruise: for a day or two, cadets and deckboys were left to find their sea legs, to learn their way round the rigging by night and day while accustoming themselves to the motion of the sea, and to get over their sea-sickness. The boys helped the experienced seamen to work the sails and the gear, while the cadets were kept together in a group under the tutelage of an officer from the Naval Academy, who explained everything to them as it was done. In this way, they began with a good idea of the theoretical side as well as the practical. They had to go aloft, too.

By the time the *Sagres* reached Madeira everyone had settled down. At anchor off that lovely island, instruction really began. The whole ship was a workhouse of instruction, from seven in the morning until six in the evening. Her three class-rooms—one on deck and two below—were filled for session after session with boys learning Portuguese, learning geography, learning arithmetic; with petty officers struggling with the higher intricacies of their profession; with cadets mastering English, electronics, trigonometry. Of the 383 people aboard, not more than 60 or 70 were in the class-room at any one time. There was plently of diversity. Others were in groups on deck or in the rigging, under boatswains and boatswain's mates, learning practical seamanship. Others were off in the ship's two schooners, which were put overside and, quickly rigged with their two masts and jibbooms, showed that they had a lively turn of speed. Still other lads pulled boats, learned to swim by the gangway, practised signalling, heaving the lead and giving the proper calls, or did splices in rope and wire, and intricate fancy-work. Some were away ashore—a certain number each day—taken on excursions into the lovely mountains of Madeira, for the cruise was a practical lesson in geography, too.

A week at Madeira sped by on sunlit wings, and the ship sailed on before the northerly wind down to the north-east trades, and so among the Canary Islands and to the Cape Verdes, where she anchored in the big windy bay of St. Vincent. At sea, the lads learned to steer and there were plenty of exercises aloft. A navy's manning problems are by no means the same as those of a merchant service. A naval ship must always be crowded with men enough to fight her as well as to sail her, to look after signals, equipment, guns, and so forth. A merchantman goes about her voyage in the fastest and most economical way she can and her crew is the minimum necessary, each concerned with the skilful performance of duties he well knows, or should know. But the naval seaman may have many diverse duties, and he must know how to conduct himself, individually and as one of a disciplined crowd, upon them all, both ashore and afloat. Above all he must learn to become a unit of an orderly team of men trained in the skilled performance of whatever functions are necessary to the fighting, the working, and the daily maintenance of the ship and are allocated to his charge. He has to learn to be a dependable unit in a precise routine which can be relied upon to remain effective and disciplined, no matter what strains may be placed upon it. He must react instantly and correctly to orders, and the *Sagres* vocational training was in large measure directed —and properly directed—towards this end. The sail-handling was generally done by drill, controlled by an officer on the poop with a microphone and the loudspeaker system.

This was the first time I had seen sails handled by naval drill, but I soon realised that there is no better medium than a mast of square sails for the purpose of organising clear-headed and intelligent drill. Things went with a swing and a great pride in performance. The drill, ragged at first—naturally, for there were many raw recruits—soon went like clockwork, and the lads were obviously not only taking a great pride in their development but enjoying it, enjoying it all the time and wholeheartedly. The food was good, the living conditions excellent, and day after day the big barque's lovely sails blew her steadily along—now at ten knots, now at six. The diesels were silent, by order. The life was quiet and the nights were silent. The ship sailed upright and graceful, moving across the quiet dark sea in a pool of her own graceful shadows, with a touch of phosphorescence where she trod the water down at her bows, and a slip of whitened wake upon the sea astern. The lads reacted to all this as sea-minded boys have always done, and the value of the sailing-ship's indoctrination was immense and obvious.

"I believe in sail-training," said Captain Dentinho. "It develops initiative and self-confidence. It is the way to begin at sea."

At St. Vincent, in the wide bay and in the channel between

the islands where the trade wind blows with almost gale-like freshness, the schooners were sailing again and the boats were away being pulled. Each officer and each petty officer was an instructor—usually in several subjects—in addition to taking a share of the ordinary shipboard routine. It was a full life for everyone. Physical training, instruction, running over the mast-heads, deck and rigging work of all kinds, kept all hands occupied from dawn to dusk. Classes filled the ship from the knight-heads right for'ard to the end of the spanker-boom beyond the stern. Two weeks of this: and then away again, with a beam wind to sail westwards to the Azores, the north-east trade serene and wonderful—a great and orderly source of power left now to go to waste—the wide Atlantic a glorious blue, white-flecked where the seas broke in a gentle, lovely line, and the flying-fish skimmed away before the bows. The wind sang in the high rigging with its old, old song, and the white sails (carrying on their foresides the red Cross of Christ as the Portuguese discoverers did) pulled the ship along beautifully. Youth reacts well to such conditions, which are not to be artificially contrived. I had not thought to know trade wind days like that again.

So to the Azores, and more boat-handling and schooner-sailing, which gave the cadets and boys more opportunity to develop and to show individual initiative. The two things worked very well together—sailing the ship as a team, and sailing the schooners and the boats with individual turns at command. From the Azores, the *Sagres* sailed back to Ferrol and, with a call at Leixoes (near Oporto), was back in Lisbon again a little over three months from the time she had sailed. What a difference those three months had made to the cadets and boys! They were now well on the way to becoming sailors, good and worth-while members of their chosen profession. They had a different look to them: there was a different swing to the whole ship. I had wondered, at first, how so vast a crowd *could* benefit from a run in an old Cape Horn ship. At any hour of the day or night there were always at least three score hands on deck, and some-times 300. Yet I was convinced. The ship took care of them all. There is no doubt whatever, to my mind, that such an experience is invaluable to any youth destined for the sea, whatever type of ship he seeks to serve, merchant service or naval.

The *Sagres* is an expensive ship for a small navy to maintain, but the Portuguese are very wise.

In Britain there has long been emphasis on pre-sea training, and lads who wished to go to sea are usually required to go first to one of the seamen's schools. There are some stationary ships which admit young children and bring them up with a healthy bias towards the sea (many of these enlist as boy-entries in the navy). The Marine School at South Shields was established in 1837 and is the oldest of the other type of school, the short-term establishment which gives lads a few months' preparation in order to make them useful when they first join a merchant ship. There are many such establshments in Great Britain, preparing boys for the deck, engine-room, and catering branches. There are also the two stationary school-ships, the *Conway* * and *Worcester*, which take lads at 12 to 15 and prepare them for a cadet-ship with the purpose of becoming executive officers, and there are two excellent establishments ashore which do the same thing, at Pangbourne and near Southampton. All these are vocational, though the cadets' schools provide something like the background of the more usual public school, as well. The purpose is to prepare lads for the profession of seamanship as it is practised today aboard powered vessels. Of all these schools, only that at Southampton makes use of a sailing-ship or, indeed, of any ship. The Southampton establishment uses the yacht *Moyana*, but she does not often go beyond the immediate area of the Solent. They would be glad to use a larger ship, if they had one.

In America, the great officers' training establishment at King's Point, Long Island, is world-famous, as it deserves to be. I have nothing but praise for the manner in which it is conducted and the good quality of its products. It is concerned solely with providing the American merchant marine with qualified and competent officers who, at the same time, form an excellent cadre

* The old *Conway*, a former wooden line-of-battle ship, has since stranded and become a constructive total loss. She will be replaced.

Captain J. B. Junker, 20 years Master of the *Georg Stage*. He evolved the very satisfactory training system used aboard.

The *Georg Stage* under sail

The Danish ships train
young boys for the
merchant service. →

The *Georg Stage* is one of
Danish school-ships. Here
is at anchor, exercising bo
←

→
Cadets lay aloft
to stow sail.

←
On the way
to oblivion

↓ The U. S. Coast Guard's school-ship *Eagle*. She was formerly German.
A sister-ship is a Brazilian training-ship, another is Russian.

of the naval reserve. It is a good many years now since the State
Maritime Academies of Massachusetts and New York ran sailing
school-ships. The old *St. Mary's* of New York is still well remembered, and so is the *Nantucket* of Massachusetts. These ships did
good work, and the indoctrination they provided has left its mark.
There are many senior officers in the U.S. service today who
remember gratefully their first voyage in these sailing-ships,
and they would not exchange the experience for a doctorate in
applied electronics, naval architecture, or any other of the divers
and complicated branches of the maritime calling today.

There is a considerable wastage from the sea of the King's
Point boys, and such wastage is expensive. Three or six months
in some American *Georg Stage*, or even a Grand Banks schooner,
might effectively restrict the advantages of the splendid training
offered to those who would most profit by it and permanently
apply its lessons in the service of their country's ships. The King's
Point Academy did have such a ship—a three-masted schooner—
but its use had to be given up on the score of economy.

The Outward Bound ketch *Warspite* and the schooner *Prince
Louis* do excellent work, short-term as it is. Boys rarely serve
in either vessel for more than a few days at a time, for the Outward Bound Sea Schools both in Wales and Scotland offer short
courses only. They are for character development, not vocational
training. They train boys through ships and the sea, not necessarily as seafarers. They certainly succeed. I sailed the *Warspite*
for some time, summer and winter, when the Marine Society
first sent her round to Aberdovey, and the good which that little
ship was able to do for so many boys was almost miraculous. My
experience in the *Warspite* and in the *Sagres* astounded me, for
I learned in both that the sailing-ship, large or small, has a very
great value in the development of sea sense (which is just another
name for common-sense) and character. Until then I had thought
that to be of real value such experience should be continuous

ABOVE LEFT   The *Sagres* is probably the last ship to carry a sailing master.

ABOVE RIGHT   Navigation lesson aboard the *Sagres*

BELOW   The big barque *Sagres*. She began life as the cargo-carrying
Rickmer Rickmers. In 1953 she still sails, as a Portuguese
naval school-ship.

←

and not shared with crowds: I was wrong. But the Outward
Bound has great need of a little barque, or perhaps a brigantine,
an ocean-going vessel, which would both provide vocational training—as well as further character building—for a selected group
of youths and, at the same time, actively preserve the ancient art
of square-rigged ocean voyaging.

It is, I think, foolish of great maritime nations to throw this
science right away. The great artifice of modern power-driven
fleets hangs often on a perilously fragile thread. The greater the
ship the greater the rust-heap, if she can no longer be run properly,
through any reason. Before all else, ships depend on men. More
than any other property, ships can be ruined quickly and irrevocably by mistakes of men, and maritime nations will go to their
ruin with them. One wonders sometimes just how healthy the
cumbrous, tax-ridden, over-regulated and over-capitalised body
of our shipping is, on both sides of the North Atlantic. Ships now
have become so costly that the wealth they represent staggers
the imagination. The men in them have better conditions and
better pay than they ever had, and no one quarrels with this.
(There have been times in the past—the recent past—when
both conditions and the pay were appalling.) Yet it is arguable
that too many of those men no longer serve their ships with the
same spirit which their forefathers did.

The wastage from the sea is great and shows no diminution.
The official statistics issued monthly by the British Ministry of
Transport are enlightening but not encouraging. The figures
issued in March, 1953, show that of a total strength of 144,306
men serving in just over 3000 ships, no fewer than 16,216 engineer officers, of a total of 23,758, were uncertificated. The in-
ference is plain. The uncertificated officer can scarcely claim that
he is properly qualified, though he has his useful place in the
smaller ships and in junior capacities. But he is not only found
in the smaller ships today, nor in junior capacities. One notes
that a great liner, belonging to a famous company, outward
bound from Tilbury for Australia with a full passenger list which
included a governor-general designate of the Commonwealth,
scarcely was outside the Thames estuary before some engine

breakdown forced her to return, ignominiously to land her people, and go into dry-dock for repairs which surely should never have been necessary. Within a week, another liner of the same company, coming out of dry-dock, promptly began to list heavily at her berth, through some oversight. Yet another, belonging to an associated company, reported a serious engine failure in the Australian Bight. Too many great vessels are breaking down, unnecessarily.

There will always be accidents, of course. But expensive great ships, whose excuse for existence is their continued efficient and economic service, ought not to break down in this almost wanton manner. Great ships are national assets, though the Lord forbid that they should ever be nationalised. It would be ironic if the effective use of the complicated and tremendously expensive fleet of modern ships was made uneconomic or impossible because of lack of men properly to serve them with the skill, the tireless devotion, and the spirit of service which they demand and must be given. Perhaps an Outward Bound School for young engineers would do some good.

A nation is most vulnerable in its ships. Today I note that whole crews of mariners must be flown about the earth in costly, noisy aircraft, to relieve their brethren who have perhaps served a twelve-month away from home. An enormous London building full of bureaucrats sits upon the shipping industry, with its branches in every port, and a case can be made out that every single person in that great place is necessary to administer and generally to look after some aspect of the thousands of regulations, documents, requirements and so forth without which ships cannot move today. It is a logical consequence of over-government and it applies not only in Great Britain. There is a much larger building, for example, in Washington. Nation-wide organisations of shipowners, of officers, engineers, wireless operators, seamen, firemen, and stewards look after their sectional and joint interests and do it very well: but who looks after the long-term public good in this vital matter? Of what use will the bureaucrats be if any thread holding up this vast industry should snap, as snap it well may, at any time? We live in a curious haze if we believe that the civilisation we have contrived, unlike all others, will endure without our constant full efforts to make it do so and to improve it. Too many seafarers today are only half at sea. Half their minds are left ashore, and they have always been so since first they stepped aboard a powered vessel. They have never been jolted out of their land-bound ways of thought. Their vocational training may have been excellent: but that is not enough.

The value of the little sailer in character-building can be tremendous. More than that, an engineless small barque of a few hundred tons—even a little brigantine of 150—could at least retain for us the old sailing skill, the ability to make free use of the ocean winds, which will always be with us and now are wasted. It seems to me just plain sense to build such a vessel—I am not interested in great four-masters: in any event it is too late now for these—and to sail her on the ocean routes while we still have some men who can handle her, and pass the torch along. Even a feeble glimmer is better, surely, than no light at all: if it were ever necessary it could be fanned to strong life again.

It could be necessary, almost any day.

Appendix

APPENDIX A

RECORD SAILING-SHIP VOYAGES

THE following particulars of record sailing-ship voyages were compiled for Lloyd's by the late Mr. Basil Lubbock, and are printed here by the kind permission of the Editor of Lloyd's Calendar. All vessels are British except those marked A, which are American, or A b, British-owned and American built, and G, which are German. All the vessels are full-rigged ships, except where otherwise stated:

Date	Vessel	Tons	Record DAYS	Record HRS.	Remarks
UNITED KINGDOM TO AUSTRALIA					
1868–9	Thermopylae, comp.	948	60	0	London to Melbourne (pilot to pilot)
1870–1	Thermopylae, comp.	948	60	0	London to Melbourne (pilot to pilot)
1854	James Baines (A b), wood	2,275	63	0	Liverpool to Melbourne
1874–5	Ben Voirlich, iron	1,474	63	0	London to Melbourne (pilot to pilot)
1874–5	Thermopylae, comp.	948	64	0	London to Melbourne (pilot to pilot)
1868	Theophane, iron	1,525	65	0	Liverpool to Melbourne (pilot to pilot)
1875–6	Cutty Sark, comp.	921	64	0	Lizard to Cape Otway
1874–5	Cutty Sark, comp.	921	66	0	Start to South Cape, Tasmania
1869	Patriarch, iron	1,339	68	0	London to Sydney (pilot to pilot)
1880–1	Torrens, comp.	1,276	65	0	Plymouth to Adelaide
1883	Maulesden, iron	1,500	69	0	Greenock to Maryboro'
1891	Oweenee, steel 4-mast bq.	2,432	66	0	Prawle Pt. to Port Pirie

381

Date	Vessel	Tons	Record DAYS	HRS.	Remarks

EUROPE TO AUSTRALIA

Date	Vessel	Tons	DAYS	HRS.	Remarks
1873	Thomas Stephens, iron	1,507	66	0	Ushant to Melbourne
1896	Wendur, iron, 4-mast ship	1,982	81	0	Fredrikstad to Melbourne
1933–4	Padua (G), steel 4-mast bq.	3,064	66	0	Hamburg to Wallaroo

AUSTRALIA TO UNITED KINGDOM

Date	Vessel	Tons	DAYS	HRS.	Remarks
1853	Lightning (A b), wood	2,090	63	0	Melbourne to Liverpool
1856	Heather Bell, wood	479	64	0	Melbourne to Liverpool
1869	Patriarch, iron	1,339	68	0	Sydney to Ushant
1885	Cutty Sark, comp.	921	67	0	Sydney to Ushant
1887	Cutty Sark, comp.	921	70	0	Sydney to Channel
1887	Cutty Sark, comp.	921	69	0	Newcastle, N.S.W., to Channel
1894	Swanhilda, steel 4-mast bq.	1,999	66	0	Wallaroo, S.A., to Queenstown

UNITED KINGDOM TO INDIA

Date	Vessel	Tons	DAYS	HRS.	Remarks
1860	Alnwick Castle, wood	1,087	67	0	Channel to Sandheads
1863	The Tweed, wood	1,745	77	0	London to Bombay
1875	Accrington, iron	1,831	74	0	Liverpool to Calcutta
1876	Ailsa, comp.	1,061	76	0	Liverpool to Calcutta
1877	Coriolanus	1,046	70	0	Channel to Calcutta
1880	Star of Italy, iron	1,571	77	0	London to Calcutta
1883	Glengarry, iron	1,769	76	0	Liverpool to Calcutta
1884	Cedric the Saxon, iron	1,619	71	0	Lizard to Calcutta
1894	Armida, steel	1,642	75	0	Liverpool to Calcutta

Date	Vessel	Tons	Record DAYS	HRS.	Remarks
UNITED KINGDOM TO CHINA					
1866–7	Ariel, comp.	853	80	0	London to Hongkong
1898	Muskoka, steel 4-mast bq.	2,357	86	0	Cardiff to Hongkong
1898	Metropolis, iron 4-mast bq.	1,811	91	0	Cardiff to Hongkong
CHINA TO UNITED KINGDOM					
1869	Sir Lancelot, comp.	886	89	0	From Foochow *
1852	Witch of the Wave (A), wood	1,200	90	0	From Whampoa †
1855	Nightingale (A), wood	1,066	91	0	From Shanghai †
1869	Thermopylae, comp.	948	91	0	From Foochow *
1871	Titania, comp.	879	93	0	From Foochow *
1873	Hallowe'en, iron	920	89	0	From Shanghai †
1874	Hallowe'en, iron	920	90	0	From Shanghai †
1875	Hallowe'en, iron	920	92	0	From Shanghai †
CHINA TO UNITED STATES					
1847–8	Sea Witch (A), wood	890	78	0.	From Canton
1845	Natchez (A), wood	—	78	6	Macao to Boston
1848–9	Sea Witch (A), wood	890	79	0	From Canton
1847	Sea Witch (A), wood	890	81	0	From Canton
1852	N. B. Palmer (A), wood	1,490	84	0	From Canton
1895	Alcides, steel 4-mast bq.	2,704	83	0	From Hongkong

* Monsoon unfavourable
† Monsoon favourable

Date	Vessel	Tons	Record DAYS	HRS.	Remarks
EUROPE TO WEST COAST SOUTH AMERICA					
1903	Preussen (G), steel 5-mast ship	5,081	57	0	Lizard to Iquique
1904	Eudora, iron 4-mast bq.	1,991	57	16	Eddystone to Coquimbo
1892	Placilla (G), steel 4-mast bq.	2,845	58	0	Lizard to Valparaiso
1900	Potosi (G), steel 5-mast bq.	4,027	59	0	Dover to Valparaiso
1905	Potosi (G), steel 5-mast bq.	4,027	59	0	Isle of Wight to Valparaiso
WEST COAST SOUTH AMERICA TO EUROPE					
1903	Potosi (G), steel 5-mast bq.	4,027	57	0	Iquique to Prawle Point
1900	Pindos (G), steel 4-mast bq.	2,484	61	0	Tocopilla to Dunkirk
1893	Placilla (G), steel 4-mast bq.	2,845	70	0	Iquique to Lizard
1903	County of Anglesea, iron bq.	1,103	67	0	Pisco to Falmouth
1895	Pamelia (G), steel barque	1,438	68	0	Iquique to Prawle Point
1904	Preussen (G), steel 5-mast ship	5,081	61	0	Iquique to Lizard
UNITED STATES TO UNITED KINGDOM					
1853	Typhoon (A), wood	1,610	13	6	Portsmouth, N.H., to Liverpool
1854	James Baines (A b), wood	2,275	12	6	Boston to Liverpool
1854	Red Jacket (A b), wood	2,035	13	1	Sandy Hook to Liverpool
1854	Dreadnought (A), wood	1,413	13	11	New York to Liverpool

Date	Vessel	Tons	Record DAYS	HRS.	Remarks

UNITED STATES TO UNITED KINGDOM (continued)

1859	Dreadnought (A), wood	1,413	13	8	New York to Liverpool
1852	Fidelia (A), wood	1,000	13	7	New York to Liverpool
1864	Adelaide (A), wood	—	12	8	New York to Liverpool

UNITED KINGDOM TO UNITED STATES

1824	Emerald (A), wood	359	17	0	Liverpool to Boston
185[?]	Fidelia (A), wood	1,000	17	6	Liverpool to New York
1855	Mary Whitridge (A), wood	978	14	9	Liverpool to Baltimore
1860	Andrew Jackson (A), wood	1,676	15	0	Liverpool to New York
1892	Howard D. Troop, steel	2,165	14	0	Greenock to New York
1892	Procyon, steel barque	2,122	15	0	Leith to New York

SAN FRANCISCO & PUGET SOUND TO UNITED KINGDOM
OR UNITED STATES (EAST COAST)

1891–2	Falls of Garry, iron 4-mast bq.	2,088	88	0	'Frisco to Queenstown
1891–2	Alcinous, iron ship	1,662	93	0	'Frisco to Queenstown
1892	Machrihanish, iron ship	1,758	91	0	Portland, Ore., to Queenstown
1893	Andelana, steel 4-mast ship	2,579	89	0	'Frisco to Brow Head
1895	Principality, iron 4-mast bq.	1,757	95	0	Astoria to Queenstown
1895	Susquehanna (A), wood 4-mast ship	2,745	94	0	'Frisco to Queenstown
1892	Benjamin F. Packard (A), wood	2,156	89	0	'Frisco to New York

Date	Vessel	Tons	Record DAYS	HRS.	Remarks
UNITED STATES (EAST COAST) TO SAN FRANCISCO					
1851	Flying Cloud (A), wood	1,793	89	0	From New York
1854	Flying Cloud (A), wood	1,793	89	0	From New York
1860	Andrew Jackson (A), wood	1,676	89	0	From New York
1852	Swordfish (A), wood	1,036	90	0	From New York
1853	Flying Fish (A), wood	1,505	92	0	From New York
1853	John Gilpin (A), wood	1,089	93	0	From New York
1856	Sweepstakes (A), wood	1,735	94	0	From New York
1851	Surprise (A), wood	1,361	96	0	From New York
1854	Romance of the Seas (A), wood	1,782	96	0	From New York
UNITED KINGDOM TO SAN FRANCISCO					
1887–8	Merioneth, iron	1,366	96	0	Cardiff to 'Frisco
1889	Senator, iron ship	1,762	90	0	Cardiff to 'Frisco
1871	Archibald Fuller, iron ship	700	100	0	Liverpool to 'Frisco
1894	Eudora, steel 4-mast bq.	1,992	99	0	Lundy Island to 'Frisco
MISCELLANEOUS					
1852	Swordfish (A), wood	1,036	32	9	San Francisco to Shanghai
1896	Wendur, iron 4-mast ship	2,046	29	13	Newcastle, N.S.W., to Valparaiso
1896	Loch Torridon, iron 4-mast bq.	2,081	30	2	Newcastle, N.S.W., to Valparaiso

Date	Vessel	Tons	*Record* DAYS	HRS.	Remarks

MISCELLANEOUS

Date	Vessel	Tons	DAYS	HRS.	Remarks
1870	Thermopylae, comp.	948	28	o	Newcastle, N.S.W., to Shanghai
1853	Hornet (A), wood	1,426	34	o	San Francisco to Callao
1897	Bernares, iron 4-mast bq.	1,721	40	o	Table Bay to New York
1897	Foyledale, steel	1,765	25	o	Hiogo to Tacoma
1888	British Ambassador, iron	1,794	39	o	San Francisco to Newcastle, N.S.W.
1895	Siren, iron	1,478	28	o	Table Bay to Sydney
1894	Drumrock, steel 4-mast bq.	3,182	5	6¼	'Frisco to Tacoma
1891	Dundee, iron 4-mast bq.	2,063	31	o	Cardiff to Rio
1895	Bangalore, iron ship	1,746	88	o	Calcutta to New York
1909	Howard D. Troop, steel 4-mast bq.	2,165	21	o	Yokohama to Astoria
1911	Lancing, iron 4-mast ship	2,764	44	o	Montevideo to New Caledonia
1899	Glenesslin, iron	1,743	74	o	Portland, Ore., to Algoa Bay
1894	Lord Spencer, iron	2,675	29	o	Capetown to Newcastle, N.S.W.
1927	Oaklands, iron bq.	990	5	21½	Gravesend to Viborg

FASTEST DAY'S RUN

*Nautical
Miles*

December 11–12, 1854   The CHAMPION OF THE SEAS (Black Ball Liner)   465

March 1, 1854   The LIGHTNING (Black Ball Liner)   436
when crossing from Boston to Liverpool on her maiden voyage. Her position on February 28 was Lat. 52.38N., Long. 22.45W. Log entry reads as follows: "Wind, south. Strong gales; bore away for the North Channel; carried away the foretopsail and lost jib; hove the log several times and found the ship going through the water at the rate of 18 or 18½ knots; lee rail under water and rigging slack."

March 19, 1857   The LIGHTNING (Black Ball Liner)   430
when running Easting down bound out to Melbourne. Her position on March 18 was, Lat. 42.34S., Long. 17.04W., March 19, Lat. 43.0S. Long. 7.17W. Extract from "Lightning Gazette" (paper published on board) reads for March 19: "This is perhaps the most uncomfortable day we have had yet. It is very wet and there is a heavy sea on. In the middle of the day the wind lulled a bit, then turned over to the starboard quarter, and, as if relieved by the change, set to work snoring again as hard as ever."

February 27, 1855   The DONALD MACKAY (Black Ball Liner)   421
when crossing from Boston to Liverpool on her maiden voyage. Extract from log reads:—"First part, strong gales from north-west; middle, blowing a hurricane from west-north-west, ship scudding under topsails and foresail at rate of 18 knots; latter part, still blowing from west-north-west with heavy hail squalls; very high sea running."

February, 1855   The JAMES BAINES (Black Ball Liner)   420
when running Easting down bound out to Melbourne.

December, 1856   The GREAT REPUBLIC   413
in North Atlantic when bound from New York to San Francisco. She averaged 19 knots for 19 hours out of the 24.

March 18, 1853   The SOVEREIGN OF THE SEAS   411
in passage Honolulu to New York in Lat. 52.12S., Long. 91.28W.; strong N.W. wind and rough sea.

APPENDIX B

SOME LAEISZ SAILING RECORDS

THE following records are from the annals of the Deutsche Seewarte, from the logs of the ships in the Laeisz office at Hamburg and, in some instances, from the records kept by the well-known Hamburg sailing-ship historian, Captain Erwin F. A. Kornitzer. It is significant that no Laeisz ship ever claimed to have sailed more than 380 nautical miles in a day. The big five-masters could touch 17 knots, under very good conditions, but the four-masters did fifteen at their best and no more. Kornitzer once asked Hilgendorf what he thought of 420-mile day's runs, but Hilgendorf smiled.

Close examination of the logs and voyage records in the Deutsche See-warte, covering more than sixty vessels over a period of thirty years, shows that the average speed recorded by wooden full-rigged ships 205 feet long running in a favouring gale of wind was 9.5 knots, iron ships 220 feet long, 10.1 knots, four-masted barques of 2,600 tons and 310 feet long, 11 knots, the *Potosi*, 13.1 knots and the *Preussen*, 13.7. Under the same conditions but close-hauled, the smallest ships logged 5 knots in a wind of Force 8, the iron full-riggers 6.1 knots, the four-masted barques 6.3 knots, the *Potosi* 7.5 and the *Preussen* 8.2 knots. All the ships were a shade faster sailing close-hauled in winds of Beaufort Force 7.

These figures show that the nitrate ships' good times were made by good voyages, and not by good bursts of speed.

Here are some Laeisz records as collected by Captain Kornitzer:

Year	Ship	Rig	Voyage	Days
1881	Papa	wooden barque	Channel–Valparaiso	74
1884	Parnass	" "	" "	70
1884	Parnass	" "	" "	74
1886	Plus	iron barque	" "	61
1888	Pirat	" "	" "	71
1889	Potrimpos	steel barque	" "	61
1889	Pergamon	" "	" "	65
1889	Palmyra	" ship	" "	63
1889	Parchim	" "	" "	65
1890	Prompt	" barque	" "	64
1892	Paposo	iron barque	" "	67
1892	Placilla	st. 4m barque	" "	58
1892	Potosi	st. 5m barque	" "	58
1895	Pamelia	steel barque	" "	62
1895	Potosi	st. 5m barque	" "	64
1901	Potosi	st. 5m barque	" "	64
1903	Preussen	st. 5m ship	" Iquique	57

(To equator 13 d. 8 hrs.—the record)

Other good passages listed by Captain Kornitzer include the *Pisagua's* 32 days from Spencer Gulf to Taltal. His record of 600 Chilean voyages show that the average number of days taken from the nitrate port to the Lizard was from 96 to 103 days, while at the same time the average of 120 Laeisz voyages in the same trade was only 78 days.

These excellent voyages went on well into the twentieth century, as is shown by the following list of voyages which I have from Mr. Erich Laeisz. The number of days taken to beat round Cape Horn, from 50 South in the Atlantic to 50 South in the Pacific, is of particular interest:

FROM THE LIZARD TO VALPARAISO

Name	Master	Passed Lizard	Line crossed	50° S Atlantic	50° S Pacific	Arrived Valparaiso	Total days
Persimmon	Horn	7. 8.04	8. 9.	1.10.	10.10.	16.10.	74
Palmyra	Paulsen	31. 8.04	3.10.	16.10.	7.11.	13.11.	74
Pangani	Schmidt	11. 9.04	28.10.	28.10.	5.11.	13.11.	63
Pera	Teschner	2.10.04	30.10.	23.11.	5.12.	11.12.	70
Plus	Petersen	27.11.04	21.12.	15. 1.05	28. 1.	7. 2.	72
Potosi	Nissen	20. 1.05	7. 2.	4. 3.	13. 3.	20. 3.	59
Pampa	Schröder	23. 2.05	11. 3.	5. 4.	17. 4.	22. 4.	58
Pangani	Schmidt	17. 4.05	7. 5.	31. 5.	13. 6.	20. 6.	64
Pera	Frömcke	16. 7.05	8. 8.	1. 9.	12. 9.	20. 9.	66
Posen	Schütt	1. 8.05	30. 8.	21. 9.	5.10.	14.10.	74
Potosi	Nissen	24. 9.05	23.10.	16.11.	29.11.	5.12.	72
Petschili	Teschner	11.10.05	4.11.	28.11.	10.12.	18.12.	68
Pamir	Prützmann	9.11.05	29.11.	25.12.	8. 1.06	19. 1.	70
Prompt	Miethe	23.11.05	20.12.	13. 1.06	29. 1.	7. 2.	76
Pangani	Junge	1. 1.06	25. 1.	21. 2.	3. 3.	9. 3.	67
Pisagua	Dehnhardt	20. 2.06	10. 3.	4. 4.	19. 4.	30. 4.	69
Pera	Allwardt	18. 3.06	12. 4.	9. 5.	19. 5.	1. 6.	75
Posen	Paulsen	11. 4.06	4. 5.	3. 6.	18. 6.	25. 6.	75
Plus	Pötscher	5. 6.06	2. 7.	25. 7.	9. 8.	20. 8.	76
Potosi	Nissen	19. 6.06	14. 7.	2. 8.	12. 8.	21. 8.	63

Petschili	Teschner	29. 8.06	24. 9.	20.10.	30.10.	5.11.	68
Parchim	Oetzmann	19. 9.06	16.10.	9.11.	24.11.	1.12.	73
Pangani	Junge	8.10.06	1.11.	26.11.	7.12.	12.12.	66
Peiho	Frömcke	3.11.06	25.11.	25.12.	7. 1.07	14. 1.	72
Pamelia	Dahm	4. 4.07	29. 4.	26. 5.	5. 6.	14. 6.	71
Potosi	Nissen	6. 6.07	3. 7.	30. 7.	6. 8.	20. 8.	75
Petschili	Teschner	10. 7.07	7. 8.	2. 9.	15. 9.	22. 9.	74
Pamir	Prützmann	15. 7.07	15. 8.	9. 9.	18. 9.	28. 9.	75
Parchim	Oetzmann	2. 8.07	29. 8.	22. 9.	3.10.	14.10.	73
Pangani	Junge	15. 8.07	10. 9.	1.10.	18.10.	28.10.	74
Pisagua	Dehnhardt	19. 9.07	18.10.	13.11.	1.12.	7.12.	76
Pommern	Allwardt	20.10.07	12.11.	6.12.	17.12.	24.12.	65
Pera	Hildebrandt	6.11.07	29.11.	22.12.	3. 1.08	13. 1.	68
Posen	Paulsen	25.12.07	13. 1.08	13. 2.	27. 2.	6. 3.	72
Pirna	Wendler	4. 1.08	28. 1.	23. 2.	5. 3.	18. 3.	74
Pitlochry	Miethe	6. 4.08	26. 4.	20. 5.	3. 6.	12. 6.	67
Pampa	Hamm	21. 5.08	17. 6.	15. 7.	28. 7.	5. 8.	76
Pisagua	Frömcke	27. 7.08	20. 8.	8. 9.	22. 9.	30. 9.	65
Peiho	Wist	27. 7.08	26. 8.	21. 9.	2.10.	9.10.	74
Pirna	Wendler	21.12.08	17. 1.09	12. 2.	24. 2.	3. 3.	71
Pangani	Junge	13. 8.09	6. 9.	28. 9.	15.10.	24.10.	72
Pampa	Hamm	17.10.09	10.11.	10.12.	21.12.	30.12.	74
Pinnas	Eck	8.11.09	9.12.	5. 1.10	19. 1.	25. 1.	78
Potosi	Frömcke	19.12.09	14. 1.10	4. 2.	16. 2.	24. 2.	67
Parchim	Becker	22. 3.10	16. 4.	18. 5.	29. 5.	8. 6.	78
Peiho	Wist	16. 4.10	11. 5.	15. 6.	24. 6.	3. 7.	78
Pirna	Siemer	11. 5.10	1. 6.	3. 7.	14. 7.	25. 7.	75
Pommern	Allwardt	28. 6.10	22. 7.	13. 8.	31. 8.	6. 9.	70
Pampa	Hamm	1. 7.10	25. 7.	17. 8.	30. 8.	5. 9.	66
Pangani	Junge	8. 8.10	6. 9.	27. 9.	17.10.	26.10.	79
Parchim	Becker	12.12.10	11. 1.11	9. 2.	22. 2.	1. 3.	79

Name	Master	Passed Lizard	Line crossed	50° S Atlantic	50° S Pacific	Arrived Valparaiso	Total days
Persimmon	Oetzmann	22.12.10	15. 1.11	9. 2.	25. 2.	4. 3.	72
Petschili	Teschner	28. 1.11	19. 2.	24. 3.	10. 4.	17. 4.	79
Peiho	Wist	9. 2.11	1. 3.	2. 4.	13. 4.	21. 4.	71
Ponape	Hamm	6. 3.11	24. 3.	25. 4.	4. 5.	16. 5.	71
Pampa	Jürs	4. 4.11	28. 4.	26. 5.	13. 6.	21. 6.	78
Pommern	Allwardt	3. 5.11	27. 5.	30. 6.	13. 7.	20. 7.	78
Pangani	Junge '	29. 5.11	23. 6.	19. 7.	1. 8.	9. 8.	73
Pamir	Miethe	29. 6.11	25. 7.	19. 8.	2. 9.	11. 9.	74
Peking	Nissen	8.10.11	6.11.	4.12.	15.12.	23.12.	76
Pirna	Wolf	19.10.11	13.11.	10.12.	23.12.	31.12.	75
Pampa	Jürs	18.12.11	14. 1.12	10. 2.	20. 2.	28. 2.	72
Penang	Eck	3. 1.12	30. 1.	23. 2.	6. 3.	14. 3.	71
Passat	Wendler	4. 1.12	29. 1.	23. 2.	6. 3.	14. 3.	72
Pangani	Junge	17. 3.12	17. 4.	10. 5.	20. 5.	26. 5.	70
Potosi	Miethe	8. 4.12	27. 4.	21. 5.	8. 6.	14. 6.	67
Pitlochry	Horn	23. 5.12	19. 6.	16. 7.	29. 7.	10. 8.	79
Peiho	Eck	7. 9.12	10.10.	4.11.	14.11.	20.11.	74
Pampa	Jürs	22. 9.12	20.10.	12.11.	1.12.	9.12.	78
Passat	Wendler	3.10.12	31.10.	23.11.	5.12.	11.12.	69
Penang	Oetzmann	9.11.12	28.11.	27.12.	14. 1.13	21. 1.	73
Pommern	Frömcke	9.11.12	26.11.	23.12.	6. 1.13	13. 1.	65
Pinnas	Radfan	16.11.12	10.12.	8. 1.13	21. 1.	30. 1.	75
Peking	Nissen	16.12.12	9. 1.13	4. 2.13	15. 2.	24. 2.	70
Pitlochry	Horn	18. 2.13	14. 3.	13. 4.	24. 4.	7. 5.	78
Pinguin	Petersen	24. 3.13	20. 4.	20. 5.	2. 6.	10. 6.	78
Pirna	Jürs	10. 5.13	31. 5.	29. 6.	13. 7.	22. 7.	73
Ponape	Hamm	6. 6.13	5. 7.	30. 7.	15. 8.	23. 8.	78
Pommern	Frömcke	23. 7.13	20. 8.	13. 9.	29. 9.	10.10.	79
Peking	Nissen	3. 9.13	28. 9.	28.10.	10.11.	16.11.	74
Pinnas	Oetzmann	6. 9.13	5.10.	5.11.	13.11.	19.11.	74

Pinguin	Ehlert	13. 1.14	2. 2.	1. 3.	14. 3.	21. 3.	67
Pirna	Brockhöft	17. 1.14	10. 2.	7. 3.	17. 3.	23. 3.	65
Pommern	Ravn	18. 4.14	17. 5.	14. 6.	24. 6.	3. 7.	76
Peking	Oetzmann	11. 6.14	7. 7.	4. 8.	28. 8.		79
Potosi	Miethe	11. 7.14	11. 8.	2. 9.	14. 9.	23. 9.	74
Priwall	Brockhöft	9. 7.21	8. 8.	2. 9.	16. 9.	25. 9.	78
Peiho	Oellrich	24.10.21	16.11.	18.12.	1. 1.22	7. 1.	75
Parma	Nissen	15. 1.22	14. 2.	9. 3.	26. 3.	3. 4.	78
Peking	Oellrich	2. 5.23	24. 5.	18. 6.	28. 6.	8. 7.	67

Here are some other records:

SMART PASSAGES CHANNEL
TO LINE BEFORE 1898

1896	"Pampa"	Capt. Steinicke	15 Days
1892	"Placilla"	" Hilgendorf	15 "
1894	"Pisagua"	" Bahlke	16 "
1896	"Pisagua"	" Bahlke	15 "

BEST PASSAGES CHANNEL TO 50° S IN
THE PACIFIC IN THE YEARS 1895-1908

1896	"Pampa"	52 Days
1896	"Pisagua"	46 "
1903	"Preussen"	46 "
1904	"Preussen"	46 "
1903	"Potosi"	54 "
1898	"Potosi"	52 "
1906	"Potosi"	54 "
1896	"Preussen"	57 "
1899	"Potosi"	57 "
1908	"Pisagua"	57 "
1906	"Pamir"	53 "
1904	"Preussen"	54 "
1905	"Preussen"	54 "
1903	"Potosi"	49 "
1895	"Plus"	55 "

SMART PASSAGES LINE—50° S

1895	"Pampa"	Capt. Steinicke	20 Days
1896	"Potosi"	" Hilgendorf	18 "
1896	"Preussen"	" Schmidt	19 "
	("Posen")		

CHANNEL 50° S

1892	"Placilla"	Capt. Hilgendorf	40 Days
1894	"Pisagua"	" Bahlke	40 "
1894	"Potrimpos"	" Hellwege	42 "
1896	"Potosi"	" Hilgendorf	41 "

ROUND CAPE HORN (50° S to 50° S)

1884	"Parnass"	Capt. Früdden	7 Days
1884	"Parsifal"	" Hilgendorf	7 "
1894	"Parchim"	" Jäger	8 "
1895	"Peru"	" Ohling	7½ "
1938	"Priwall"	Capt. Hauth	5 Days 14 Hours

Here are ten passages of the "Preussen" and the "Potosi"

"PREUSSEN"					"POTOSI"				
Depar-ture	Channel −Line	Line −50°S	50°S 50°S	Total to 50°S	Depar-ture	Channel −Line	Line −50°S	50°S 50°S	Total
4. 5.01	20,3 d	23,3 d	8,3 d	51.9 d	5. 8.02	22,2 d	22,1 d	9,0 d	53.3 d
30. 1.02	29,1	23,3	21,3	75.7	5. 3.03	13,2	23,0	10,3	46.5
25. 9.02	30,4	22,2	11,5	64.1	26. 8.03	26,3	22,0	11,5	59.8
15. 4.03	16,5	27,0	11,0	54.5	2. 3.04	16,3	22,0	8,0	46.3
5.11.03	29,0	17,3	13,0	59.3	11. 9.04	26,0	19,3	8,0	53.3
25. 5.04	24,0	20,3	11,3	55.6	5. 3.05	21,0	21,0	16,0	58.0
20. 1.05	18,3	25,0	9,0	52.3	16. 9.05	27,3	18,0	10,0	55.3
24. 9.05	29,2	24,4	12,0	65.6	21. 3.06	18,1	30,0	18,3	58.4
19. 6.06	25,3	19,0	9,3	53.6	23. 9.06	26,1	22,2	8,3	56.6
5. 6.07	28,3	25,3	9,0	62.6	11. 5.07	27,0	21,0	20,0	68.0
average	25,0	22,9	11,6	59.5	average	22,4	22,1	11,1	55.6

The best round-trip ever was made by the "Preussen" under command of Capt. Boye Petersen, from Hamburg to Iquique and back in 146 days.

Lacking cargo, she went out in ballast. The crew started dumping sandballast soon after crossing 50° S in the Pacific so that she arrived with only about 600 ts sandballast + 550 ts waterballast at Iquique.

She commenced loading the next day and the usual Laeisz charter party-clause "as fast as ship can load" provided sufficient nitrate. She sailed again inside a week.

Quick despatch in ports of discharge and loading is, of course, just as indispensable as smart passages that do not vary very much in length to make a ship pay her way.

When only the *Padua* and the *Priwall* were left to fly the house-flag of the Laeisz Line, they were still making records. Here are some of the *Padua's* last passages, for example:

Master	Passage	Left	Arrived	Days
H. Piening	Channel–Line	2 Aug. 1929	25 Aug.	23
	Line–50 S Atlantic	25 Aug.	20 Sept.	26
	50 S–50 S	20 Sept.	2 Oct.	12
	50 S–Corral			3
				64
R. Clauss	Channel–Line	3 Nov. 1936	27 Nov.	24
	Line–50 S	27 Nov.	23 Dec.	26
	50 S–50 S	23 Dec.	31 Dec.	8
	50 S–Corral			4
				62
H. R. Wendt	Channel–Line	22 Oct. 1938	12 Nov.	21
	Line–50 S	12 Nov.	5 Dec.	23
	50 S–50 S	5 Dec.	18 Dec.	13
	50 S–Corral			4
				61

On this 61-day passage, the *Padua* had logged 9,390 nautical miles, at an average speed of 6.4 knots. The same ship, on her passage from Valparaiso in ballast to Port Lincoln in South Australia in 1939, averaged 7.2 knots, when she covered 9014 nautical miles in 52½ days. Homeward bound from Port Lincoln to Queenstown in Ireland (Cobh) with a cargo of 52,804 sacks of wheat, she covered 14,962 miles at an average speed of 6.7 knots, which was better than the speed of advance of too many convoys in the war which was then about to break out.

Here is the complete record of the voyages made by the *Potosi* under the German flag:

		Days			Days
1895	Channel to Iquique	66	1905	Channel to Valparaiso	59
	Iquique to Channel	68		Caleta Buena to Channel	85

		Days
1896	Channel to Caleta Buena	65
	Caleta Buena to Channel	78
	Channel to Valparaiso	59
1897	Iquique to Cuxhaven	84
	Channel to Valparaiso	70
	Iquique to Channel	77
1898	Channel to Valparaiso	62
	Caleta Buena to Cuxhaven	74
	Channel to Iquique	62
1899	Iquique to Channel	74
	Channel to Iquique	68
	Caleta Buena to Channel	70
1900	Channel to Valparaiso	55
	Iquique to Channel	73
	Channel to Iquique	61
	Iquique to Channel	73
1901	Channel to Valparaiso	63
	Iquique to Channel	79

(The *Potosi* was commanded by Robert Hilgendorf throughout these voyages. Her next commander was Schlüter)

1902	Channel to Valparaiso	86
	Iquique to Channel	76
	Channel to Tocopilla	78
	Caleta Buena to Channel	77

(Captain H. Nissen then took over command)

1903	Channel to Iquique	68
	Iquique to Channel	57
	Channel to Valparaiso	68
1904	Caleta Buena to Channel	74
	Channel to Iquique	71
	Iquique to Channel	86

		Days
	Channel to Valparaiso	74
	Iquique to Channel	86
1906	Channel to Valparaiso	65
	Iquique to Channel	76
1907	Channel to Valparaiso	78
	Iquique to Channel	87
	Channel to Coquimbo	79
1908	Tocopilla to Channel	56

(This was the occasion when the *Potosi* sailed 2958 miles in eleven days)

1909	(Captain Frömcke)	
	Channel to Taltal	62
	Taltal to Channel	62
	Channel to Valparaiso	67
1910	Taltal to Channel	79
	Channel to Talcahuano	61
	Tocopilla to Cuxhaven	76
1911		
	Channel to Talcahuano	69
	Caleta Buena to Channel	77

(Frömcke went to the *Pommern* for a rest, but died there)

1912	(Captain Niethe)	
	Channel to Valparaiso	67
	Mejillones to Channel	79
1913	Channel to Valparaiso	84
	Mejillones to Channel	84
	Channel to Valparaiso	69
1914	Iquique to Falmouth	77
	Channel to Valparaiso	74

The *Potosi* arrived at Valparaiso on September 23, 1914, and that was the end of her great voyages. Though she went to sea briefly again, it was not under the Laiesz flag nor did she make Laeisz voyages.

Here is a record of the *Preussen's* voyages:

		Days			Days
1902	Channel to Iquique	65		Channel to Taltal	69
	Iquique to Channel	79	1907	Taltal to Channel	62
1903	Channel to Iquique	57		Channel to Valparaiso	80
	Iquique to Channel	68		Tocopilla to Channel	62
1904	Channel to Tocopilla	72	1908	Cuxhaven to New York	33
	Tocopilla to Channel	74		New York to Lombok Straits	73
				New York to Yokohama	112
	Channel to Tocopilla	62			
	Tocopilla to Channel	79		(On this passage the *Preussen* once sailed 3020 miles in eleven consecutive days)	
	Channel to Iquique	62			
	Iquique to Channel	69			
1905	Channel to Iquique	78		Yokohama to Taltal	75
	Iquique to Channel	78		(To 180 Deg. in 12 days)	
			1909	Tocopilla to Cuxhaven	75
	Channel to Iquique	67		(C. Horn to the Line in 22 days)	
	Iquique to Channel	71			
				Channel to Taltal	74
1906	Channel to Taltal	69		Tocopilla to Channel	83
	Taltal to Channel	73	1910	Channel to Taltal	68
				Taltal to Channel	75

The *Preussen* was lost by collision in the Channel when outward bound on her next voyage. Captain Boye Petersen had handed over command to Captain Nissen in April, 1909. These were the only officers who commanded the five-masted ship.

The Laeisz fleet usually consisted of between twenty and twenty-two big square-rigged ships, up to 1914. In 1908, for example, in addition to the five-masters *Preussen* and *Potosi,* it included twenty other barques, ships, and four-masted barques. These were the *Palmyra, Pamelia, Pamir, Pampa, Pangani, Parchim, Parnassos, Peiho, Pira, Persimmon, Petschili, Pindos, Pirat, Pirna, Pisagua, Pitlochry, Plus, Pommern, Posen* and *Prompt. Every one* of these ships was making excellent passages. There were not only a crack few. For example, that year the *Pamelia* sailed from the Channel to Valparaiso in 74 days and back in 77; the *Petschili* out in 78 and back in 89; the *Pamir* out in 83; the *Pisagua* out in 79 and the *Parchim* with the same passage; the *Pommern* (under the redoubtable Frömcke) out in 65 and back in 75; the *Pera* out in 72; the *Posen* in 78, *Pirna* 74, *Persimmon* 67, *Pitlochry* 71, the *Pampa* 76. So it went, year after year.

APPENDIX C

INSTRUCTIONS TO LAEISZ MASTERS

THE Laeisz ships were owned outright by the firm of F. Laeisz, who took a keen personal interest in all his ships, and his sons and grandsons did likewise. Each master of a Laeisz ship received a copy of instructions drawn up personally by the head of the Line. This is a translation of those put aboard the new *Preussen* at Hamburg in 1903.

"My ships can and shall make *fast* voyages. Therefore all necessary gear, sails, cordage, wire, etc. must be on board and must be properly cared for at all times. Equipment which is lost or damaged must be replaced. The rules laid down in the Inventory book must be complied with strictly: the highest possible standard in this vital matter of their gear is the only acceptable standard in my vessels.

"The Master is fully responsible that everything he requires is aboard the ship before he leaves Hamburg . . .

"As well as strict application to the navigation of the vessel I demand economy, and attention to improvements wherever these are possible. . . . My Captains are never to be under the influence of liquor: any contrary information coming to my notice will lead to instant dismissal. Neither may the Mates be under the influence of liquor. If any are, or are found asleep on watch, they are to be dismissed and never employed in my ships again.

"All the crew must be medically examined before going aboard. Only healthy seamen shall be shipped.

"Only such officer-aspirants may be shipped as may be personally selected by myself. I wish to take only the sons of sailors who have been brought up by the coast. Only such may be recommended to me by the Captain.

"When overtime has to be worked by the crew, the Captain must draw up a statement immediately upon leaving the port where the overtime has been worked. This statement must have the crew's agreement, in order to avoid possible future difficulties.

"In view of the present Social-Democratic tendencies of seafaring men, the Captain must be careful in handling the crew and must advise the Mates accordingly. Discipline must be maintained by the exercise of tact not force, by leadership not driving.

"If there be any case of insubordination it must be recorded in the ship's Official Journal, read aloud to those concerned and signed by witnesses.

"Remember there can never be too much fresh air in the quarters. Whenever it is at all possible, skylights, ports, and companion-ways must be kept open.

"If any vessel be communicated with while on voyage, this must be recorded in the Journal and reported to me.

"There must be a daily record of the quantity of cargo worked each day, and of the number of persons employed at the ship's expense. Demurrage must not in any circumstances be incurred by my vessels.

"The Captain is responsible for the quality and quantity of dunnage provided, which must always be sufficient to avoid damage to the cargo.

"Should any coastal cargoes be shipped, a copy of the Manifest is to be forwarded to me.

"The Captain must see that all possible discounts and rebates are credited to me, as owner. This applies to all manner of gratuities, perquisites, etc. It is not to be tolerated that my Captains will accept anything of the sort from anyone other than myself.

"It is in the Captain's interests as much as it is in mine, that he should at all times pay the strictest attention to the safety and safe-handling of the cargo. . . . If there be average claims I must be informed by cable, in detail, and, if it is possible, my instructions in such matters are always to be awaited. Arrangements must be made that commissions payable to agents are an agreed percentage of the repair bill, and not a percentage on the value of the ship and/or her cargo. . . . Such an agreement must be drawn up and signed before the Captain consigns the vessel to anyone. Likewise I give warning against so-called 'good friends' of ships and helpful advisers, especially shipchandlers. The ship has two good friends, the Owner and the Captain. . . . My ship concerns no one else, for she is not insured.

"I recognise the difficulties imposed upon a Captain in times of trouble, when he is resisting insurance representatives, agents, surveyors, and so forth, the more particularly if any of these gentlemen have consular support. But my Captains must never forget that, as the uninsured owner, I have an important influence and, I should think, the right to the last word in such matters.

"My Captains will be in a better position if this facet of my views is explained to the consul in a tactful and polite manner. In consequence, unnecessary and expensive inspections or other actions of that sort may be avoided or at any rate put off until I have had an opportunity of making my reply to the first extensive report.

"All reports above averages and other unpleasant events are to be forwarded to me by the Captain in a separate envelope marked 'Private'.

"The Captain, as my representative, has to preserve secrecy regarding fixed freight-rates and other important matters of that sort.

"I have insured the belongings of Captains, Mates, sailors, and cooks, to the following limits:

Captains	Marks	1000
Mates (1st)	"	800
Mates (others)	"	600
Carpenters, sailors, and cooks	"	300

"This includes damages: if any wishes higher cover he must give notice, and pay the higher premium himself."

APPENDIX D

A VOYAGE IN THE POTOSI

THE following is an account, from the able seaman's point of view, of a voyage in the *Potosi*. It was written for me by Charlie Müller, a very experienced sailing-ship sailor.

"I shipped in the *Potosi* March 26th 1901. She was bound to Valparaiso with a general cargo, and we left Hamburg the same day we signed on. All hands were on board by noon and we never had a chance to spend our 2 months advance. There were 41 souls on board: Captain, 3 officers, 2 Boatswains, 2 carpenters, 2 sailmakers, cook and cook's mate, 1 steward, 20 able seamen, 4 ordinary seamen and 4 boys. There was a passenger on board too in the shape of a German sheep-dog, which had to be delivered safe and sound in Valparaiso. It was.

"The captain was that famous master of Cape Horn ships, Robert Hilgendorf. He was a driver but nevertheless a fair man, not given to hazing his men. The mate was a giant of a man named Schütt, the second mate a man named George Lessel, with whom I had been shipmates before the mast in the bark *Prompt*. The third mate was a young man just out of navigation school. The two boatswains were both elderly men who had been in Laeisz's ships for years. The sailmaker was a Norwegian, his name was Nils Larsen, if I recollect right. His mate was a Dane from Korsör. The two carpenters were both Germans and the cook and his mate also. A good half of the able seamen were Scandinavian, mostly Danes and Swedes, men who had sailed in German ships for years. The ordinary seamen and the boys were all Germans.

"We towed as far as Beachy Head where we got a fair wind which took us in 3 weeks down to the Line. We had about 5 days of doldrums and had a fairly strong South East trade. Before we got into the North East trades, we shifted sails, that is we bent the second best suit, good enough for the Trade winds, and then we bent the heavy canvas again after we left the South East trades; this shifting of sails tooks us just one day. All hands were kept at it. The watch from 4 to 8 a.m. got everything ready, rove off gantlines and got the sails which were to be bent out of the sail locker. At ½ past seven a.m., all hands had breakfast and at 8 all hands turned to. One gang worked aloft, unhanding the sails, and sent them down, and the gang on deck sent up the new sails and stowed away the unbent ones. By 8 o'clock p.m., every sail on those 5 masts had been shifted and everything cleared up.

"We had a good slant around the Horn; it took us just one week from 50 south on the Atlantic side to 50 south on the Pacific side. Anyway, after an uneventful passage of 62 days from the Channel, we dropped anchor in Valparaiso Bay. We had the privilege to be tied alongside the only pier for quick discharging, but every night after knock off time, we had to heave the ship off from the pier for the night, and in the morning before 6 o'clock we had to go alongside again. As it was the time for those dreaded Northers, we had to send the royal yards down. By rights we should have sent down the topgallant yards as well and house the topgallant mast, but Capt. Hilgendorf said it won't be worth it, because he won't stay more than a week at the utmost. As it turned out, we stayed 9 days, discharging a full cargo of general goods. We had enough ballast in her to sail her up the coast to Iquique, which took us 5 days. In Valparaiso we loaded some bales of hay and straw and also a couple of hundred chickens, which we let run loose in the lower hold. In Iquique we had quite a job catching those hens in that large hold and I am afraid not all of those fowls got ashore!

"In Iquique Capt. Hilgendorf sailed his ship right into the pier, without the aid of a tug. We came in late at night and were kept at it till she was moored fore and aft, two anchors forward and two anchors aft. At six next morning we started discharging the bales of hay out of one hatch, while saltpeter for stiffening was taken on board in the other hatches. Twelve days it took us to put her down to her marks. While we were loading, three men were in the punt over the side putting hot tallow on her plates, which would be under the water. We had 6,300 tons of saltpeter in her by the time she was loaded, and no sooner was the last bag on board, we started to heave up our moorings and again without a tug, slid out of the harbour, homeward bound. We had again a good run around the Horn and nothing out of the common happened till we ran out of the North East trades and into a calm, which lasted for quite a long time. Anyway, we had a long passage of 78 days to the chops of the Channel, and Capt. Hilgendorf was not too pleased about it.

"We had three more men aboard homeward bound. In Chile it was the custom for the Laeisz's ships to take a few cadets from the Chilean Navy on board. On this trip we had 3 of those youngsters, and I must say they were real good boys and they learned fast what they did not know. We did not go through the English Channel, but went around the North of Scotland, because there was a headwind for us in the Channel.

"I was paid off November 13, 1901. The whole round trip lasted just 5 months and 19 days.

"I did not stay ashore very long, on account of having had a small pay day. I shipped in the 4 m. Bark *Octavia,* the former *Loch Nevis,* for a voyage to Santa Rosalia with a cargo of coke."

APPENDIX E

INSTRUCTIONS TO A SHIPMASTER

THE following, given here by permission of The Trident, are the owners' instructions to the master of a Cape Horn sailing-ship. The master was Captain T. C. Fearon, the ship the full-rigged ship *Fitzjames* (which later was to become the Laeisz Line's *Pinnas*), the owners W. Montgomery and Company, of London, who also owned the *Grace Harwar*, the *Eva Montgomery*, and the *Ladye Doris*. Captain Fearon was a most experienced and highly respected shipmaster who had distinguished himself by sailing the *Grace Harwar* from Chile to Falmouth without her bowsprit. The bowsprit had been shorn off in a collision. No spars were available for replacements. Nothing daunted, Fearon took the deep-loaded full-rigger home round the Horn with the headstays taken to the stump of the bowsprit, and temporary jibs rigged on them. To repair the ship in Chile would have meant waiting for a new bowsprit to be shipped out from England.

63, MARK LANE,
LONDON, E.C.
May 12, 1902

CAPT. T. C. FEARON,
SHIP *Fitzjames*,
GLASGOW

DEAR SIR,—We may preface the General Instructions we are about to record by stating that in appointing you to the command of the *Fitzjames* we have done so in the firm conviction that you are in every way fitted for the responsibilities devolving upon you, and we beg to assure you that you enjoy to the fullest extent, as far as we are concerned, that confidence which should always exist mutually between employer and employed.

CARE OF SHIP AND NAVIGATION IN CHANNEL. You will at all times conduct the business of the ship as if she were your own and uninsured; in case of accident you can never be wrong in acting on that principle. You will give your whole attention to the navigation of the ship in Channel, keep a good lookout and, on approaching land, we particularly impress upon you the necessity of keeping the *Lead* going; also your *Sidelights* must be well attended to *At All Times* as in case of accident these are very important points both as regards the owners and yourself.

CONDITION AND MAINTENANCE OF SHIP. You are now in command of an exceptionally fine vessel and we are sure that you will take a pride in her and do all that lies in your power to keep everything connected with her, inside and outside, in first rate order. We need not remind you that a new ship on her first voyage requires a very exceptional amount of care, especially with regard to caulking decks, in view of which you are carrying a carpenter's mate. Always remember that a steel ship requires much more care than an iron one and, if neglected, soon sustains damage which is irremediable, or at any rate terribly expensive to repair.

INSIDE from limbers to deck should be kept perfectly clean and free from dirt, and where there is any sign of rust thoroughly scrape and paint at once. Give special attention to the *Reverse Frames* and take every opportunity of raising the ceilings and examining the state of the *Floors,* cleaning and re-cementing, whenever necessary. It is always better to do this abroad as, if it is left for a home port, the expense incurred is very great. Take great care as to condition of *Peaks,* and whenever it is time to take out the *Mast Wedges* do not fail to do so and scrape and paint the masts where the wedges have been. When painting your *Holds,* for which purpose we always supply a sufficiency of material, take care that careful supervision is exercised and that every inch of metal is thoroughly well coated.

OUTSIDE. It is hardly necessary for us to recapitulate many points which were dealt with in our letter of March 5th, which no doubt you have by you, but we would specially urge upon you the necessity of keeping all moveable iron-work in order so that it does not get "froze". Great care has been exercised with regard to brass bushing wherever possible, but none the less all such moveable parts must be constantly looked to. Look well after your *Boats* and see that everything whether lowering tackles or equipment is kept in readiness and thorough repair. Always keep *Topsides* well cleaned and painted, also the *Hull* as low down as possible. This last should be done by your own men as the ship lightens during discharge.

PROVISIONS. These have been provided on a very liberal scale and you are doubtless well acquainted with the system of feeding your crew, which we recommend. In cold weather more food is consumed than in hot and as long as there is *No Waste* the men need not be tied to the fixed scale. Although we are aware that same is sufficient, a very strict account of all stores used must be kept by your steward who must regularly, say once a week, submit his books for your inspection. The mate must also rate in his log the beef and pork as it is broached and the depth of water in the tanks. Beef and pork must be kept as cool as possible and we recommend that you should have the bungs out during the voyage to examine the state of the pickle and if it appears poor or at all stale run it off and have fresh pickle put in; this will only involve trifling labour and will greatly improve the meat.

CARE OF CARGO. This is so important that we must urge upon you to see to it personally as far as you possibly can. Every care and precaution that experience can suggest must be taken of cargo when loading or discharging. When you have general cargo on board it is almost certain to include intoxicants and strict watch must invariably be kept on the stevedores to prevent pillage and the vexatious claims consequent thereon. It is unnecessary for us to warn an experienced shipmaster like yourself to take every means you can devise to prevent broaching by the crew, an occurrence far too common and fraught with terrible consequences. If you load coals always see that temperature tubes are properly fixed and used, and that shifting boards are not overlooked.

Nitrate of Soda is a cargo you are almost certain to carry and requires the greatest of care. Always look well after the weighing of your cargo and see that you get good weights and good bags. Every particle of loose nitrate whether in lighters alongside or on board must be picked up. When bags are lifted from lighters, canvas or tarpaulin should be placed over the side and on to the lighter so that if any bags break in the slings the contents may be saved. Good and reliable men must be placed in the hatchways to gather up and bag any spilt nitrate and if any broken bags come on board they must be needled up at once. This work, especially the picking up, is always shirked and not constantly looked after. The bottom of the hold should be well and carefully dunnaged and all beams and stanchions protected by old canvas and wooden battens. Never allow bags to be in contact with the sharp edges of beams, as the natural settlement of the cargo will cut them to pieces, and on no account allow mats of any description to be used either under cargo or on beams.

When the loading is completed the hatches must not be taken off except in case of absolute necessity. All ventilators should be fitted with canvas covers so that nothing can be thrown down them. There is also the necessity of avoiding the slightest risk of fire, which has been the finish up of many of the nitrate ships, including one of our own. All smoking in the hold must be prevented, nor must lighted pipes be allowed near open hatchways, or any naked lights below.

VENTILATION must be carefully attended to, especially when coming into cold weather. Your ship is amply provided with permanent ventilators and in addition you must use every opportunity of allowing heated air to escape from your holds.

BALLASTING. In ballasting your ship, always be careful that you have enough. You will no doubt have discussed this very important question with your predecessor and are perfectly certain in your own mind as to the quantity she requires to stand in dock and how much more is necessary for moving in river, stream or tideway. Always take too much rather than too little, it is always best to be on the safe side. Never forget that for a voyage in ballast (or with coal) shifting boards are an absolute necessity and you are never on any account whatever to dispense with them. The ship should never have less than 250 tons of stiffening in her to be quite safe, even in dock.

DRAFT OF WATER. You must never fail to advise us of the draft fore and aft on arrival at a port, and of the loaded draft, when you finish taking in cargo, also your draft when you leave any port in ballast. You are, of course, aware of the Act of Parliament at present in force with regard to draft of ships. The marks, showing the depth to which your ship may be loaded are clearly marked on her side and you will always take care that under no circumstances whatever is the line across the disc ever to be submerged.

ACCIDENT. Should you unhappily meet with an accident bear in mind that it is your duty to act as if the whole venture, ship and cargo, were your own and uninsured. You will not give up command of your ship to Lloyd's agents, coastguard people or anybody else. Should you find it advisable to secure their assistance, you will consider them your servants and be held responsible for their acts. Make a special bargain for all assistance from steamers or others in writing, if practicable on the "no cure no pay" principle. Claims for salvage often arise when a little foresight and presence of mind would prevent all dispute.

When, however, time will permit, you will advise us by cable and await instructions from us, and in the event of repairs to the ship being absolutely necessary you will telegraph giving the best estimate you can of the probable cost. But we trust you will never go into any port for either supplies or repairs unless absolutely compelled to do so, and you know that repairs done abroad have almost always to be done over again at home.

REPORTING AND SPEAKING. Whenever in the English Channel and the opportunity offers do not fail to report yourself to the signal stations, and at sea whenever possible to homeward-bound vessels. If requested, as sometimes happens, by a disabled ship, or indeed any vessel to report them, do not fail to do so immediately on your arrival at your first port, giving as full and accurate details as you can.

TELEGRAMS. You will see that a cablegram is invariably sent us advising your arrivals and departures from port. This is very important and we wish you always to see to it yourself and not leave it to agents or anyone else. You will always use Scott's Code 1896 Edition, of which a copy is supplied to the ship, and we shall use the same code in telegraphing to you.

ABSTRACT LOG. We have provided you with forms for making this out. It will give you but little trouble to keep it up day by day when at sea and we should always like one sent us in your first letter after arriving at a port whether at home or abroad.

NEGLIGENCE CLAUSE. When signing Bills of Lading or Charter parties always take care that it is inserted in both. We append a copy of its provisions:—

"The Act of God, Perils of the Sea, Fire, Barratry of the Master and Crew, Enemies, Pirates, assailing Thieves, arrest and restraint of Princes, Rulers and People, Collisions, Stranding, and other accidents of navigation excepted; even when occasioned by the negligence default or error in judgment of the Pilot, Master, Mariners, or other Servants of the Shipowner."

CONTRACTS. You will be duly notified of any existing at ports where you may be going. We enclose copy of one with Messrs. T. & A. Brown, of Newcastle, N.S.W., for towage; also another for stevedoring with Mr. . . ., Sydney. We did not quite like another of our master's account of . . .'s proceedings and it will be as well for you to keep a good look out in any dealing with him. If you think it desirable to employ a surveyor at Sydney, you cannot do better than Captain Vine Hall.

OFFICERS are sometimes rather difficult to find. It is best never to be in a hurry over the selection of them. We always prefer that the first mate should be in possession of a Master's certificate. Always be extremely careful whom you take and make thorough sobriety a 'sine qua non,' both as regards mates and tradesmen.

APPRENTICES. We wish you to make them your especial care. You are starting with six, all green, although four of them have served two years in training ships. Be very particular as to their conduct, especially when in foreign ports. Do all you can to inculcate a system of thorough and steady discipline; give them every opportunity and all the assistance you can in the study of their profession, whenever you perceive a willingness to learn. Try and turn them out smart and efficient young officers by the time they are due to pass their examinations, so that if we are able to continue to employ them we may find them of real use to us and a credit to their captain and themselves.

CREW. We leave their number entirely to your discretion so long as the ship is thoroughly and efficiently manned. We prefer always your carrying a sailor too many, rather than one short. Whenever possible we prefer a British crew. If, however, you find it impossible to obtain really good and efficient Britishers and have to take foreigners, Scandinavians appear to answer as well as any. All our ships are entered in the Shipping Federation and their agents at the various British ports are always able and willing to assist you. As a rule, men holding the Federation tickets are the most desirable. A crew well treated will generally work well and be more likely to complete the voyage in the ship. If you have to replace deserters abroad, you will hardly be likely to get better seamen than at home and the rate of pay is sure to be higher.

Advance as little as possible to your sailors and apprentices that they may have less inducement to leave the ship and in the event of your discharging any of your crew abroad, be careful where an allotment note has been given, to keep back a sufficient sum to cover two months' allotments; should it not be required the man or his relations can get the balance afterwards. No allotments should be given to the crew except in the case of officers or petty officers, and only when required. In discharging men abroad, after showing in your wages book the balance due to each of them and paid over, state at foot the amount in currency and the rate of exchange to assist us in checking your account. In cases of desertion, be particular to give us timely notice by cable to stop allotments (See Scott's Code page 236) and when writing advise us of the names of any men who have quitted the ship to enable us to reply to enquiries.

The health of your sailors is a matter of great importance and we trust you will be watchful and careful with them and insist on cleanliness, which is the mainspring of health. A bathroom for the use of the crew is provided and arrangements should be made so that it is always accessible at suitable times to men who wish to use it.

Everything should be done to enable the men to get their meals in decency and comfort. Proper dishes for the food are provided and must be regularly used. We have also supplied a plate, mug, knife and fork and spoon for each of the foremast hands, to be issued to them free and returned when they leave the ship. You are already in possession of our wishes as regards supplying milk to the crew in their tea and coffee.

CREW LIST. When leaving a port never omit to send us a list of everyone on board with their rating and pay.

ECONOMY AND DISBURSEMENTS. Be as strict and as rigid on this point as is consistent with keeping the vessel in a sound state of safety and efficiency. A shipmaster is, we need not remind you, in a position of great trust and cannot be too careful in regard to money matters. Make a bargain for everything you find it necessary to buy and always take care that the price includes delivery free on board. Never deal with any but first-class and thoroughly respectable tradesmen. You will allow your consignees to pay all bills after you have examined and signed same, excepting in cases where a commission is charged to us on disbursements. You will then, if directed by us to do so, draw the money yourself for your crew and other expenses. You must get all accounts rendered in duplicate and retain a copy yourself, but have all vouchers sent home *at once* either by yourself or the consignees.

Also, before leaving port be very particular to examine the consignees' account carefully and minutely before you sign it as correct; render us an account of all cash drawn and disbursed or received and take care always that the rate of exchange, should there be one, is clearly stated. Be especially careful that before leaving port you have everything on board of provisions and stores which you require for the voyage. We have an especial objection to stores of any description, save in cases of actual necessity, being purchased from other vessels on the high seas.

We have on this occasion nothing further to add save to assure you of our best wishes for your new command.

We remain, Dear Sir,

Yours very truly,

W. MONTGOMERY & CO.

APPENDIX F

BALANCE SHEET
OF A SAILING-SHIP'S VOYAGE

DEVITT & MOORE'S OCEAN

Dr.   Sailed from London 16th September, 1911, for Sydney,

	£	s.	d.	£	s.	d.
To Stock of Provisions brought from last voyage				80	0	0
" Outfit and General Expenses in London, including Provisions bought in London	2,867	5	4			
" Discount and Address Commission on Outward Freight, as per Charter	141	5	9			
				3,008	11	1
" Expenses in Sydney, Inward and Outward	2,254	3	6			
" Agency Fee, Sydney	25	0	0			
" Agent's Loading Commission on Homeward Freight	244	0	6			
				2,523	4	0
" Expenses at Newcastle, N.S.W., Inward and Outward	144	18	10			
" Agent's Fee, Newcastle	5	5	0			
				150	3	10
" Rebates on Homeward Freight paid in Sydney	524	12	5			
" Cost in London of forwarding part of Cargo to destinations	236	12	7			
				761	5	0
" Exchange on Captain's Draft for Disbursements at Sydney				60	8	0
" Expenses in London, Inward, viz.: Towing, Pilots, Dock Dues, Discharging Cargo, &c.				932	13	6
" Insurance on Ship, Freight, &c.				455	0	5
" Portage Bill, Crew	1,206	14	10			
" Portage Bill, Captain, 12 months at £25 per month	300	0	0			
				1,506	14	10
" Captain's Expenses in London and Sydney				32	3	3
" Our Commission on Midshipmen's Premiums				82	5	0
" Our Commission on Midshipmen's Premiums, Outward Freight				115	18	5
" Our Commission on Midshipmen's Premiums, Homeward Freight				55	14	2
" Our Commission on Midshipmen's Premiums, Passage Money				11	3	6
" Management Fee				199	8	0
" Postages and Petty Expenses				21	0	0
" Profit on the Voyage				28	16	5
				£10,024	9	5

Examined and found correct, 30th November, 1912

99, Cheapside,
LONDON, E.C.

T. EDW. GOODYEAR,
Chartered Accountant

TRAINING SHIPS, LIMITED

THE SHIP *"Port Jackson,"* 1911–12

and arrived in London 7th June, 1912   *Cr.*

	£	s.	d.	£	s.	d.
By Midshipmen's Premiums				1,645	0	0
" Freight London to Sydney				2,318	8	8
" Passage Money London to Sydney				145	0	0
" Passage Money Sydney to London				65	0	0
" Board of Passenger in Sydney				13	10	0
" Freight Sydney to London	5,570	17	5			
Less Due but not received	2	0	0			
				5,568	17	5
" Sale of Wine, Spirits, and Sundry Stores				95	4	6
" Fees recovered from Seamen				0	8	0
" Stock of Provisions carried to next Voyage				160	0	0
" Interest at 4 per cent. on this account						
to 30th November, 1912				13	0	10

£10,024 9 5

E. & O. E.

LONDON, 30th *November*, 1912   DEVITT & MOORE

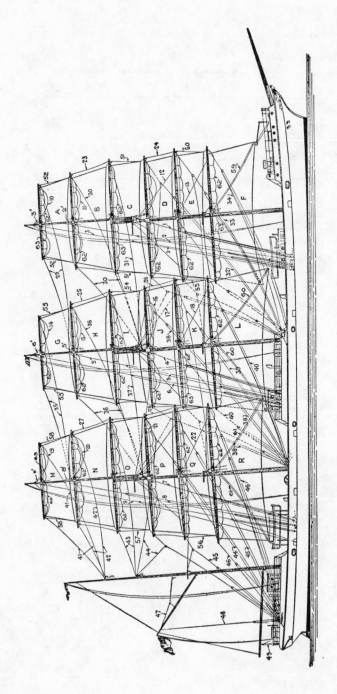

SQUARE SAILS AND RUNNING RIGGING
OF A 20TH CENTURY STEEL FOUR-MAST BARQUE

A   Fore royal
B   Fore upper topgallant sail
C   Fore lower topgallant sail
D   Fore upper topsail
E   Fore lower topsail
F   Foresail (or forecourse)

G   Main royal
H   Main upper topgallant sail
I   Main lower topgallant sail
J   Main upper topsail
K   Main lower topsail
L   Mainsail (or main course)

M   Mizzen royal
N   Mizzen upper topgallant sail
O   Mizzen lower topgallant sail
P   Mizzen upper topsail
Q   Mizzen lower topsail
R   Crojack (or crossjack)

1 Fore topsail halliards
2 Fore topgallant halliards
3 Fore royal halliards
4 Main topsail halliards
5 Main topgallant halliards
6 Main royal halliards
7 Mizzen topsail halliards
8 Mizzen topgallant halliards
9 Mizzen royal halliards
10, 14, 19 Royal lifts
11, 15, 20 Topgallant lifts
16, 21 Topsail lifts
12, 17 Lower topsail lifts ‡
13, 18, 22 Course lifts
23, 25, 27 Upper topgallant downhauls
24, 26, 28 Upper topsail downhauls
29 Fore royal braces
30 Fore upper topgallant braces
31 Fore lower topgallant braces
32 Fore upper topsail braces
33 Fore lower topsail braces
34 Fore brace
35 Main royal braces
36 Main upper topgallant braces
37 Main lower topgallant braces
38 Main upper topsail braces

‡ Not always rigged.

39 Main lower topsail braces
40 Main braces
41 Mizzen royal braces
42 Mizzen upper topgallant braces
43 Mizzen lower topgallant braces
44 Mizzen upper topsail braces
45 Mizzen lower topsail braces
46 Crojack (or mizzen) braces
47 Span
48 Vang
49 Spanker sheets
50 Fore lower topsail clewline
51 Fore lower topgallant clewline
52 Fore royal clewline
53 Main lower topsail clewline
54 Main lower topgallant clewline
55 Main royal clewline
56 Mizzen lower topsail clewline
57 Mizzen lower topgallant clewline
58 Mizzen royal clewline
59 Fore clewline *
60 Main clewline *
61 Crojack clewline *
62 Footropes
63 Stirrups

* It was more usual for these clewlines to be rigged to the yardarms.

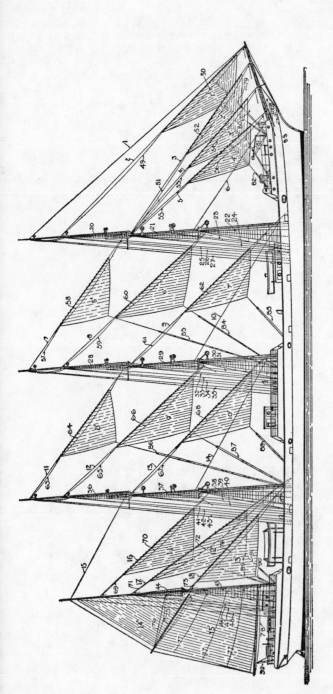

MODERN CLYDE-BUILT STEEL FOUR-MAST BARQUE

1 Fore royal stay
2 Fore topgallant stay
3 Outer jib stay
4 Inner jib stay
5 Fore topmast stay
6 Forestay
7 Main royal stay
8 Main topgallant stay
9 Main topmast stay
10 Mainstay

11 Mizzen royal stay
12 Mizzen topgallant stay
13 Mizzen topmast stay
14 Mizzen stay
15 Jigger royal stay
16 Jigger topgallant stay
17 Jigger topmast stay
18 Jigger stay
19 Vangs
20 Fore topgallant rigging

21 Fore topmast rigging
22 Fore shrouds
23 Fore cap-backstays
24 Fore topmast backstays
25 Fore topmast cap-backstay
26 Fore topgallant backstay
27 Fore royal backstay
28 Main topgallant rigging
29 Main topmast rigging
30 Main shrouds

31 Main cap-backstay
32 Main topmast backstays
33 Main topmast cap-backstay
34 Main topgallant backstays
35 Main royal backstays
36 Mizzen topgallant rigging
37 Mizzen topmast rigging
38 Mizzen shrouds
39 Mizzen cap-backstays
40 Mizzen topmast backstays
41 Mizzen topmast cap-backstay
42 Mizzen topgallant backstays
43 Mizzen royal backstays
44 Jigger topmast rigging
45 Jigger shrouds
46 Jigger topmast backstays
47 Jigger topgallant backstay
48 Jigger royal backstay
49 Flying-jib halliards
50 Outer-jib halliards
51 Outer-jib downhaul
53 Inner-jib halliards
54 Inner-jib downhaul
55 Fore topmast staysail halliards
56 Fore topmast downhaul
57 Main royal staysail halliards
58 Main royal downhaul

59 Main topgallant staysail halliards
60 Main topgallant' staysail down-haul
61 Main topmast staysail halliards
62 Main topmast staysail downhaul
63 Mizzen royal staysail halliards
64 Mizzen royal staysail downhaul
65 Mizzen topgallant staysail hal-liards
66 Mizzen topgallant staysail down-haul
67 Mizzen topmast staysail halliards
68 Mizzen topmast staysail down-haul
69 Jigger topgallant staysail hal-liards
70 Jigger topgallant downhaul
71 Jigger topmast staysail halliards
72 Jigger topmast staysail downhaul
73 Jigger staysail halliards
74 Jigger staysail downhaul
75 Span
76 Spanker head outhaul
77 Brails (for working spanker)
78 Spanker foot outhaul
79 Flying-jib sheets
80 Outer-jib sheets

81 Inner-jib sheets
82 Fore topmast staysail sheets
83 Main royal staysail sheets
84 Main topgallant staysail sheets
85 Main topmast royal staysail sheets
86 Mizzen royal staysail sheets
87 Mizzen topgallant staysail sheets
88 Mizzen topmast staysail sheets
89 Jigger topgallant staysail sheets
90 Jigger staysail sheets
91 Jigger topmast staysail sheets
92 Spanker sheet
1′ Flying-jib
2′ Outer jib
3′ Inner jib
4′ Fore topmast staysail
5′ Main royal staysail
6′ Main topgallant staysail
7′ Main topmast staysail
8′ Mizzen royal staysail
9′ Mizzen topgallant staysail
10′ Mizzen topmast staysail
11′ Jigger topgallant staysail
12′ Jigger topmast staysail
13′ Jigger staysail
14′ Gaff topsail
15′ Spanker

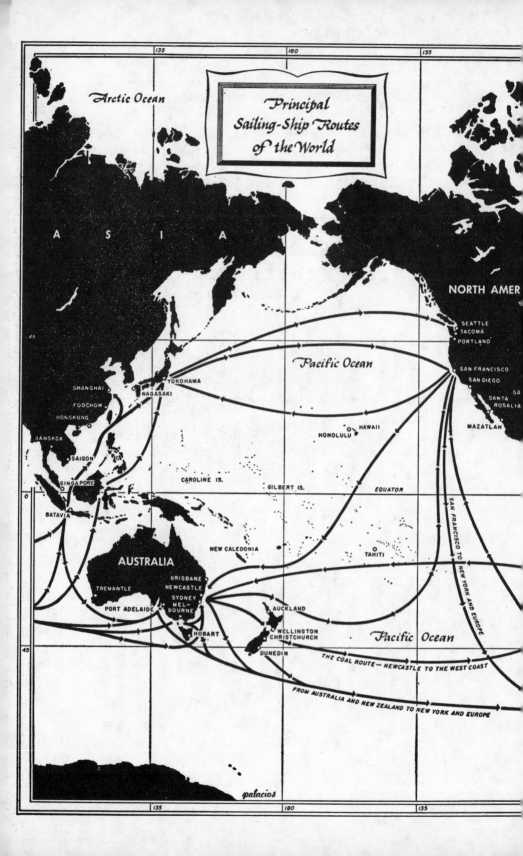

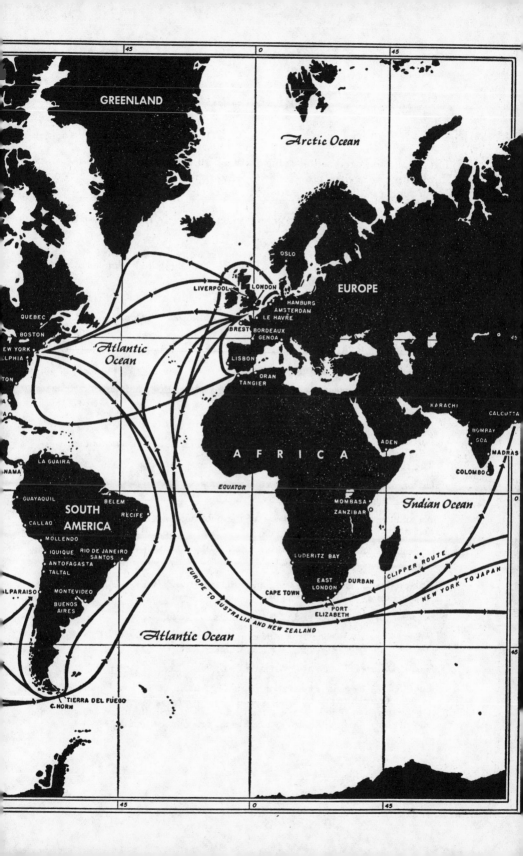

BIBLIOGRAPHY

Tis makes no pretence of being a list of all books dealing with the Cape Horn ship, for such a list would be almost endless. These are the books I have found useful, and have studied and enjoyed.

Last of the Windjammers, Vols. I and II, BASIL LUBBOCK. Brown, Son and Ferguson, Glasgow, 1929.

> These are excellent works, real treasure-houses of information. Much of the books consists of histories of particular ships but it is all spiced with anecdotes and personal reminiscences.

The Colonial Clippers, BASIL LUBBOCK. Brown, Son and Ferguson. Glasgow, 1924.

> Another of the excellent Lubbock sailing-ship histories. This deals mainly with the Australian trade.

The Down Easters, BASIL LUBBOCK. Brown, Son and Ferguson, Glasgow, 1929.

> Another Lubbock, giving the story of the New England wooden ships.

The Maritime History of Massachusetts, SAMUEL ELIOT MORISON. Houghton Mifflin Company, Boston, 1941.

> Abounds in good stories and good history, all very well written.

The Clipper Ship Era, ARTHUR H. CLARK. Putnam and Company, London.

> The classic for the period 1843 to 1869.

American Merchant Ships, 1850–1900, FREDERICK C. MATTHEWS. Marine Research Society, Salem, Mass., 1930.

> An excellent piece of work, as are all the publications I have ever seen from this Society.

Five Hundred Sailing Records, CARL C. CUTLER. The Marine Historical Association, Mystic, Conn., 1952.

> The product of much painstaking and original research, this gives many interesting sailing records of U.S.-built ships.

Greyhounds of the Sea, CARL C. CUTLER. Putnam, 1930.

> An excellent book about the American clippers, written by the Curator of the Marine Historical Museum at Mystic, Conn.

Falconer's Marine Dictionary, WILLIAM FALCONER. London, 1789.

> Subtitled "A Copious Explanation of the Technical Terms and Phrases employed in the Construction, Equipment, Furniture, Machinery, Movements, and Military Operations of a Ship," this is a fascinating work, well illustrated with diagrams and drawings. My edition is described as a "new one, corrected."

Dana's Seaman's Manual, R. H. DANA. London, 1873.

Called *Dana's Seaman's Friend* in America. "It is to be hoped that the various classes of society which are led by their callings, duty, or affection, to take an interest in sea-faring men, and who may wish to know something of their business and their language, will find this little Manual useful," says the English editor. He need not have been so apologetic. The book is comprehensive and most interesting.

Wrinkles and Suggestions for Sailing Vessels, J. C. B. JARVIS, Extra Master. Dundee, William Kidd, Whitehall Street, 1897.

This is Captain Jarvis' own little book on his very practicable ideas for improving the working rig of square-rigged ships.

Master in Sail, CAPTAIN JAMES S. LEARMONT. London, Percival Marshall, 1950.

An original document—a straightforward account of an outstanding master and his career under sail, full of absorbing source material. Not very well written, but that is no blemish on its historical worth.

Under Gustaf Erikson's Flagga, GEORG KÅHRE. Mariehamn, Åland's Nautical Club, 1948.

Interesting account of Sailing-ship Owner Gustaf Erikson. (In Swedish.)

The Nitrate Clippers, BASIL LUBBOCK. Brown, Son and Ferguson, Glasgow, 1932.

Good account of Laeisz and A. D. Bordes ships, but not up to this writer's usual standard.

The Log of the Cutty Sark, BASIL LUBBOCK. Brown, Son and Ferguson, Glasgow. New edition 1945.

This is comprehensive, thorough, and interesting throughout—a first-class piece of work.

The China Clippers, BASIL LUBBOCK. Brown, Son and Ferguson, Glasgow. New edition 1946.

This book deals with all the famous clippers of the China trade. Like all Lubbock's work, it is the product of original and comprehensive research. These books are recommended without reserve to the student of the sailing-ship.

The Return of the Cutty Sark, C. FOX SMITH. Methuen and Co., London, 1924.

Out of print. An interesting and well-written account of the *Cutty Sark* up to the time of her restoration by Captain Dowman.

The Cutty Sark—*The Last of the Tea Clippers,* DR. C. NEPEAN LONGRIDGE. Percival Marshall, London, 1933. 2 Vols.

Out of print. Comprehensive study of the ship especially valuable to the model-maker.

The Tea Clippers, DAVID R. MACGREGOR. Percival Marshall, London, 1952.

A first-class study of the subject with many good plans and illustrations.

The Composite Tea Clipper Cutty Sark, by CAPTAIN G. C. STEELE, V.C., R.N.

Article in the MARINER'S MIRROR—the journal of the Society for Nautical Research, July, 1939.

Various articles in the magazine SEA BREEZES, the nautical magazine published by Charles Birchall and Sons, 17 James St., Liverpool: and in the NAUTICAL MAGAZINE, published by Brown, Son and Ferguson, Glasgow.

THE AMERICAN NEPTUNE ⎫ Various articles.
THE MARINER'S MIRROR ⎭

Ocean Passages for the World, Admiralty (Hydrographic Dept.), published by H.M. Stationery Office.

Contains sailing routes, charts, weather maps, route maps for both sailing-ships and steamships, but does not pretend to give sailing routes in full detail.

Explanations and Sailing Directions, to Accompany the Wind and Current Charts, M. F. MAURY. Many editions, published by U.S. Hydrographic Office.

Another classic, providing a useful analysis of sailing conditions for global voyages.

Deep-Water Sail, HAROLD A. UNDERHILL. Brown, Son and Ferguson, Glasgow, 1952.

A thoroughly competent and profusely illustrated account of the types of ship and the manner in which they were rigged.

Masting and Rigging: The Clipper Ship and Ocean Carrier, HAROLD A. UNDERHILL. Brown, Son and Ferguson, Glasgow, 1946.

Mr. Harold Underhill is a naval draughtsman by profession. He has made a lifelong study of the sailing-ship and this work contains the fruits of his study.

The Sailing Ship, ROMOLA and R. C. ANDERSON. London, George G. Harrap and Company, 1926.

The best of the brief historical accounts of the development of the sailing-ship.

Der Seewart, Nautische Zeitschrift der Deutschen Seewarte, Hamburg. Various numbers, reprints, and extracts.

Articles in this publication deal exhaustively with the question of sailing-ship speeds, record voyages, and allied subjects.

Tabellarische Reiseberichte, published by Deutsche Seewarte, for 1903 to 1910.

Gives voyage details compiled from logs of German deepsea sailing-ships.

Index

INDEX

Workmen's Compensation Act, 222
World War I, 25, 38, 48, 68, 171, 189, 214; and death of training under sail, 334-36, 341-42
World War II, 68
Wrinkles and Suggestions for Sailing Vessels, by Jarvis, quoted, 126
Wyoming, 13

Yachts, 8, 9, 86, 135-40; *illus.*, 9; yachting, 135-39, 147, 150
Yards, 108-9, 111-13, 121, 124-25, 129-32; *illus.*, 130, 410-13; crojack, 110; fore-yard, 110; halliards, 109; jackstay, 128; main, 110; royal, 128; steel, 100-102, 109, 113, *illus.*, 106; topgallant, 128; topsail, 109, 128